W9-AFB-039

Women, Crime, and the Criminal Justice System

Women, Crime, and the Criminal Justice System

Lee H. Bowker
University of Wisconsin
with contributions by
Meda Chesney-Lind
Joy Pollock

Lexington Books
D.C. Heath and Company
Lexington, Massachusetts
Toronto

Library of Congress Cataloging in Publication Data

Bowker, Lee Harrington.
Women, crime, and the criminal justice system.

Includes index.
1. Female offenders. 2. Drugs and women. 3. Women—Crimes against. 4. Criminal justice, Administration of. I. Chesney-Lind, Meda, joint author. II. Pollock, Joy, joint author. III. Title.
HV6046.B82 364.3'74 78-57180
ISBN 0-669-02374-4

Second printing, March 1980.

Published simultaneously in Canada.

Printed in the United States of America.

International Standard Book Number: 0-669-02374-4

Library of Congress Catalog Card Number: 78-57180

Contents

List of Figure and Tables

Figure

Tables

Acknowledgments

No work of scholarship can be completed without the assistance of library staff members. In my early studies of female drug use and sex roles, Lorraine Reed, a librarian at Whitman College, was my lifeline to the international scholarly community. More recently, Jessica Brown and her staff in the interlibrary loan office at the University of Wisconsin-Milwaukee were incredibly successful in obtaining obscure publications for my use. In an area such as the one treated in this book, it is essential to be able to tap resources beyond those available in local libraries and these women have been more than equal to the task.

Some of the empirical material on drug use and abuse presented in this book was collected under grant number 1-D20-00931-01 from the National Institute of Mental Health. Part of the literature search was funded by the Drug Abuse Prevention Office, Office of Community Development, State of Washington, under grant number 033-F135-NA-6691. A series of three grants from the Aid to Faculty Scholarship Committee of Whitman College supported additional computer processing, travel costs for library research at the University of Washington, and manuscript typing costs. Professor Richard Thomassen, a specialist in computer technology among other talents, contributed many days of hard work in the processing of the data from a number of the drug surveys.

Many scholars have contributed comments, constructive criticisms, technical reports, and unpublished data to this project. These include Malcolm Klein, Carol Smart, John Quicker, Beth Vanfossen, Jacqueline Boles, G.F. Kirchoff, Duncan Chappell, Michael A. Hagstad, Jennifer James, Barbara Sherman Heyl, Gary D. Hill, M.W. McIsaac, Michael Hindelang, and Bill Feyerherm from academic institutions. Officials in governmental agencies, research institutes, and other agencies were generous in their sharing of material on international female crime. I am particularly thankful to S.D. Gokhale and N.K. Sohoni (India), Fidel V. Ramos (The Philippines), Osamu Mzumachi (Japan), Monica M. Gutierrez (Chile), J. Nepote (Interpol), Penny Reedie (Canada), S. Faissol (Brazil), D.F. MacKenzie and P.M. Kershaw (New Zealand), David Biles, Ian S. Cox, and M.D. Giles (Australia), H.K. Huh (Republic of Korea), W.T. Fook (Malaysia), Arne Lonberg (Denmark), W. Buikhuisen (The Netherlands), Matti Joutsen (Finland), Eva Roussakoff (Sweden), D. Bruce (Scotland), G.C. Biddulph and Anne B. Dunlop (England). Much of the material on international female crime has informed the discussion in Chapter 9, but has not been specifically analyzed in this book. Data collection is continuing, and a comprehensive report on the subject will be forthcoming.

I am particularly grateful to my coauthors, Joy Pollock and Meda Chesney-Lind, whose contributions to this project extend beyond the chapters they wrote. Gregory M. St. L. O'Brien, Dean of the School of Social Welfare at the University of Wisconsin-Milwaukee, was generous in granting me released time in which to complete the book. Along with other faculty and staff members, he helps to create an atmosphere at UWM that is conducive to scholarly work. Molly McAfee typed the manuscript and has greatly increased the efficiency of the Criminal Justice Program office since her arrival. Finally, my wife, Dee, has stimulated my interest in female crime and victimization, and suffered as a "writer's widow" during several periods of intense work on the book.

Introduction

After being ignored in most investigations of criminal behavior down through the years, female crime has suddenly become a popular subject. New courses on the subject are being offered on university campuses, articles and books are appearing in the popular press, and scholars are beginning to turn their attention to studies of women and crime. The purpose of this book is to contribute to the developing literature in women's studies by illuminating the multiple relationships among women, criminal behavior, and the criminal justice system. What kinds of crimes do women commit? What are the trends in the incidence of female crime in the United States and around the world? Why are there differences between the crimes perpetrated by men and those committed by women? Are women commonly the victims of crime, particularly violent crime? Is "the new female criminal" a fact or a myth? How are female criminals and victims treated by practitioners in the criminal justice system? Is sexual discrimination as severe among deviants and criminals as it appears to be in the world of legitimate business? To what extent are conditions and services in correctional institutions for women and girls conductive to their growth and healthy development into law-abiding citizens? Why do women enter into a life of crime? These are the questions that we have tried to answer on these pages.

An intellectual history of the project is a fitting subject for an introduction. My interest in female deviance and criminality grew out of my early studies of college student drug use. The first of a long series of studies on drug use and abuse was my doctoral dissertation, which revealed a large number of differences between male and female drug use. More important were a series of in-depth interviews that were used to increase my understanding of the quantitative data derived from a questionnaire survey. The female students in these interviews indicated that their drug-use patterns were not independent of their dating activities. Subsequent studies concentrated more on this topic, and produced evidence that even young women in drug-using subcultures are not free from the disadvantages of sexual oppression. In my efforts to understand female participation in the drug scene, I gradually moved toward a consideration of factors in general female deviance, which in turn led to an examination of female criminal behavior. The social control mechanisms used by young men to reduce the degrees of freedom available to young women in the drug scene fascinated me and stimulated me to look more carefullly at cross-sex social control mechanisms in America's middle and lower classes. The criminal justice system, a behemoth dominated by men and male ways of looking at the world, represents the most formal development of cross-sex social controls in human society.

The book is divided into two parts. Part I concentrates on the "facts" of female crime and early theoretical explanations advanced on the subject. It also includes a summary of the work on female drug use that led me to a broader interest in female crime and deviance. Part II focuses on the relationship between women and the criminal justice system but also includes material on gang behavior, prostitution, the victimization of women, and female crime in other countries. The treatment of women and girls by the police, the courts, and correctional personnel is discussed in some detail. It is hoped that readers of this volume will have gained an increased sensitivity to the ways in which the criminal justice system systematically puts at a disadvantage the women and girls it processes. Criminal justice administrators, instructors in women's studies courses, activists in the women's movement, and anyone interested in sexual equality should find something of interest in these pages.

Part I
The Theoretical and Empirical Setting

1 Statistics on Female Crime

Female crime can be estimated in two ways, by official statistics, which include arrest statistics and statistics on correctional populations, and through self-report surveys in which girls and women answer questionnaire or interview items about how often they have engaged in illegal behavior of various kinds. In this chapter, we will begin by having a look at some of the more useful kinds of official statistics, followed by an examination of self-report studies of female crime and delinquency. We will consider how self-report data differ from official data, as well as how female crime and delinquency have changed historically, both in absolute terms and in comparison with male crime and delinquency.

Official Statistics

The *Uniform Crime Reports* series published by the Federal Bureau of Investigation has serious deficiencies, but it is the best official source of data on female crime and delinquency in the United States. Each case listed in the *Uniform Crime Reports* has survived a number of levels of discretion, as well as possible reporting errors. For most crimes, no legal action can occur unless a citizen reports the crime to the police. If the police receive a crime report, they may decide to ignore it or they may try to make an arrest. If they fail to solve the crime, no arrest can take place. In some cases, police officers "know" who committed a crime but lack sufficient evidence to make an arrest that would lead to successful prosecution. Another problem is that not all police departments report their arrests to the Federal Bureau of Investigation. Even worse, historical comparisons are damaged by the fact that the number of police departments in the Uniform Crime Reporting System has increased over the years, and differential applications of police and citizen discretion almost certainly impact male-female comparisons of arrest statistics. Differential discretion not only operates historically, it also occurs between jurisdictions in the same time frame, so that forty-three shoplifting arrests in Tampa do not mean quite the same as forty-three shoplifting arrests in Detroit, an effect which is heightened by differences in legal definitions and court precedents from one jurisdiction to another.

An earlier version of this chapter appeared in the *International Journal of Women's Studies* under the title "The Incidence of Crime and Delinquency—A Comparison of Official and Self-Report Statistics." See the March-April 1978 issue, 1 (2): 178-92.

One could go on criticizing the *Uniform Crime Reports* for an entire chapter, but this would not serve any purpose in a book on female crime and delinquency. For the moment, it is better to suspend criticism in order to get on with the task of examining the data at hand. The FBI arrest data have included some breakdowns by sex since the first report was published in 1930. We will look most closely at the period from 1966 to 1976, which is summarized in table 1-1. This table gives figures on female crime as a percentage of all reported crime for 1966 through 1976. General summary data for violent crime, serious property crime, and total arrests are presented, plus information on selected specific offenses.

The female contribution to the arrest totals rose steadily from 12 percent in 1966 to 16 percent in 1976. In similar fashion, the female contribution to serious property crime rose from 15 percent in 1966 to 22 percent in 1976, but female violent crime rose only from 9 percent to 10 percent during this period. Looking at the individual offense categories, it is evident that some have increased, others have decreased, and a number have remained steady. The crime categories that experience about the same proportion of female arrests today as they did in 1966 are murder and nonnegligent manslaughter, robbery, aggravated assault, burglary, narcotics, and curfew and loitering. Larceny-theft, forgery and counterfeiting, fraud, embezzlement, vagrancy, and runaways have had a proportionate increase in female arrests, and female arrests for prostitution and commercialized vice have decreased proportionately.

Despite the relative decrease in female arrests for prostitution and commercialized vice, these are still the only offense categories dominated by females. Seventy-one percent of all 1976 arrests in these areas were of females, compared with 57 percent of the runaways, 37 percent of the frauds, 31 percent of both larceny-theft and embezzlement, and 30 percent of forgery and counterfeiting arrests.

Another way to look at female arrest statistics is to calculate the ratio of arrests for each offense to total female arrests. If we do this, we see that only one in every thirty female arrests is for prostitution. In 1976, the most common female arrest was for larceny-theft. Twenty-three percent of all female arrests in 1976 were for larceny-theft, followed by runaways at 8 percent, disorderly conduct at 7 percent, drunkenness and narcotics at 6 percent, driving under the influence of alcohol and fraud at 5 percent, and nonaggravated assaults at 4 percent. Historically, the probability of the arrested female's being charged with prostitution, disorderly conduct, drunkenness, or curfew and loitering violations has decreased, while the probability of being charged with larceny-theft, fraud, narcotics, and driving under the influence is up. As compared with male crime, female crime in 1976 was more heavily concentrated in the areas of larceny-theft, forgery and counterfeiting, prostitution and commercialized vice, and runaways,

Table 1-1
Female Crime as a Percentage of All Reported Crime in the United States, 1966-1976

	Year										
Offense	*1966*	*1967*	*1968*	*1969*	*1970*	*1971*	*1972*	*1973*	*1974*	*1975*	*1976*
Murder and non-negligent manslaughter	16	16	16	15	15	16	15	15	15	16	15
Robbery	5	5	6	6	6	6	6	7	7	7	7
Aggravated assault	13	13	12	13	13	13	13	13	13	13	13
Burglary	4	4	4	4	5	5	5	5	5	5	5
Larceny-theft	23	24	24	26	28	28	30	32	31	31	31
Forgery and counter-feiting	20	21	22	23	24	24	25	27	29	29	30
Fraud	22	23	24	26	27	29	30	31	33	34	37
Embezzlement	19	19	20	21	25	25	26	24	26	31	31
Prostitution and com-mercialized vice	80	78	78	80	79	78	74	76	76	74	71
Narcotics	14	14	15	16	16	16	15	14	14	14	14
Vagrancy	9	10	10	11	20	22	35	34	12	10	22
Curfew and loitering	18	18	19	20	21	21	20	19	23	20	20
Runaways	48	48	49	51	52	55	56	56	57	57	57
All violent crime[a]	9	10	9	10	10	10	10	10	10	10	10
Serious property crime[b]	15	15	16	17	19	19	20	21	21	22	22
All arrests	12	12	13	14	14	15	15	15	16	16	16

Source: *Uniform Crime Reports* (Washington, D.C.: FBI, U.S. Department of Justice, 1966-1976).

[a]Violent crime includes murder, forcible rape, robbery, and aggravated assault.
[b]Serious property crime includes burglary, larceny-theft, and motor vehicle theft.

but male crime was more heavily concentrated in the areas of burglary—breaking and entering, vandalism, narcotics, driving under the influence, and drunkenness.[1]

Arrests for FBI index crimes, generally the most serious crimes, comprised 20 percent of all female arrests in 1966, but this rose steadily up to 29 percent in 1976. This rise was almost entirely due to index property crimes. The index violent crime rate for females rose only from 2.5 percent to 2.9 percent of all female crimes over the period.[2]

The *Uniform Crime Reports* also include data on city, suburban, and rural arrests by sex of offender. In 1966, females were involved in about the same proportion of arrests in the city and suburbs, but in a considerably smaller proportion of rural arrests. This rural-urban differential has continued up through 1976, when 16 percent of the city arrests, 16 percent of the suburban arrests, and only 12 percent of the rural arrests were of females.[3]

There has been much publicity in the popular press over the fact that female crime has been rising much more rapidly than male crime. This is generally true, and it is true of both young people under age eighteen and of adults. The latest issue of the *Uniform Crime Reports* indicates that, among juveniles, arrests rose 68 percent for females and 30 percent for males between 1967 and 1976. For arrests at all age levels, females rose 64 percent and males rose 15 percent. There are individual crime categories for which the difference is much larger. To take just one example, the arrest rate for driving under the influence of alcohol rose 389 percent for male delinquents, 963 percent for female delinquents, 126 percent for all males, and 198 percent for all females during this period.

The misleading thing about these percentage differences is that they are based on 1967 figures that are very small, so that only small increases in absolute terms turn out to be huge increases when presented as percentages. The male increase in arson arrests between 1967 and 1976 was 53 percent and the female increase was 158 percent, but the number of male arrests rose from 4,790 to 7,343, an increase of 2,553, while the number of female arrests rose from 370 to 955, an increase of only 585 arrests. Female arrests for arson are not rising more rapidly than male arson arrests in absolute terms. It only appears that way when the rises are calculated in percentage terms from baseline statistics collected in years when female arrests were very low. Even in larceny-theft, where females have made their greatest gain, the absolute rise in male larceny-thefts is 164,812 and the absolute rise in female larceny-thefts is 114,627.

Between 1975 and 1976, total female crime decreased 1 percent and total male crime decreased 6 percent. Among juveniles, female crime and delinquency decreased 5 percent and the decrease for males was 7 percent. In every case, the decreases for violent crimes and for serious property crimes were greater than the figures for total crimes, and in every case, males decreased more than females. Violent crimes were down by 7 percent for all females and 8 percent for juveniles.[4]

It is quite possible for summary statistics collected over a wide and diverse area to mask many opposing trends occurring in portions of that area. To test that possibility for U.S. arrest data, it is necessary to examine arrest data produced by individual states. In Pennsylvania, 14 percent of all 1976 arrests were of females, including 29 percent of larceny-thefts, 30 percent of the forgery and counterfeiting arrests, 36 percent of the frauds, and 53 percent of the runaways. As compared with 1975, female arrests were up 4 percent while male arrests declined 1 percent. In the previous year, female arrests had risen 11 percent and male arrests had risen 8 percent.[5]

Females comprised 21 percent of all people arrested for index crimes in Wisconsin in 1976 and 19 percent in 1975. In 1969, it was only 17 percent. Table 1-2 presents data for FBI index crimes (the index is the summation of offense figures for Type I offenses in the *Uniform Crime Reports*, and these are criminal homicide, forcible rape, robbery, aggravated assault, burglary, larceny, and auto theft) and selected lesser offenses. Although some categories have very few offenses recorded in a given year, which makes for a great deal of statistical variability from year to year in offenses such as

Table 1-2
Female Crime as a Percentage of All Reported Crime in Wisconsin, 1969-1976

	Year							
Offense	*1969*	*1970*	*1971*	*1972*	*1973*	*1974*	*1975*	*1976*
Murder[a]	14	15	21	14	14	6	18	13
Robbery	7	5	4	5	6	7	7	8
Aggravated assault	12	10	13	11	10	11	10	12
Burglary	3	4	5	4	3	4	5	5
Larceny-theft	25	28	29	31	29	28	27	30
Motor vehicle theft	5	5	6	6	6	7	8	8
Prostitution and commercialized vice	95	87	94	84	85	77	86	85
Embezzlement[a]	5	28	22	10	15	22	0	45
Forgery	22	23	25	27	31	27	28	33
Fraud	28	30	31	32	34	33	33	35
All crime index offenses	17	20	21	22	21	20	19	21

Source: *Wisconsin Crime and Arrests* (Madison: Crime Information Bureau, Department of Justice, 1969-1976).

[a]When working with very small numbers of cases, a greater amount of statistical variability between years will be found than when working with large numbers of cases.

murder and embezzlement, the general pattern exhibited in the Wisconsin statistics is similar to the pattern for the nation as a whole. The female contribution to the major violent crime is essentially steady, prostitution and commercialized vice are down, and property crimes are up across the board.

In *Crime in the State of Washington*, Schmid and Schmid include information on female crime up to 1970. In the years from 1945 to 1970, females accounted for between 15 and 20 percent of the arrests. Excluding those arrested for drunkenness, females comprised more than 30 percent of the arrestees in 1945 (an effect of World War II), which declined gradually until 1959 and was largely steady at 15 percent from then to 1970. In this twenty-five-year period, the female contribution to arrests for murder, robbery, aggravated assault, larceny, forgery and counterfeiting, and fraud and embezzlement increased, though the increase for murder was very small. Female narcotics arrests declined in comparison with total arrests between 1945 and 1970.[6]

Combining annual data from 1968 through 1970, Schmid and Schmid constructed ratios of male to female arrests. The only crime categories with a preponderance of female arrests were prostitution and commercialized vice, where the ratio was 3.6 female arrests to each male arrest. Arranged in order, the other arrest ratios (male over female) listed by Schmid and Schmid are forgery and counterfeiting, 3.1; larceny, 3.2; murder and nonnegligent manslaughter, 4.0; fraud and embezzlement, 5.4; disorderly conduct, 5.8; narcotics, 6.0; vandalism, 8.5; weapons possession, 8.7; drunkenness, 9.7; nonaggravated assault, 9.8; drunken driving, 10.6; robbery, 11.2; liquor laws, 11.9; aggravated assault, 12.5; vagrancy, 12.8; sex offenses other than prostitution and commercialized vice, 16.5; stolen property, 19.0; burglary, 36.5; and auto theft, 39. During this period, arrestee rates per 100,000 population were not constant for the different racial and ethnic groups in Washington. The arrestee sex ratio was 5.0 for Native Americans, 5.1 for blacks, 5.3 for Chinese Americans, 7.8 for Caucasians, 8.8 for individuals of a Filipino heritage, and 11.1 for Japanese Americans.[7] Since these figures are adjusted by considering the population at risk, they are more useful than the crude, unstandardized percentages given in the *Uniform Crime Reports*.

Nebraska is a small, rural state. The number of female arrests in some categories is so small that table 1-3 presents raw arrest data rather than percentages. Not many Nebraska females commit murder, and the number has been decreasing since 1973. The only other crimes showing decreases in table 1-3 are drunkenness, which peaked in 1972, disorderly conduct, which also peaked in 1972, and runaways, which have been declining since 1974. Offenses showing sharp rises are burglary, larceny-theft, forgery and counterfeiting, fraud, prostitution, and narcotics. Though there are some differences, Nebraska's female crime picture approximates the national

Table 1-3
Female Arrests in Nebraska, 1971-1976

	Year					
Offense	*1971*	*1972*	*1973*	*1974*	*1975*	*1976*
Murder and manslaughter	4	12	14	12	12	6
Robbery	22	33	36	41	52	34
Felony assault	68	96	85	87	102	104
Burglary-breaking and entering	56	55	86	103	91	103
Larceny-theft	1283	1331	1722	2473	2810	2712
Auto theft	39	36	38	42	68	68
Misdemeanor assault	170	155	164	228	220	257
Forgery and counterfeiting	54	81	64	104	154	149
Fraud	282	266	324	397	583	676
Embezzlement	7	8	4	7	8	9
Stolen property	42	42	63	58	50	79
Prostitution and commercialized vice	45	44	89	95	100	121
Narcotics	259	465	561	680	597	609
Drunkenness	1171	1332	1101	1164	1090	855
Disorderly conduct	418	592	335	306	337	311
Vagrancy	115	115	101	51	26	126
Runaways	499	578	711	713	632	346
Total arrests	6284	7238	7793	9067	9678	9773

Source: *Crime in Nebraska* (Lincoln: Nebraska Commission on Law Enforcement and Criminal Justice, 1971 and 1973) and *Nebraska Uniform Crime Report* (Lincoln: Nebraska Commission on Law Enforcement and Criminal Justice, 1974 and 1976).

distribution. Perhaps the most interesting difference is that while total female crime in the United States decreased about 1 percent from 1975 to 1976, female crime in Nebraska rose by just under 1 percent in the same period. It could be that if urban female crime declines slightly in the coming years, rural female crime will slowly rise, reducing but not eliminating the rural-urban continuum. In a recent study of juvenile delinquency in eight North Dakota counties, Thilmony and McDonald found that there was greater proportion of "criminal" case referrals to the district court from small towns than from the larger urban centers.[8]

Considering these four examples, as well as other states that have not been mentioned above, it seems that national patterns and state patterns in female arrest statistics are comparable. Whatever broad social forces have been responsible for changes in female criminal behavior as well as for the responses of citizens and the police to female crime seem to be operating in all the individual American states as well as in the nation as a whole.

A Note on Female Violence

In the "Message from the Director" in the May 1977 issue of the *FBI Law Enforcement Bulletin*, Clarence Kelley bemoans the rise in female crime. Though the hard statistics he gives are mostly for property crimes, the emphasis in his article is on violent crime. He mentions one seventeen-year-old girl who had been charged with assault with intent to murder, two women who are believed to have held up three Los Angeles banks, and that although the first woman was not added to the FBI's "Ten Most Wanted Fugitives" list until 1968, there were four women on the list by 1970. He also points to the participation by females in terrorist activities such as those carried out by the Weather Underground and the Symbionese Liberation Army.[9]

The newspapers also contain many articles about female violence. For example, a recent *Milwaukee Journal* article was headlined "Women Deeply Involved in European Terrorism." This article gives many examples of female terrorism in West Germany, Italy, Sweden, and The Netherlands, but the only "hard" data provided is that "a good half of the unflattering pictures on the latest wanted posters in office buildings are of women."[10]

Despite assertions and reports such as these, the arrest statistics contained in the *Uniform Crime Reports* are clear. Female violent crime is up, but only as much as male violent crime, with the result that the female contribution to all arrests for violent crimes has been steady at 10 percent every year since 1969. Female property crimes are definitely up, both absolutely and proportionately, but in violent crimes they are just keeping pace with males. When one begins to look behind the headlines, the violence is muted. In the April 1968 Washington, D.C., riot associated with the death of Dr. Martin Luther King, Jr., 437 women were arrested and committed to the Women's Detention Center. Of these, 276 were for curfew violation, 75 were for looting, 36 for drunkenness and 27 for disorderly behavior, and 23 for other violations, only a handful of which were serious violent crimes. Curfew violators were young employed women who did not know a curfew was in effect, were curious and went to see the looting, or were just continuing their normal life patterns, such as walking their dog in the evening. Looting suspects were a bit older, and more likely to be unemployed. Many had had no intent to steal, but were just in the area and got caught up in the contagion of crowd behavior. Those arrested for being drunk or disorderly (really interchangeable categories) were generally women over forty-five who were employed in low-paying service occupations. They hardly knew what they were doing.[11] In short, when the background statistics are available, it is evident that much seeming female violence is greatly overstated in the popular press and by criminal justice system spokespeople who have a vested interest in maximizing the furor over female criminality.

Female homicide has also become a popular topic in the last decade. The tone of most studies of the subject is exemplified by this quotation from Sparrow's *Women Who Murder.* "We have seen our women murderers at work, pursuing their evil in stealth and with cunning."[12] The value-laden terms used to describe women in these books would be more honestly represented if they were retitled with captions such as *Female Murderers: The Woman as Vampire.* Are female murderers really more sinister than male murderers? Down through history, much has been made of the evilness of women, and the emphasis on the extreme perversity of female murderers is just one of the many manifestations of that trend. If we turn from treatments of the subject that are based on only a few cases, carefully selected to support the stereotypes of the authors, what does the scientific evidence show?

Rosenblatt and Greenland report that, in Canada, homicides by females were much more likely to occur in the home than those committed by males.[13] Harlan also found that most female homicides were committed at home in his study of 500 Birmingham, Alabama, murders between 1937 and 1944.[14] For murders of adults in Canada, females were more likely to use guns than any other weapon. They were also much more likely than men to murder someone with whom they were intimate—lovers or family members. Men were much more likely to murder strangers.[15] In a sample of female homicides up for review in California in 1965, Cole *et al.* also found that most female murderers chose victims with whom they were intimately associated (20 percent of the victims were children, 47 percent other intimates, and 33 percent acquaintances or strangers) and that guns were the most popular method, at 37 percent, followed by knives at 32 percent and hands in 13 percent of the cases.[16] In India, as in Canada and the United States, female murderers were most likely to victimize intimates. It was found that more than four of every five female murderers chose victims to whom they were related by kinship ties in a study of murders by women in three Indian states.[17]

Data for female offenders at the California Institution for Women were gathered in the early 1960s and then for a second time in 1968. Again, homicide victims were mostly husbands, lovers, and children. Guns and knives or similar sharp tools were about equally popular as weapons in the homicides, though no weapon at all was used in nearly a quarter of the cases. Ward *et al.* estimated that physical strength was required in only four out of every ten murders. Though most of the victims were adult males, they were often incapacitated by being drunk, ill, off-guard, or asleep. In the 1968 sample, the women were more likely to use guns than in the early 1960s, and they were more likely to play active criminal roles instead of being only conspirators or accessories. This change in roles was more evident in the statistics for robbery than for assault and murder, but it was present in all three categories of violent crime.[18]

From these studies, it seems that females are more likely than males to murder those who are close to them, which largely reflects their more restricted range of social involvements as well as their dependence on intimate social relations to meet their needs. It would also seem that stealth and evil are no more a part of female murders than male murders. A direct approach is indicated by the use of guns and knives. Poison is not used nearly as often as is commonly thought.[19] However, because of the difference in strength between most females and their adult male associates, they may have to depend on catching a man off-guard in order to be sure of murdering him. Anecdotal evidence suggests that in many cases these women have earlier been the victims of assaults by their adult male victims, so that their homicidal actions often take on the character of misguided attempts at self-defense.

As with most mythic stereotypes,there is a kernel of truth in the image of the evil female murderer: she does have to pick carefully the right time to strike, and her victim is likely to be a family member or sexual intimate, which infers that she is "betraying" the trust of her victim. The betrayal theme is really only applicable to cases of fatal child abuse, in view of the open and often violent conflict that commonly precedes a woman's killing of an adult male companion. To the extent that these themes have any validity at all, they are reflections of the enforced underdevelopment of women in human societies, not to any inborn biological or psychological characteristics. If women have to be careful about how they attack men, it is more due to lack of training in physical skills than to the necessary biological differences between the sexes. When women choose their victims from within their own intimate associates and family members, it is largely due to their exclusion from many kinds of meaningful relations outside the home and to their less frequent use of certain social settings, such as bars, in which many homicides and assaults occur between men.

Self-Report Studies

There are other kinds of official statistics besides the arrest data contained in the *Uniform Crime Reports*, but these statistics portray females in judicial and correctional situations that are even further from the actual commission of crimes than arrest data. The further we go from the site of the crime, the larger the number of filtering processes that occur and the lower the resemblance between the criminals described and any representative sample of actual criminals. Recent studies by Klein[20] and Hindelang[21] illustrate the strength of these filtering processes. In a sense, judicial and correctional statistics tell us more about the responses of the criminal justice system to female crime than they do about female crime itself. They form a basis for an analysis of how females are mistreated or aided by the system, or of organizational and administrative problems that need to be dealt with, but it is exceedingly dangerous to make any generalizations about female crime and delinquency on the basis of these statistics. For this reason, a consideration of these data sets will be reserved for later chapters in which we discuss females in the criminal justice system.

The only way to reduce the number of biasing variables in the process of generalizing from arrest data to actual criminality is to ask the criminals themselves. Self-report studies of crime and delinquency are a fairly recent innovation of social science methodology, so comparisons between these studies and arrest data must be limited to the past several decades. Within this time frame, the self-report statistics should give us an improved estimate of the true level of female criminality over arrest data, and should also allow us to make some statements about the discretionary biasing factors that intercede between crime commission and arrest.

In celebrating the validity of self-report data, it would be a mistake to ignore the biases that can creep into these data. These biases revolve around the factors of sampling, honesty, and communication. Most self-report studies are of limited local samples rather than national samples. They also have to depend on official permissions in the case of institutional entry and on individual cooperation in all cases. As a result, the relatively powerful are underrepresented in self-report surveys. As examples of this, juveniles are studied more often than adults, institutional populations more than samples of people in their homes, and public schools more often than elite private schools.

Assuming that sampling problems are solved to everyone's satisfaction, there is still the problem of communication. Is a printed questionnaire phrased so clearly that all subjects understand exactly what is desired? Some terms will be clear to certain groups of subjects but not to others, and then there are those subjects who can hardly read at all. There are all kinds of response biases, such as the tendencies to pick the first example in every multiple-choice question, to always agree with what is presented, and to heap numerical estimates around round numbers. In interviews, the characteristics of the interviewer interact with the responses given. Even worse, the interviewer's biases may be consciously or unconsciously communicated to the subject, thus influencing the answers given, since most subjects are quick to try to please the interviewer by saying what they think is expected of them.

Even if the subject understands exactly what is to be done, and receives no biased signals from external sources, there may still be biases that are generated internally. People like to project certain images, even to themselves when there is no external observer. Although they may have accepted the researcher's assurance that their responses will be completely anonymous, they may still overreport certain behaviors and underreport others. A man may underreport behaviors that he defines as unmasculine, perverted, or sick, but overreport behaviors that reinforce his self-image as masculine, in the swing of things, and healthy. Similarly, a woman may underreport masculine, deviant, or negative behaviors while overreporting their opposites.

No scientific study is perfect, but they are also not equally biased. There are methodological techniques for minimizing biases due to weaknesses in sampling design, communication, and respondent honesty, and the competent researcher applies these as fully as possible, given the constraints of time, budget, and other external conditions. Each self-report study must be judged on its own merits after carefully examining the methodological safeguards employed. Luckily, the rigorous evaluations by editors and anonymous reviewers assure us that, by the time a self-report study appears in a sociological journal, it is worthy of our consideration. At this level of sophistication, self-report studies are generally considered to be much more accurate representations of criminal behavior than any known set of arrest statistics.

Because of the paucity of self-report information on the criminal behavior of adults, the analysis that follows will be limited to self-report studies of female juvenile delinquency. In the 1950s, Nye and Short published the first important studies using the self-report approach to juvenile delinquency with general adolescent populations. In *Family Relationships and Delinquent Behavior*, Nye presented data from youths in three small western towns.[22] In a series of subsequent articles, these data were compared with a sample drawn from three towns in the Midwest by Short. In Nye's sample, young men reported higher levels of offenses ever committed and offenses committed more than once or twice for all twenty-four offense categories listed. Short's sample showed the same pattern except for "defied parents' authority" (both "ever committed" and "committed more than once or twice") and "taken things of large value ($50)" (only "committed more than once or twice"). None of these three differences was statistically significant, nor were a few of the differences on items like running away from home and drinking, on which females showed relatively high rates. For all other offenses, the male preponderance was large enough to be statistically significant, and this was consistently true at both the "ever committed" and "committed more than once or twice" levels of measurement.[23] Dentler and Monroe found the same pattern for thefts by junior high school students in three Kansas communities.[24]

Two studies from the mid-1960s added to the store of knowledge about female juvenile delinquency. Clark and Haurek administered questionnaires to youngsters aged eleven to nineteen in four unidentified (but presumably midwestern) communities, finding that the male to female ratio of all offenses was 2.3 to 1 and of chronic offenses, 3.7 to 1. Interestingly, the sex ratio for "major theft" was only 1.4 to 1. The offense sex ratio was lowest in the lower-class urban community (2.16), followed by the industrial city (2.54), upper-middle-class urban community (2.71) and rural farm community (4.18).[25]

The other study from the mid-1960s is of middle-class juvenile delinquency. Barton's unpublished doctoral dissertation is based on her study of 589 adolescents in an upper middle-class Connecticut suburb. Of thirty-five specific offense comparisons, young men were higher on every one except running away from home, and there the difference was not statistically significant. In general, gender differences were smallest in alcohol, driving, and inferred sex offenses and largest in vandalism and assaultive offenses. The most common delinquencies by young women were "given or attended parties where liquor was served" (58 percent), "bought or drunk beer, wine, or liquor" (51 percent), "skipped school without excuse" (41 percent), and "taken things of little value" (35 percent). Twenty-one percent had participated in fist-fighting, 4 percent took part in gang fights, and 2 percent admitted carrying a concealed weapon.[26] Though young men were more likely to commit delinquencies than young women, and were more likely to repeat offenses, the patterns of repetition were the same for both male and female repeaters.[27]

Barton makes an effort to compare her findings to Short's data from three towns in the Midwest, finding that there are few differences between the frequencies of delinquent offenses for young men and women in the two samples. Barton's young women reported higher percentages of participants in theft and alcohol offenses, but lower percentages of participants in assault incidents. The male-female delinquency ratios are about the same, and in both samples are much smaller than offense ratios derived from official data.[28]

An outstanding exponent of the self-report technique, Martin Gold, has published a number of reports including information on female juvenile delinquency. In his best-known study, published as *Delinquent Behavior in an American City*, Gold supervised the interviewing of a random sample of 522 youngsters aged thirteen to sixteen in Flint, Michigan, during 1961. Although there was some indication that young women underreported certain offenses, it was evident that the actual rate of juvenile delinquency was far below that of the young men. For the total sample, females were responsible for 50 percent of the reported incidents of hitting parents, 45 percent of the runaways, 40 percent of the drinking incidents, 35 percent of truancy and illegal entering, 25 percent of threatened assault, shoplifting, and trespassing, and 20 percent of unlawful automobile driving, fornication, theft, and false age identification. They committed only 15 percent of assaults, extortion, gang fighting and property destruction, 10 percent of the concealed weapons incidents, and none of the armed robberies and thefts of items from automobiles.[29]

A national sample conducted in 1967 confirmed the preponderance of males in self-reported delinquencies for the country as a whole,[30] and a similar survey in 1972 allowed comparisons to be made over time.[31] As compared with 1967, males reported more drug use, but less larceny, threatened assault, trespassing, forcible and nonforcible entry, and gang fighting in 1972. Females also reported more drug use, but less larceny, property destruction, and breaking and entering. Delinquent incidents decreased 9 percent for males and increased 22 percent for females. Aside from drug offenses, male delinquency was down 20 percent and female delinquency stayed about the same. A seriousness index of delinquent acts also showed stability from 1967 to 1972 for young women, but a 14 percent decrease for young men.[32]

In table 1-4, the 1967 and 1972 data sets for sixteen-year-olds are presented in the form of incidents per capita. We see that, in 1967, sixteen-year-old females were more likely to commit truancy than any other offense, followed by drinking, illegal entry, fraud, theft, property destruction, and trespassing. In 1972, drinking had become the most common offense, followed by truancy, drug use, fraud, trespassing, illegal entry, and theft. The increase in delinquency occurred at all age levels, but was strongest at age fifteen and rather weak at age thirteen. Even male delinquency increased at age fifteen but decreased sharply at the other age levels. Counting only serious incidents, males aged fifteen increased, but there was a significant decrease at all other ages. Strangely, serious offenses by females decreased somewhat at age fifteen at the same time that total offenses increased sharply.[33]

Hindelang's 1969 dissertation[34] and several journal articles derived from it[35] report on the delinquent involvements of youngsters in a Catholic high school in Oakland, California. Males reported higher levels of delinquent acts than females for all offenses, with the highest sex ratios being for promiscuous sexual behavior, gambling, major theft, and group fist-fighting. Despite these absolute differences, the patterns of involvement were highly similar between the sexes. At least in this 1968 data set, the main male-female difference in delinquency was in total frequency, not in the distribution of offenses. Young women reported an average of 10.2 delinquencies in the past year, as compared with 26.1 for the young men, but the rank order correlation for the mean frequencies of the delinquent acts of males and females was .92. The most common delinquencies for females were drinking and cheating on school exams, making up 20 and 15 percent of all female

Table 1-4
Self-Reported Delinquency of Sixteen-Year-Olds, 1967-1972

	Incidents per Capita			
	1967		*1972*	
Delinquency	*Male*	*Female*	*Male*	*Female*
Running away	.10	.13	.10	.07
Hit a parent	.08	.20	.11	.11
Truancy	1.40	.97	1.10	1.00
Property destruction	.78	.25	.57	.17
Fraud	.51	.41	.63	.52
Confidence game	.16	.08	.14	.12
Theft	.83	.40	.70	.37
Assault	.64	.14	.44	.08
Threat	.45	.22	.23	.15
Trespass	.97	.25	.57	.49
Illegal entry	.69	.51	.43	.43
Drinking	1.60	.91	1.40	1.30
Gang fighting	.55	.08	.36	.05
Concealed weapon	.24	.02	.18	.04
Auto theft	.19	.10	.21	.01
Illegal drug use	.06	.10	.61	.59

Source: Martin Gold and David J. Reimer, *Changing Patterns of Delinquent Behavior Among Americans 13 to 16 Years Old, 1967-1972* (Ann Arbor: Institute for Social Research, University of Michigan, 1974), 193-94.

offenses, respectively. For males, the most common delinquencies were drinking (14 percent), minor theft (9 percent), and cheating on school exams (just under 9 percent).[36]

Another significant dissertation is Weis's study of eighth- and eleventh-grade students in an upper-middle-class community, completed in the early 1970s. As in the Hindelang data, the young men committed many more delinquencies than the young women, but the patterns were the same. The male-female rank order correlations for mean offense frequencies were .92 for eighth graders and .97 for eleventh graders. In absolute terms, the most noticeable difference between the sexes was that females committed very few violent acts. Among eighth-grade females, the most common offenses, listed in order of decreasing frequency, were curfew violations, smoking marijuana, drinking, becoming drunk, and cutting classes in school. The eleventh graders had much lower levels of delinquency. For the females, curfew violations were still the most common, followed by cheating, cutting classes, shoplifting, and smoking marijuana.[37]

In a recent unpublished paper by Stewart *et al.*, 1973 data on the delinquencies of young women in a midwestern suburban community of 25,000 were presented. All students attending the suburb's public junior and senior high schools on the day of the survey were included in the sample. The 937 young women in the study engaged in a wide range of antisocial behavior. At least 10 percent of the sample reported committing all of the offenses listed on the questionnaire, except weapon use (9 percent) and narcotics use (4 percent). The most commonly reported nonstatus offenses were shoplifting (58 percent), assault (34 percent), stealing money (33 percent), vandalism (32 percent), marijuana use (31 percent), sedative use (19 percent), and reckless driving (17 percent). Status offenses included skipping school (56 percent), drinking alcohol last month (50 percent for beer, 48 percent for wine, and 32 percent for whiskcy), heavy petting (38 percent), sexual intercourse (22 percent), and running away from home (18 percent). Young men reported higher delinquency levels than young women for all items listed, but a number of them were by rather slight margins. The least sexually differentiated offenses were smoking (male/female ratio of 1.06), drinking whiskey last month (1.19), shoplifting, drinking beer last month, and taking sedatives (1.20), skipping school (1.21), and running away from home (1.22). The largest gender differences were for fist fighting (2.86), weapon use (2.49), narcotics use (2.17), and reckless driving (2.08).[38]

The similarity in the pattern of offenses between the sexes is indicated by a rank order correlation of .89 among the twenty-two categories of offenses committed by each gender. A gender difference was that male offenses were more highly intercorrelated (.35) than female offenses (.25), which suggests that young women are less likely than young men to be involved in an integrated set of deviant activities. From the pattern of intercorrelations between different delinquent acts, it appears that illegal drug use is the central core of female juvenile delinquency in this sample. Stewart *et al.* also asked their respondents about eleven types of psychological stress, finding that there were few substantial relationships between measures of stress and any of the forms of delinquent behavior. For young women, the only stress items that were relevant were suicidal thought ("I have thought of different ways of committing suicide") and, to a lesser extent, rage ("I have felt like smashing things").[39]

A number of self-report studies of juvenile delinquency have appeared in print in the last two or three years. For our purposes, the best of these are by Jensen and Eve,[40] Walberg and Yeh,[41] and Kratcoski and Kratcoski.[42] Kratcoski and Kratcoski studied eleventh and twelfth graders in three public high schools, using an updated version of Short and Nye's delinquency checklist. In terms of offenses ever committed, female delinquency was closer to male delinquency than in many earlier studies. In fact, slightly higher percentages of females than males reported running away from home, defying parental authority, buying or drinking alcohol, and using or selling drugs. Offenses with less than a 10 percent excess of male over female admittees were truancy, school probation or expelled, homosexual intercourse, sending in false fire alarms, and arson (these last three small differences being misleading because only small percentages of either sex admitted committing these acts). The delinquencies in which males dominated most heavily were fist fights (90 to 38 percent), gambling (79 to 31 percent), and deliberately damaging property (53 to 15 percent). On the crucial dimension of theft, young men were more likely than women to report the theft of items under $2 in value (73 to 53 percent), items worth $2 to $50 (48 to 22 percent), and items worth more than $50 (16 to 3 percent).[43]

Walberg and Yeh's study of 400 Chicago high-school students in randomly selected English classes is valuable because it breaks down the data simultaneously by ethnicity (black, white, Latin) and social class (dichotomized into lower and higher). Looking first at ethnic comparisons between young women in the lower of the two social class categories, it is evident that blacks were more likely to report fist fights, strong-arming for money, beating up others, and gang fights, and whites were more likely to report thefts of minor and medium size, as well as offenses related to automobiles. Young women of Latin origin were much less delinquent in all areas. In the higher social class group, whites reported more delinquencies than blacks in nearly all categories, with blacks reporting higher levels of only fist fights and beating up others. Too few Latin females were present at this social class level to make any generalizations about them. By social class, lower-status black females reported higher levels of almost all offenses than upper-status black females, but there was no clear relationship between status and delinquency for the white females. In the lower-status category, there were six cases in which more females admitted offenses than males—fist fights (black), running away (black, white), theft under $2 (Latin), gang fights (black), and drugs (black). In the higher-status category, the only cases in which more young women admitted offenses were running away, theft under $2, alcohol use, and beating up others, all for blacks only. In this highly urban sample, females committed less violent delinquencies than males, but the differences were surprisingly small for all ethnic groups in the lower-status category and for blacks at the higher-status category.[44]

The Jensen and Eve article, though published in 1976, uses data on 4,000 Richmond, California, youngsters that were gathered ten years earlier. When simultaneously broken down by sex and race, the data show that blacks are less sexually differentiated than whites with respect to violent offenses, but more sexually differentiated than whites with respect to property offenses.[45] Jensen and Eve report larger gender differences than Walberg and Yeh do, probably because their study is much older. This fact notwithstanding, they did find "numerous subcategories of females with rates of delinquency involvement similar to or greater than other subcategories of males."[46]

A study so recent that it is not yet published except as a research report of the Institute of Juvenile Research examined the delinquent behavior of 3,112 Illinois males and females between the ages of fourteen and eighteen. Improper behaviors such as running away from home, making anonymous phone calls, cheating on exams, and being truant from school were exhibited about equally by the two sexes. Young women were *not* more likely than young men to run away from home. For various kinds of alcohol violations, there was no gender difference among whites, but nonwhite males were more likely to be violators than nonwhite females. Six kinds of illegal drug use were similarly distributed between males and females. On automobile offenses, males were higher than females, and this difference was larger for nonwhites than for whites.[47]

Young men reported committing more property offenses—petty theft, shoplifting, keeping or using stolen goods, damaging property, larceny, and breaking and entering. The greatest gender differences were in the percentages of whites who ever commmitted these offenses. Nonwhites were less differentiated than whites on offenses ever committed, and both whites and nonwhites were less sexually differentiated on offenses committed more than once or twice than on offenses ever committed. The only category in which a higher proportion of females admitted to committing more offenses than males was shoplifting, in which more non-white females than males aged fourteen to fifteen and sixteen to eighteen reported offenses committed more than once or twice.[48]

For each of five violent acts specified in the self-report questionnaire, nonwhite (essentially black) females showed higher percentages admitting to the offenses than white females. The large racial differences in young women ever participating in fist fights, carrying weapons, gang fights, using weapons, and strong-arming were also found among those reporting that they had committed these acts at least a few times or often. White females showed a general decrease in violence from the lower class through the upper middle class, with the surprising exception that middle-class females were more likely than young women from the working class to participate in some form of violence. This trend was accentuated among non-whites, where violence admitted to by young women from the working class was much lower than violence admitted to by those lower or higher in status. Young men admitted to much higher levels of violence than young women for whites in all social classes. This pattern was not repeated in the violence figures for non-whites. There, lower-class females were, as a whole, slightly more violent than lower-class males, though nonwhite males were quite a bit more violent than nonwhite females at higher class levels. Even then, there were instances of higher female violence. For example, only 8 percent of the nonwhite males from the working class had ever used weapons, as compared with 20 percent of the nonwhite females with working class backgrounds.[49]

Conclusions

Though it is probable that self-report studies provide a more accurate picture of female delinquency than official statistics, the lack of studies using adult females limits the usefulness of this technique for overall policy development. In addition, it must be remembered that the usefulness of different methodological techniques is dependent on the purposes to which they are put. All research strategies have advantages and disadvantages, and the calculus changes as the research problem changes. The superiority of the self-report technique over official data for an estimate of the "real" incidence of female crime and delinquency is a matter of degree, and is not a black and white case.

Taking all the self-report studies together, they clearly show smaller gender differentials than official arrest statistics. The general pattern of offense statistics is similar for both self-report and official data. It is mostly the frequencies for each offense that differ rather than the overall pattern of the relative frequencies of offenses by females or the relative differences between the sexes. Where differences are found between official data and self-report studies, they suggest that officials working in the criminal justice system tend to underreport female property offenses more than serious violent offenses, and that they are likely to sexualize female offenses inappropriately from time to time. When a young women has committed a string of delinquencies, she is more likely to have the sexual delinquency recorded as official than would be expected if no biases were operating. The reverse tendency to protect girls' and women's reputations can also be discerned by the large number of general offenses attributed to them in official statistics, such as curfew, loitering, and incorrigible offenses. In general, offenses that are inconsistent with the American stereotype of the female role are underreported more in official statistics than offenses which seem to be compatible with the stereotype.

Other general trends supported by the official and self-report data available at this time are that (1) female crime and delinquency increased steadily up to about 1975 and then began to decrease; (2) in the past several decades, offenses committed by young women have risen more rapidly than those committed by adult females; (3) in the same period, serious property crime has risen equally for female delinquents and adults, but violent crimes and other crimes have risen much more among female delinquents than women; (4) total male-female crime differentials have been decreasing throughout this period; (5) these decreases have been greater for adolescents than for adults; (6) what appears to be a large rise in female violent crime is inflated because of the small base statistics on which this rise is calculated; (7) in absolute terms, the increase in the number of violent crimes by males has been much greater than the increase by females; (8) the significant change in female illegal behavior has been in property rather than violent offenses; (9) at least with respect to delinquency, male-female differences are more in the total frequencies of the offenses than in the patterns of the offenses; and (10) there is some evidence that females are playing more active roles in criminal and delinquent incidents than they did in earlier decades.

Notes

1. *Uniform Crime Reports* (Washington, D.C.: FBI, U.S. Department of Justice, 1976).
2. *Uniform Crime Reports* (Washington, D.C.: FBI, U.S. Department of Justice, 1966-1976).
3. Ibid.
4. *Uniform Crime Reports*, 1976.
5. *Crime in Pennsylvania, Uniform Crime Report* (Harrisburg: Bureau of Research and Development, Pennsylvania State Police, 1975, 1976).
6. C.F. Schmid and S.E. Schmid, *Crime in the State of Washington* (Olympia: Law and Justice Planning Office, Planning and Community Affairs Agency, 1972), 199-202.
7. Ibid., 197-98.
8. J.T. Thilmony and T.D. McDonald, "Rural Sociocultural Change and Its Relationship to the Female Delinquent," paper presented at the Annual Meeting of the American Society of Criminology, Tucson, November 1976, 8.
9. C.M. Kelley, "Message from the Director," *FBI Law Enforcement Bulletin* 46 (May 1977), 1, 2.
10. "International Dateline: Women Deeply Involved in European Terrorism," *Milwaukee Journal* (August 21, 1977), 2.
11. E.E. Miller, "The Woman Participant in Washington's Riots," *Federal Probation* 33 (June 1969), 3-34.
12. G. Sparrow, *Women Who Murder* (London: Barker, 1970), 156.
13. E. Rosenblatt and C. Greenland, "Female Crimes of Violence," *Canadian Journal of Criminology and Corrections* 16 (1974), 177.
14. H. Harlan, "Five Hundred Homicides," *Journal of Criminal Law and Criminology* 40 (1950), 736-52.
15. Rosenblatt, 176-77.

16. K.E. Cole, G. Fisher, and S.S. Cole, "Women Who Kill, A Sociopsychological study," *Archives of General Psychiatry* 19 (1968), 1, 2.

17. R. Ahuja, "Female Murderers in India—A Sociological Study," *Indian Journal of Social Work* 31 (1970), 273.

18. D.A. Ward, M. Jackson, and R.E. Ward, "Crimes of Violence by Women," in *Crimes of Violence*, Volume 13, D.J. Mulvihill, M.M. Tumin, and L.A. Curtis, eds. (Washington, D.C.: National Commission on the Causes and Prevention of Violence, 1969), 868-907.

19. E. Nau, "Homicide by Females," unpublished translation of a German text, available through the Document Loan Program of the National Criminal Justice Reference Service (Washington, D.C.: National Institute of Law Enforcement and Criminal Justice, 1975).

20. Malcolm Klein, "The Diversion of the Female Delinquent," paper delivered at the annual meeting of the American Society of Criminology, Atlanta, 1977.

21. Michael J. Hindelang, "With a Little Help from Their Friends: Group Participation in Reported Delinquent Behavior," *The British Journal of Criminology* 16 (April 1976), 109-25.

22. F.I. Nye, *Family Relationships and Delinquent Behavior* (New York: Wiley, 1958). Prior to this time, the only self-report survey was of a limited sample of Texas college students by Porterfield. See: A.L. Porterfield, *Youth in Trouble* (Fort Worth, Texas: Leo Potishman Foundation, 1946), 38-41.

23. J.F. Short, Jr. and F.I. Nye, "Extent of Unrecorded Juvenile Delinquency: Tentative Conclusions," *Journal of Criminal Law, Criminology and Police Science* 49 (1958), 296-302.

24. R.A. Dentler and L.J. Monroe, "Social Correlates of Early Adolescent Theft," *American Sociological Review* 26 (1961), 733-43.

25. J.P. Clark and E.W. Haurek, "Age and Sex Roles of Adolescents and Their Involvement in Misconduct: A Reappraisal," *Sociology and Social Research* 50 (1966), 496-508.

26. N.J. Barton, *Disregarded Delinquency: A Study of Self-Reported Middle-Class Female Delinquency in a Suburb*, unpublished doctoral dissertation (Indiana University, 1965), 211-23. See also: N.B. Wise, "Juvenile Delinquency Among Middle-Class Girls," in *Middle-Class Juvenile Delinquency*, E.W. Vaz, ed. (New York: Harper and Row, 1976), 179-88.

27. Ibid., 241.

28. Ibid., 230-33.

29. M. Gold, *Delinquent Behavior in an American City* (Belmont, California: Brooks, Cole, 1970), 61-70.

30. J.R. Williams and M. Gold, "From Delinquent Behavior to Official Delinquency," *Social Problems* 20 (1972), 209-29.

31. M. Gold and D.J. Reimer, *Changing Patterns of Delinquent Behavior Among Americans 13 to 16 Years Old, 1967-1972* (Ann Arbor: Institute for Social Research, University of Michigan, 1974).

32. Ibid., 43-55.

33. Ibid.

34. M.J. Hindelang, *Personality Attributes of Self-Reported Delinquents*, unpublished doctoral dissertation (University of California, Berkeley, 1969).

35. M.J. Hindelang, "Age, Sex, and the Versality of Delinquent Involvements," Social Problems, 18 (1971), 522-35; and M.J. Hindelang and J.G. Weis, "Personality and Self-Reported Delinquency: An Application of Cluster Analysis," *Criminology* 10 (1972), 268-94.

36. Hindelang, "Age, Sex, and the Versatility of Delinquent Involvements," 524-27.

37. J.G. Weis, *Delinquency Among the Well to Do*, unpublished doctoral dissertation (University of California, Berkeley, 1974), 369-79.

38. Cyrus S. Stewart, Mary M. Zaenglein-Senger, Arthur M. Vener, and L.R. Krupka, "Patterns of Delinquency Among Adolescent Girls," unpublished manuscript (Michigan State University, 1977), 3-4, 10.

39. Ibid., 5-11.

40. G.J. Jensen and R. Eve, "Sex Differences in Delinquency: An Examination of Population Sociological Explanations," *Criminology* 13 (1976), 427-48.

41. H.J. Walberg and E.G. Yeh, "Family Background, Ethnicity, and Urban Delinquency," *Journal of Research in Crime and Delinquency* 11 (1974), 80-87.

42. P.C. Kratcoski and J.E. Kratcoski, "Changing Patterns in the Delinquent Activities of Boys and Girls—A Self-Reported Delinquency Analysis," *Adolescence* 10 (1975), 83-91.

43. Ibid., 86-87.

44. Walberg, 86.

45. Jensen, 434.

46. Ibid., 444.

47. G. Schwartz, "Summary and Policy Implications of the Youth and Society in Illinois Reports," unpublished research report, Institute for Juvenile Research (Chicago, 1977), 3-50.

48. Ibid., 63.

49. Ibid., 83.

2 Early Theories of Female Criminality

Joy Pollock

Through the years research on female criminality has proceeded along different lines and at a different rate than research on male criminality. Recently, there has been a proliferation of studies and the equality of research has improved, but this has not always been the case. Historically, in literature, science, and popular thought, women have either been idolized or maligned. The images of women have fluctuated from paragons of virtue to devious enchantresses; unfortunately, these myths persisted in scientific research. Instead of exposing these misconceptions, early social scientists often based theories on them. In general, women were believed to be very different from men and almost always inferior. Whether they regarded women as infantile, amoral children or as pampered slaves, early sociologists were guilty of gross sexism.[1] As one writer concludes, the founding fathers were "sexists to a man."[2]

In criminology, this bias was seen in theories which simplified causality and stereotyped female criminality. Recent reviews of the literature remark on these dominant trends in past studies. Rasche describes five chronological stages in research and literature. The first stage was the prescientific stage, which continued up until the twentieth century. The few things written about female criminality in this stage concentrated on environmental causes, but women were not taken seriously as criminals and were not considered worthy of the attention of researchers. A stage which emphasized constitutional causes followed. This stage was composed of studies that looked at physiological and mental causes of crime. The third stage, which occurred in the 1930s, combined constitutional causes with environmental. In the 1940s, research turned to "numbers and offenses"—the fourth stage. The fifth and last stage of research was the women's prisons stage, which existed until very recently.[3] Rasche found that research on females paralleled their place in society. For instance, during the constitutional/environmental cause stage, women were seen as the protectorates of males, and research was gingerly conducted in order to protect their privacy and virtue.[4] In this stage, the interest in women as research subjects was a change from earlier times when they were not considered worthy of attention.[5]

Klein writes that, even when female criminals were studied, the research was done under contradictory beliefs. Women were seen as malicious and deceitful, and, at the same time, loving and caring. The stereotypes continued and were reflected in research because they were never recognized as such.[6] Klein found that research on females never left the "medico-psychological" realm as had the research on males. Women were regarded as behaving under biological laws and inherent qualities.[7] This viewpoint completely negated the possibility that the female criminal was a victim of the social structure or of a social critic.[8] Other writers have remarked on the tendency of early theorists to see female crime in a unicausal light.[9] Crime was defined as deviation from a male-imposed normative structure; the female criminal, in this case, may only have been an individual who was reacting or adapting to society in ways that were perceived as deviant.[10]

In this chapter we provide a review of the major studies on female crime. The historical sequence revolves around three dominant theorists. The first is Caesare Lombroso, who exemplified the extreme of pseudo-science in studies on women. W.I. Thomas is the second major theorist. He applied a psychological model of crime consistent with the emerging gestalt of the 1920s and 1930s. The third pivotal theorist is Otto Pollak. His study on women criminals in 1950 is probably the most ambitious work ever completed on the subject.

One other major influence was not an individual theorist but a school. The American Statisticians were a group of American researchers who used the same methodology of measurements and testing to produce a substantial body of literature in the 1920s and 1930s. The statisticians' studies are interesting in two ways. First, they preceded any serious investigation of that type on men, and second, the majority of the researchers were women. The value of women professionals so early in the game was significant despite the fact that their work was influenced by the biases of their time. The women of the American Statistician school were not the earliest examples of female criminologists; Pauline Tarnowsky and Dora Melegari wrote much earlier and were contemporaries of Lombroso. Tarnowsky contributed data to Lombroso's book, *The Female Offender,* in 1894. It is regrettable, but understandable, that, without exception, early female theorists operated under the same myths and biases toward women that handicapped the thinking of male researchers. It is only very recently that female writers have started to reexamine female criminality from a feminist perspective.

Before Lombroso

The type of literature on female crime that existed in the early 1800s was primarily editorial, though some writers did start seriously to investigate female criminality. Pauline Tarnowsky studied Russian peasant murderesses, and found that they were biologically different from normal women in cranial capacity, height, weight, and other features.[11] She also found that poison was the most frequent method used; it was employed thirty-five times in 100 cases while no other method was used more than sixteen times.[12] Tarnowsky concluded that there was definitely a quantitative sex differential in the commission of crime and this differential was due to biological and social influences.[13]

Ryckere wrote about "babyfarming" in 1898. This was the practice of paying a sum of money for "care" of a child. There was a tacit understanding that the care meant the child was to be killed outright or by neglect and abuse.[14] Babyfarming was a type of crime that was mainly practiced by women; they were both the customers and the "farmers." A large amount of literature was written about this sex-specific crime. When it was brought to public attention, there was a general outcry of horror. The literature reflected the shock of seeing women, stereotyped as nurturers, acting so differently from what was expected of them.[15]

An early work by Pike explored crime historically. He saw a sex differential in crime rates and explained it as the social aftereffect of an early biological limitation. Pike believed that, at some early point in man's existence, females were physically restricted from engaging in criminal acts by their weakness. Even after urban life became the norm and physical strength was no longer a necessity for crime, women were still influenced by their early biological heritage through the process of social conditioning. Other theorists that approached female crime using a social conditioning model believed that women's lower crime rates were due to social inequalities. They predicted that as women gained social equality their rates would go up correspondingly. This was different from other writers, such as Proal, who believed that women committed less crime because they were inherently morally superior to men.[16]

An example of the most common type of literature is George Ellington's *Women of New York.* This rambling, unscientific treatise made many assertions and conclusions based on myths, apparent reality, and examples. It appears to be, at best, a phenomenological study of one part of New York's underworld. Ellington gave interesting descriptions of the confidence games and the daily life of criminals, such as the methods prostitutes used to steal from their clients. He believed that victims and police were reluctant to identify and treat females as criminals. These tendencies made official female crime rates much lower than the actual crimes committed.[17]

Ely van de Warker was a theorist who followed Quetelet in his belief that crime was an inevitable part of society. He believed that society "prepared the crime." Because of certain social conditions, a criminal was naturally going to turn to crime as the path of least resistance when satisfying the artificial wants defined by society. According to van de Warker, a woman's relation to crime was determined by "social conditions" and "sexual conditions." Social conditions included occupation, opportunity, and marriage; sexual conditions referred to an almost biological need of women to secure the permanent attentions of one man. This drive was so strong that the female would commit serious crimes to achieve it. In this analysis he was referring to the high number of infanticides committed by unmarried females. Presumably the need to appear chaste in order to catch a husband was much stronger than conflicting feelings of motherhood, and the child was killed. An interesting part of van de Warker's theory was his belief that women had a biological pride for adornment. This mental trait supposedly explained why female domestic servants stole even when they were adequately fed and clothed. Men, van de Warker explained, committed crime when they were hungry or poor; women committed crime because of mental traits that drove them to it.[18] Van de Warker believed that the social condition of women limited their involvement in criminal acts, but he did not feel that there was a large differential in criminal tendencies between the sexes.

Lombroso and Ferrero

Caesare Lombroso and William Ferrero wrote the first edition of *The Female Offender* in 1894. In this book, Lombroso continued to use the analytic framework he had developed in *The Criminal Man,* which had been published in 1870. As the founder of the Positivist school, Lombroso infused criminology with a new energy. No longer was it the philosophical ruminations of men like Tarde or Beccaria that dominated criminological thinking. A new direction emerged; these writers were eager to legitimize criminology as a science. They had a dogmatic faith in the scientific method.

Lombroso's initial research was done with male criminals. He had been an army doctor and also a prison physician. Data collected from these two positions were used as groundwork for further research.[19] Lombroso's basic theory was that the criminal was a biologic throwback to a primitive breed of man. Criminal types could be recognized by various "atavistic" degenerative body characteristics. To prove his theory he measured a number of body parts and noted such things as low foreheads, excessive facial hair, and large mandibles (jawbones). Prisoners from various prisons and jails were used as the criminal sample.

Eventually his interest turned to the female criminal. In conjunction with his son-in-law, William Ferrero, he wrote *The Female Offender.* Lombroso and Ferrero applied the thesis that crime was "biologically predisposed" and recognizable by physical stigmata to female criminality. Their research took them to the prisons for women and to courts dealing with women offenders. As with the male offenders earlier, Lombroso measured various body parts and noted physical irregularities. Such things as cranial capacities, facial anomalies, facial angles, and brain weights were analyzed. He decided that the number and type of body abnormalities were more significant than cranial and body measurements. Criminals could be categorized by the type of anomalies they possessed. For instance, a prostitute was likely to have very heavy lower jaws, large nasal spines, simple cranial sutures, deep frontal sinuses, and wormian bones. A "fallen woman" usually possessed occipital irregularities, a narrow forehead, prominent cheekbones, and a "virile" type of face.[20]

Lombroso found less degenerative physical characteristics among women criminals than he had found in males. He believed this was due to the fact that women, as a whole, were biologically more primitive and had evolved less than men. In measurements, female criminals were found to be physically similar to ancient males rather than normal modern women or men. Prostitutes were found to have more atavistic qualities than other female criminals. This followed logically from the belief that prostitutes were more primitive than either normal or criminal women. According to Lombroso, primitive women were rarely criminal, but almost always prostitutes.[21]

Criminal women were found to possess many male characteristics, both physical and mental. This masculinity suppressed female maternal drives and induced even greater criminality. At the same time, female characteristics contributed to make the woman criminal more "terrible" than the male. Insensitivity to pain was found to be a common quality of the subjects. This obviously explained why the female criminal was so cruel and unmerciful. The analogy between women and children was brought up again and again in early theories of female criminality, and Lombroso's was no exception. All women were thought to be big children with no moral sense and no maturity. Law-abiding women were only amoral children held in check by their characteristics of piety and sobriety.[22]

Lombroso sought to explain why there were far fewer women offenders than male. Female criminals possessed fewer atavistic characteristics than males. He concluded that this was because of a sexual selection factor. In evolution, those physical qualities odious to the eye were bred out of the female population, hence less stigmata in modern women. Because stigmata and criminality were correlated, this also meant less criminality was present. Women were organically conservative and passive, according to Lombroso. This, and feminine qualities such as piety, maternal instinct, and weakness, served to repress criminal tendencies. When these were lacking or were overcome by strong passions or drives, the result was a criminal more cruel, more deviant, and less penitent than the male.[23]

Lombroso applied the typology developed for male criminals to women. The "born criminal" type was the biological criminal, the woman who possessed a large number of degenerative stigmata. This type was found less frequently than in the male sex because of the biological and constitutional differences of the female. His statistics indicated that only 14 percent of the prisoner sample had the four or more degenerative characteristics required to be considered in this type.[24] In effect, the born criminal was an exception twice—as a criminal among normals and as a woman among criminals.

A more frequent criminal type was the occasional criminal. This type possessed few or no degenerative features; in addition, her "moral equipment" approximated that of a normal woman's. The occasional criminal committed crime at the suggestion or by the influence of a male (in most cases a lover). Lombroso believed that higher education, by preventing marriage and increasing want, also induced crime. Temptation was another factor that he believed initiated offenses. Women, again described as children, did not have the respect for property that men had. The occasional criminal was a woman who, by suggestion or circumstance, found herself engaged in crime. Rehabilitation was possible, even probable. Guidance and control by a judicious father or husband was needed to make her law-abiding.[25]

Another criminal type was the hysterical offender. Lombroso found this type to be rare—only 3.9 percent in a prison population. His description of the hysterical offender followed closely to current descriptions of schizophrenia including rapid mood changes, delusions, and destructive behavior. Still another type was the offender who committed crimes of passion. These individuals were also devoid of physical degeneracy but did possess excessive virile characteristics. Moral qualities were present but there was an excess of strong feelings. The causes of crime for this type included passion for love or material riches. Lombroso categorized suicides as a separate type. His interpretation of available statistics led him to believe that women committed suicide less often than men because they were more adaptable to changed living conditions and had less pride than men had.[26]

Criminal female lunatics and epileptic delinquents comprised the last two types of criminals. Lunatics followed the same pattern as criminals; that is, there were less female lunatics than male lunatics, but when they existed they were more depraved and more aberrant. Female epileptic delinquents were also found to be rare. The rarity of lunatics and epileptics was in proportion to the small degree of criminality among women.[27]

In brief, Lombroso postulated a biological theory of crime. The criminal was a primitive breed recognizable by physical, atavistic qualities. Women were, on the whole, less inclined to criminality because of constitutional and psychological factors. They were organically conservative. Atavistic qualities had been bred out by sexual selection, and feminine qualities such as piety and maternal affection further worked against criminal tendencies. When criminality overcame these factors and "reared its ugly head," it was much worse than criminality as it appeared in the male. The predominant type of criminal was the less serious occasional offender. This type only committed crime under the influence of a male or in a situation of extreme temptation.

Probably more critiques have been written on Lombroso than on any other theorist in the field. Criticism focuses on two main categories; inadequacies in his methodology, and his general theoretical assumptions. Although Lombroso seemed fanatically attached to figures and statistics, he evidently was unaware of basic statistical methods. First, all of his data came from prisoners. It is true today, and no doubt was the case in Lombroso's time, that criminals who are caught are only a small proportion of the total number who commit crime. Furthermore, criminals who are convicted are a still smaller proportion, and, finally, those who are sentenced form a very small percentage of the total number of criminals. If his findings had any validity at all they would still have only applied to that minuscule proportion. In other words, the most he could be sure of was that atavistic qualities were correlative with prison commitment.

The most serious inadequacy of his study was his small sample size. The major part of his work was based on data from seventy-two criminals and forty-seven prostitutes. Later he brought in other studies to make his total closer to 1,000, but then the problem was that the data were compiled from several studies which were carried out by different people in different areas. It would have been difficult to standardize measurements that were used in all the studies, especially when judging the anomalies. One wonders how it was determined when a cheekbone was prominent or a forehead receding. The variable of different ethnic types would also affect some of the data. For instance, Lombroso's finding that criminals had dark, coarse hair could possibly be attributed to the fact that a large proportion of the sample was taken in Rome in the southern part of Italy, where dark skin and dark hair predominated.

Lombroso's findings were not statistically significant. Differences he found could easily have been explained by the range of human variability. The control groups of normal women were very inadequate. Lombroso remarked on this problem himself in an amusing way. Excusing the small "normal" sample of fourteen, he explained that it was difficult to obtain permission to measure the circumference of a lady's neck, legs, and thighs.[28] Lombroso falls into the all too easy practice of using examples to illustrate points. It is forgivable to use this occasionally, but he abused it to an extreme. In the latter half of his book, Lombroso used examples exclusively to prove his assertions about the characteristics of criminal types. He also attributed motives to offenders and then used the motives as proof of his theory. Often the same individual was used to exemplify different parts of his theory. Examples were sometimes cases known to him, but he often used popular accounts of sensational criminals. An example of this was his description of Belle Starr, the American female outlaw. Lombroso's description reads more like a dime-novel idolization than a scientific analysis.

All of these inadequacies contributed to make the study statistically invalid. As many critics have said of Lombroso's work, "They're just numbers." If Lombroso would have had a larger sample and had refrained from using examples as proof, there would still have been criticism. The general assumptions under which he operated would have been challenged again and again. Even if he had proved a correlation between criminality and physical characteristics, a causal link would not have been established. There was no proof that crime was caused by atavistic qualities, or that those qualities were prerequisite to being criminal. A strong possibility was that a third variable, namely socioeconomic class, was a causal factor in both crime and the physical symptoms of degeneracy.

Another mistake Lombroso made was attributing biological bases to clearly subcultural traits. For instance, tatooing, drinking, and overeating were all subsumed under biological auspices instead of environmental causes. Assumptions about women in general were made with no scientific facts. If women were docile and pious, it was more likely due to social conditioning than to organic, constitutional factors as Lombroso believed. His theory that the woman criminal was more terrible than the male was only a reflection of the common stereotype of women. When a murderess was described as inherently more depraved than a murderer, it was because she deviated so much from the female norm. These same norms and attitudes about how a woman should behave influenced Lombroso and other social scientists to impose artificial double standards for men and women. They then labeled them criminal when they deviated from those standards. Klein, in a review of the literature, describes Lombroso as having a racist and classist view of femininity. What he classified as normal was subjective judgment masquerading as scientific fact.[29]

Recent critics have attacked Lombroso on his confusion of sex and gender. Since the biological definition of sex is not immutable, attributing characteristics to females on the basis of their sex was not well founded. Secondly, the terms masculine and feminine are unquestionably based on social context and should not have been used in any other way. That is, to explain deviousness as a feminine trait only explained it as a personality trait that females acquired through socialization.[30] Lombroso followed a common pattern when he related any aspect of women, whether it was emotion, criminality, or character, back to their sexuality. While the possibility of environmental conditions was allowed for male offenders, females were seen to commit crime only because of inherent primitiveness, moral immaturity, or biological nature. Many of the themes initiated by Lombroso and Ferrero permeated research for decades; sociocultural factors, confounding variables, and environmental causes were developed fairly soon to replace Lombroso's biological theories of male crime, but research on female crime shed his influence less rapidly.

Contemporaries of Lombroso

Several authors were more or less contemporary with Lombroso. Each followed different lines of research. Prinzing looked at marriage rates in Germany. He found that criminals who were married were more likely to be female except in the oldest age groups, where just the opposite was true: males were more likely than females to be married. While Prinzing's study was statistical, Puibaraud's was psychological. He cited various motives that were attributable to female crime and not to male crime. Among these motives were sex repression, envy, jealousy, and vengeance.[31]

There were several who responded to Lombroso's work very soon after it was published. Three of these were Arthur Griffiths, Frances Kellor, and Hargrave Adam. Griffiths felt that physical, anthropological theories did not explain criminal progression, which was moving from less serious to more serious types of crime. He believed, as did Puibaraud, in psychological motives for female crime. Vengeance, feminine rage, and jealousy were cited as the common motives of serious crime. Poisoning, he believed, was the favorite method of murder. He observed that less-serious criminals possessed common traits, such as vanity, intolerance of control, persistent misconduct, and "fluent, shrewish tongues." He disagreed with Lombroso's opinion that maternal affection was absent in the female criminal. Griffiths' work was mainly based on observations he made in a prison for women. He included a few statistics, such as the fact that in the time period of 1882-83 to 1892-93 female crime decreased by 41 percent. This statistic was broken down to show that serious crime decreased 72 percent and lesser offenses decreased 33 percent. He also employed individual case studies and personal observations.[32]

Frances Kellor tested several of Lombroso's conclusions in American prisons and institutions, including the Geneva Reform School, Joliet Penitentiary, Cincinnati Workhouse, Ohio State Penitentiary, and New York City's Blackwell's Island Workhouse and Penitentiary. The normal group used for comparison consisted of a group of fifty-five students. The items measured were weight, height, sitting height, strength of chest, hand grasp, cephalic index, distance between eyes, crown to chin, nasal index, length of ears, of nose, of middle fingers, of thumbs, width and thickness of mouth, height of forehead, anterior and posterior diameters. Very few of

Lombroso's findings were substantiated by Kellor. Several of the items were too influenced by nationality to be valid. Other findings were not replicated—prostitutes were not found to live longer than males, physical features such as large lower jaws and projecting cheekbones were not found to characterize prostitutes, nor did they possess masculine voices or handwriting.[33] Kellor made other tests, such as for memory, fatigue, pain, taste, smell, and hearing. Compared to normals, these findings showed that criminals generally were inferior in all tests, but Kellor wisely attributed this not to criminality *per se* but to the social environment from which the criminals had come.

An intriguing test Kellor described used a machine called a kymograph. Evidently it was a forerunner of the lie detector since it measured changes in a subject's respiration in reaction to stimuli. An individual was connected to a respirator and when s/he inhaled or exhaled, air was forced up or down rubber tubing. This was attached to a pointer which drew corresponding lines on smoked paper which revolved around a drum. The testing showed that subjects responded more dramatically and took longer to recover from surprise than it took for them to recover from pain. Fear produced either a straight line, when they held their breath, or a ragged line of varied amplitude. No comparisons were made with normal subjects.[34]

In an additional article, Kellor describes the results of other testing. It was found that workhouse and reformatory residents differed from penitentiary criminals. Generally, the workhouse and reformatory offenders were recidivists and had lower scores in all tests administered. They were also more apt to come from poverty backgrounds than were the penitentiary population.[35] The most common occupation of female criminals was in domestic service. This was because of the lack of education and inability of the subjects to pursue other types of employment. Kellor cites several reasons why this occupation contributed so frequently to the criminal class: (1) there were a large number of women in this category of employment, so proportionally it should have been higher; (2) inadequate salaries that characterized the occupation spurred workers to steal; (3) workers engaged in this type of employment were generally unable to do anything else; (4) it was an easy route to prostitution, and, related to this point, (5) employment bureaus were often procurement places for prostitution.[36]

Kellor recognized that the myth of the greater depravity of women criminals was the result of the different standards set for the two sexes. This work was a theoretical bridge between the statistical methods of Lombroso and Ferrero and the in-depth research which came later by the American Statisticians at Bedford Hills. Kellor must be admired for recognizing the influence of social factors and the presence of several false assumptions in the existing research literature on female criminals.

There is not much to be admired in Adams's book, *Women and Crime.* Although he scoffed at Lombroso's findings, Adams operated under many of the myths Lombroso had, such as the greater depravity of female criminals. He made blanket assumptions about female nature, often contradicted himself, and was not consistent from men to women when explaining personality traits. For instance, Adams talked of women devoted to men as exemplifying the female trait of lack of willpower and "tendency to excess." When he spoke of men devoted to women, it was explained by the woman's hypnotic powers! This hypnotic power women were supposed to possess was always a "malign influence," and the more evil a woman was, the greater was her power. Adams wrote that the purpose of his work was to analyze and trace the motives of female crime. Actually, all that he did was retell many newspaper accounts of murders and other crimes and superficially explain them with confused beliefs, double standards, and a patronizing sexism.[37]

In the early 1900s there were a few studies done that appear to be statistically adequate. Hoegel found a sex differential in crime rates for the period 1886-1895. Female crime rates were found to decline much more slowly than male crime rates. Statistics showed that, in the twenty-one to twenty-five age group, male convictions were 7.5 times higher than female, while in the forty to fifty age group the differential was smaller; males committed crimes only 3.3 times as often as females. Dora Melegari also used statistics to study female crime. She found an age differential in criminality peaks of Italian criminals. Males reached a peak of criminal activity in their twenties, while women peaked in their thirties. This finding contradicted the assumption that women would peak earlier due to their more rapid adolescent maturation. She concluded that, because of social conditioning, females did commit less crime, but probably the rates were underreported because male victims were less likely to complain. An Austrian study done by Herz found that in 1899 13.9 per 100 total convictions were workmen while 30.3 per 100 convictions for murder were of women. Other findings were that robbery was committed by 4.8 women out of 100 convictions, arson was committed by 19.5 women out of 100 convictions. Italian figures by Roncoroni showed similar differentials. In 1885-1886, 3.4 women per 100 men were convicted for murder.[38]

Other writers took a psychological view. Hans Gross, for instance, looked at qualitative aspects of female crime. He postulated that deceitfulness was a trait common to all women and came naturally from a history of concealment (of menstruation and socially disapproved aggression). Gross believed menstruation was a causal factor in crime. He attempted to show its role in shoplifting, arson, and homicides. Another writer, Fischer, believed that pregnancy was a causal factor in crime. Granier wrote of the sex-specific crime of infanticide. He said that the fear of dismissal in domestics and the inability to provide for the child were major reasons for murdering infants. As the first thought of the woman was to stifle the baby's cries, smothering was the common method employed.[39]

In 1910 and shortly after, there were several studies published. Leale analyzed statistics to determine if there were a differential in the crime rates. He concluded that both sexes probably committed equal amounts of crime. Conyngton found that women in manufacturing and mechanical occupations in the United States composed 16.7 percent of the criminals arrested, while that occupation comprised 28.4 percent of the total work force. Commerce occupations, which were 10.0 percent of the working population, accounted for only 3.3 percent of offenders. Fully 77.5 percent of criminals arrested came from the domestic and personal service occupations, which comprised 40.4 percent of the total working force. Aschaffenburg looked at arrest statistics and found that in 1909 there were 20.0 women arrested for every 100 men. For the crime of murder, 16.6 women were arrested per 100 men. Thirty-one women per 100 men were arrested for petit larceny, while 7.3 per 100 were arrested for grand larceny. Another set of German statistics, these for the year 1896, showed 17.9 women per every 100 men were arrested.[40]

A Chicago study also looked at conviction rates. It was found that, of those arrested, 44.8 percent men were convicted. Of the women arrested, 48.1 percent were convicted, but they were more likely to receive fines than sentences; in the men's case, just the opposite was true.[41] Finally, Anderson did a study in the court system of Boston. One hundred "offenders against chastity" were studied. The following results were obtained: the average age was twenty-six years; 49 percent had a mental level of below twelve years; 48 percent had serious mental handicaps; and 34 percent were alcoholics. Anderson suggested preventive treatment, including supervision instead of imprisonment for certain types of offenders.[42]

The American Statisticians

Fairly early in the 1900s, research was conducted at Bedford Hills Reformatory for Women in New York. Weidensall was one of these early researchers. Her study compared reformatory inmates to working girls and school girls in a variety of tests measuring intelligence, skill, and mechanical ability. Additional tests measured height, weight, strength of grip, and visual acuity. The reformatory inmates generally did worse on all tests. They were slow to understand directions, and this dullness lowered their scores. The criminal women's scores formed a bimodal distribution with a group clustered higher than the working or school girls and a group clustered much lower. A clear correlation between an individual's place on this curve and years in school was indicated.[43]

Criminal women were found to be emotionally unstable, suspicious, and unthinking. One test which had the subject trace a star figure indicated that the criminal group gave up easily when faced with difficulty. Weidensall was the superintendent of the institution and seemed to be fairly progressive for her time. She encouraged and supported the psychological testing done in the Laboratory of Social Hygiene, as it was called, because of its potential for guiding classification restrictions. Weidensall believed there were different types of criminals. Some were intelligent but too lazy to go to work; some were truly criminal; and some were just so unintelligent they drifted into crime. She believed that this type, through guidance and training, could be turned into upstanding and moral workers.[44] This study points to mental ability as a causal factor in crime. It was believed that criminals formed bad habits and did not break away from them because no one had shown them a better way. Social conditions were given short shrift by Weidensall. Why, she asked, did those in the working-women sample who came from the same socioeconomic class as the offenders not become criminal?

Another study was done by a group of authors using statistics from the State Prison for Women at Auburn, New York County Penitentiary, New York City Workhouse, the New York Magdalen Home, and a group of probationers. The methodology was to collect a mass of data from these groups and obtain large numbers of case studies. With this data, extensive information was accumulated about the offender's background. The material that was compiled ranged from the subject's home condition to her age at first sexual experience and the offense charged in her first arrest. Two general causal factors were identified: (1) poor economic background and the resulting home environment it produced; and (2) inferior mental ability. It was found that recidivism occurred more often with misdemeanants than with felons; that the average age at first conviction was twenty-seven; that more criminal women were unmarried, but if they were married, their husbands tended to be older; and that the native born were overrepresented as opposed to immigrant groups. On a scale of good, fair, mediocre, and poor, the economic statuses of the offenders were 45 percent fair or mediocre, moral standards were 46 percent mediocre to fair, and parental supervision was 46 percent poor. There were 49 percent who had defective strains within their family (that is, alcoholic, feebleminded, neurotic, or "sexually irregular").[45]

Sexual bias was apparent in the study of the women's backgrounds. A major portion of the acquired information was the sexual history of the women—when they first had intercourse, with whom, how often, and so on. This was used in a determination of their moral characters. The researchers wrote that only 16 percent of the women were not serious sex offenders.[46] This is a good example of the practice in which the early researchers identified different moral standards as criminal behavior. In other ways, however, the study was relatively good. The authors' conclusions were cautious and they recognized the unlikelihood that a well-defined type of individual could be identified as inherently criminal.

Guibord did still another study at Bedford Hills. This time only the physical states of the women offenders were examined. Her main finding was that only 13.5 percent of the cases studied were free from any syphilis. Additional conclusions were that the group had high degrees of physical defectiveness, that these conditions were largely preventable since they were caused by such factors as faulty nutrition and bad hygiene, and that the defects had some part in causing delinquency. Guibord believed that simple poverty was too often overlooked as an important cause of crime.[47] This rather straightforward study is exemplary of a trend at that time which thought female criminals should be treated more as juveniles than male criminals, even to the use of the term "delinquency" instead of crime. Many felt that all the female offender needed was a good meal and a bath to set her back on a law-abiding path.

Edith Spaulding undertook a study of 400 women prisoners to form a working classification of offenders; that is, who could do what types of work in the institution, and whose chance of success on the outside was greatest. This was done by investigating the education, home environment, and physical condition of the prisoner. In a ranking system, Spaulding concluded that 23 percent were capable of most work, 36.5 percent had mediocre skills, and 40 percent were totally incapable of work. The average age of the offender was 27.4, and the average years in school were 7.4. Signs of mental subnormality were present in 26 percent, and fully 86 percent were found to be infected with venereal disease.[48]

This compiling of data from case records was the beginning of an ambitious plan of filing and cross-referencing all inmates in regard to their physical and mental capacities. Many ideas and projects were undertaken in this time period by the energetic and competent women professionals who were working in women's corrections. Also, small numbers of female criminals were easier to work with, and the general feeling was that women needed to be taken care of and treated rather than punished.

Another publication by Spaulding relayed the progress of one of these projects. At Bedford Hills, an experiment was undertaken to deal with a number of intractable and troublemaking inmates. A separate facility was built which included several cottages, each with a capacity of eighteen, an occupational room, clinics, and staff rooms. The unstable, emotional, "psychopathic" prisoners were moved to this building and a form of self-government was instituted. The hypothesis behind the experiment was that separation from the general population would decrease encouragement for violent outbursts. Another advantage was that having them all together would be useful for research purposes.

As with most correctional experiments, this one did not succeed as well as hoped. The inmates did not turn into model prisoners and they wore down the staff by the frequency and extent of their outbursts. Soon discipline included wet packs and isolation. Spaulding observed that extreme irritability and outbursts were associated with menstrual periods. Another causal factor was what she termed the "herd instinct," which she associated with race. Factors from the environmental background of the offender were also involved. These included illness, sudden death of parents, poor supervision during adolescence, the influence of undesirable companions, and early marriage. As for inheritance itself playing a role, Spaulding concluded that it was definitely not a factor in 49.5 percent of the cases and only a possibility in 39.4 percent. She wrote that it was impossible to separate the influences of inheritance and environment on a person's entry to crime.[49]

Spaulding believed that, because of their upbringing, the women had never had to face the consequences of their actions. The outbursts were signs of immaturity bordering on insanity, although they never completely lapsed into insanity because they loved life. Very few were intellectually deficient according to the psychological tests done on them. Her study reported that 33.3 percent of the graduates of the hospital were doing well three to four years after release.[50] The program, however, like many of its kind, was soon closed due to budgetary cutbacks.

William Healy and Augusta Bronner wrote an essay on the treatment of male and female delinquents in Boston. It is a good example of the practice of linking a woman's criminality to her sexuality. Women who were immoral were automatically considered to also be criminal. The best chance of rehabilitation for the female was marriage to a "good man" who would guide her morally and keep her in line.[51] Numerous other studies were done under this same general methodology.[52] All concluded that both environmental background and hereditary factors played a part in criminality. This time period had a protective, treatment-oriented attitude toward the female offender. Her bad habits and especially her sexual immorality were disapproved of, but the common tendency was to think that all she needed was a good bath, or, even better, a good husband.

The 1930s

The remainder of the 1920s produced few additional studies other than those already mentioned in the American Statistician school. Published articles on female criminals increased in the 1930s and 1940s, although they were small in number compared to the flood of studies on male criminals. Articles on women offenders were either statistical explorations of a specific subtopic of female crime, statistical reports much like the earlier ones done by Spaulding and the other statisticians, or psychological theories of female criminality.

Those investigating a specific aspect of female criminality included Kopp and Taussig, who both studied abortions. Kopp found that, of 10,000 abortions in New York City, 1,863 were self-induced and 7,667 were criminal abortions performed by a midwife or doctor. Taussig believed there were 700,000 abortions a year in America of which 30 percent were criminal.[53] In another study, Morton explained the infanticide law passed in 1922 that declared it to be manslaughter instead of murder if a woman killed a newborn child. This leniency was due to the belief in "puerperal" or "lactational" insanity which could affect women in the months following birth. Morton believed that most infanticide was caused by a mental breakdown from fatigue and overwork. He noted an absence of vengeance, that most regretted the act, and that many offenders linked infanticide to suicide attempts.[54]

Kingsley Davis analyzed prostitution in an article published in 1973. He believed that society disapproved of prostitution because its ends were pleasure and not procreation. Davis did not attach much weight to economic factors in entry to prostitution, but instead believed that the demand for prostitution would always maintain the profession. In other words, if the regular wages of working girls were raised, the prices paid for prostitutes would also increase, so there would always be a proportion of females that would rather prostitute than do legitimate work. In order to eliminate prostitution, Davis believed that the whole social structure which institutionalized and rigidified sexual behavior would have to change. Even then, the demand for prostitutes would likely continue since there would always be a number of men who could obtain sexual gratification in no other way.[55]

In England, Bishop reported that the average number of shoplifters caught was twenty per week per store and the individual store's losses averaged 15,000 to 20,000 British pounds per year. The reluctance of stores to report these crimes stemmed from the bad press they would have received, the importance of some of the customers, and the loss of work time by employees who would have to serve as witnesses. All of these contributed to make underreporting very serious. Bishop believed that published figures represented only 2 percent of the actual shoplifting incidence.[56]

A general study was done by Radzinowicz, who used statistics from Poland with some comparison data from other countries. Sex ratios of crime varied considerably from country to country. Belgium had the lowest ratio with 100 males being arrested for every 34.1 females, and Finland had the highest ratio, with only 4.1 females being arrested for every 100 males. Sweden's ratio was 6.7; Japan's, 6.9; Hungary's, 31.3; France's, 10.1; Germany's, 18.2; and Italy's, 20.2. Radzinowicz found that the female arrest rates in each individual country systematically varied by age and residence. For example, 81.2 women aged sixty and over were arrested per 100,000 persons, while those in the thirty to thirty-nine age group had a coefficient of 196.2, nearly two and one-half times greater. Women living in rural districts were arrested 100.5 times per 100,000, but those who lived in towns were arrested three times as often. Radzinowicz concluded that these variables influenced sex ratios and made the analysis of statistics more complex than many researchers realized. He cited several reasons why reported figures were not true indications of actual crimes committed. Women, he said, generally had lower conviction rates, and they were often not reported because their crimes were less serious. In many crimes women took part as inciters and accomplices and therefore were not caught. Finally, the courts were not as severe on females as they were on males.[57]

Several studies published in the 1930s were very similar to those of the early statisticians. Growden investigated the intelligence and other mental traits of Ohio offenders. He used the Army Alpha test, the Pintner Nonlanguage test, and the Ohio Literacy test, and also interviewed the subjects. Growden found that black and white misdemeanants and black and white females all had lower scores than noncriminal women. The differential between offenders and normal women, however, was larger for the whites than for the blacks. One interesting finding that emerged was that white forgers and embezzlers had higher mental ages than those of an army control group. There did not seem to be any correlation between mental age and criminality.[58]

A study done at a correctional school for girls in Wisconsin showed that home environment played a role in commitment. Lumpkin found that, of the offenders studied, 83.4 percent had been influenced by bad companions; 63.5 percent came from broken homes; 30.4 percent were from families with more than one delinquent member; 25.0 percent had mothers who worked; 22.0 percent had worked themselves before the age of fifteen; and 63.9 percent came from homes which had had contact with one or more social agency. She concluded that bad home environment played a more influential role in the commission of minor offenses than in the case of major crimes.[59]

The Gluecks

Another study done in the tradition of the statisticians was one by Sheldon and Eleanor Glueck. This mammoth undertaking covered every aspect of the lives of 500 Massachusetts offenders from their childhood to after they were paroled. The Gluecks not only presented their findings, they also made criticisms of and recommendations for the entire criminal justice system. The system of data collection was painstakingly thorough, and fully one-fourth of the book is devoted to appendixes on methodology and charts and tables showing their findings. The purpose of the study, as in the earlier studies, was to determine what factors were causal in delinquency. They sought to determine the best methods of classification to use in treatment, and attempted to identify variables to use in predicting successful rehabilitation. The data covered five areas—the offender's personal history, her family history, her reformatory history, her parole history, and her postparole history. Every conceivable type of information was collected—court records, school records, personal interviews, physical examination records, parole reports, and arrest records. All information was verified as much as possible.

The Gluecks' findings were endless, but not always very useful. Family history showed that 60 percent had foreign-born parents. The religions of the offenders' families were 54 percent Catholic and 35 percent Protestant. Seventy-seven percent of the offenders had parents who had not attended school. Parents of 27 percent of the offenders were day laborers, while 25 percent had parents who were skilled workers and 19 percent had parents who were factory workers. Only 1 percent of the parents were professionals, and 44 percent were either unemployed or employed irregularly. Seventy-eight percent of the families lived in "marginal" economic circumstances. Mental disease was present in 58 percent of the families, and other delinquency occurred in 81 percent of the families.[60]

The offenders' educational background broke down as follows; 21 percent had had six years of schooling; 15 percent, seven years; 22 percent, eight years; 21 percent, nine years; and 18 percent, ten years. Sixty percent were classified as poor students. The majority (51 percent) left school for economic reasons, and the mean age at first employment was 14.9 years. They did not have overwhelmingly good work records; 58 percent were judged poor by their employers. The sexual history of the offenders was investigated as thoroughly as possible. A large proportion, 86 percent, were determined to have bad sex habits. Prostitution was broken down into types from the professional prostitute down to the "doubtful good girl." Most (42 percent) fell into the occasional prostitute category. This determination was separate from the women's current sentence, which showed that 52 percent were convicted of prostitution. Venereal disease was found to afflict 67 percent of the offenders. About half the women had never been married. Of those who were, 41 percent of the husbands had criminal records. Only 1 percent of the marriages were judged successful.[61]

In the data gathered from the reformatory, the Gluecks found that only 33 percent of those incarcerated were not psychotic, psychopathic, epileptic, alcoholic, addicted to drugs, psychoneurotic, or of marked unstable personality. Nine-tenths had never been in the reformatory before, and the mean time spent at the reformatory was only fifteen months. After release on parole, 60 percent were not arrested within five years, but delinquent activity of minor sorts continued in 76 percent of the cases. The Gluecks found that, in all factors recorded, the group that was successfully rehabilitated fell between the non-delinquent group and the recidivists. Other factors that were thought to be helpful in rehabilitation included a good marriage and the responsibility of bringing up children, the weakening of promiscuous urges with age, the absorption in a new vocation, and a move to a new community. Ideally, they thought scores should be given to offenders on such indexes as delinquency, leisure habits, school record, church attendance, industrial adjustment, neighborhood influence, mental condition, and homemaking competence. These scores could then be used to predict recidivism.[62]

In their conclusion, the Gluecks wrote that environmental and biological conditions combined to make rehabilitation difficult for offenders. Furthermore, criminality was likely to be passed down to the women's children and succeeding generations. All that could be done to aid rehabilitation should be, urged the Gluecks. This included instigating indeterminate sentencing, moving women to the jurisdiction of the juvenile courts, and making community agencies more preventive. The Gluecks' study was a comprehensive one for its time. Biases and sexist attitudes influenced what they looked at and their interpretation of data. The sexual histories were examined as a matter of course and were used as a measure of an offender's character whenever she became involved in the criminal justice system. This happened despite the fact that the offense might be completely unrelated to sexual behavior. All of these studies paid close attention to the sexual lives of their subjects. This interest was somewhat justified due to the large proportion who were incarcerated for prostitution, but for other crimes the sexual history of the offender was important only because she was a woman. This is clear when we attempt to find studies of the immoral behavior of male offenders. Another aspect of this sexism was the Gluecks' conclusions regarding rehabilitative factors. A good marriage, they wrote, was a strong factor in preventing further delinquency. What a woman needed, in other words, was the iron hand of a man. It may have been true that the economic and emotional security marriage provided decreased the delinquent activity of women offenders; it is harder to believe that it was the benevolent dictatorship of a husband that accomplished rehabilitation. It would be unlikely, in fact, since the Gluecks had shown in their study that women ran away from such authoritarian rule by their fathers.[63]

Their most blatant bias was in relation to the seeming inevitability of criminal tendencies passed down from generation to generation. If it was incurable, at least it should be contained, according to the Gluecks. To do this they wanted a sterilization program instituted on a wide scale, since the women evidently were incapable of controlling themselves. The other alternative was to isolate those judged to be "defective delinquents" to prevent them from procreating. Thus, the Gluecks advocated keeping large numbers of women locked up in prisons and reformatories indefinitely for the sole purpose of keeping them from getting pregnant.[64] This solution to the problem was blind to the ethical and legal implications of such an act. It is fortunate that the Gluecks' recommendations were not instituted to a large degree.

Eugenia Lekkerkerker

A completely different type of study was written by Lekkerkerker, a Dutch lawyer. She traveled all over the United States, visited many reformatories and correctional agencies, and published her findings in 1931. Her book is a descriptive and analytic account of the women's reformatory system in America. Lekkerkerker's objective perspective and penetrating insight make her prose fascinating reading, even today. She observes that women offenders were regarded as "erring and misguided" and in need of protection and help. Shame was an important tool in rehabilitation attempts with females. The reformatory system for women was more influenced by this line of thinking than by the tradition of the existing penitentiary system. Directors were chosen outside of correctional backgrounds and instructed to develop homelike atmospheres. The purpose of the institution was to instill "standards of sexual morality" and "sobriety." Also, the reformatory trained the women in duties as homemakers.[65]

Lekkerkerker believed that the activism of Americans made them more likely to accept environmental theories rather than fatalistic, biological theories like Lombroso's. She saw the experimentation and research that was going on as part of a social-engineering tendency in Americans. The reformatory system, however, was not operated by any general theory or set of principles. According to Lekkerkerker, it developed by happenstance through legislation, economic considerations, and special-interest groups.[66] Her book includes material not only on reformatories but also on legislation, the court system, and police agencies as they were involved in female crime. This is a very good study and an important one for any student of female criminality.

W.I. Thomas

A psychological approach was taken by Thomas in *The Unadjusted Girl.* In this work, females were seen as the passive opposites of males, who were the active, dynamic sex. The theory Thomas proposed was a dyadic goals-means conflict. Every human, he believed, had basic desires. The desire for new experience and the desire for response were two that influenced criminality. A woman entered prostitution to satisfy a desire for excitement and response; as a woman, prostitution in one form or another was the most likely avenue to satisfy those needs.[67]

Environmental factors were not ignored by Thomas. In fact, a large part of the book was devoted to criticism of the community, which he felt was not doing its job as a socializing agent. Thomas believed that the school should identify maladaptive, predelinquent children very early and treat them before they progressed further in criminal careers. He urged that the community assume its responsibilities in providing legitimate opportunities for attainment of needs.[68]

Contemporary writers criticize Thomas for his liberal paternalism. He believed in manipulating people's lives "for their own good" to conform to social norms that were not necessarily universal. His theories were sexist in that females were identified as offenders through sexual behavior. The sexual standards of society were rigid, and female deviators were castigated more harshly than were male deviators. The significance of this in sociology was that a man's sexual behavior was only one facet of his total character, whereas a woman was actually defined by her sexuality.[69] Thomas also assumed many things that had not been and still are not proved, such as the maternal instinct and the female's greater need for response.[70]

Thomas did make several important observations, such as that crime was one representation of the same creative drive that produced legitimate innovations. He did not, however, break out of the mold set by the dominant liberal social workers. Instead, his theory was a pseudopsychological justification for continuing the rehabilitation methods that were presently being employed. Hence, we continued to "treat" the offender and make only minor changes in the structure of society.

The 1940s

The theories of the 1940s could be easily categorized into those with a psychological framework and those which developed along sociological lines. Tappan looked at the court records of New York. He found that the court system was a moral enforcer as well as a legal body. Wayward girls, those identified as flaunting social standards, were given harsher sentences than those who were judged morally superior. This was the case even when the latter committed more serious crimes. The court had tremendous power in that it often interceded in cases where no criminal offense had been committed. Tappan made many recommendations based on his study. He believed the court should have restricted itself to the legal realm and not acted as a moral enforcer. Additionally, he recommended that probation or other alternatives be used for those girls convicted of a criminal offense. Those not convicted of a criminal offense should never have been committed to institutions, according to Tappan. He wrote that agencies should be coordinated to avoid duplication of efforts. Research, both in causes of delinquency and the success of treatment modes, was needed. Finally, Tappan believed that sociology and the legal system should work together but should not supplant each other's spheres, for they each had different functions.[71]

Other sociological theorists continued to use statistical methods of investigation. Diggs investigated the girl runaway and concluded that her delinquent behavior was the result of disturbances in her life. Diggs compared runaways to delinquent nonrunaways. The findings showed that runaways were more likely to be illegitimate; the educational status of their parents was lower; runaways were more likely to be the oldest child in the family, and they were generally in worse physical condition than nonrunaways.[72] Curran studied 270 female prisoners admitted to Bellevue Hospital in 1940. The average age of the offender was 36.5 years with 58 percent in their twenties and thirties. Twenty percent were black, 24 percent were foreign born, and 47 percent were Catholic. Almost two-thirds of the women had only eight years of schooling. Those with more education seemed more likely to have committed crimes from psychological causes. The marital-status data showed that only 27 percent of the women were married. Regarding offense, 67 percent were committed for prostitution, disorderly conduct, vagrancy, drug addiction, alcoholism, or shoplifting. Only 18 percent were committed for serious crimes. Curran wrote that 40 percent of the cases were psychotic and thirty-three others had psychopathic personalities. Alcoholism played a part in 12 percent of the cases, and mental deficiency was present in 10 percent. Only 16 percent had venereal disease, but 60 percent had other medical or surgical conditions. He concluded that women tended to commit crimes against persons rather than property.[73]

A more useful statistical study was done by von Hentig, who investigated the criminality of black women and found that some of the apparent racial differences were spurious. Statistics showed that prison commitments were twenty black to five white women, but this greater criminality could partially be explained by the higher number of blacks in the crime-prone age group of fifteen to thirty-nine. Another factor that influenced crime was the sex ratio of the population. It was found that, in the age group of twenty to twenty-nine, there was a proportion of black females in excess of black males; in the white population just the opposite was true. Von Hentig believed that this was a factor in racial differences in crime rates. He explored other variables such as mortality, insanity, education, marital status, and occupation. All of these factors contributed to produce a tremendous influence on the criminality of the two groups so that race could scarcely be said to be a factor in itself. Police discrimination was found to be less influential than the demographic variables listed above.[74]

The psychological theorists attributed female criminality to motivations or conflicts in the personality of the offender. These traits were defined most often as inherently female, although Belby believed that female criminals possessed an abundance of masculine traits which caused them to commit crime.[75] Porterfield developed a theory that was very similar to the theory of Thomas in that he postulated a desire-means dichotomy. The adolescent, according to Porterfield, had basic drives that were repressed because of the good examples set by parents. The child was then forced into a criminal subculture to act out her forbidden desires. He also believed that the community played a crucial role in instilling values in potential delinquents.[76]

The most interesting psychological theory was one proposed by Cassity. He wrote that psychological differences explained why females committed less crime than males. He also cited the reasons for different physical capabilities of women, the protective attitudes of society, the female's preoccupation with her home, and her economic and psychological dependency. He found that aggressive crime was higher in females; 12 percent of male crime was aggressive while 20 percent of female crime was. He believed this reflected repressed aggression in the female. Larceny was explained as the woman's desire to please a father image. Cassity was blatantly sexist in his attribution of motives and explanations of crime. He used examples in place of statistics throughout the article, and when he included statistics he did nothing to explain them. For instance, the aggressive nature of 20 percent of female crime only indicates the proportion to total female crime, which was very small compared with male crime, but Cassity led his readers to believe that the female was a volcano ready to explode at the slightest provocation. In a classic example of scientific chauvinism, he admitted that, although females committed less crime, female crime had deeper psychological meaning.[77]

The other literature in the 1940s was of the type exemplified by Monahan.[78] She wrote of her experiences as the warden of the Minnesota Reformatory and the Illinois Training School during the 1920s through the 1940s. This biography has no theoretical or statistical value, but it is interesting in that it gives the reader an insight into the type of thought dominant in the correctional field at that time. Finally, there were some books that did nothing but sensationalize individual women criminals, such as the one by Jenkins.[79]

Pollak

Pollak's book is included in this chapter on classical theories even though it was published at a fairly late date. It capped all the studies made in the field up to 1950. In *The Criminality of Women* Pollak integrated data collected from a comprehensive survey of American, English, French, and German studies. He analyzed the conflicting results and theories and came to his own conclusions regarding female criminal behavior.

Several requirements of a good study were cited by Pollak in his introduction. It should include the ways in which women create crime, the real (as opposed to the apparent) amount of female crime, specificity of female crime, the personal characteristics of female offenders, and the unique factors of causation affecting females. He used criminological sources, medical literature, biographies, psychological research, and trade journals in compiling data to answer the questions he raised.[80]

Pollak decided that women's crime figures did not show the full extent of criminality because of a number of factors. The types of crimes committed by women were petty offenses (such as shoplifting) that were not likely to be prosecuted. In addition, many types of crime that were prosecuted if committed by males were either not identified or ignored if committed by females (such as homosexual behavior and exhibitionism). Because men were socialized to protect women, it was likely that they would not report being the victim of a female offender. In the type of crime committed, Pollak believed that social inequality forced the women to play the part of instigator. If she did play a central role, either her method or her choice of a victim was likely to mask the crime from the public eye. Even when a woman was identified as a criminal, she was likely to receive differential treatment from the criminal justice system. Pollak wrote that male officers experienced conflict in reconciling social norms with their professional duty when it came to dealing with women criminals. In court, women were more likely to be acquitted.[81] Pollak concluded that in answer to the three questions regarding female crime—Are they underreported? Are they less detected? Do they receive more leniency?—the response was a definite yes.

In the second chapter, Pollak looked at the methods females used in committing crimes. He agreed with the theories that described women as more deceitful than men. Various factors went into this conclusion. The relative weakness of the female made deceit necessary as a defense, subversion was found to be a common tactic of all oppressed classes; the biology of the female enabled her to deceive (she could fake orgasm while men could not), and her socialization taught her to conceal many things (menstruation, aggression, and marital frustration). This predilection toward deceit resulted in hidden crime. Women were likely to use methods such as poison that were difficult to detect. They also tended to choose family members as victims, either husbands or, more commonly, children.[82]

In crimes against persons, female crime was predominantly manifested in babyfarming, infanticide, false accusation (usually of a sexual nature), aggravated assault (usually of a lover), and sex offenses against children. Crimes against property included robbery and burglary (usually as accomplices), larceny, pickpocketing, prostitution, shoplifting, blackmail, and fraud. In these types of crimes, Pollak found that women were likely to use their sex role to the victim's disadvantage. The best example of this is the prostitute, but in the other crimes it was also the case. For instance, the female was more likely to create an incident to blackmail a victim, to lure watchmen away from a burglary target, to use sexual advances to pick pockets, and to use her female "enigma" to aid her mystic role in fraud attempts.[83]

Pollak believed that if the amount of hidden crime, such as shoplifting, were projected, the female figures would surpass the figures for males. Even if male hidden crime were to be added in, the differential would still be lower because of the higher number in each group. In other words, when the raw rates were 100 to 10, the differential would be 10 to 1; if the true crime rate were more like 200 to 110, the differential would then be only 1.8 to 1.[84]

Pollak studied the conflicting data, which related increasing social equality of women to their rising crime rates. He had to conclude that there did seem to be a correlation. His statistics on crime rates during the war years showed that, when women entered the mainstream of society by necessity, they also engaged in greater amounts of crime. Pollak cautioned researchers to accept the apparent correlations with reservation since other factors such as prosecution policy, methods of reporting, and changes in the law might affect the results. Regarding specificity of crime, he found that the only crimes that could truly be defined as sex-specific were prostitution and infanticide. He found that age and marital status influenced criminality more than any other factors. Statistically, females were more likely to be criminal if they were in the age group of twenty-five to thirty and married. Domestics predominated in the occupation category, and relatively lower intelligence was likely.[85]

Looking at biological factors, Pollak believed that the generative phases of a woman—menstruation, menopause, and pregnancy—were more influential than either physical weakness or the rate of physiological development. Influential social factors included differential association, the cultural basis of forming desires, and the accessibility of objects for criminal attack. The last factor was very important according to Pollak. The woman's domain, so to speak, was the home, and in it she was virtually invisible from the public eye. This enabled her to commit crime, whether it be poisoning her husband or beating her children, with little chance of detection.[86]

In his summary, Pollak wrote that men had idolized or maligned women because they did not understand them. This, and the tradition of chivalry, masked a large amount of female crime. He predicted that social emancipation would increase the total amount of female crime, but it would not decrease the hidden crime occurring in the home because that would still be the woman's domain.[87] Pollak recognized that social factors such as the oppression of women and the social norms they were forced to comply with affected female crime. His conclusion regarding the influence of social equality was fairly valid. Finally, his was a study that looked at all aspects of female criminality and identified it as a valuable object of research.

Major criticisms have been leveled against Pollak in regard to his statistical conclusions and biases in his assumptions. Smart provides a good critique that covers these points. She objects to Pollak's prison statistics as indicative of the greater aggressiveness of female crime. The leniency that Pollak had already said existed in the courts would make it natural that those women in prison would likely be there for a violent offense. The male's statistics, on the other hand, would be eclipsed by the large amount of property crime. Pollak felt confident in projecting a large amount of hidden female crime and denied the existence of a similar amount of crime for males. Smart writes that both are mere speculations on Pollak's part, and, in fact, it was likely that a large amount of hidden male crime existed in the form of wife beating and child abuse. Smart believes that Pollak's theories on causation were heavily influenced by Freudian analysis and therefore are subject to the same criticism that has been raised against Freudian theory. The assumptions of penis envy and sexual passivity in the female have no proof and were poorly chosen for use in a causal theory.[88] While Pollak recognized the leniency present in the court system, he did not mention the bias in the other direction. The court's power in controlling the social and sexual behavior of women by labeling them deviant was very prevalent.

Conclusions

The literature on female crime contains many attempts to explain why the female seems to commit fewer crimes than the male. Some theorists like Proal believed this differential was due to the greater morality of women. Lombroso and others believed it was due to the biological nature of the female. Still others such as van de Warker and Thomas attributed it to inherent psychological traits of the female. Many theorists believed in an interplay of biological and social conditions. Thus women were believed to commit less crime because of their passive nature, and, reinforcing that, their role defined for them by society. All of these theories had similar classist and sexist notions of what was normal and natural.

In these theories, we see that women were defined by their sexual behavior. They were seen to be influenced by psychological or biological drives to a greater extent than were males. Most theorists, in fact, took a unicausal view whereas theories on males regarded crime as a more complex phenomenon. The theories on female criminality were generally contaminated by popular stereotypes and myths regarding women. Unfortunately, the women criminologists were also guilty of these biases. This shows how powerful socialization can be, even when tempered with scientific training. Only when female crime rates started to rise was serious attention directed toward the field. Contemporary criminologists, especially women such as Rasche, Klein, and Smart, in analyzing these classic studies from feminist perspectives, have done much to expose many of the myths that have existed for so long in the literature.

Notes

1. Herman Schwendinger and Julia Schwendinger, *Sociologists of the Chair* (New York: Basic Books, 1973), 310.
2. Ibid., 290.
3. Christine E. Rasche, "The Female Offender as an Object of Criminological Research," *Criminal Justice and Behavior* 1 (1974), 307-14.
4. Ibid., 304.
5. Ibid., 307.
6. Dorie Klein, "The Etiology of Female Crime: A Review of the Literature," *Issues in Criminology* 8 (1973), 29.
7. Ibid., 28.
8. Ibid., 29.
9. Rita James Simon, *The Contemporary Woman and Crime* (Washington, D.C.: Government Printing Office, 1975), 4.
10. Ibid., 5.
11. Caesare Lombroso and William Ferrero, *The Female Offender* (New York: Appleton, 1920), 45-75.
12. Pauline Tarnowsky, *Les Femmes Homicides* (Paris: Felix Alcan, 1908). As cited in Otto Pollak, *The Criminality of Women* (Philadelphia: University of Pennsylvania Press, 1950), 16.
13. Tarnowsky in Pollak, xvii.
14. Raymond de Ryckere, *La Femme en Prison et devant le mort, Etude de Criminologie* (Lyon: A. Storck, 1898). As cited in Pollak, 37, 112.
15. Pollak, 13, 19-20. Publications about babyfarming include Robert J. Parr, *The Baby Farmer* (London: National Society for the Prevention of Cruelty to Children, 1909); Benjamin Waugh, "Babyfarming," *Contemporary Review* 57 (1890), 700-14; Arthur A. Guild, *Baby Farms in Chicago* (Chicago: Juvenile Protection Association, 1917); and Frances H. Low, "A Remedy for Babyfarming," *Fortnightly Review* 63 (1898), 280-86.

16. Luke Owen Pike, *A History of Crime in England* (London: Smith, Edler and Co., 1876); Cornelis Loosjes, *Bijdrage Tot De Studie Van De Criminaliteit Der Vrouw* (Haarlem: De Erven Loosjes, 1894); Napolione Colajanni, *Sociologia Criminale, II* (Catania: F. Tropea, 1889); and Louis Proal, *Le Crime et La Peine* (Paris: Felix Alcan, 1892). As cited in Pollak, xvi-xviii.

17. George Ellington, *The Woman of New York* (New York: The New York Book Company, 1864). As cited in Pollak, 33-34.

18. Ely van de Warker, "The Relations of Women to Crime," *Popular Science Monthly* 8 (1875-1876), 1-16.

19. Walter C. Reckless, *The Crime Problem* (New York: Appleton-Century-Crofts, 1967), 246.

20. Lombroso and Ferrero, 27-28.

21. Ibid., 23, 104, 111.

22. Ibid., 151.

23. Ibid., 109, 151.

24. Ibid., 104.

25. Ibid., 204, 207.

26. Ibid., 218-35, 245, 269.

27. Ibid., 297.

28. Ibid., 56.

29. Klein, 10.

30. Carol Smart, *Women, Crime and Criminology, A Feminist Critique* (London: Routledge and Kegan Paul, 1977), 35.

31. Fr. Prinzing, "Der Einfluss der Ehe duf die Kriminalitat des Mannes," *Zeitschrift Fur Sozial Wissenschaft, II Atte Folge* (1899), 433-50; and Louis Puibaraud, "La Femme Criminelle," *Grande Agview* 12 (1899), 415. As cited in Pollak, 109, 140.

32. Arthur Griffiths, "Female Criminals," *North American Review* 161 (1895), 145-52.

33. Frances A. Kellor, "Psychological and Environmental Study of Women Criminals," *American Journal of Sociology* 5 (1900), 527, 531.

34. Ibid., 542.

35. Frances Kellor, Criminal Sociology—Criminality Among Women," *Arena* 23 (1900), 516-24.

36. Kellor, "Psychological and Environmental . . . ," 675-76.

37. Hargrave Adams, *Women and Crime* (London: T. Warner Laurie, 1914), 17. Other books that were more or less similar to Adams's were: Mrs. Cecil Chesterton, *Women of the Underworld* (London: Stanley Paul and Co., Ltd., 1928), and Netley Lucas, *Crook Janes, A Study of the Women Criminal the World Over* (London: Stanley Paul and Co., Ltd., 1926).

38. Hugo Hoegel, "Die Straffaligkeit de Weibes," *Archiv fur Kriminal*

Anthropologie 5 (1900), 231-89; Dora Melegari, "La Femme Criminelle en Italie," *Le Correspondant* 210 (1903), 524-49; Hugo Herz, "Die Kriminalitat des Weibes nach den Ergebnissen der neueren osterreichischen statistik," *Archiv fur Kriminal-Anthropologie* 18 (1905), 285-303; and L. Roncoroni, "Influenza del Sesso sulla criminalita in Italia," Archivio di Psichiatria, *Science Penalt et Antropologia Criminale* 14 (1893), 1-14. See Pollak, 80, 89, 98, 99.

39. Hans Gross, *Kriminal psychologie* (Leipzig: F.C.W. Vogel, 1905); Max Fischer, "Schwangerschaft und Diebstandi," *Allgemeine Zeitschrift fur Psychiatrie* 111 (1904), 312-54; and C. Granier, *La Femme Criminelle* (Paris: Octave Doin, 1906). Another later study analyzed the statistics on infanticide. Suffocation and strangulation occurred in twenty-five cases out of sample of forty-nine in a study by G. Puppe, "Zur Psychologie und Prophylaxe des Kindesmordes," *Deutsche Medizinische Wochenschrift* 43 (1917), 609-13. As cited in Pollak, 9, 12, 21, 22, 136.

40. H. Leale, "De la Criminalite des Sexes," *Archives of Anthropologie Criminelle* 25 (1910), 401-30; Mary Conyngton, "Relation Between Occupation and Criminality of Women," *Report on Conditions of Women and Child Wage Earners in the United States* 15 (1911), 61st Congress, 2nd Session, Senate Document no. 645; and Gustav Aschaffenburg, *Crime and Its Repression* (Boston: Little, Brown and Co., 1913). As cited in Pollak, xviii, 111, 112.

41. Maurice Parmelee, *Criminology* (New York: The Macmillan Company, 1918); and *City Council Committee on Crime of the City of Chicago, Report of* (Chicago, 1915). As cited in Pollak, 5, 112.

42. V.V. Anderson, "The Immoral Woman as Seen in Court," *Journal of the American Institute of Criminal Law and Criminology* 8 (1917-18), 904, 908.

43. Jean Weidensall, *The Mentality of the Criminal Woman* (Baltimore: Warwick and York, 1916), 18, 250.

44. Ibid., 223, 284, 286.

45. Mabel Fernald, Mary Hayes, and Almena Dawley, *A Study of Women Delinquents in New York State* (New York: Century Company, 1920), 127-68, 214, 242, 525.

46. Ibid., 528.

47. Alberta S.B. Guibord, "Physical States of Criminal Women," *Journal of the American Institute of Criminal Law and Criminology* 8 (1917-18), 91-94.

48. Edith S. Spaulding, "The Results of Mental and Physical Examinations of 400 Women Offenders—With Particular Reference to their Treatment during Commitment," *Journal of the American Institute of Criminal Law and Criminology* 5 (1914-15), 704-717.

49. Edith Spaulding, *An Experimental Study of Psychopathic Delinquent Women* (New York: Rand McNally, 1923), 50, 96-97, 102, 112.

50. Ibid., 71, 99, 105.

51. William Healy and Augusta Bronner, *Delinquents and Their Criminals: Their Making and Unmaking* (New York: Macmillan and Company, 1926), 56.

52. See Anne Bingham, "Determinants of Sex Delinquency in Adolescent Girls Based on Intensive Studies of 500 Cases," *Journal of Criminal Law and Criminology* 13 (1922-23), 494-586; Edith N. Burleigh and Frances R. Harris, *The Delinquent Girl* (New York: The New York School of Social Work, Studies in Social Work, Child Welfare Series, Monograph, no. 3, 1923); Sophonisba Breckinridge and Edith Abbott, *The Delinquent Child and the Home* (New York: Charities Publishing Committee, 1912); Augusta Bronner, A Comparative Study of the Intelligence of Delinquent Girls (New York: Teacher's College, Columbia University Contributions to Education, no. 68, 1914); Julia Mathews, "A Survey of 341 Delinquent Girls in California," *The Journal of Delinquency* 8 (1923), 196-231; and Winifred Richmond, *The Adolescent Girl* (New York: Macmillan Co., 1926).

53. Marie E. Kopp, *Birth Control in Practice* (New York: Robert M. McBride and Company, 1934); and Frederick J. Taussig, *Abortion Spontaneous and Induced, Medical and Social Aspects* (St. Louis: C.V. Mosby Co., 1936). As cited in Pollak, 47, 48.

54. J.H. Morton, "Female Homicides," *Journal of Mental Science* 80 (1934), 70-71.

55. Kingston Davis, "The Sociology of Prostitution," *American Sociological Review* 2 (1937), 744-56. Other studies on prostitution include Gladys Hall, *Prostitution in the Modern World* (New York: Emerson Books, Inc., 1936) and Howard Woolston, *Prostitution in the United States* (New York: Century Company, 1921).

56. Cecil Bishop, *Women and Crime* (London: Chatto and Windus, 1931). See Pollak, 24, 49.

57. Leslie Radzinowicz, "Variability of the Sex Ratio of Criminality," *Sociological Review* 29 (1937), 90-98.

58. Clarence H. Growdon, "The Mental Status of Reformatory Women," *Journal of the American Institute of Criminal Law and Criminology* 22 (1931-32), 196-220. For a similar study conducted in Nebraska, see T.E. Sullenger, "Female Criminality in Omaha," *Journal of Criminal Law and Criminology* 27 (1936-37), 706-11.

59. Katherine Lumpkin, "Factors in the Commitment of Correctional School Girls in Wisconsin," *American Journal of Sociology* 37 (1932),222-30.

60. Sheldon and Eleanor Glueck, *Five Hundred Delinquent Women* (New York: Alfred A. Knopf, 1934), 64-67, 340.

61. Ibid., 78-94, 101.

62. Ibid., 130, 193, 236, 264, 282.

63. Ibid., 89, 302-21.

64. Ibid., 309-22.

65. Eugenia Lekkerkerker, *Reformatories for Women in the United States* (Groningen, The Hague: J.B. Wolter, 1931), 163-64.

66. Ibid., 131, 140, 169.

67. W.I. Thomas, *The Unadjusted Girl* (Boston: Little, Brown and Company, 1937), 6, 30, 109.

68. Ibid., 56, 199.

69. Smart, 37.

70. Thomas, 21, 67.

71. Paul Tappan, *Delinquent Girls in Court* (New York: Columbia University Press, 1947), 92-102, 224-26.

72. Mary Huff Diggs, "The Girl Runaway," in National Probation and Parole Association (ed), *Current Approaches to Delinquency* (1949), 72.

73. Frank J. Curran, "Specific Trends in Criminality of Women," *Journal of Criminal Psychopathology* 3 (1941-42), 605-24.

74. Hans von Hentig, "The Criminality of the Colored Woman," in *University of Colorado Studies*, Series C. Volume 1, No. 3 (1942), 231-60.

75. Jose Belby, "Female Delinquency," *Archives de Medicina Legal Argentina* 12 (1942), 3-20.

76. Austin L. Porterfield, *Youth in Trouble* (Ft. Worth: Leo Potishmen Foundation, 1946), 100.

77. J.H. Cassity, "Socio-psychiatric Aspects of Female Felons," *Journal of Criminal Psychopathology* 3 (1941-42), 597-604.

78. Florence Monahan, *Women in Crime* (New York: Ives Washburn, Inc., 1941).

79. Elizabeth Jenkins, *Six Criminal Women* (Freeport, New York: Books for Libraries Press, 1949).

80. Pollak, xix-xx

81. Ibid., 1-4.

82. Ibid., 10-13.

83. Ibid., 20-25, 31-42.

84. Ibid., 48-54.

85. Ibid., 59-64, 84-113.

86. Ibid., 122-46.

87. Ibid., 149-55.

88. Smart, 50-52.

3 Women and Drugs: Beyond the Hippie Subculture

Data on sex differences in the use of legal and illegal drugs have been collected more extensively than the data on any other type of deviant behavior. These data establish the fact that males and females evince rather different patterns of drug use, and in addition reveal different combinations of variables that are causally associated with drug use. In this chapter, we will look at these patterns and variables. In addition, information will be presented in support of the idea that some of the differences between male and female drug use are caused by the sexual oppression of women.

Sexual Differentiation in the Use of Legal and Illegal Drugs

To justify treating females as a special group, it must be shown that they have patterns of drug use and abuse that are different from male patterns, or at least that different factors are associated with female drug use than with male drug use. In this section, we present the results of a survey of over 200 research reports containing data on drug-use differences between the sexes. These data establish beyond any reasonable doubt that there are large male-female differences in drug use at every age level.

Table 3-1 presents male-female comparisons of gross frequencies of use for eleven categories of drugs, based on an extensive survey of the literature. Males exhibit higher levels of drug use at all age levels for marijuana, hallucinogens, alcohol, nicotine, and illegal drugs in general. They also predominate among the school children who use narcotics and solvents, the college students who use narcotics, barbiturates, and amphetamines, and the adults who use solvents. Females show a clear preponderance of use for the ingestion of tranquilizers and legal drugs in general at all ages and for the use of amphetamines and barbiturates among adults. There are four categories of drugs for which approximately the same proportion of males and females are users or regular users. These are the use of solvents by college students and amphetamines and barbiturates by school children.

This chapter is a revision and condensation of Lee H. Bowker, *Drug Use Among American Women, Old and Young: Sexual Oppression and Other Themes* (Palo Alto, CA: R&E Research Associates, 1977), and also relies on material derived from Lee H. Bowker, "The Relationship Between Sex, Drugs and Sexual Behavior on a College Campus," *Drug Forum* 7 (1978), 69-80.

Table 3-1
Female-Male Comparsons of Drug-Use Frequencies

Drug and Age of Subjects	*Studies in which Males Show Higher Use Rates*	*Studies in which Females Show Higher Use Rates*	*Studies in which Male and Female Approximately Equal*
Marijuana			
School children	23	0	4
College students	40	1	11
Adults	7	0	0
Hallucinogens			
School children	13	0	5
College students	20	0	2
Adults	4	0	0
Alcohol			
School children	25	0	3
College students	20	0	5
Adults	10	0	1
Narcotics			
School children	7	0	2
College students	14	0	3
Adults	4	5	0
Nicotine			
School children	10	2	5
College students	8	3	3
Adults	6	0	0
Solvents			
School children	8	0	3
College students	2	2	0
Adults	1	0	0
Amphetamines and other "uppers"			
School children	3	3	10
College students	13	2	7
Adults	0	7	2
Barbiturates and other "downers"			
School children	2	3	8
College students	10	6	5
Adults	0	7	1
Tranquilizers			
School children	0	3	6
College students	0	14	3
Adults	0	10	0
Illegal drugs in general[a]			
School children	8	0	1
College students	13	0	2
Adults	2	0	0
Legal drugs in general[a]			
School children	0	3	0
College students	0	7	0
Adults	3	12	3

[a]Many studies listed only illegal or legal drugs in general, rather than specific drugs in either category.

The drug categories discussed here can be simultaneously classified by degree of legality and purpose of use. This classification is presented in table 3-2. Male use predominates in every drug that is used mostly for recreational purposes, which also includes all those drugs that are illegal, or legal only for adults. A large majority of the males using tobacco and alcohol as adults began as adolescents, when the use of those drugs was either illegal or at least prohibited by administrative regulation. There would seem to be a relationship between a drug's illegality and its predominant use by males.

"Uppers" and "downers" are extensively prescribed by physicians, mostly for females, but are also widely available on the street, where the proportion of male users rises drastically. As a result of these two conflicting trends, the use figures are rather inconsistent for adolescents and college students. At the adult level, male use of illegal drugs decreases as compared with younger males, though sexual differentiation in the use of illegal drugs increases due to the fact that female illegal drug use decreases even more steeply than male illegal drug use. Because of this decrease in male illegal use of "uppers" and "downers," legal prescription use by females predominates, which is why no study shows higher adult use of these drugs by males than females.

Males report higher use levels of narcotics than females at all ages, and, among adults, of other pain-reducing preparations such as aspirin. In contrast, females invariably use more tranquilizers, legal psychoactive drugs, and prescription drugs in general than do males. How do these two groups of drugs differ? None of the drugs is completely illegal, nor are any of these mainly used for recreational purposes. The male corner on narcotics use may be related to the fact that there is extensive use of narcotics obtained illegally (heroin, etc.) among males, but comparatively less nonlegal use by

Table 3-2
Drug-Use Categories Classified by Legal Status and Purpose of Use

	Legal Status			
Purpose of Use	*Legal*	*Legal for Adults*	*Legal by Prescription*	*Illegal*
Recreational		alcohol nicotine		marijuana hallucinogens solvents illegal drugs in general
Partially Medical	legal drugs in general		narcotics "uppers" "downers"	
Medical	aspirin		tranquilizers prescription drugs	

females. Another factor is that it is acceptable for males to use drugs for recreation (marijuana, alcohol, etc.) or physical pain (narcotics, aspirin), but not for mood modification, particularly in adult life.

The material in this section establishes beyond any doubt that there are considerable differences between the sexes in drug-consumption habits. It is the task of the remainder of this chapter to attempt to provide a meaningful explanation of these differences. Significant differences are not necessarily total differences. In fact, total differences rarely occur in human behavior. In statistical terms, what we have is not a matter of two discontinuous curves, but rather two distributions that have more overlap than difference.

As a footnote to this section it should be mentioned that, in addition to engaging in different patterns of drug use, males and females may also experience different effects from the use of the same drugs. There is not yet enough research in this area to make a strong statement, but MacLennan mentions a British study in which drugs from the amylobarbital and trifluopenazine groups did have different effects on males and females in a double-blind experimental design.[1] Whether this could be due to innate biological differences, socialization patterns, or both remains to be seen. One aspect of differential drug effects that is due to biological differences is the impact of weight. Women weigh less than men on the average, and the severity of the effect of most drugs is inversely associated with weight. Green and Nemzer have pointed out that when one takes the weight difference into account, a lower rate of consumption by women does not necessarily mean lower toxicity or psychopharmacological effects, since these effects are determined by consumption per pound rather than per person, regardless of weight.[2]

Female Drug Use in a Rural County

The author conducted nine surveys of drug use and abuse in Walla Walla County, Washington, between 1972 and 1974. These were initially summarized in a monograph,[3] four technical reports,[4] and six journal articles.[5] Seven of the nine surveys were completed under an implementation and development grant funded by the National Institute of Mental Health (NIMH) and the other two were additional surveys of one of the three local colleges.

Walla Walla County is a rural county of about 50,000, located in eastern Washington and having an economy based largely on agriculture. It has more of the rich and the poor than most American counties, and a correspondingly small middle class. Minority individuals are relatively few in number, but retired persons are heavily overrepresented. The isolation and conservatism of the county is somewhat relieved by the unusual circumstance of the presence of three colleges and a number of federal or state institutions.

All data are not of the same quality. Three estimates of the quality of data presented are provided by (1) the quality of questions asked, (2) the setting under which they are asked, and (3) the proportion of respondents contacted who complete the questionnaire or interview. In all the surveys, questions were developed after a careful analysis of the literature which included obtaining the best questionnaires available from other researchers in the field. In addition, the questionnaires were pretested on volunteer subjects before reaching their final form. Finally, the NIMH questionnaires were each examined and criticized by a committee of informed citizens and professionals. While the final products were less than perfect, the use of these three filters produced questionnaires of acceptable quality.

Setting is crucial to all research with human subjects. There were slight variations in technique, but basically the studies incorporated a number of mechanisms to ensure respondent anonymity as well as to make sure that the respondents were confident that their responses were anonymous, a condition that does not automatically follow from the researcher's intention of anonymity. Not only did the questionnaires state that no names were to be used, but trained research aides reinforced this point verbally when they gave out the questionnaires. At the same time, they gave each subject an unmarked envelope into which the completed questionnaire was to be sealed, and displayed a sealed box with a slit in it, explaining that the envelope containing the completed questionnaire was to be inserted in the box by the subject and that only the director of the project could open the box to collect the questionnaires. If the subject was unable to read or write well, research aides were instructed to provide whatever help was requested, including reading the entire questionnaire to them if necessary. These and other mechanisms designed into the research setting give us some assurance that the majority of subjects saw the questionnaire as safe, worthwhile, and professional.

The third factor, response rate, is a reflection of both the quality of the questionnaire and the setting. If these are inferior, the response rate will certainly be too low. Even if they are well constructed, other factors may combine to lower the response rate. One simple way of looking at response rates is to label less than 70 percent as inadequate, 70 to 80 percent as good, 80 to 90 percent as very good, and over 90 percent as excellent.

The response rate in the 1972 college study was 95 percent, and the resurvey of this population in late 1974 achieved a 94 percent rate. In between, this institution was one of three area colleges surveyed under the NIMH drug study. These three NIMH surveys were "farmed out" to research associates employed by the grant because a number of studies were being conducted simultaneously. Apparently, this allowed a decline in quality control, for the response rates on the three colleges were 67 percent, 62 percent, and 51 percent. Due to the inadequacy of these rates, the discussion of college student drug use in this monograph is based almost entirely on the 1972 and 1974 privately conducted studies.

The three private schools surveyed were all associated with religious denominations. The questionnaires were administered by project personnel in the classrooms without the presence of the teachers. The response rate was 100 percent in each school, though some students did not answer every question on the questionnaire and a few who were absent on the testing day were not included in the survey.

The NIMH adults study utilized a multi-stage random sampling design, starting with city blocks and then moving to occupied dwelling units and finally to a random selection of the adult residents within each occupied dwelling unit. The response rate was 71 percent. The 29 percent nonrespondents included both those actively or passively refusing to participate and those who could not be contacted after repeated callbacks. Anecdotal evidence from the research aides suggests that heavy drug users were underrepresented among those completing questionnaires.

In the three private schools surveyed, the ever-use statistics for females were 3 percent for LSD, 3 percent for narcotics, 11 percent for amphetamines, 15 percent for tranquilizers, 17 percent for barbiturates, 20 percent for marijuana, 32 percent for nicotine and 48 percent for alcohol. Thirty percent had used over-the-counter drugs and 35 percent had used other prescription medicines within the past twelve months. Forty-six percent reported using aspirin at least once per month, and 32 percent used caffeine at least once a week. Weekly use of alcohol was reported by only 5 percent and weekly use of marijuana by 6 percent. Tables 3-3 and 3-4 present these data, with male rates added for comparison. These figures are unusually low due to the high percentage of Seventh-Day Adventist students in the samples. It is relatively certain that the percentages of use would be

Table 3-3
Marijuana and Alcohol Use by Students in Three Walla Walla County Private Schools, by Sex of Respondent

	Male				*Female*			
	Marijuana		*Alcohol*		*Marijuana*		*Alcohol*	
Never	119	(72%)	78	(51%)	147	(80%)	94	(52%)
Less than once a week	19	(11%)	52	(34%)	25	(14%)	78	(43%)
Once a week or more	28	(17%)	23	(15%)	11	(6%)	10	(5%)
Total	166	(100%)	153	(100%)	183	(100%)	182	(100%)

Table 3-4
Selected Drugs Ever Used by Private-School Students in Walla Walla County, by Sex of Respondent[a]

(Percentage)

	Male	*Female*
Barbiturates	14	17
LSD	11	3
Narcotics	8	3
Amphetamines	14	11
Tranquilizers	17	15

[a]*N*s varied slightly from drug to drug, but were approximately 165 for males and 180 for females.

higher for non-Adventist public-school children. Despite the small numbers involved, it bears mentioning that females using recreational drugs at least once a week were as likely to use marijuana as alcohol.

The reported drug use of opposite-sex close friends influenced females to use alcohol themselves more than it did males. For same-sex close friends, males were more influenced to drink than females. Exactly the same pattern was formed for marijuana use of boys and girls. Tables 3-5 and 3-6 show these relationships for marijuana use. What all this means is that girls are more influenced to use the major recreational drugs of alcohol and marijuana by their boyfriends than by their girlfriends. The causal chain influencing use is heterosocial, from boys to girls. On the other hand, boys are more influenced by their close male friends, so for them the causal chain is homosocial. One might hypothesize from these findings that drug use spreads in an age-specific cohort of youngsters from a few male drug users to a larger number of boys, and then from the boys to the girls. There is much evidence in support of this in other Walla Walla studies, as well as in published data from other parts of the nation.

Though males generally consumed larger amounts of drugs than females, most other dimensions showed no significant differences between the sexes, including tardiness in school, skipping classes, grades, attendance at dances, dates and movies, church attendance, and perceptions of quality of life in both the present and the future. One variable that did show a modest difference was stealing. Nineteen percent of the boys and only 10 percent of the girls admitted having stolen things in the past.

Both boys and girls were strongly influenced by the perceived drug use of their parents and siblings. In general, parental and siblings alcohol use influenced girls to use alcohol or marijuana more than it did boys. Girls were also more likely than boys to use over-the-counter medicines if their

Table 3-5
Self's Marijuana Use and the Perceived Drug Use of Opposite-Sex Close Friends, for Males and Females

	Perceived Opposite-Sex Friends' Drug Use					
	Male[a]			*Female*[b]		
Self's Marijuana Use	*Less than Self*	*Same*	*More*	*Less than Self*	*Same*	*More*
Not this year	12 (33%)	67 (81%)	15 (68%)	12 (67%)	86 (90%)	36 (67%)
This year	24 (67%)	16 (19%)	7 (32%)	6 (33%)	10 (10%)	18 (33%)
Total	36 (100%)	83 (100%)	22 (100%)	18 (100%)	96 (100%)	54 (100%)

[a] $\chi^2 = 25.435, p < .001$, gamma = –.50.
[b] $\chi^2 = 13.518, p < .01$, gamma = .27.

Table 3-6
Self's Marijuana Use and the Perceived Drug Use of Same-Sex Close Friends, for Males and Females

	Perceived Same-Sex Friends' Drug Use					
	Male[a]			*Female*[b]		
Self's Marijuana Use	*Less than Self*	*Same*	*More*	*Less than Self*	*Same*	*More*
Not this year	8 (73%)	57 (69%)	30 (64%)	7 (44%)	94 (85%)	32 (80%)
This year	3 (27%)	26 (31%)	17 (36%)	9 (56%)	17 (15%)	8 (20%)
Total	11 (100%)	83 (100%)	47 (100%)	16 (100%)	111 (100%)	40 (100%)

[a] $\chi^2 = 0.506$, not significant, gamma = .12.
[b] $\chi^2 = 14.152, p < .001$, gamma = –.29.

mothers did, but the sexes were equally influenced by what they perceived to be the use of over-the-counter medicines by their fathers and siblings. The perceived nicotine use of mother, father, and siblings was more likely to be associated with marijuana use in boys than girls. Exactly why girls seemed to be more sensitive to family alcohol use and boys to nicotine use was not revealed by the study, but it may be linked to the norms for appropriate sex-role behavior.

Ever-use statistics for female college students in the 1972 survey were 9 percent barbiturates, 19 percent for hallucinogens, 18 percent for amphetamines, 24 percent for tranquilizers, and 50 percent for marijuana. Nearly one-third of those females who tried marijuana currently used it more than once a month. At the level of use once or more per week, 14 percent used nicotine, 26 percent used aspirin, 33 percent used other legal drugs, and 39 percent used alcohol. Table 3-7 presents detailed drug-use information for four of these drugs.

The data from the 1972 college study offer some support for the theory advanced by Cooperstock in "Sex Differences in the Use of Mood-Modifying Drugs: An Explanatory Model" that drug use is sexually differentiated along an instrumental-expressive continuum. She believed that male drug use tended to be seen as useful in ways such as aiding in studying for exams, decreasing physical pain, or in relaxing at parties, while females tended to use drugs to modify moods rather than to accomplish utilitarian or social tasks.[6] But her theory does not explain why female use is only higher for legal drugs. We suggest that it is access to (and control of) the illegal drug distribution system that is the primary factor in higher male rates of the use of certain kinds of drugs.

In addition to examining causal relationships for individual categories of drugs, the 1972 study summed all rates of drug use into an index of total drug use. Using this index as the dependent variable, we found that females were more influenced to use drugs by what they believed to be the drug use of their boyfriends than males were by their girlfriends. Although the relationships are weaker, females were also more influenced by what they believed to be the drug use of their female friends than males were by their male friends. On the other hand, males were more influenced to use drugs than females by what they believed to be the drug use of other students in the college. Table 3-8 summarizes these relationships. Taken together, these findings support the idea of the male as the carrier of drug-use patterns to females. They also suggest that females may be more sensitive to social stimuli in their immediate life space, while males' sensitivity is greater for the more distant social environment.

It was decided to restudy the college population that had been surveyed in 1972 in order to gain further information about the ways in which males controlled the drug distribution system and encouraged females to use

Table 3-7
The Use of Alcohol, Amphetamines, Marijuana, and Hallucinogens by Male and Female College Students

	Male								Female							
	Alcohol		*Amphe-tamines*		*Mari-juana*		*Hallu-cinogens*		*Alcohol*		*Amphe-tamines*		*Mari-juana*		*Hallu-cinogens*	
Never used	23	(7%)	243	(74%)	117	(36%)	245	(78%)	25	(8%)	256	(82%)	153	(50%)	248	(81%)
Used, but not last year	13	(4%)	13	(4%)	25	(8%)	21	(7%)	9	(3%)	9	(3%)	21	(7%)	16	(5%)
Used less than once a month	59	(19%)	58	(18%)	51	(16%)	37	(12%)	64	(21%)	36	(12%)	40	(13%)	37	(12%)
About once a month	82	(26%)	7	(2%)	41	(13%)	12	(4%)	89	(29%)	3	(1%)	40	(13%)	6	(2%)
About once a week	106	(33%)	3	(1%)	37	(12%)	1	(0%)	96	(31%)	6	(2%)	23	(8%)	1	(0%)
2-4 times a week	34	(11%)	3	(1%)	41	(13%)	0	(0%)	23	(7%)	1	(0%)	16	(5%)	0	(0%)
5 or more times a week	1	(0%)	0	(0%)	9	(3%)	0	(0%)	3	(1%)	0	(0%)	11	(4%)	0	(0%)
Total	318	(100%)	327	(100%)	321	(101%)[a]	316	(101%)[a]	309	(100%)	311	(100%)	304	(100%)	308	(100%)

[a]Where percentages do not add to 100, it is due to rounding error.

Table 3-8
The Specification by Sex of Relationships[a] between Measures of the Perceived Peer Drug Environment and College Student Drug Use

	Male	*Female*	*Total*
Perceived opposite-sex best friend's drug use × self's drug use	−.34	.30	−.04
Perceived same-sex best friend's drug use × self's drug use	−.10	.22	.06
Perceived drug use of other students × self's drug use	.34	.18	.26

[a]Correlations are gamma correlations, based on the analysis of 2 × 2 and 2 × 3 tables.

drugs, including alcohol. By asking how drugs came to be in the possession of the students, it was found that males generally bought their drugs while females were more likely to be given their drugs. Only 11 percent of the females always bought their drugs, but 67 percent were usually or always given the drugs they used. Among males, 70 percent normally bought their own drugs. Females were much more likely than males to engage in sexual relations of some sort with their drug suppliers. Twenty-three percent of the females reported currently receiving their drugs from someone they were sexually involved with, and 49 percent reported either a current or a past involvement. Comparable figures for males were 6 percent and 21 percent.

The most common drug used as a tool in sexual seduction was alcohol. Marijuana was far less popular, and no other drug saw much use at all for this purpose. Forty-eight percent of the males and 56 percent of the females reported participating actively or passively in a date where alcohol was used to make one of the partners more sexually willing or responsive. Marijuana was mentioned in this context by only 31 percent of the males and 32 percent of the females.

Males were slightly more likely than females to approve of "a girl offering drugs to a guy," but females were more likely to approve of a girl's paying her own way on a date. There was no sex difference in the level of approval of "a guy offering drugs to a girl," nor were there statistically significant differences between the sexes in the levels of social and sexual interpersonal activity. Males showed stronger support for the legalization of marijuana, as they usually do in surveys of college populations.

The initial "turn-on" with marijuana, alcohol, and other recreational drugs was same sex for males but opposite sex for females. That is to say, females were likely to be "turned on" by males, but the reverse was not true. Approximately nine of every ten males who started using recreational drugs were initially "turned on" by males, as compared with same-sex female drug introductions of only 52 percent for alcohol, 41 percent for marijuana, and 28 percent for other recreational drugs. The same pattern continued in later uses of recreational drugs. Females were less likely than males to use marijuana or alcohol with same-sex friends, but more likely to use it in mixed groups of males and females. They were also more likely to receive drugs from the opposite sex on a continuing basis. One reason for this imbalance was undoubtedly that males knew more people who could supply them with alcohol, marijuana, or pills. For example, nearly half the women did not know anyone who would supply them with drugs in pill form, but more than two-thirds of the males did know a source of pills.

Approximately six in every ten females had at least tried marijuana, and one in six had tried some other illegal recreational drug (not counting alcohol). Males used these drugs more heavily than females, but there was no significant sex difference in alcohol consumption. Although male and female alcohol consumption did not differ greatly, the perceived effect of the drug differed, with females being more likely to feel that alcohol increased their level of sexual behavior. Marijuana and other recreational drugs did not increase sexual behavior for college women any more than for college men.

Respondents were directly asked whether they had ever used any drugs to seduce members of the opposite sex. Approximately half of the independent men and nearly two-thirds of the fraternity members admitted using drugs in this fashion at least once, as compared with less than a quarter of the co-eds. These research findings establish more clearly than any other studies published to date the way in which males use drugs to reduce the freedom of females in dating activities.

Some of the drugs included in this study may be used to encourage or facilitate sexual behavior. None of them can be said to be an aphrodisiac in a technical sense because none has the same impact on sexual behavior every time it is taken. The effect of a given drug varies with such factors as the personality and biophysical makeup of the user, the characteristics of the immediate setting, and the more general culture in which they are embedded. Adolescents and young adults use alcohol, marijuana, and occasionally other drugs as if they were true aphrodisiacs, even though they are not. Not only do they generally reduce inhibitions, but they also help to set a norm-breaking mood which encourages people to "let go."

The 1974 college study broke down many bivariate relationships by introducing affiliation (fraternity and sorority or independent) as a control variable. The data thus obtained support to some degree the common stereotype of fraternity men as more sexist than independents. However, the similarities between affiliated students and independents were more important than the differences. The imbalance between the sexes in the control of the drug distribution system was found to be considerable among independents, and even greater between fraternity and sorority members. The correlation between mode of drug reception (bought or given) and sex was slightly higher for affiliated students than for independents. In addition, correlations between sex and both having sex with your drug supplier and active drug seductions were quite a bit higher for affiliated students than for independents.

Fraternity members are not unusual people. Their sexism is only a slightly concentrated reflection of the pervasive homosocial climate that exists in America. In a homosocial society, males' social behavior is primarily oriented toward other males, with females playing a secondary role. This general American characteristic is always accentuated wherever males are relatively isolated, as in prisons, military organizations, and in the boarding-school atmosphere of single-sex college residence halls and fraternities.

As a rule of thumb, males can be considered to be homosocial when even their interaction with members of the opposite sex is indirectly oriented toward other males. The ultimate development of the homosocial orientation occurs when the main motivation for a fraternity member's heterosexual activity is the status it gains him among his fraternity brothers. When intensely involved with his date, the thought occurs to him, "Oh boy, wait till the brothers hear about this!" It is to be expected that sexual exploitation will be the goal of many college men, for it would take considerable strength of personality and an unusual experience of childhood socialization to ignore the combined forces of homosocial status pressure from the social system and sexual desire from the physical organism. It is unfortunate that this kind of undergraduate experience tends further to socialize men to engage in sexist and exploitive relations with women in adult life.

What the data presented in this section suggest is a model which includes inputs of sexist norms, beliefs, and values from the larger society on a cultural level, of sexual desire from the biological and psychological system, and of ecological living patterns on the structural, or sociological, level. Two years of personal observation as a faculty resident in a co-ed residence hall suggest that the strength of the input from the structural level is at least as strong as the other determinants of heterosexual exploitation. In the co-ed residence hall, exploitive behavior between the sexes seemed to be remarkably reduced as compared with relationships between young men and women housed in separate dorms, and this perception was shared with the author by the students involved.

An exception to the general pattern in the data was that a higher proportion of independent women than sorority sisters received all of their marijuana, alcohol, and pills from men. This was probably a reflection of the tendency of some affiliated women to supply their sorority sisters with drugs on an informal basis. Men seemed to dominate the distribution system slightly more among independents than affiliated students, but more independent women paid for their drugs, thus presumably retaining a greater degree of independence in their heterosexual relationships.

It is evident that the drug scene at this college is controlled by men. Women are introduced to drugs through men and largely supplied with their drugs by men on a continuing basis. A number of women have never received drugs from another women—an amazing situation in a residence college where most women live in intimate contact with small groups of other women in the residence hall.

Where is the line between control and exploitation? Women do not generally buy their drugs. They are given to them, commonly by their boyfriends or other male associates. Doesn't this reduce their freedom to resist sexual advances, and in other ways to be a free and equal partner in the dating relationship? It is not surprising that a significant number of women have had sexual relations with their drug suppliers. This is consistent with the data on the use of drugs by males in drug seductions. In using the concept of the drug seduction we do not mean to imply that females enjoy sex less than males, but rather that their selection of possible male partners is unnaturally attenuated by the male domination of the drug distribution system. As a matter of fact, it is probable that in some cases females are using sex to seduce males into providing them with drugs rather than the reverse. There are always secondary gains associated with minority-group status, and this would be an example of the use of limited resources to obtain desired goods in the sexual marketplace.

Do the findings presented here justify defining the male college student as a sexual predator, who counts drugs among his many tools to be used in the conquest and use of females as objects for his own pleasure? They certainly are not conclusive in this respect, but they do suggest that the image of the sexual predator is not without some validity. We need additional research to sharpen this image and to produce an estimate of the extent of sexual predation on the college campus, as well as to develop a typology of morphological entities and levels of severity in the male use of drugs to increase his dominance over women in intimate relationships.

In the sample of adults from Walla Walla and College Place, females used drugs at a lower rate than has been found in various national studies. This result was mainly due to the large population of Seventh-Day Adventists in the Walla Walla area, a group that is strongly opposed to recreational drug use. Ever-use statistics were 35 percent for tranquilizers, 28 percent for barbiturates, 25 percent for narcotics, 12 percent for marijuana, and 4 percent for the stronger hallucinogens. Only 63 percent reported using alcohol in the last year, and less than half of these drank more often than once a month. Twenty-five percent took aspirin more commonly than once a month, 44 percent used other prescription medicines for more than a short period, 42 percent used over-the-counter medicines for more than a short period, and 26 percent used nicotine more than five times per week. The full distributions for adult female use of all kinds of drugs are given in table 3-9.

Respondents were asked to indicate which of eight categories of needs (physical/sensory, to relieve tension, to socialize, to rebel, to become more alert, aesthetic appreciation, to increase life's meaning, and for adventure) were met by twelve kinds of drug use. Adults used nicotine and alcohol for the same reasons, to relieve tension and to socialize. Amphetamines were used to relieve tension and to increase alertness. Caffeine combined elements of all three of these drugs. It was used for increasing alertness and to socialize.

A second group of drugs was used mainly for physical/sensory reasons. This group was composed of aspirin, narcotics, other prescription medicines, and other over-the-counter medicines. Barbiturates and tranquilizers were also used for physical/sensory reasons, but they met the additional need of relief from tension.

Hallucinogens met a very different pattern of needs. They were used because they heightened aesthetic appreciation and for adventure and kicks. Marijuana was found to be a unique drug, for it satisfied a larger range of needs than any of the other drugs. It relieved tension, enhanced socializing, heightened aesthetic appreciation, and gave a sense of adventure, thus combining many of the properties of the common social drugs, barbiturates, tranquilizers, and hallucinogens.

The adult need patterns were further broken down into patterns for males and females. There were slight differences between the sexes, with drugs meeting basically the same needs for Walla Walla County adults regardless of sex. Of the ninety-six cells formed by the intersection of twelve drugs and eight motives, only five showed a male-female difference of 15 percent or more. Table 3-10 presents data on needs met by drugs for the women in the Walla Walla study.

Taking all drugs and all motives together, females in general reported a level of motive satisfaction through drug use that was about 10 percent above the male level. By drug, female motive satisfaction exceeded male satisfaction by 15 percent or more for hallucinogens, nicotine, and other prescription medicines. Male motive satisfaction exceeded female satisfaction by 15 percent or more for only marijuana and barbiturates. On the other drugs, the sexes were approximately equal. By motive, and using the same 15 percent standard, females found drug use to be more satisfying than males for social, political, and adventure/curiosity reasons, while males exceeded females only on the creative/aesthetic motive.

Why do females report greater motive satisfaction through drug use than males? One reason may be that since societal norms forbid most kinds

Table 3-9
The Use of Drugs by Women in Walla Walla and College Place, Washington

	Alcohol	*Amphetamines*	*Aspirin*	*Barbiturates*	*Hallucinogens*	*Marijuana*	*Narcotics*	*Nicotine*	*Other Prescription Medicines*	*Other Over-the-Counter Medicines*	*Tranquilizers*
Never Used	95 (35%)	218 (82%)	28 (10%)	195 (72%)	263 (96%)	240 (88%)	206 (75%)	172 (63%)	34 (13%)	52 (20%)	174 (65%)
Used, but not last year	7 (3%)	15 (6%)	9 (3%)	12 (4%)	3 (1%)	4 (1%)	15 (5%)	15 (5%)	26 (10%)	16 (6%)	28 (10%)
Used, but for a short period only	6 (2%)	16 (6%)	36 (13%)	28 (10%)	6 (2%)	12 (4%)	37 (14%)	9 (3%)	93 (34%)	84 (32%)	31 (12%)
Less than once a month	60 (22%)	3 (1%)	78 (29%)	9 (3%)	0 (0%)	6 (2%)	7 (3%)	3 (1%)	20 (7%)	44 (17%)	11 (4%)
About once a month	29 (11%)	5 (2%)	54 (20%)	9 (3%)	2 (1%)	3 (1%)	1 (0%)	1 (0%)	16 (6%)	33 (12%)	8 (3%)
About once a week	32 (12%)	1 (0%)	30 (11%)	5 (2%)	0 (0%)	5 (2%)	1 (0%)	0 (0%)	7 (3%)	12 (5%)	6 (2%)
2-4 times a week	33 (12%)	5 (2%)	22 (8%)	6 (2%)	0 (0%)	0 (0%)	1 (0%)	1 (0%)	10 (4%)	9 (3%)	2 (1%)
5 or more times a week	12 (4%)	3 (1%)	16 (6%)	5 (2%)	0 (0%)	4 (1%)	5 (2%)	72 (26%)	65 (24%)	14 (5%)	8 (3%)
Total	274 (101%)[a]	266 (100%)	273 (100%)	269 (98%)[a]	274 (100%)	274 (99%)[a]	273 (99%)[a]	273 (98%)[a]	271 (101%)[a]	264 (100%)	268 (100%)

[a]Where percentages do not add to 100, it is due to rounding error.

of drug use more strongly for females than for males, only those females who experience particularly high motive satisfaction from drug use will initiate or continue with the use of most drugs. An alternative way of looking at this is to say that females using drugs need to define them as more satisfying than males do in order to justify using them to themselves as well as others.

Another point of some interest is that males and females were equally satisfied by drugs on the emotion motive. The popular stereotype is that females are more emotional than males, but if this were so we would expect them to report greater emotional satisfaction from drug use. That there was no evidence at all to support this in the data represents one stone turned out of the foundation of the old sexist stereotype that females are more emotional than males, and therefore weaker in some fundamental way.

One would expect that, where males are heavier users of drugs than females, they would be less likely to disapprove of drug use and more likely to see drug use as beneficial rather than harmful. It was found that males were slightly less likely than females to disapprove of marijuana use (82 percent to 88 percent), with few respondents of either sex approving of any kind of illegal drug use. For legal alcohol use, however, there was no difference between the sexes, with only about 40 percent of each sex disapproving.

Respondents were asked to rate eight categories of drugs on a beneficial-harmful continuum. For those drugs used more heavily by males, males were slightly more likely to see the drugs as beneficial. Just the reverse was true for drugs like barbiturates that were more commonly used by women, and there were approximately equal evaluations of the drugs that were used at the same levels by men and women. All differences were quite small, which suggests that general socialization is a much more important determinant of beliefs about drugs than sexual differentiation.

Another set of questions were asked about the drug use of close friends and spouses. Men were likely to see their spouses as using less drugs than themselves and women to see their spouses as using more drugs than themselves, an accurate reflection of the drug-use rates established by the survey. Both were likely to see their friends as using more drugs than themselves. About 90 percent of both men and women were willing to seek help for a drug problem should one arise, nearly all of them in their home town. Ten percent cited fear of legal difficulties as a reason why they would not seek help for a drug problem. A possible solution to this problem would be to guarantee no legal action for people seeking help for a drug-related problem. Eighty-eight percent of the men and 93 percent of the women said they would support a program developed along these lines. Again, general socialization patterns seem to be more important than sexual differentiation.

Table 3-10
Number of Women Reporting the Needs Met by Twelve Types of Drugs[a]

Needs	*Alcohol*	*Amphet-amines*	*Aspirin*	*Barbi-turates*	*Caffeine*
Physical/sensory relief from pain	8	7	188	17	8
To relieve tension, anxiety, bad moods	39	11	28	15	34
To socialize, peer pressure, to communicate	89	1	0	3	50
To rebel against others—to be anti-establishment	2	1	2	1	0
To expand mental alertness, mental capacities, to solve problems	0	9	1	1	30
To increase the appreciation of beauty enjoy art or music	2	2	1	2	1
To find meaning in life, to establish a personal image	0	3	2	1	2
Adventure, kicks, curiosity, other unknown reasons	11	2	0	3	4

[a]N = 274. Respondents were free to check more than one need per drug.

A final set of questions asked whether parents would give their children permission to use various kinds of drugs at home. Few parents of either sex were willing to give their children permission to use even over-the-counter drugs at home, to say nothing of illegal drugs. There was indirect evidence that parents using amphetamines and barbiturates, in contrast to the general pattern, were particularly likely not only to give their children permission to use these drugs, but actually to allow them to use pills from their own prescriptions.

Alcoholism and Narcotic Addiction among Women

The United States has had extensive problems with narcotic addiction over the last century. Cuskey *et al.* cite early studies completed in Florida, Tennessee, Iowa, and Michigan between 1877 and 1915 as all showing that female rates of narcotic addiction were well above male rates.[7] In the years

Hallu-cinogens	*Marijuana and Hashish*	*Nar-cotics*	*Nicotine*	*Other Prescription Medicines*	*Other Over-the-Counter Medicines*	*Tran-quilizers*
0	2	27	10	115	90	22
1	5	3	36	22	13	44
2	9	0	22	3	2	0
2	2	1	4	2	2	1
3	1	1	4	2	4	1
2	4	2	2	1	3	0
1	1	0	0	0	1	0
4	10	3	2	3	2	1

before narcotics became illegal without a prescription, it was possible to become addicted to various over-the-counter medicines that contained narcotics, as well as to be permanently maintained in addiction by a physician's prescription. One of the unintended consequences of outlawing self-medication with narcotics was the shift from female to male predominance in use rates, as well as the change of the source and circumstances of obtaining the drugs.

A group of studies of patients at the narcotics treatment facility in Lexington, Kentucky, in the 1960s shows that there are still some visible effects of the old pattern of female narcotics addiction. Williams and Bates questioned 172 consecutive female Lexington admissions in 1965. They found that 38 percent reported a *legal* source of drugs (generally a physician). This proportion rose to 67 percent among patients from the Southeast.[8] O'Donnell, using a different series of patients, reports that only 21 percent of the females (as against 43 percent of the males) obtained most or all of their narcotics from illegal sources.[9] In still another study, Chambers *et al.*

report that the majority of black female addicts received their drugs from illegal sources, but the majority of white female addicts obtained them legally.[10]

In the 1969 O'Donnell study, female addicts were more likely than male addicts to have become addicted through treatment for an illness. Treatment-addicted females were less involved in the addict subculture than males, but women were more involved than men if addicted through the recreational use of narcotics. O'Donnell comments, ". . . Women are less likely to become deviant, but . . . those women who do are likely to go the whole distance, and become more deviant than men."[11] Henderson offers some support for this thesis with his finding, based on 438 British Columbia addicts, that, once females began using narcotics, they became addicted more quickly than males. Nineteen percent of the male addicts became addicted within seven weeks of their first use of narcotics, as compared with 26 percent of the female addicts. In contrast, 40 percent of the males and only 25 percent of the females managed to avoid addiction for at least a year after beginning narcotics use.[12]

Brown *et al.* found that female addicts were more likely than male addicts to cite the influence of friends or relatives (66 percent to 47 percent) or relief from a personal disturbance (20 percent to 7 percent) as reasons for first using heroin, and that males were more likely to cite the biological system reason of drug-related physical problems as a factor in their first withdrawal from the drug (46 percent to 19 percent).[13]

Surveying the field of addiction, Kaubin concludes that sexism contributes to both initial female addiction and later difficulties in treatment. She points out that the often-used excuse that female drug use is less than male could not possibly apply to the field of legal psychoactive drugs, where female use is generally greater. As a result of sexism, there are too few beds and other facilities for the treatment of female addicts. A radical feminist approach, she feels, could be an important factor in the treatment of female addicts who have poor self-images.[14]

The quality of most studies published on female addiction to narcotic drugs is not impressive, and it is also true that most of them are not relevant to the thesis developed in this chapter. For these reasons, this section is uncommonly short. Readers desiring a fuller acquaintance with this literature should consult items 13 through 81 in *Women and Drugs: An Annotated Bibliography*, which has been recently published by the National Clearinghouse for Drug Abuse Information.[15]

According to Cahalan, approximately 40 percent of American males and 15 percent of the females have at least some psychological dependence on alcohol. Twelve percent of the males and 8 percent of the females in a 1967 national sample reported having had a health problem connected with drinking during the past three years. Women's drinking problems were few in the twenties and fifties, but concentrated in the thirties and forties—middle age. Cahalan says, ". . . While men may generally get introduced to heavier drinking by other men when they are young, women more often get involved in heavier drinking relatively later, perhaps as a result of their husbands' or men friends' influence."[16]

In another national sample, interviewed in 1964-65, Cahalan *et al.* found that females were more likely than males to increase alcohol consumption because they were going out more (20 percent to 9 percent) or for social reasons, including spouse's influence (36 percent to 20 percent). When depressed or nervous, females were more likely to eat, take tranquilizers or other pills, work harder, pray, or talk with friends and relatives, but men were more likely to drink and smoke. Female heavy drinkers were more differentiated from other females than male heavy drinkers were from other males in that they showed a greater increase in alienation and neurotic tendencies. In general, females were more influenced by the drinking of their spouses and social acquaintances than were males.[17]

Gordon Bell argues that female alcoholics might be as prevalent as male alcoholics, but that they conceal it more effectively because they are better at manipulating their environments to support their drinking.[18] Lindbeck's opinion is that "it is probably true that the greater condemnation, fear of ostracism, and guilt suffered by the female alcoholic contribute both to the concealment of her drinking and to its telescoped development."[19] There is no question about the fact that married females have a good opportunity to hide their alcoholism, particularly if their husbands cooperate in the deception. One of the reasons for the ease of concealment may be that females often drink small amounts of alcohol all day long, thus being able to continue to function in what looks like a normal fashion.[20]

Finding an effective method of geting these women to "come out of the closet" and accept treatment is an important task to be accomplished. There is abundant empirical evidence based on anonymous surveys that documents two crucial facts about female alcoholism: (1) rates are high, but not nearly as high as male alcoholism rates, even allowing for concealment; and (2) female rates are rapidly rising, and will eventually catch up to and surpass male rates if the current trend continues.

Three common theories about the etiology of female alcoholism are deprivation, deviant sex-role adaption, and the "empty nest." In deprivation theory, female alcoholics are seen as much more likely than male alcoholics to have suffered deprivation, loss of significant others, etc. Presumably, it takes this sort of tragedy to push many females into heavy alcohol use in the face of strong societal norms against "unladylike drinking." Some of the research findings and theoretical statements supporting this position are given below.

1. Beckman indicates that female alcoholics are more likely than male alcoholics to have suffered loss of a parent through divorce, desertion, or death, and to have experienced more emotional trauma. Women are more sensitive to social environmental circumstances than men. What appears to be greater maladjustment in female alcoholics than male alcoholics may be due to a more negative reaction by the representatives of the social order rather than by any initial condition.[21]
2. In an experimental situation, Wilsnack found that nearly all heavy-drinking women studied named specific traumatic experiences that occurred just prior to their onset of heavy drinking, and half of them defined these experiences as having a causal role in their heavy drinking.[22]
3. Lisansky reports that female alcoholics were more likely than male alcoholics to come from a home having parental problem drinking, and to have alcoholic spouses. They were also twice as likely to cite specific experiences such as parent's death, a divorce, a bad love affair, or postpartum depression as immediately preceding the beginning of uncontrolled drinking.[23]
4. Female alcoholics were more likely than male alcoholics to suffer the death of a significant other, physical illness, miscarriage, pregnancy, childbirth, loss of spouse, or marital problems as preceding the onset of their latest period of drinking, in a study by Hoffman and Noem.[24]
5. In another article, female alcoholics were more likely than male alcoholics to suffer parental loss at age six to sixteen. De Lint believes that the causal chain consists of early parental loss, causing reduced tendency to deal with anxiety by affiliating with others, which in turn causes heavy drinking to be used as a substitute crutch.[25]

A number of studies report that female alcoholics are more likely than male alcoholics to have an alcoholic spouse, which is a deprivation of sorts, but Lisansky correctly points out that since there are more male than female alcoholics this finding does not necessarily mean that female alcoholics are more sensitive to trauma of an alcoholic spouse than males.[26]

The second theory is that female alcoholism is related to deviant sex-role adaptation. For example, Parker found that female alcoholics were higher than moderate female drinkers on emotionality, and lower on femininity.[27] In a later study, he extended his theory to heavy-drinking college females, who tended to reject some of the aspects of the traditional female role. These young women had scores on the femininity and neuroticism scales that were similar to those of the adult female alcoholics in the 1972 study.[28] This is a particularly important finding, since it suggests that the sex-role deviance precedes the development of true alcoholism by a considerable period of time, extending back at least to the period of pre-alcoholic heavy drinking by college girls.

Wilsnack reports that, in the structured situation she created, female heavy drinkers were more power oriented and valued motherhood more than lighter-drinking women. These heavy drinkers had had more reproductive problems and expressed "genuine disappointment about their inability to have children or to have as many children as they wanted."[29] She suggests a negative response cycle in which heavy alcohol use increases threats to femininity through deteriorating performance, and hence leads to even more use. Both the low femininity and the trouble with reproduction indicate problems with traditional sex-role identification.[30]

There is evidence that alcohol does help females to meet certain needs. In an experimental study of a garden club by Durand, middle-aged females decreased their need for power and affiliation after moderate alcohol consumption. Commenting that this pattern is very different from the male pattern, the author recommends that both theoretical explanations and therapies should be different for the two sexes.[31]

A third theory explaining some of the variance in female alcohol consumption is the "empty nest" theory. Curlee studied the consecutive admission of 100 males and 100 females at a private alcoholism treatment center. Of the thirty females who associated one particular factor with the onset of alcoholism, twenty-one cited a middle-age identity crisis in which they lost their husband, entered menopause, or had their children leave home. Curlee describes these women as conscientious, conforming, and unhappy. Within a few months to a year or two of their first heavy drinking, they had become alcoholics. Her theory is that the "empty nest" is related to lowered self-esteem, which leads to heavy drinking and poor performance at home, which continues the cycle by lowering self-esteem still further.[32]

Wanberg and Knapp agree about the rapid onset of alcoholism among middle-aged females, noting that females in their study were more likely than males to drink alone, to drink at home, and to drink with only their spouses. They suggest the possibility of a lonely-housewife syndrome.[33] Female alcoholics in Scotland studied by Sclare reported a decline in sexual interest and drive that was greater than the decline among male alcoholics—a point that supports both the "empty nest" and the deviant sex-role theories. Sclare believes that there are three groups of women who abuse alcohol—teenagers with boyfriends, early middle-agers who are what we might call "swingers," and middle-agers who become depressed through marital problems.[34]

Reporting on a 1970-71 national study, Parry *et al.* say that males are twice as likely as females to use alcohol as a coping mechanism to deal with depression and anxiety. This was true for all age groups and in all regions of the country.[35] The weakness of the "empty nest" theory of female alcoholism as a general explanatory theory is precisely that it is males, not females, who are most likely to use alcohol to cope with depression and anxiety. Women prefer prescription psychotherapeutic drugs for this purpose, which leads us to the topic of housewife drug problems and their medical correlates.

Housewife Drug Problems

There is now a considerable amount of knowledge in existence about housewife drug problems. Before 1970, only four studies were published on the topic. Even if we count only those with some theoretical value, twenty-one have come into print during the 1970s. The discussion which follows is based on these twenty-five studies, but it cannot do justice to their complexity. Readers with a particular interest in this subject are urged to consult the original sources listed in the notes.

Perhaps the best place to start is to note the observation made by Cuskey *et al.* that the contemporary sedative-hypnotic and stimulant abuse pattern among middle-aged females parallels the old narcotics pattern in six ways: (1) the drugs are obtained legally, (2) the users are respectable citizens, (3) there is a concentration among the housewives and women working outside the home, (4) the drug abuse is not widely condemned, (5) the abuse is not very noticeable, and (6) the drugs are used to combat stress, pain, and fatigue.[36] Previous sections in this chapter have established that adult females predominate in the use of psychoactive prescription drugs, and that although alcoholism and narcotics addiction are less common among females they are a particularly grave danger for middle-aged women. If it is true that the general pattern outlined by Cuskey *et al.* extends back perhaps as far as a century, how can we explain this unusual regularity?

Contemporary explanations generally focus on the relationships between women and their physicians. In an analysis of 1965-66 Toronto prescriptions, Cooperstock notes that 69 percent of all prescriptions for psychotropic drugs were written for women, while only 56 percent of patient visits to general practitioners were by women. She believes that the excess of female prescription psychotropic drug use develops in a five-stage process. Initially, the norms in Western cultures permit greater expression of feeling in females than males. This is not to say that there is any biological difference to start with. That is a completely different question. In stage two, the greater expression of feeling permits women to perceive more emotional problems in themselves, which leads to the third stage, in which they are more likely to attend physicians to gain relief from these emotional problems. Stage four focuses on the physician, who expects greater female emotional expressiveness from general cultural socialization as well as from experience in practicing medicine. In stage five, the physician expects women to need mood-modifying drugs, and so physician and patient agree on a psychotropic drug course of treatment.[37]

In a later publication, Cooperstock offers additional evidence in support of her model. She shows that in one study, at every age level from twenty to thirty-nine through sixty and over, females are more likely than males to be defined by their doctors and/or to define themselves to their doctors as having the symptoms of lassitude, fatigue, vertigo, and headache. Females outnumber males in the display or definition of mental disorders at all age levels, but particularly so at ages forty to fifty-nine and sixty and over.[38] Hindmarch agrees that middle-aged females are particularly prone to drug abuse. He believes that women's problems in adjusting to middle age produce depression, anxiety, and sleeplessness, for which physicians prescribe psychoactive drugs. This may be a long-term affair, for Hindmarch cites a study showing that 50 percent of the patients of general practitioners who have prescriptions for amphetamines or barbiturates have had refills for four years or longer, 25 percent for eight years or longer, and 9 percent for sixteen or more years.[39]

Shapiro and Baron studied New York area physicians' prescriptions in eleven insured medical plans for a one-week period in 1959. They note for males, age-specific prescription rates increased gradually from age one to fourteen to retirement, but for females, there was a huge increase that occurred in the age range fifteen to forty-four.[40] Fejer and Smart found that 73 percent of all the people with prescriptions in Toronto were female. An interesting sidelight of this study was that while males and females were equally likely to have tried stimulant drugs, females were more frequent users and obtained their drugs by prescription 79 percent of the time. Males, on the other hand, obtained only 25 percent of their stimulant drugs by prescription.[41] The rest must have come illegally, though this does not necessarily mean that they were all bought on the street.

Manheimer, Mellinger, Balter, Parry, and Cisin have published a number of reports on adult psychotropic drug use based on samples drawn first in the San Francisco area and then nationally. Commenting on the first study, completed in San Francisco proper, Mellinger *et al.* say that the difference between the male and female use of psychotherapeutic drugs is entirely due to an excess of medical prescriptions to females. By avoiding physicians as much as possible and using recreational drugs instead of prescription drugs, men are able to obtain emotional relief without threatening their masculine self-images.[42] In the national sample the sex difference in prescription psychotherapeutic drug use declined from about four to one (female over male) at age eighteen to twenty-nine, to three to two by age sixty to seventy-four. Although females were more likely than males to use prescription psychotherapeutic drugs, males were slightly more likely to progress from occasional use to heavy use. One may assume that once a male has broken through the sociocultural normative barrier against prescription psychotherapeutic drug use and solved the masculine self-image problem caused thereby, there is no reason not to use the drugs heavily. Alternatively, one could argue that, to break the norm, the problem had to be severe enough to demand heavy drug use in treatment. Mellinger *et al.* found that females were somewhat more likely than males to report a high level of life crises (35 percent to 29 percent) and much more likely to report high psychic distress (34 percent to 19 percent). Even when distress and life crisis were controlled, female use of prescription psychotherapeutics was still higher than male use. They conclude that this higher use is due to three factors. First, females are more likely to report emotional distress. Second, they are more likely to seek medical care and thus gain access to the prescribing system. Finally, America being less tolerant of alcohol use by females, they are encouraged to find nonalcoholic ways of reducing their psychic pain.[43]

Since there is general agreement that physicians prescribe an excessively large proportion of psychotherapeutic drugs to females, the question is, why? Certainly some of the variance is due to the female propensity to visit physicians when psychologically distressed[44] or for any reason at all.[45] There is also considerable evidence that females are more likely to define themselves as having a chronic health problem,[46] including psychological and physical anxiety, poor physical health, and immobilization.[47] In one study, females were more likely to define a past problem in mental-health terms (27 percent to 19 percent), but of those making this definition males and females were about equally likely to obtain professional help.[48] Phillips and Segal refine this picture, reporting on their 1964-66 Lebanon, New Hampshire, study. They indicate that females in this New England town scored much higher on psychological and psychophysiological symptoms, with the sexes being equal on physiological symptoms and males being higher on ambiguous symptoms. Although both physician diagnoses and self-reports showed approximate sexual equality with respect to physical illness, females reported more symptoms at each level of physical illness.[49]

There is also a social dimension in this situation. Women may talk with each other about symptoms and psychotherapeutic drugs, in sort of a gender subculture. In doing so, they may promote sensitivity to certain symptoms and knowledge of how psychotherapeutic drugs would help these symptoms. As Linn and Davis put it, psychotherapeutic drug use "is related to participation in drug and health-oriented social circles in which discussions about medication, pharmaceutical products, and health problems are frequent and in which exchange of information and practices are common."[50]

There is also empirical conformation that some of the variance in psychotherapeutic drug prescriptions by sex is due to distortions or stereotypes on the part of the physician. For example, Lennane and Lennane show that physicians generally take dysmenorrhea (ovulation pain), nausea of pregnancy, labor pains, and infantile colic to be psychogenic rather than organic in origin, even though current research (which is typically ignored in medical texts) shows that these have organic origins.[51] Linn found that 87 percent of the Los Angeles physicians he studied legitimated the daily use of librium by a middle-aged housewife having marital problems, a much larger proportion than the 57 percent who supported its use for a college student suffering from high anxiety.[52] *Prescribed and Nonprescribed Medicines, Type and Use of Medicines, United States—July 1964-June 1965*, a 1967 report from the U.S. Public Health Service, showed that females used more prescribed medicines than males for most illnesses, the largest difference being that females used 243 percent of the male prescription drug rate for mental illness and epilepsy. On over-the-counter drugs, the sexes were nearly equal.[53]

One reason for the high level of drug prescribing may be that doctors use the prescription as a way of terminating the examination and moving patients out of the office. Muller indicates that physicians have only about seventeen minutes per patient.[54] The textbook socialization into sex-linked patient stereotypes that occurs in medical school has its correlate in drug advertisements that appear in medical journals. Prather and Fidell found a relationship between type of illness and sex of patient in drug advertisements in three medical journals and one psychiatric journal. Females were overrepresented as having emotional illness and underrepresented as having somatic (physical) illness. Men were seen as needing psychotropic drugs because of work pressures, and females because of diffuse anxiety and tension.[55] The constant, though subtle, pressure on the medical profession from the drug industry should not be ignored as a source of sex-role stereotypes.

Becker argues that a physician's prescription is aimed at what the physician wants to accomplish rather than what the patient wants. The physician may choose not to give the patient all available knowledge about the drugs prescribed because this may cause the patient to disobey the doctor's orders or to imagine symptoms.[56] Females are particularly a target for many of the new psychoactive and contraceptive drugs on the market. Becker says that, "to produce a *noticeable* improvement, company recommendations, insufficient research, and physician inclinations combine to produce a tendency to prescribe dosages larger than required for the desired medical effect, large enough to produce serious side effects."[57] Eventually, sufficient research and patient suffering accumulate for the drug companies and physicians to lower dosages and thus relieve many of the excessive side effects. It seems likely that females suffer from this destructive cycle much more than males.

Sexism is present in all aspects of our society. The studies discussed on these pages illuminate only a few dimensions of the complex relationships that condition female drug problems. Many others remain to be examined in future studies. All of them will doubtless be progressively modified as sexual equality spreads across America. Sexual discrimination is not unrelated to the present forms of female drug use and abuse. It certainly increases the suffering of many female drug users. However, it would be a superficial and ideologically distorted analysis that concluded that the alleviation of sexist discrimination would solve all female drug problems overnight.

Males as Carriers of Drug Use to Females

The only available study concentrating entirely on male domination of females in the drug scene is reported in "An Anatomy of Male Dominance: Sexual Differentiation in the Drug Scene," an expanded treatment of which recently appeared in *Drug Forum*.[58] There are, however, a number of partial findings that have appeared in other publications in recent years. These are briefly summarized below.

1. In a study of the use of seventeen categories of drugs in New York State, Chambers obtained data on the proportion of drugs obtained illegally for each category and the sex of users. Our secondary analysis of this data yields a Spearman rank-order correlation of −.77 between percent male use of a drug category and percent of the drugs in that category obtained legally. This indicates a strong relationship in which males are more likely to use drugs obtained illegally and females are more likely to use drugs obtained legally. The drugs with the lowest percentages of female users were methedrine (17 percent), solvents and inhalants (20 percent), heroin (31 percent), cocaine (33 percent), and marijuana, including hashish (34 percent). The highest percentages of female users were reported for diet pills (80 percent), nonheroin narcotics (76 percent), stimulants other than amphetamines and cocaine (75 percent), antidepressants (72 percent), and relaxants or minor tranquilizers (70 percent).[59]
2. Lisansky feels that socioenvironmental factors are more important in causing alcoholism in females than in males. She points out that women start later but seem to go through the stages of alcoholism more quickly. They also seek treatment more quickly after the onset of alcoholism than males.[60]
3. Among British Columbia narcotics addicts studied by Henderson, females were more likely than males to first hear about drugs from their spouse or boyfriends or girlfriends and males were more likely to first hear from their male chums and gang members. Females were more likely to

have lost one or both parents, and males were more likely to have been in a reformatory or prison. During adolescence, the preaddict girls were slightly more socially isolated then their male counterparts (presumably from same-sex friends). Later on, the female addicts were more likely to have been married and to be currently living with their husbands. There is some evidence that females were more likely than males to have entered the criminal subculture before becoming addicted, for they were more likely to have an adult criminal conviction before becoming addicted (73 percent to 48 percent). Having mostly addicts for friends depressed the number of voluntary abstentions from heroin more among females than males, but males were more negatively influenced when it came to the length of time that the abstentions lasted.[61]

4. Eldred and Washington found that the majority of female addicts entering an urban treatment program had been introduced to heroin by males. They were more likely than males to use drugs with the opposite sex, to have another person obtain their drugs for them, to support their habit with money from their spouse, to have drugs provided free by others, and to live with a current or ex-narcotics user. They were less likely to buy their own drugs.[62] The authors believe that these sex-linked differences may be due to "the power structure or status hierarchy implicit in male-female relationships, as well as the relative importance of same-sex and opposite-sex relationships for men and women."[63]
5. Taking the use of four or more different recreational drugs as an index of full entry into the drug subculture, Goode found that the percentage of females having sexual intercourse rose from 34 percent to 71 percent as they moved from the use of no illegal drugs to four or more. Similarly, the number having sexual relations with four or more partners rose from 2 percent to 24 percent.[64] In his book *The Marijuana Smokers* Goode concludes that drug use spreads from the males to the females. Those females who associate most frequently and intimately with males are the ones likely to be using recreational drugs, provided that there is a high level of drug use in the social milieu.[65]
6. In a study of needle sharing in the Haight, Howard and Borges found that females were more likely than males to not have their own "outfits" for "shooting" drugs, to share needles with other users, to have never shot alone, and to be both "tied off" and "hit" by someone else in the same drug-use incident. They report a revealing quotation by one male addict, who said that "shooting" a woman made her seem submissive.[66]
7. Baseloga found that females were more likely than males to say that they started using drugs because of the influence of friends. He comments that the female's role in drug use is passive. She never proselytizes and is never a pusher. Baseloga also found that female drug

users had a greater affective dependence on their families than male drug users.[67]

8. In one of the finest books ever written on drug abuse, Johnson pinpointed the selling of drugs as a crucial variable in the movement of young people into the drug subculture, and noted that this was true even more for females than for males.[68] Johnson says at one point, "This may indicate that when persons are pressured by some friends who want them to use cannabis and by other friends who would prefer that they avoid it, males will try cannabis and females will avoid it."[69] As compared with males, females who tried marijuana were less likely to progress to regular marijuana use, and regular users were less likely to sell narcotics. But as their subcultural participation increased, they learned values suggesting not only that sex is fun, but that drugs make sex better. There is considerable pressure to behave consistently with expressed values in the drug scene, as there is in all other forms of social life.
9. MacDonald *et al.* report that the number of hours their subjects felt that they ought to spend socializing with friends and the number of hours actually spent socializing with friends were related to four of five measures of drug use. Social participation was higher for marijuana users than for nonusers, but there was no statistically significant difference between users of only marijuana and users of multiple illegal drugs.[70]
10. Wohlford proposes that girls have a more difficult socialization task than boys, for which reason they may be more likely than boys to select peers or siblings as role models. Though the relationships were not strong, imitation of parental smoking by children of the same sex was greater than imitation by opposite-sex children.[71]
11. Girls were more sensitive to peer pressure than boys on all four drug dimensions tested (but only one difference was large enough to be statistically significant) in a ninth-grade sample studied by Schuman and Polkowski.[72]
12. "The Social Context of First Marijuana Use," by Freeland and Campbell, provides evidence that males are the carriers who introduce both males and other females to marijuana use. The authors found that, in dyadic introductions to marijuana use, 95 percent of the males and only 23 percent of the females were by the same sex. In group introductions, 68 percent of the males were in the company of only other males, but only 12 percent of the females were in all-female groups.[73]
13. Several articles report on a 1969 survey at a large university on the East Coast. Milman and Anker indicate that the increase in female marijuana use that accompanies dating suggests the extent to which women's activities are influenced by men.[74] There is no parallel pattern

of male marijuana use increasing as dating increased. This sex-linked difference was stronger for graduate students than for undergraduates.[75]

14. Walters *et al.* found that beginning drug use increased females' sexual behavior more than males' among college students. Comparing illegal drug users with nonusers, we find that the percentage of nonvirgins climbed from 46 percent to 80 percent among males, a difference of 34 percent. For females, the percentage having sexual intercourse rose from 36 percent to 88 percent, a difference of 52 percent. By the time that hallucinogen use was begun, 92 percent of the women and all the men were having sexual intercourse.[76]
15. Sex of respondent was found to be related to initiation of drug use but not to frequency of use among users in a study by Henley and Adams. Females were less likely than males to begin using drugs, but equally likely to progress to heavy use once they had started.[77]
16. At Bishop's University in Canada, Campbell found that female drug users were more likely than female nonusers to have had delinquent friends during adolescence, while there was no difference in adolescent relationships with delinquents between male users and nonusers.[78]
17. Rosenberg *et al.* point out that because of the social pressure to be datable, it may be difficut for a girl to refuse to please her date by "turning on."[79]
18. Snow's 1970 study of high-school drug users suggests that girls may be using drugs to be social with boys rather than in response to deep personality problems. Boys started drug use earlier than the girls, but then the girls caught up by tenth grade (perhaps due to dating activities). After that they increased their drug use more slowly than boys, which Snow thinks may be because they had found a social life outside of drug-using groups.[80]
19. Klinge *et al.* studied adolescent inpatients at the Lafayette Clinic in Detroit, Michigan, who were admitted between 1966 and 1971. They found that nearly half of the females, but less than a third of the males, obtained most of their drugs through personal friends. Males were more likely to obtain drugs directly from a dealer, to sell drugs, or to steal drugs. Only the first and the last of these four sex-role differences were statistically significant, which may be related to the smallness of the sample studied. Males were three times as likely as females to work for their drug money.[81]
20. In his Ph.D. thesis, Sadava found that ". . . in general the intensity and duration of drug-using behavior seems to be much more responsive to social reinforcement for females than males."[82] Furthermore, "in many cases, the female is led by a male important to her into deeper involvement with drugs, and is likely to wait for his lead."[83] Among

female college students, those who have low expectations for social love and affection are likely to begin and persist in illegal drug use, but there is no similar relationship for males. Sadava reasons that because of restrictive social norms that single out females for "proper" behavior, they require greater social support and more positive reasons in order to engage in illegal drug use.[84]

21. Rouse and Ewing found that among college women marijuana use was associated with an increased probability of using alcohol, smoking, or having sexual relations as a way of coping with being nervous and depressed. There was also an increased chance of using alcohol to relieve menstrual pain.[85]
22. In a 1961 study of drinking in twenty-one North Carolina colleges, Alexander and Campbell found that females were more likely than males to have never been encouraged by their friends to drink and to have actively discouraged others from drinking. Among abstaining frequent churchgoers, females were more likely than males to feel that drinking was wrong as a matter of principle, but once they began to drink the sex-linked difference diminished.[86]
23. Citing an unpublished study done in South Wales, Oakley concludes that best friends are more important for adolescent females than for males.[87]
24. Brunswick and Tarica found that the most significant predictor of drinking among black adolescent girls was pregnancy. Number of health problems was more strongly related to drinking among girls than boys.[88]
25. Using 1967 data, Wolk reports that females were more likely than males to become uninhibited as a result of using marijuana (62 percent to 47 percent). They were also more likely to become quiet and introspective, but less likely to work more effectively afterwards or to become frightened and tense.[89]
26. Robbins *et al.* found that parents were seen as more opposed to the use of illicit drugs (thirteen of fifteen tests) and alcohol or tobacco (seven of ten tests) by females than by males. On the other hand, they were perceived as being more tolerant of female students' use of medicinal drugs in twenty of twenty-four tests.[90]

It is difficult to integrate these diverse findings into one theory of female drug use during the formative years of adolescence and early adulthood. Figure 3-1 presents diagrammatically a process model of adolescent and college-student use of recreational drugs, in which we see males and females coming to the dating marketplace from very different backgrounds. With the exception of certain gang and sorority members, females have been relatively isolated from drugs, the norms governing drug

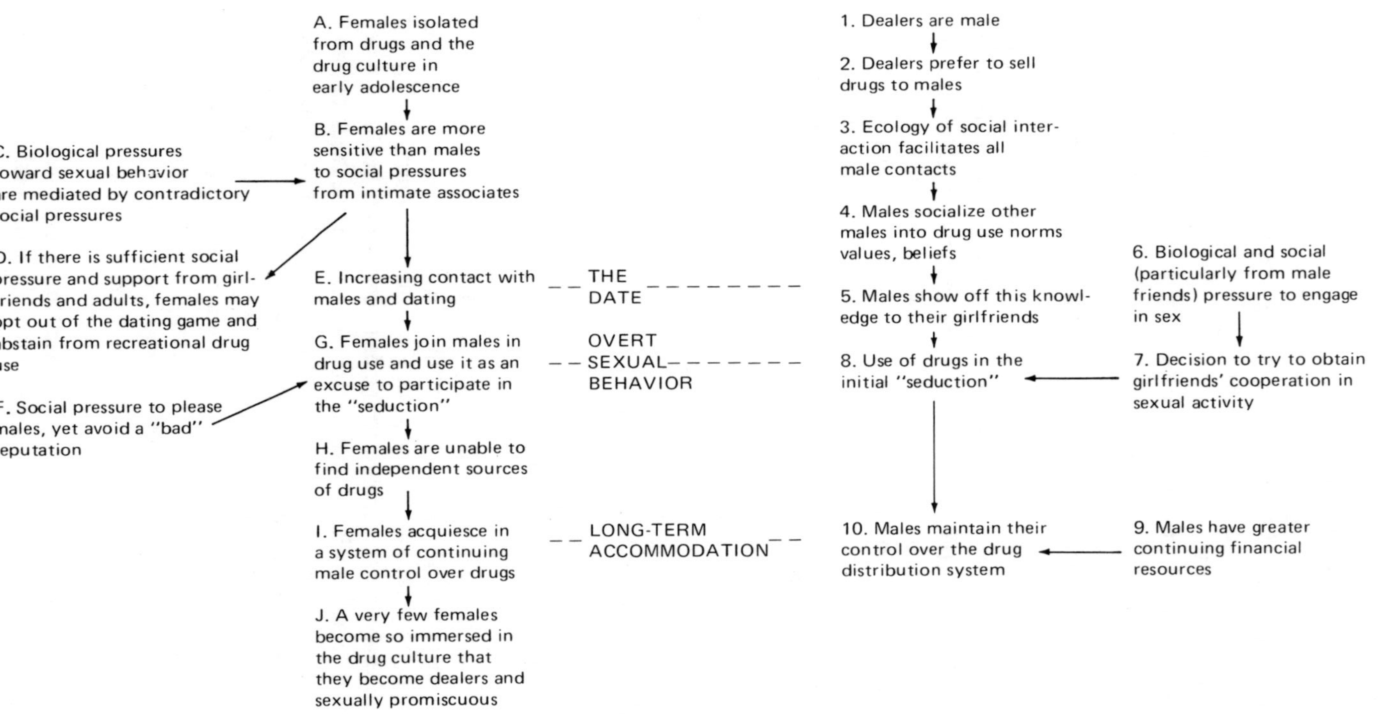

Figure 3-1. A Process Model of Adolescent and College Student Use of Recreational Drugs and its Relationship to Heterosexual Behavior

behavior, and knowledge about drugs. Their natural biological pressure toward sexual bonding is mediated by social pressures that may be either strongly negative, positive, or mixed. The problem is compounded by a special sensitivity to social pressures from intimate associates. Males come out of an environment in which there is a greater likelihood of meeting with and being socialized by drug dealers. The dealers (who are also males) and their male customers frequent the same ecological areas (in which females are at least rare, if not excluded) and so have continuing possibilities for social interaction. The male customers socialize each other and are at the same time socialized by dealers in the norms, values, and beliefs governing drug behavior.

Females who are part of groups that negatively sanction drug use may refrain from participating in the dating game and, in doing so, avoid recreational drug use entirely. (Of course, there are many exceptions; all the statements in the model are probable, not absolute.) If the social and biological pressures combine to favor increased heterosexual interaction, the females begin to date, and it is on these dates that their boyfriends show that they are "in the right crowd," "with it," and so on by displaying their newly gained sophistication about the norms, values, and beliefs of the drug culture. The males believe that this will make them appear more sociosexually desirable, but in fact more females are threatened than attracted, and many relationships with "fast" males end at this point.

The combination of biological and social pressures may lead to ambivalence about sex among females. For males the pressures are all toward engaging in sexual behavior. As a result, males try to get their girlfriends to agree to participate in sexual intercourse. Females are socialized to please males (on dates and everywhere else), yet expected to avoid pleasing them so much that they ruin their reputations. A reasonable solution to this double-bind dilemma is for females to join their boyfriends in recreational drug use and use it as an excuse for participation in initial and subsequent drug seductions ("I'm not that kind of girl, but I was just so drunk . . .").

Initially, the only female pipeline to the drug dealer may be through her boyfriend. Most females will, for one reason or another, not seek out and find a direct drug source of their own that is independent of their sexual dating relationship. Because of the drug isolation of the ecological niche in which most females are situated, they would have to be very aggressive to locate alternative sources of drugs, and in doing so would face the possibility of being stigmatized as unfeminine. To fit into the social order and be accepted as normal, most females find it easier to acquiesce in a system wherein males have continuing control over their source of recreational drugs. Males are delighted to maintain this control, since it also reduces the females' degrees of freedom to resist male sexual advances when they might desire to do so. The greater financial capability of most males also contributes to their ability to dominate the drug distribution system.

For most females, their level of recreational drug use is always moderate and tied to dating activities. There are a few who go deeper into the drug world, with its concomitants of heavy drug use and relatively promiscuous sexual behavior. These women may make enough contacts in the drug subculture to become dealers themselves, though this is very rare. By this time, they are thoroughly immersed in a contraculture in which the norms, values, and beliefs no longer fit those that characterized the earlier stages of the process.

The large majority of the young women who avoid a full entry into the drug subculture are still not free of sex-linked drug problems. Marriage removes them from the dating game, with its structured sexual inequality, only to plunge them into a world in which the sources of drugs are still largely controlled by males. Now the men are their physicians (and occasionally husbands, as among heroin addicts and many female alcoholics) instead of boyfriends. The women are still expected to accept the advice of these "wise" and powerful males. Their dating experiences have socialized them to fit into the mold described in the section on housewife drug problems.

General Sociological Theory on Female Drug Use

It is generally thought that girls are less delinquent than boys because their sex-role socialization inclines them in that direction rather than because they were born more pure.[91] As Heidensohn says, "Not only do women appear to be remarkable conformists, they seem to have consistently lower rates of deviance than men, with a fairly constant ratio which remains despite fluctuations in rates over time."[92] Cohen *et al.* show that, under certain conditions, females conform less rather than more than males, so we must be careful not to overgeneralize on this point.[93] According to Heise, females are also more likely than males to condemn deviant behavior, especially of a serious nature.[94]

Pollak's theory in 1950 was that sex differences in crime were not as large as they appeared, since many female crimes were hidden from public view.[95] Perhaps this is true, for an increasing number of female offenses have been coming to light in recent years as it has become less fashionable to cover up and excuse away female delinquencies. Heise believes that females are more deviant than males only where this fits well with the stereotype of femininity or where there is a greater opportunity to do so, so one could reason that, as sex-role norms become more flexible, females will display increased deviancy.[96]

There is much evidence in support of some degree of convergence in deviant behavior by males and females, particularly among adolescents. For example, Giordano *et al.* found that there was an increase in delinquent involvement reported by girls incarcerated in two training schools in 1975, as compared with data from a 1960 study.[97] Some changes in self-report data may be due to females admitting more offenses because it is more socially acceptable to do so. Phillips and Clancy indicate that females may be more sensitive than males to providing the "right" answers when questioned.[98] However, it is likely that there are also gross changes in real behavior in addition to distortions in reporting trends caused by the decline of the stereotype of the "pure" woman.

Jensen and Eve analyze 1964-65 data from Western Contra Costa County in California, finding that even as of that date sex of respondent explained no more than 2 percent of the variance in delinquency when introduced into a multiple regression analysis with other variables.[99] Bosse and Rose are among those to note the rapid converging of rates of cigarette smoking,[100] and Green and Menzer note that if we adjust for sex differences in body weight, males and females were smoking about the same number of cigarettes per pound in 1970.[101] Smart and Fejer show a strong trend toward convergence in drug-use data obtained from six years of surveys of student drug use in Toronto.[102]

The most common sociological explanation for the rise in female deviance (or the convergence of male and female rates, which amounts to the same thing) is that it is due to decreases in sexism, however defined. For example, Smart and Fejer state that the decline in sex differences on drug use rates " . . . may be related to the recent concern given to sexual equality in many areas of life."[103] Projecting into the future, Suffet and Brotman predict that as women assert themselves and gain more freedom in their private lives, their use of recreational drugs will increase.[104] But there are cautions against applying this theory uncritically. Giordano *et al.* point out that it is very unlikely that the women's movement has had a direct impact on female juvenile delinquency. Instead, it has helped to create a social context in which female juvenile delinqueny is encouraged more than it was in the past by subtle changes in dating patterns, opportunities for advancement, sex-role stereotypes, and so forth.[105]

The most up-to-date word on this topic comes from Weis, who organizes theories of criminal behavior into three groups. The first is the masculinization of female behavior, in which it is thought that deviant females are more masculine than conforming females. The sociological version of this is that liberation has allowed women to increase their (masculine) criminal activity.[106] Weis quotes Adler (1975: 3) as saying that "women are committing more crimes than ever before. Those crimes involve a greater degree of violence."[107]

The second group of theories may be titled role convergence, in which it is assumed that females are temporarily increasing their criminal behavior as male and female roles become more alike, but that as the roles converge, the crimes of both males and females should decrease in number. Role validation, or sexism, comprises the third group of theories. In this view, females who engage in crime are validating their femininity illegally, not denying femininity and becoming more masculine. "In short, female criminal behavior is an illegitimate expression of legitimate female role expectations and opportunities."[108] Weis tested these theories against national arrest data and a study of public-school children in an upper-middle-class suburban community. He found that role validation was more consistent with the evidence than masculinization, liberation, role convergence, etc. However, he admits that the evidence is not strong enough to be conclusive.[109]

Anyone who is administering a treatment program has to decide which theories are the most valid and then develop the treatment plan out of these theoretical assumptions. At the present state of the art, there is no one set of theoretical assumptions that is clearly preeminent. The one thing that can be stated without any doubt is that women's drug problems will no longer be ignored. The first National Forum on Drugs, Alcoholism and Women was held in Miami Beach in 1975.[110] The Services Research Branch of the Division of Resource Development, National Institute of Mental Health, now has a Women's Project that includes treatment demonstration programs, a central data collection and analysis system, an information system, and a consultant group of treatment and research professionals.[111] It is likely that additional organizations will shortly be unveiled. Granting agencies now look favorably on projects dealing with female drug problems, whereas before 1975, they were likely to put their money elsewhere. In this "boom" situation, it is not likely that practitioners will have long to wait for improved theoretical and empirical guidance on women's deviance in general and women's drug problems in particular. Whether they will seek out and make use of this knowledge is a question to which the answer may not be so positive.

Notes

1. Anne MacLennan, "Sex and Personality Influence Drug Actions," *The Journal* 3 (issue 10, 1974), 16.

2. Dorothy E. Green and Daniel E. Nemzer, "Changes in Cigarette Smoking by Women—An Analysis, 1966 and 1970," *Health Service Reports* 88 (1973), 631-36.

3. Lee H. Bowker, *Drug Use at a Small Liberal Arts College* (Palo Alto, CA: R & E Research Associates, 1976).

4. Lee H. Bowker, "Drug Use Among Adults in Walla Walla County" (Report # 74-2); "Drug Use in Our Schools" (Report # 74-5); and "A Causal Analysis of the Drug Scene at a Seventh Day Adventist College"

(Report # 74-8). All reports produced in 1974 for the Walla Walla County Drug Project, Whitman College, Walla Walla, Washington.

5. Lee H. Bowker, "Student Drug Use and the Perceived Peer Drug Environment," *International Journal of the Addictions* 9 (1974), 851-61; "College Student Drug Use: An Examination and Application of the Epidemiological Literature, "*Journal of College Student Personnel* 16 (1975), 137-44; "The Incidence of Drug Use and Associated Factors in Two Small Towns—A Community Study," *United Nations Bulletin on Narcotics* 28 (1976), 11-25; "The Influence of the Perceived Home Drug Environment on Student Drug Use," *Addictive Behaviors* 1 (1976), 1-6; "The Relationship Between Sex, Drugs, and Sexual Behavior on a College Campus," *Drug Forum* 7 (1978) 69-80; and "Motives for Drug Use: An Application of Cohen's Typology," *International Journal of the Addictions* 12 (1978), 983-91.

6. Ruth Cooperstock, "Sex Differences in Use of Mood-Modifying Drugs: An Explanatory Model," *Journal of Health and Social Behavior* 12 (1971), 238-44.

7. Walter R. Cuskey, T. Premkumar, and Lois Sigel, "Survey of Opiate Addiction among Females in the United States between 1850 and 1970," *Public Health Reviews* 1 (1972), 8-39.

8. J.E. Williams and W.A. Bates, "Some Characteristics of Female Narcotic Addicts," *International Journal of the Addictions* 5 (1970), 245-56. *Public Health Reviews* 1 (1972), 8-39.

9. J.A. O'Donnell, *Narcotic Addicts in Kentucky* (Washington, D.C.: Government Printing Office, 1969).

10. Carl D. Chambers, R.K. Hensley, and M. Moldestad, "Narcotic Addiction in Females: A Race Comparison," *International Journal of the Addictions* 5 (1970), 257-78.

11. O'Donnell, 248.

12. Irwin Henderson, *An Exploration of the Natural History of Heroin Addiction* (Vancouver: Narcotic Addiction Foundation of British Columbia, 1970).

13. Barry S. Brown, Susan K. Gauvey, Marilyn B. Myers, and S.D. Stark, "In Their Own Words: Addicts' Reasons for Initiating and Withdrawing from Heroin," *International Journal of the Addictions* 6 (1971), 635-45.

14. Brenda J. Kaubin, "Sexism Shades the Lives and Treatment of Female Addicts," *Contemporary Drug Problems* 3 (1974), 471-84.

15. *Women and Drugs: An Annotated Bibliography* (Rockville, MD: National Clearinghouse for Drug Abuse Information, 1975).

16. Don Cahalan, *Problem Drinkers* (San Francisco: Jossey-Boss, 1970), 42.

17. Don Cahalan, Ira H. Cisin, and Helen M. Crossley, *American*

Drinking Practices, A National Study of Drinking Behavior and Attitudes (New Brunswick, NJ: Rutgers Center for Alcohol Studies, 1969), 105-108, 150-97.

18. Gorden Bell, cited in Kaubin, 473.

19. Vera L. Lindbeck, "The Woman Alcoholic: A Review of the Literature," *International Journal of the Addictions* 7 (1972), 569.

20. E.S. Lisansky, "Alcoholism in Women: Social and Psychological Concomitants," *Quarterly Journal of Studies on Alcohol* 18 (1957), 588-623.

21. L.J. Beckman, "Women Alcoholics, A Review of Social and Psychological Studies," *Journal of Studies on Alcohol* 36 (1975), 797-824.

22. Sharon C. Wilsnack, "Femininity by the Bottle," *Psychology Today* 6 (1973), 39-43.

23. Lisansky, 600, 620.

24. Helmet Hoffman and Avis A. Noem, "Social Background Variables, Referral Sources and Life Events of Male and Female Alcoholics," *Psychological Reports* 38 (1976), 79-84.

25. J.E.E. De Lint, "Alcoholism, Birth Rank and Parental Deprivation," *American Journal of Psychiatry* 120 (1964), 1062-65.

26. Lisansky, 603.

27. Frederick B. Parker, "Sex-role Adjustment in Women Alcoholics," *Quarterly Journal of Studies on Alcohol* 33 (1972), 647-57.

28. Frederick B. Parker, "Sex-role Adjustment and Drinking Disposition of Women College Students," *Journal of Studies on Alcohol* 36 (1975), 1570-73.

29. Wilsnack, 102.

30. Ibid., 39-43.

31. Douglas E. Durand, "Effects of Drinking on the Power and Affiliation Needs of Middle-Aged Females," *Journal of Clinical Psychology* 31 (1975), 549-33.

32. Joan Curlee, "Alcoholism and the Empty Nest," *Bulletin of the Menninger Clinic* 33 (1969), 165-71.

33. K.W. Wanberg and J. Knapp, "Differences in Drinking Symptoms and Behavior of Men and Women Alcoholics," *British Journal of Addiction* 64 (1970), 347-55.

34. A. Balfour Sclare, "The Woman Alcoholic," *Journal of Alcoholism* 10 (1975), 134-37.

35. Hugh J. Parry, B. Mitchell Balter, Glen D. Mellinger, Ira H. Cisin and Dean I. Manheimer, "Increasing Alcohol Intake as a Coping Mechanism for Psychic Distress," in *Medical Use of Psychotropic Drugs*, ed. by R. Cooperstock (Toronto: Addiction Research Foundations, 1974), 119-44.

36. Cuskey, 35.

37. Cooperstock, 238-44.

38. Ruth Cooperstock, "Some Factors Involved in the Increased Prescribing of Psychotropic Drugs," in Cooperstock, 1974, 21-34.

39. J. Hindmarch, "Drugs and Their Abuse-Age Groups Particularly at Risk," *British Journal of Addiction* 67 (1972), 209-14.

40. Sam Shapiro and Seymour H. Baron, "Prescriptions for Psychotropic Drugs in a Non-Institutional Population," *Public Health Reports* 76 (1961), 481-88.

41. Dianne Fejer and Reginald Smart, "The Use of Psychoactive Drugs by Adults," *Canadian Psychiatric Association Journal* 18 (1973), 313-20.

42. G.D. Mellinger, M.B. Balter, and D.I. Manheimer, "Patterns of Psychotropic Drug Use Among Adults in San Francisco," *Archives of General Psychiatry* 25 (1971), 385-94.

43. G.D. Mellinger, M.B. Balter, H.J. Parry, D.I. Manheimer, and I.H. Cisin, "An Overview of Psychotropic Drug Use in the United States," in *Drug Use, Epidemiological and Sociological Approaches*, ed. by E. Josephson and E. Carroll (New York: Wiley, 1974), 333-66.

44. Ann Cartwright, "Prescribing and the Relationship Between Patients and Doctors," in Cooperstock, 1974, 63-74.

45. John C. Sibley, "Drug Utilization and the Quality of Primary Health Care: A Methodology for Appraisal," in Cooperstock, 1974, 101-17.

46. Lawrence S. Linn and M.S. Davis, "The Use of Psychotherapeutic Drugs by Middle-Aged Women," *Journal of Health and Social Behavior* 12 (1973), 331-40.

47. G. Gurin, J. Veroff, and S. Feld, *Americans View Their Mental Health* (New York: Basic Books, 1960), 189.

48. Ibid., 288.

49. Derek L. Phillips and B. Segal, "Sexual Status and Psychiatric Symptoms," *American Sociological Review* 34 (1969), 58-72.

50. Linn and Davis, 338.

51. K.J. Lennane and R.J. Lennane, "Alleged Psychogenic Disorders in Women—A Possible Manifestation of Sexual Prejudice," *New England Journal of Medicine* 288 (1973), 288-92.

52. Lawrence S. Linn, "Physician Characteristics and Attitudes Toward Legitimate Use of Psychotherapeutic Drugs," *Journal of Health and Social Behavior* 12 (1971), 132-40.

53. *Prescribed and Nonprescribed Medicines, Type and Use of Medicines, United States—July 1964—June 1965* (Washington, D.C.: Government Printing Office, 1967).

54. C. Muller, "The Overmedicated Society: Forces in the Marketplace for Medical Care," *Science* 176, #4034 (1972), 488-92.

55. J.E. Prather and L.S. Fidell, "Pressure for Providing Psychoactive

Drugs to Women," paper presented at the annual meeting of the American Sociological Association (New Orleans, 1972).

56. Howard S. Becker, "Consciousness, Power, and Drug Effects," *Journal of Psychedelic Drugs* 6 (1974), 67-76.

57. Ibid., 73.

58. Bowker, *Drug Forum*, 69-80.

59. Carl D. Chambers, "An Assessment of Drug Use in the General Population," in *Drug Use and Social Policy*, ed. by J. Susman (New York: AMS Press, 1972), 50-123.

60. Lisansky, 608-609.

61. Henderson, 101-24.

62. Carolyn A. Eldred and Mabel N. Washington, "Interpersonal Relationships in Heroin Use by Men and Women and Their Role in Treatment Outcome," *International Journal of the Addictions* 11 (1976), 117-30.

63. Ibid., 128.

64. Erich Goode, "Drug Use and Sexual Activity on a College Campus," *American Journal of Psychiatry* 128 (1972), 1272-76.

65. Erich Goode, *The Marijuana Smokers* (New York: Basic Books, 1970).

66. J. Howard and P. Borges, "Needle Sharing in the Haight: Some Social and Behavioral Functions," *Journal of Health and Social Behavior* 11 (1970), 220-30.

67. E. Baselga, "Younger Drug Users: Sociological Study of One Sample," *Bulletin on Narcotics* 24 (1972), 17-22.

68. Bruce D. Johnson, *Marijuana Users and Drug Subcultures* (New York: Wiley, 1973).

69. Ibid., 61.

70. A.P. MacDonald, R.T. Walls, and R. LeBlanc, "College Female Drug Users," *Adolescence* 8 (1973), 189-96.

71. Paul Wohlford, "Initiation of Cigarette Smoking: Is It Related to Parental Smoking Behavior?" in *Drug Use and Social Policy*, 323-26.

72. Stanley H. Schuman and Jane Polkowski, "Drug and Risk Perceptions of Ninth-Grade Students: Sex Differences and Similarities," *Community Mental Health Journal* 11 (1975), 184-94.

73. Jeffrey B. Freeland and Richard S. Campbell, "The Social Context of First Marijuana Use," *International Journal of the Addictions* 8 (1973), 317-24.

74. Doris H. Milman and Jeffrey L. Anker, "Pattern of Drug Usage Among University Students: IV. Use of Marijuana, Amphetamines, Opium and LSD by Undergraduates," *Journal of the American College Health Association* 19 (1971), 178-86.

75. Jeffrey L. Anker, Doris H. Milman, Stuart A. Kahan, and Carlo Valenti, "Drug Usage and Related Patterns of Behavior in University

Students: I. General Survey and Marijuana Use," *Journal of the American College Health Association* 19 (1971), 178-86.

76. P.A. Walters, G.W. Goethals, and H.G. Pope, "Drug Use and Life-Style among 500 College Undergraduates," *Archives of General Psychiatry* 26 (1972), 92-96.

77. James R. Henley and Larry D. Adams, "Marijuana Use in Post-Collegiate Cohorts: Correlates of Use, Prevalence Patterns, and Factors Associated with Cessation," *Social Problems* 20 (1973), 514-20.

78. I.L. Campbell, "Non-Medical Psychoactive Drug Use at Bishop's University, 1965-1970," Unpublished report, Bishop's University, Lennoxville, Canada, 1970.

79. Janis S. Rosenberg, S.V. Kasl, and R.M. Berberian, "Sex Differences in Adolescent Drug Use: Recent Trends," *Addictive Diseases* 1 (1974), 73-96.

80. Mary Snow, "Youth and Drugs: A Pilot Study of Use, Attitudes, and Knowledge of Drugs Among Students in Two New York City Schools," New York: Narcotic Addiction Control Commission, 1970.

81. Valerie Klinge, Habib Vaziri, and Kathleen Lennox, "Comparison of Psychiatric Inpatient Male and Female Adolescent Drug Abusers," *International Journal of the Addictions* 11 (1976), 309-23.

82. Stanley W. Sadava, "College Student Drug Use: A Social Psychological Study," Ph.D. dissertation (University of Colorado, 1970), 116.

83. Ibid., 90-91.

84. Ibid., 101, 156-57.

85. Beatrice A. Rouse and John A. Ewing, "Marijuana and Other Drug Use by Women College Students: Associated Risk Taking and Coping Activities," *American Journal of Psychiatry* 100 (1973), 486-90.

86. Norman C. Alexander and Ernest Q. Campbell, "Normative Milieux and Social Behaviors: Church Affiliations and Collegiate Drinking Patterns," in *The Domesticated Drug, Drinking Among Collegians*, ed. by G.L. Maddox (New Haven, CT: College and University Press, 1970), 268-85.

87. Ann Oakley, *The Sociology of Housework* (New York: Pantheon, 1974), 8.

88. Ann F. Brunswick and Carol Tarica, "Drinking and Health: A Study of Urban Black Adolescents," *Addictive Diseases* 1 (1974), 21-42.

89. D.J. Wolk, "Marijuana on the Campus: A Study at One University," *Journal of the American College Health Association* 17 (1968), 144-49.

90. L. Robbins, E. Robbins, S. Pearlman, A. Philip, E. Robinson, and B. Schmitter, "College Students' Perceptions of Their Parents' Attitudes and Practices toward Drug Use," paper presented at the annual meeting of the Eastern Psychological Association (New York, 1971).

91. Don C. Gibbons, *Delinquent Behavior* (Englewood Cliffs, NJ: Prentice-Hall, 1976).

92. F. Heidensohn, "The Deviance of Women," *British Journal of Sociology* 19 (1968), 161.

93. Bernard P. Cohen, L.D. Flanders, Karen Glenney-Smith, and T.G. Rundall, "Do Females Conform More than Males: The Wrong Questions," paper presented at the annual meeting of the Pacific Sociological Association (San Diego, 1976).

94. David R. Heise, "Norms and Individual Patterns in Student Deviancy," *Social Problems* 16 (1968), 78-92.

95. See Christine E. Rasche, "The Female Offender as an Object of Criminological Research," *Criminal Justice and Behavior* 1 (1974), 301-20.

96. Heise, 83.

97. Peggy C. Giordano, S.A. Cernkovich, and C.L. Baker, "Continuing Patterns of Female Delinquency," paper presented at the annual meeting of the Society for the Study of Social Problems (New York, 1976).

98. Derek L. Phillips and Kevin J. Clancy, "Some Effects of 'Social Desirability' in Survey Studies," *American Journal of Sociology* 127 (1972), 92-940.

99. Gary J. Jensen and Raymond Eve, "Sex Differences in Delinquency, An Examination of Popular Sociological Examinations," *Criminology* 13 (1976), 427-48.

100. Raymond Bosse and Charles L. Rose, "Smoking Cessation and Sex Role Convergence," *Journal of Health and Social Behavior* 17 (1976), 53-61.

101. Green and Nemzer, 631-36.

102. Reginald G. Smart and D. Fejer, "Six Years of Cross-Sectional Surveys of Student Drug Use in Toronto," *Bulletin on Narcotics* 27 (1975), 11-22.

103. Ibid., 21.

104. Frederic Suffet and Richard Brotman, "Female Drug Use: Some Observations," *International Journal of the Addictions* 11 (1976), 19-33.

105. Giordano, 7.

106. Joseph G. Weis, "Liberation and Crime: The Invention of the New Female Criminal," *Crime and Social Justice* 6 (Fall-Winter 1976), 17-18.

107. Freda Adler, *Sisters in Crime: The Rise of the New Female Criminal* (New York: McGraw-Hill, 1975), 3.

108. Weis, 19.

109. Ibid., 23-25.

110. Gary Seidler, "Report from the First National Forum on Drugs, Alcoholism and Women," *The Journal* 4, 12 (1975), 5.

111. George M. Beschner, "The Women's Project, Report I," unpublished paper (Rockville, MD, 1975).

Part II
Females and the Criminal Justice System

4 A Scream in the Night: Women as Victims

We will begin this chapter with a general treatment of the extent and conditions of the criminal victimization of women in the United States between 1965 and 1975 and will then present detailed examinations of four specific types of female victimization. The first is forcible rape, which more than any other crime symbolizes the condition of women in American society. The only more serious personal crime than rape is murder, and that is the second type of female victimization to receive special treatment in this chapter. The third topic is wife-beating, which follows from homicide by virtue of the fact that so many instances of wife-beating lead to murder. Finally, there is a discussion of the physical abuse of female infants and girls.

The Criminal Victimization of Women in America

Until 1965, little was known about the characteristics of the victims of crime in the United States. Except for the crimes of murder and rape, the *Uniform Crime Reports* do not go into detail on the characteristics of victims. The main interest of the FBI is in the characteristics of the criminals, as presented in arrest statistics. The identification of patterns and rates for female victimization had to await the development of self-report victimization survey methodology. The first survey of this type was conducted in 1965-66 by the National Opinion Research Center of the University of Chicago for the President's Commission on Law Enforcement and Administration of Justice. This survey was based on a national sample of 10,000 households, which allowed its results to be generalized to the entire population of the United States. The most important finding of the NORC Survey was that self-reports of crimes were much higher than official crime statistics. For example, the *Uniform Crime Reports* violent crime rate for 1965 was 184.7 per 100,000 Americans, but NORC found 357.8 violent crimes per 100,000, an increase of 94 percent over the *UCR* data. Similarly, the *UCR* property crime rate was 793.0 and the NORC rate was 1,761.8, an increase of 122 percent. Not all crimes were underreported to the police to the same degree. The most underreported of all crimes was forcible rape, for which the NORC self-report rate was nearly four times the official *UCR* rate.[1]

For all crimes reported in the NORC survey, the ratio of female to male victimizations was .34. That is to say, women were victimized only one-third as often as men. Except for burglary, for which the ratio of female to male victimizations was .20, the ratios for all major crimes were higher than the average figure of .34. For larceny of $50 or more, the female/male ratio was .40; for aggravated assault, .41; for motor vehicle theft, .49; and for robbery, .69. This suggests that when women were victimized the crime was more likely to be a serious one than for men. NORC data also revealed that women were most likely to be victimized between the ages of twenty and twenty-nine, with a secondary peak between forty and forty-nine. Every one of the specific crimes was higher in the twenty to twenty-nine age bracket than at any other age, except for larceny of $50 or more, which was highest at age forty to forty-nine.[2]

The President's Commission also sponsored a study of 13,713 cases of assaultive crimes against the person other than homicide from the files of the Chicago Police Department. The run of cases was from September 1965 to March 1966. For these assaultive crimes, black women were nearly eight times as likely to be victimized as white women. Among white women, 62 percent of the assaultive victimizations were by white men, 26 percent by black men, 8 percent by white women, and 3 percent by black women. The cross-sex, intraracial character of white female assaultive victimizations was replicated for black women. Eighty-seven percent of their assaultive victimizations were by black men, 11 percent by black women, 2 percent by white men, and only a fraction of one percent by white women. The Chicago Police Department data also revealed that while men were most likely to be assaulted in the street, women were most likely to be assaulted in their homes.[3]

Instead of following up on the NORC self-report survey strategy, the National Commission on the Causes and Prevention of Violence elected to expand on the analysis of police reports that the President's Law Enforcement Commission had carried out in Chicago and elsewhere. The Violence Commission sponsored a study of a 10 percent random sample of 1967 offense and arrest reports from seventeen large U.S. cities. This strategy did not allow them to generate rates for the entire population of the nation, but it did provide details about criminal victimization in the highest crime areas of the country. In their sample of cases, women comprised all of the victims of rape, 21 percent of the victims of homicide, 34 percent of aggravated assault, 11 percent of armed robbery, and 29 percent of unarmed robbery. The overwhelming majority of these incidents were perpetrated on the women by men—approximately four of every five homicides and aggravated assaults, nine of every ten robberies, and all the forcible rapes.[4]

Much more detailed information on the victimization of women became available when the Law Enforcement Assistance Administration began its series of victimizaation surveys in large cities in 1972 and in the nation as a whole in 1973. Table 4-1 presents a basic set of national victimization statistics for 1973, 1974, and 1975. Three years is too short a time to do a trend analysis, but it is better than nothing, and limited comparisons can be made with the 1965-66 NORC data. The only reasonable comparable figures for female victimization are for rape, robbery, and aggravated assault. They indicate that between 1965-66 and 1973 rape increased 125 percent, the robbery of women was up by 375 percent, and aggravated assaults of women increased by 333 percent. Over the shorter span of time from 1973 to 1975, males experienced a nonlinear increase in victimization experiences of 3 percent, and females had a linear increase of 6 percent. These increases did not change the basic differences between male and female victimization. Approximately fifteen in every 100 men reported being victimized in 1975, as compared with eleven out of every 100 women.

The only substantial changes for women between 1973 and 1975 were in

Table 4-1
Victimization Rates[a] for the United States, 1973-1975, by Sex of Victim

	Victimization Rates		
Sex and Crime	*1973*	*1974*	*1975*
Females			
Rape	1.8	1.8	1.7
Robbery	3.8	4.3	4.0
Aggravated assault	5.2	5.2	5.4
Simple assault	10.9	10.4	11.9
Total crimes of violence[b]	21.6	21.7	22.9
Personal larceny with contact	3.4	3.2	3.3
Personal larceny without contact	76.8	79.1	81.5
Total crimes of theft	80.3	82.3	84.8
Total victimizations	101.9	104.0	107.7
Males			
Rape	0.1[c]	0.1[c]	0.1[c]
Robbery	9.9	10.3	9.8
Aggravated assault	15.2	16.0	14.1
Simple assault	19.0	18.8	19.5
Total crimes of violence[b]	44.1	45.1	43.5
Personal larceny with contact	2.6	3.0	2.9
Personal larceny without contact	100.2	105.7	105.1
Total crimes of theft	102.9	108.7	107.9
Total victimizations	147.0	153.8	151.4

[a]Rates are per 1,000 residents aged twelve and over.

[b]Since these are self-report statistics, murder is not included.

[c]Estimates based on approximately ten or fewer cases are statistically unreliable.

Sources: *Criminal Victimizations in the United States, A Comparison of 1973 and 1974 Findings* (Washington, D.C.: Government Printing Office, 1976); and *Criminal Victimization in the United States, A Comparison of 1974 and 1975 Findings* (Washington, D.C.: Government Printing Office, 1977).

simple assaults (up to 10.9 to 11.9 per 1,000) and personal larceny without contact (up from 76.8 to 81.5 per 1,000). These two categories were mainly responsible for the increases in the totals for crimes of violence and crimes of the theft. Excluding rape, the ratio of female to male victimization incidents moved slightly closer to unity between 1973 and 1975 for each category of crime. The female/male robbery victimization ratio increased from .38 to .41, the aggravated assault ratio increased from .34 to .38, simple assault increased from .57 to .61, and personal larceny without contact increased from .77 to .78. Personal larceny with contact was the only victimization category in which women exceeded men, but that ratio decreased from 1.31 in 1973 to 1.14 in 1975. With the exception of the last ratio, which is based on a relatively small number of incidents, these changes are all unimpressive, but they for are only a two-year period. This is the stuff of which long-term trends are made. It will be some years before we can say for sure whether or not these changes are part of a long-term trend in American society or just short-term fluctuations without any theoretical relevance.

In table 4-2, rates and ratios for crimes of violence and personal-property crimes are given for men and women in thirteen cities and the United States as a whole. Each of the cities was surveyed twice, with either two or three years between the surveys. For some, the victimization year ran from July of one year through June of the following year, which is why their rates are listed for 1971-1972 or 1974-75 instead of for single years. The striking thing about table 4-2 is the difference in rates between cities. The female victimization rate for violent crime varies from 27.4 (Newark, 1974-75) to 52.6 (Detroit, 1974). For males, the range for violent victimizations is from 45.7 (New York, 1972) to 112.3 (Baltimore, 1974-75). This means that men in some cities are subject to fewer crimes of violence than women in other cities, even though they are in general much more likely to experience a violent victimization than are women. Looking at personal-property crimes, we see that the female victimization rate fluctuates from 46.5 (Newark, 1974-75) to 131.9 (Portland, Oregon, 1974-75) and the male rate varies from 42.8 (Newark, 1974-75) to 154.1 (Denver, 1974-75). Here there is a more substantial overlap between male and female victimization rates, and even some instances in which women reported more personal-property crimes committed against them than did men.

Victimization rates for the entire United States are quite a bit lower than rates recorded for the large cities. This reflects the differences in magnitude between city crime and suburban, town, and rural crime. The difference is so extreme for violent crime that the lowest city rates for both males and females are higher than the national rates. Put simply, there is not a safe city on the list. The differences for personal-property crimes are not as large,

Table 4-2
Victimization Rates[a] for Thirteen American Cities, by Sex of Victim

		Rates					
		Crimes of Violence[b]			*Personal Property Crimes*		
City and Year		*Male*	*Female*	*Ratio of Female/ Male*	*Male*	*Female*	*Ratio of Female/ Male*
Atlanta	1971-72	62.8	35.9	.57	114.1	89.2	.78
	1974-75	58.9	31.4	.53	102.0	85.9	.84
Baltimore	1971-72	78.4	37.3	.48	83.0	75.3	.91
	1974-75	112.3	50.6	.45	108.2	101.7	.94
Chicago	1972	71.1	42.5	.60	94.9	80.5	.85
	1974	81.7	42.9	.53	97.4	85.3	.88
Cleveland	1971-72	68.8	41.5	.60	76.0	66.2	.87
	1974-75	88.0	49.5	.56	99.4	73.3	.74
Dallas	1971-72	60.7	27.8	.46	102.2	91.3	.89
	1974-75	68.2	31.4	.46	129.3	105.5	.82
Denver	1971-72	89.9	47.2	.52	146.3	122.6	.84
	1974-75	98.4	47.5	.48	154.1	116.3	.75
Detroit	1972	90.8	48.5	.53	104.3	86.6	.83
	1974	107.6	52.6	.49	108.8	75.9	.70
Los Angeles	1972	71.5	36.6	.51	115.0	97.1	.84
	1974	78.0	41.8	.54	130.5	109.9	.84
Newark	1971-72	52.8	33.8	.64	45.0	54.5	1.21
	1974-75	51.7	27.4	.53	42.8	46.5	1.09
New York	1972	45.7	28.0	.61	46.8	55.4	1.18
	1974	56.7	31.5	.56	69.0	62.5	.91
Philadelphia	1972	93.4	37.9	.41	100.9	90.0	.89
	1974	72.0	30.1	.42	92.0	78.9	.86
Portland,	1971-72	76.4	43.7	.57	137.7	109.9	.80
Oregon	1974-75	93.1	51.4	.55	154.8	131.9	.85
St. Louis	1971-72	61.2	27.5	.45	72.8	72.7	1.00
	1974-75	66.4	34.9	.53	104.0	83.2	.80
United States	1973	44.1	21.6	.49	102.9	80.3	.78
	1974	45.1	21.7	.48	108.7	82.3	.76
	1975	43.5	22.9	.53	107.9	84.8	.79

Sources: *Criminal Victimization Surveys in Eight American Cities, A Comparison of 1971-72 and 1974-75 Findings* (1976); *Criminal Victimization Surveys in Chicago, Detroit, Los Angeles, New York, and Philadelphia, A Comparison of 1972 and 1974 Findings* (1976); *Criminal Victimization in the United States, A Comparison of 1973 and 1974 Findings* (1976); and *Criminal Victimization in the United States, A Comparison of 1974 and 1975 Findings* (1977). All published by the Government Printing Office (Washington, D.C.).

[a]Rates are per 1,000 residents aged 12 and over.

[b]Since these are self-report victimization rates rather than official statistics, crimes of violence do not include murder.

with some cities being safer than the national average and others being less safe. Not very many Americans move from one city to another to avoid high crime rates, but perhaps more will do so in the future, considering that violent crime is more than twice as common in some cities as others and property crime is three times as common in the most crime-prone cities as in the least crime-prone. Comparing the thirteen cities, it appears that women who live in Atlanta, Dallas, Newark, New York, Philadelphia, and St. Louis are a great deal safer than women who live in Detroit, Denver, Cleveland, Baltimore and Portland, Oregon.

Many of the cities in table 4-2 show relatively steady victimization rates between the two surveys, but others show large changes for which there is no evident explanation. For example, the violent crime rate in Baltimore rose steeply from 78.4 (male) and 37.3 (female) in 1971-72 to 112.3 and 50.6 in 1974-75 and the personal-property crime rate in Portland rose from 137.7 (male) and 109.9 (female) in 1971-72 to 154.8 and 131.9 in 1974-75. We can not attribute changes such as these to reformulations of police-department policies when we are dealing with self-report data. It could be that we could make sense of these shifts if we had separate data for the different ecological units that are present within each of these major metropolitan areas, along with demographic and other social indicator profiles for each ecological unit.

Ratios were formed for violent and personal-property crimes by dividing the female victimization rate by the male rate. This statistical device makes sexual differentiation among victims explicit, and aids in sorting out the effects of the structural characteristics of different cities from possible basic changes in the sexual composition of successive cohorts of victims. The largest ratio change for violent crime between surveys is .09 in Newark, and for personal-property crime, it is .21 in New York. The victimization ratio for violent crime declined in nine of thirteen cities and the ratio for personal-property crimes declined in eight of the thirteen cities. This means that women in most of these large cities made up a slightly smaller proportion of crime victims in 1974-75 than in 1971-72. Since the national victimization ratios increased slightly from 1973 to 1975, this implies that the ratios are rising in the suburbs, towns, and rural areas while they are declining in most major American cities.

There is no city in which women are more likely than men to be the victims of violent crime. The highest victimization ratio for violent crime is .64 for Newark in 1971-72, followed by New York at .61 in 1972. A higher proportion of personal-property crime is committed against women than the proportion of violent crime. In fact, the lowest personal-property crime victimization ratio is higher than the highest violent crime ratio. In New York during 1972 and in both of the survey periods in Newark, women made up more than half of all the victims of personal-property crime. As a rule, male and female victimization rates increased or decreased together, which indicates that changes in the structural characteristics of crime in the cities affect men and women in the same way.

We have been comparing women and men as if all women suffered the same burden of criminal victimization. Table 4-3 shows that this is an oversimplification. White women are less likely than black women or women of Spanish origin to be the victims of rape, robbery, or assault, but more likely to be victimized by crimes of theft. Women who are separated or divorced suffer higher rates of rape, robbery, and assault than other women, and their property crime victimization rate is exceeded only by the property crime rate for females who have never married, most of whom are relatively young. There is almost a perfect inverse relationship between age and both violent and property crime victimization rates. The violent crime rate increases slightly from 40.9 at age twelve to fifteen to 43.5 at age twenty to twenty-four, and then rapidly subsides. For crimes of theft, the peak comes

Table 4-3
Victimization Rates[a] for Women in the United States, 1975, by Age, Race/Ethnicity, and Marital Status of Victim

	Crime				
	All Crimes of Violence[b]	*Rape*	*Robbery*	*Assault*	*Crimes of Theft*
Age					
12-15	40.9	1.6	5.2	34.1	143.7
16-19	41.9	4.6	4.5	32.7	145.6
20-24	43.5	4.7	7.3	31.4	125.7
25-34	26.8	2.3	3.7	20.8	95.2
35-49	15.9	0.4[c]	3.5	11.9	77.9
50-64	9.6	0.4[c]	2.5	6.7	47.7
65 and over	6.5	0.1[c]	3.4	3.0	22.7
Race/ethnicity					
White	21.4	1.6	3.5	16.3	86.8
Black	34.1	1.8	7.5	24.8	73.1
Spanish origin	29.9	2.1	5.3	22.5	69.0
Marital status					
Never married	38.3	3.1	5.9	29.3	131.3
Married	12.6	0.8	2.3	9.5	70.2
Separated or divorced	64.6	4.7	9.9	50.1	107.6
Widowed	11.1	0.5[c]	3.9	6.7	34.6
Total	22.9	1.7	4.0	17.3	84.8

Source: *Criminal Victimization in the United States, A Comparison of 1974 and 1975 Findings* (Washington, D.C.: Government Printing Office, 1971).

[a]Rates are per 1,000 residents aged twelve and over.

[b]Since these are self-report statistics, murder is not included.

[c]Estimates based on approximately ten or fewer cases are statistically unreliable.

earlier, at age sixeen to nineteen, with a rate of 145.6, and decreases greatly in each succeeding age category. The danger of a young woman's being raped in the United States is three times as great between the ages of sixteen and twenty-four as at age twelve to fifteen, and twice as great as at age twenty-five to thirty-four.

A more detailed report on the 1973 national victimization survey has been issued by the Law Enforcement Assistance Administration. This confirms the effect of an urban environment on criminal victimization that was implied in the comparison of data from thirteen large cities with material from national samples. In 1973, the white female victimization rate for violent crime varied from twenty-nine per 1,000 in central cities to twenty-one in suburban areas and fifteen in nonmetropolitan areas. For black females, the violent crime victimization rate decreased from forty-one per 1,000 in central cities to thirty-eight in suburban areas and twenty-four in nonmetropolitan areas. The difference in violent crime victimization rates between central cities and nonmetropolitan areas was slightly greater for white women than for black women. The nonmetropolitan rate was 59 percent of the central-city rate for black women and 52 percent for white women.[5]

The 1973 pattern for crimes of theft was a bit different. Whites experienced the same decrease of victimization rates in suburban and nonmetropolitan areas as compared with central cities that they did for violent crime, but the theft victimization rates for both black men and black women were curvilinear, with the highest levels of victimization being reported from suburban areas rather than central cities. Another difference between violence and theft patterns in 1973 was that, while blacks suffered much higher rates of violence than whites, whites were more likely to be victimized in crimes of theft in central cities and nonmetropolitan areas, and about equally likely to be victimized in suburban areas outside of central cities. This was true for men and women, although the male victimization rates for crimes of theft were well above the female victimization rates in all areas.[6]

Another series of tables in the 1973 detailed report reveals the percent of violent victimizations involving strangers. Women were more likely than men to know their attackers, and this was true for blacks as well as whites, and at all age levels except sixty-five and over. Overall, 45 percent of the women and 29 percent of the men knew their attackers. In rape incidents, 23 percent of the women knew the offenders. There were not enough male rape victims to allow valid statistical comparisons to be made. For robberies, 22 percent of the women and 12 percent of the men knew their attackers. Assaulters were much more likely to be known to their victims than robbers, with 34 percent of the men and 52 percent of the women knowing their attackers. These patterns were similar for blacks and whites, except that black victims, both male and female, were more likely to know their attackers in assault cases than were white victims.[7]

Women were more likely than men to report violent victimizations to the police, and this was true regardless of whether or not they knew their attackers. There was no difference between men and women in the proportion of personal crimes of theft reported to the police. The crime that women were most likely to report to the police was robbery with serious injury (85 percent), followed by aggravated assault with injury (69 percent). Women were least likely to report personal larceny victimizations without personal contact (21 percent). Among violent crimes, the ones least likely to be reported by women were attempted assault without a weapon (40 percent) and rape (49 percent).[8]

Rape: A Symbol of Oppression

According to the FBI, there were 56,730 forcible rapes in the United States in 1976, or one every nine minutes,[9] and this is just the tip of the iceberg. Rape rates recalculated from FBI data show that there has been a steady rise in American rape levels since the first *Uniform Crime Reports* was issued in 1933. The only substantial exception to this upward trend was in 1945-49, when the rape rate decreased by approximately 19 percent before resuming its upward spiral.[10] The increase in rape has been far greater than the increases in other violent crimes such as criminal homicide, robbery, and aggravated assault.

Table 4-4 contains rates for attempted and completed rapes in thirteen major American cities plus completed rapes in the nation as a whole. It is evident that some cities are much safer than others, and that the same city sometimes experiences considerable fluctuations in the rape rate. Portland's rape rate increased from 4.3 to 6.8 per 1,000 women between 1971-72 and 1974-75, Atlanta's rate was steady at 4.3 in both time periods, and Detroit's rate decreased from 4.7 to 3.3 between 1972 and 1974. The U.S. rate for completed rapes was essentially steady between 1973 and 1975.

Not all rapes that are attempted result in a completed act of sexual intercourse. The victim may be successful in beating off her attacker, or something may happen in the environment to scare off the rapist. Table 4-4 shows that the attempted-rape rate is always larger than the completed-rape rate. Only in Chicago (1974), Dallas, and Atlanta (1974-75) did the completed-rape exceed 40 percent of the total rate of sexual assaults. In contrast, the proportion of rapes that included a completed act of sexual intercourse was as low as 12 percent in Philadelphia (1972), 14 percent in Baltimore (1971-72), and 15 percent in New York (1972), but all three of these proportions rose considerably by 1974-75. As a matter of fact, the completion percentage rose in all the cities surveyed except for St. Louis, Los Angeles, and Newark.

Why was the 1972 rape completion rate much lower in Chicago (23 percent) than in Los Angeles (38 percent)? Was it because Los Angeles is located in the West, which has generally high rape rates? Or perhaps it was due to the unique combination of ethnic groups in the Los Angeles area. If so, then why were the two cities reversed in 1974, when the rape completion rate was 29 percent in Los Angeles and 45 percent in Chicago? At this point, we don't have enough data to answer these questions. A possibility that bears investigation is that variations in collective definitions of what constitutes an attempted rape are to some extent a characteristic of the culture of each city or region and are also subject to rapid change due to manipulations of the public by the mass media. One thing that we can be sure of in table 4-4 is that, at any given point in time, women in the most dangerous city are two to six times as likely to be sexually assaulted as women in the least dangerous city. In the average big-city neighborhoods containing perhaps 4,000 females aged twelve and up, fourteen of these women can be expected to be sexually assaulted each year. If the risk were equally divided among all the women in the neighborhood, one in every eight urban American women could be expected to be sexually assaulted during her lifetime. In America, this is not the case. Rape risks are not equally distributed. Women who were divorced, separated, never married, black, poor, and young reported higher than average rape rates in the 1973 national survey.[11]

Rape is usually conceptualized as an act perpetrated by a total stranger, and this is generally the case, but nearly a quarter of the victims in the 1973 survey knew their attackers.[12] In the 1967 survey of reported crime in major American cities conducted by the National Commission on the Causes and Prevention of Violence, only 53 percent of the rapes were committed by strangers. The next most common category of sexual offenders was acquaintances (28 percent), followed by family members (7 percent) and neighbors (3 percent). Husbands' rapes of their wives are not counted in the family category or in any other category because the tradition in the United States has been to permit men to force their sexual attentions on their wives whenever they wish to do so.[13] In Amir's study of rape in Philadelphia during 1958 and 1960, only 42 percent of the rapes were committed by total strangers.[14] Other surveys of rapes reported to the police have shown higher percentages of rapes by strangers, ranging from 56 percent (Los Angeles, 1967) to 91 percent (Boston, 1967),[15] and self-report victimization data from 1973 show that 77 percent of the rapes were committed by strangers.[16]

As in the self-report data, single women are always more likely to be victimized than married women.[17] Most rapes are intraracial, with blacks raping blacks in 42 percent of the Tampa cases.[18] 40 percent of Oakland cases,[19] 60 percent of the cases from seventeen cities investigated by the National Commission on the Causes and Prevention of Violence,[20] 76 percent of Washington, D.C., cases,[21] and 77 percent of Philadelphia cases.[22] Black

Table 4-4
Female Rape Victimization Rates[a] for Thirteen American Cities

		Rape Rates			
City and Year		*Attempted Rape Rate*	*Completed Rape Rate*	*Total Rape Rate*	*Proportion of Rapes That Are Completed*
Atlanta	1971-72	3.3	0.9	4.3	21%
	1974-75	2.5	1.8	4.3	42
Baltimore	1971-72	1.8	0.3[b]	2.1	14
	1974-75	2.9	1.3	4.3	30
Chicago	1972	3.6	1.1	4.8	23
	1974	2.4	2.0	4.4	45
Cleveland	1971-72	2.6	0.9	3.5	26
	1974-75	2.3	1.5	3.8	39
Dallas	1971-72	2.2	1.1	3.3	33
	1974-75	1.6	1.4	3.0	47
Denver	1971-72	4.4	0.9	5.4	17
	1974-75	3.5	1.2	4.7	26
Detroit	1972	3.4	1.2	4.7	26
	1974	1.9	1.3	3.3	39
Los Angeles	1972	2.5	1.5	4.0	38
	1974	2.8	1.2	4.1	29
Newark	1971-72	1.5	0.9	2.4	38
	1974-75	2.0	0.8	2.7	30
New York	1972	1.6	0.3[b]	2.0	15
	1974	0.9	0.3[b]	1.2	25
Philadelphia	1972	2.1	0.3[b]	2.4	12
	1974	1.6	0.8	2.3	35
Portland	1971-72	3.2	1.2	4.3	28
Oregon	1974-75	4.3	2.5	6.8	37
St. Louis	1971-72	1.4	0.7[b]	2.2	32
	1974-75	1.3	0.4[b]	1.7	24
United States, Total	1973	–	–	1.8	–
	1974	–	–	1.8	–
	1975	–	–	1.7	–

Sources: *Criminal Victimization Surveys in Eight American Cities, A Comparison of 1971-72 and 1974-75 Findings* (1976); *Criminal Victimization Surveys in Chicago, Detroit, Los Angeles, New York, and Philadelphia. A Comparison of 1972 and 1974 Findings* (1976); *Criminal Victimization in the United States, A Comparison of 1973 and 1974 Findings* (1976); and *Criminal Victimization in the United States, A Comparison of 1974 and 1975 Findings* (1977). All published by the Government Printing Office (Washington, D.C.).

[a]Rates are per 1,000 female residents aged twelve and over.

[b]Estimates based on approximately 10 or fewer cases are statistically unreliable.

rapes of white women ranged from 3 percent of all Philadelphia rapes[23] to 33 percent of the rapes in Oakland,[24] and white rapes of blacks were almost nonexistent.

It is difficult to explain rape incidents in terms of the criminality of the attacker, since the majority of the attackers have no previous criminal record,[25] and although the opportunity for robbery is almost always present, comparatively few rapes are accompanied by the commission of any nonsexual felony crimes.[26] Likewise, the influence of alcohol cannot be used to explain most rapes, since Amir and Nelson found it to be present in only one-third of the cases.[27] Even if it were more prevalent, recent research has made clear that factors such as the nature of the social situation, the users' expectations of the effects of the drug, and the person's social learning history are more important than the biochemical effects of alcohol on human behavior.[28]

Most women physically resist the rapist,[29] but rapists use physical force to subdue them in two-thirds to five-sixths of the cases,[30] resulting in physical injuries to the victims beyond rape in perhaps half the cases.[31] One author who has had the opportunity to examine a large number of rape victims over the years has concluded that "if a normal, healthy adult is raped, serious injury will be found, not to the genitalia, but to other parts of the body, particularly the face, neck and extremities."[32] Rather than indicating submissiveness, the data suggest that rape victims demonstrate considerable bravery in resisting the application of physical violence by the rapist, especially when it is realized that approximately a third of the rapists employ weapons such as knives and guns to subdue their victims[33] and that about a quarter of all rapes are by multiple offenders.[34] In addition to vaginal penetration, more than a quarter of the victims of rape are subjected to further sexual acts, including fellatio, cunnilingus, and anal intercourse.[35]

Few would argue with the assertion that rape is a horrible crime and that the victims of this crime deserve much sympathy and support. For that reason, the callous response of the criminal justice system to rape complaints has drawn considerable criticism in recent years. After a sexual assault has taken place, the first step in the legal process occurs when the victim contacts the police. Approximately half of American rape victims decide not to do so, which ends the process at that point.[36] When asked why they did not report the rape incident to the police, victims gave a variety of reasons. For whites, the most common reason for completed rapes was that it was a private matter. For attempted rapes, it was the feeling that nothing could be done because of lack of proof. Blacks cited the same reason for failure to report attempted rape, but named fear of reprisal as the main reason for failure to report completed rapes.[37] In some cases, the crime may be reported by friends, neighbors, or even strangers who take it upon themselves to involve the victim in the criminal justice system.

The trauma of rape has been fully explicated by Weis and Borges,[39] and by Burgess and Holmstrom.[40] The shock of the experience is not only physical. There is a process of personal redefinition as the victim comes to terms with feelings of humiliation, pollution, degradation, and perhaps self-hate. There is always a loss of status connected with rape victimization, and this is compounded by the transformation of the self from a person into an object. Burgess and Holmstrom believe that the acute phase of the victim's reaction to rape lasts two or three weeks, to be followed by a long second phase of reorganization. During the acute phase, symptoms other than physical injury include tension headaches, fatigue, insomnia, persistent startle reactions, loss of appetite, nausea, stomach pain, vaginal discharges, self-blame, embarrassment, hatred, and fear. The personality disorganization that makes it difficult for women to give an accurate account of the rape to police persists throughout the acute phase. In the reorganization phase, only 16 percent of the women studied by Burgess and Holmstrom denied having any symptoms, as compared with 47 percent who reported moderate, severe, or compounded symptoms. Among the symptoms commonly found in rape victims during the reorganization phase are nightmares, increased motor activity in a variety of defensive reactions, and one or more phobias such as fear of being in the environment in which they were originally assaulted, fear of being alone, fear of crowds, and fear of people behind them. Even more severe is a long-term disturbance in the victim's sex life and her relations with men in general.[41]

If the rape is reported to the police, the victim is in danger of being twice victimized. Until recently, police interrogations were almost always carried out by men, and these men were often more sympathetic to the rapist than to the victim. To be fair, police officers had to be sure that the rapist was not falsely accused, an occurrence that has never been uncommon, but this hardly excuses the insensitivity, badgering, and other excesses of technique and attitude that characterized the rape investigations carried out by many officers. Male officers often "suggest that she was not *really* raped, that she enjoyed the experience, that she is not a 'good' woman, or that she encouraged the encounter."[42] They have been known to violate the victim psychosexually by asking irrelevant and obscene questions such as "How many orgasms did you have?," "How big was he?," and "What were you thinking about while he was doing it?" These are actual quotations from interviews conducted with rape victims and staff members of the Rape Crisis Center in Washington, D.C., by Pamela Wood.[43]

The police do not accept every rape complaint as valid. In a Philadelphia study conducted in 1966-67, 23 percent of the rape complaints were unfounded by the police, working together with the prosecutor's office. Rapes were least likely to be unfounded if there was evidence of physical battery. In many cases, the police did not even conduct investigations. When the victim showed no physical evidence of the rape, the police conducted investigations in only 42 percent of the cases.[44] With only limited resources at their disposal, police officers do not wish to "waste time" following up on cases that they judge to have a low probability of successful prosecution, even if they believe that the victim was actually raped. When rape victims take a bath and change their clothes after the attack, as they often do out of revulsion as much as to make themselves presentable before reporting the crime, they destroy much of the evidence that could have helped to convict their attackers.

As a result of rising rape statistics, the work of the feminist movement, and other factors, rape has increasingly been defined as an intolerable social problem.[45] The response of the criminal justice system has been surprisingly rapid, beginning with the formation of the New York Police Department's Rape Investigation and Analysis Section in 1972, which emphasized the use of sympathetic (but objective) policewomen.[46] The proliferation of these units probably has something to do with the noticeable improvement in victims' opinions of the police in recent reports.[47] Improvements in the technical and humanistic aspects of rape investigations are documented in the LEAA prescriptive package *Rape and Its Victims,* along with parallel improvements in patrol and support services, victim services, information systems, and coordination with other social-service agencies.[48]

LEAA sponsored national surveys of police departments and prosecutors in 1975 which give us considerable detail about the response of the criminal justice system to victims of forcible rape. The police survey was designed to cover departments handling 90 percent of all the officially reported rapes in America in 1974, but, due to nonresponses, the completed survey included responses from departments that handled only 60 percent of the rape cases. Still, this is an invaluable source of information on police-department operations in response to crimes of rape. When a rape is initially reported, the most readily available officer is generally sent, but the investigation is more likely to be handled by special rape-investigation units, which were in operation in two-thirds of the police departments surveyed. The number of female officers in these special units is comparatively small, with about one woman for each four men on the staff, but this is still larger than the proportion of women in other police-department units. In addition to the investigative services provided by these units, three-quarters of the jurisdictions have special medical services available, and two-thirds of the jurisdictions also offer special rape-counseling services.[49]

The police departments surveyed by the LEAA project did not all have the same working definition of what constitutes a rape incident. Twenty-eight percent of the departments required penetration, force, and either the use of a weapon or resistance by the victim (or both); 52 percent required penetration and force; 14 percent required penetration alone; and 5 percent did not require any of these factors. The departments that required weapons and/or resistance reported from 10 to 63 percent less rapes than those that didn't have these requirements, depending on the population of the jurisdiction. The departments also differed on the procedures used in unfounded rape reports. Thirty-eight percent of the agencies' unfounded rape reports were based on a combination of insufficient evidence and lack of victim cooperation; 36 percent, on lack of victim cooperation alone; 8 percent, only on insufficient evidence; and 18 percent, on too much time between the offense and the report. The most important factor in the decision to proceed with the investigation was proof of penetration, which was mentioned by 80 percent of the departments, followed by use of physical force (70 percent), promptness of reporting (49 percent), injury to the victim (44 percent), and the nature of the relationship between the victim and the suspect (41 percent). In addition to the loss of cases through lack of police attention, cases are dropped when the victims withdraw their cooperation as mentioned above. In this data set, approximately one-tenth of the women withdrew their cooperation before the investigation, one-tenth during the investigation, and a third tenth after the rapist's arrest.[50] When combined with the figures on nonreporting of rapes to the police, this indicates that victim noncooperation occurs in approximately two-thirds of all rape cases.

The survey also included police-officer estimates of the characteristics of rape cases in their jurisdictions. These data cannot be considered to be as accurate as the victimization surveys, or even as accurate as careful case-by-case rape studies of specific police-department files, but they do offer conformation of most of the patterns found in these other studies. Police respondents estimated that just over 60 percent of the rapes were by strangers; the offenders were under the influence of alcohol or other drugs in more than a third of the cases; physical force was used in more than half of the cases, as were weapons; less than a third of the victims offered no resistance; and somewhat more than half of the victims were injured in ways beyond the rape itself. Victims who offered physical resistance were more likely to suffer injuries than those who offered only verbal resistance or none at all. In approximately half the cases, sexual acts in addition to vaginal intercourse were forced on the victims. Interracial rapes were much less common than intraracial rapes, and when they occurred they were usually black rapes of white women. More than half of the cases were reported within one hour, but more than one in every ten was reported at least twenty-four hours after the incident. In nearly two-thirds of the cases, physical proof of penetration was obtained. Police estimates of the previous arrests of the offenders seem unrealistically high. According to them, nearly 80 percent had previous arrests for sex and violent crimes, a quarter of these being rapes and another quarter being other sex offenses.[51]

In a parallel survey, prosecutors' offices were contacted and asked to fill out an extensive thirty-nine page questionnaire on their experiences with rape cases in 1974. Sixty-six percent of the prosecutors' offices completed questionnaires, which limits the validity of the results to some degree, even though this is a high response rate for surveys of this type. The most common elements cited as minimum requirements for filing rape complaints were penetration (97 percent), lack of consent (82 percent), and threat of force (77 percent). In obtaining convictions on rape charges, the most important factors were estimated to be the use of physical force (mentioned by 83 percent of the respondents), injury to the victim (76 percent), and promptness of reporting (70 percent). The prosecuting officials had a less positive view than police officers of the services available to rape victims from community agencies. Only three of every five respondents reported special medical-treatment services for rape victims, and just slightly under that proportion indicated that rape-counseling services were available.[52] These discrepancies beween police and prosecutors' reports illustrate the dangers of relying on respondents' opinions of what services are available instead of performing a direct enumeration of those service programs.

The majority of prosecutors in medium- and small-sized counties sometimes used polygraph examinations of rape victims to decide whether or not to go ahead with the cases. Some used the polygraph with every rape victim, no matter how strong the evidence. In the larger counties, polygraph examinations were less commonly conducted, being sometimes used in slightly less than half the jurisdictions. In nearly six of every seven jurisdictions, evidence of the victim's prior sexual activity was admissible in court either by statute or by judicial decision, and a similar percentage of prosecutors felt that the introduction of this evidence would have a significant impact in a jury trial. A change in the admissibility of evidence about the victim's previous sexual history was the modification of existing rape laws most often cited as desirable by prosecutors. About a third of the agencies had made each of the following improvements in the previous three years: better forensic techniques, use of female deputies, special rape training, use of female investigators, and the institution of a special rape unit. A similar proportion of prosecutors' offices plan to make improvements in these areas in the near future.[53]

The final drama of the rape victim's ordeal occurs in the courtroom. She was first forced to repeat her story over and over again to police investigators. Now, when she has probably begun to recover from the experience, she is forced to dredge it all up again and to relive it in detail on the stand. When Burgess and Holmstrom observed thirteen court hearings for probable cause, they found that the issue of the victim's consent came up in all thirteen, the degree of the struggle in twelve, her sexual reputation and behavior in nine, her general character in nine, her emotional state in eight, and so forth.[54] Can the victim be blamed for thinking that it is herself rather than the rapist who is on trial? Bohmer's interviews with thirty-eight

Philadelphia judges who had handled rape cases suggest that many judges are less than objective in the carrying out of their legal duties. She found that the judges tended to classify rape cases as either (1) genuine, (2) instances of consensual intercourse, or (3) plain female vindictiveness, and she infers that they were more likely to admit damaging evidence about the victim's background and to otherwise give her a difficult time in cases they subjectively defined as vindictive or consensual than in what were taken to be genuine cases of rape.[55] The fact of the matter is that there is no crime in America for which the criminal is as well protected by statute and judicial policy as he is in the case of rape.[56]

Gerald Robin discusses five reasons that are commonly given for the stringent requirement of proof in rape cases. These are (1) the alleged frequency of women who fantasize about being raped, (2) the assumed ease of making a rape charge juxtaposed with the severity of the prescribed punishment, (3) the belief that juries are uniquely sympathetic to rape victims, (4) the history of American sexism, and (5) social-science discussions of victim precipitation in crimes of violence.[57] Women may or may not commonly fantasize about being raped. This has nothing to do with making false charges about sexual assaults. Has anyone ever suggested making it easier to convict rapists because men commonly fantasize about committing rapes? The second point is shown to be fallacious by the many accounts of the difficulty and psychic pain that are experienced by those women who dare to bring a rape report to the attention of the police. Robin cites a study by Kalven and Zeisel to show that, rather than being sympathetic to rape victims, juries are often inappropriately sympathetic to rapists.[58] There are two problems with the argument about victim-precipitated rape. The first is that the vast majority of rapes do not in any way involve the elements of victim precipitation and the second is that, even if it were present, it is not recognized as a mitigating factor under the law.

The argument about sexism in America's history is a much stronger one. Our contemporary rape laws do not constitute a sharp break from the past. At one time, women were little more than the property of their husbands, and their sexuality was usually their most valuable attribute. The unsupported testimony of a woman wasn't worth much in many early American courts, but the laws for most crimes did not explicitly state that fact. Because only women were allowed to play the role of rape victims, rape laws took on the character of the reigning stereotypical notions of the limitations of women. One of these made sexual behavior a master status for women, and thus justified including their past sexual behavior as relevant to their present testimony because it revealed the essence of their moral fiber. Another repeated the endless assertions of the emotionality, simplicity, and instability of women, and a third reminded legislators of the duplicity and special capacity for evil supposedly present in the female personality.

These and other similar stereotypes are as much the basis for American rape laws as the careful legal scholarship that is to be expected in less controversial legal areas.

Many readers may argue that although this is an admittedly deplorable situation, it has developed out of the nature of cross-sex relations in the human race, and there is not too much that we can do about it. Actually, there is more than a little evidence in support of precisely the opposite position—evidence which says that rape is indeed the all-American crime. Although rape is found in all but a few human societies,[59] it is much more prevalent in the United States than in nearly all countries for which information is available.[60] What is it about American society that produces such a high rate of sexual assault? There are many ideas about this, but no answers, as Chappell's brief survey of the social determinants of rape demonstrates.[61]

Some light can be shed on this question by examining variations in rape rates within the United States. The 1976 FBI *Uniform Crime Reports* includes data on rape, total violent crime, and total property crime for nine American regions. These regions show considerable variability in the official rape rate, with the Pacific states, at 42.0 rapes per 100,000 population, being nearly three times the 14.8 rate in New England. The other regions and their official rape rates in 1976 were Mountain, 32.6; West South Central, 28.1; South Atlantic, 27.4; East North Central, 25.6; Middle Atlantic, 22.2; East South Central, 20.9; and West North Central, 19.6. The Pacific Coast was also the highest region on the total violent crime rate and the total property crime rate. When the nine regions were ranked on all three rates, it was found that the Spearman rank-order correlation between the rape and violent crime rates was .68 and the correlation between the rape and property crime rates was .57. Both these correlations were stronger than the correlation between the property and violent crime rates, which was only .43. These correlations suggest that there must be a general violence factor and, to a lesser extent, a general criminality factor in any comprehensive explanation of sexual assault. Probably the most useful conception of such a general factor in the criminological literature is Wolfgang and Ferracuti's subculture of violence, in which subcultural norms and values favoring violence are passed down from generation to generation within specified ecological areas via processes such as differential learning, association, and identification.[62]

We have already pointed out that rape rates are higher in central cities than in towns and rural areas. These are areas in which impersonal relations, anonymity, and bystander apathy are the rule rather than the exception. It is probable that these elements foster increased rapes and other crimes by decreasing both the criminal's empathy for the victim and the perceived likelihood of the crime's being reported to the police while it is in progress. There is another characteristic of American urban areas that might relate to high rape rates, and that is high mobility, which is intertwined with social heterogeneity and lack of neighborhood or community identity. It is interesting that the Pacific and Mountain states, which report the highest rape rates of any region, are also subject to unusually high rates of immigration and other measures of geographic mobility.

A third factor in rape is that it is inversely related to social status. The lower-status groups in society generally suffer higher rape rates than higher-status groups. Aside from the obvious fact that women are raped more than men (except in prison), blacks are raped more often than whites, young people more often than old, and the poor more often than the rich. A special case of the raping of low-status individuals occurs in war, when soldiers on the winning side commonly commit thousands of sexual atrocities on women in conquered areas. One of the most horrible accounts of this practice is K.K. Ray's article on the mass rapes committed by Pakistani troops on women and girls in Bangladesh during 1971. More than 200,000 women were reported as rape victims during an eight-month period, many of them kept in army barracks for repeated sexual assaults over extended periods of time. In one such military center, nearly 500 women were kept naked with their hair cut short because so many of them attempted suicide by hanging, using their saris or hair in lieu of a rope. Group rapes and associated acts of extreme brutality and perversion were common in streets, schools, shops, and fields all over Bangladesh.[63] The Bangladesh experience is not unusual for the number of victims, but for the organized fashion in which the atrocities were carried out, reminiscent of the behavior of Nazis in World War II and the genocide of the Armenians by the Turks in World War I.

The act of rape may be the symbol of sexual oppression, but it is not a very good example of it. Wife-beating is far better, as we shall see later on in this chapter. None of the studies of sexual offenders[64] reveals behavior and motivational patterns in rapists that support the idea that rape is used as a mechanism of illegitimate social control in American society. Instead, the offenders are revealed as ". . . criminally inclined men who take what they want, whether money, material, or women, and their sex offenses are by-products of their general criminality."[65] They grew up in generally disorganized families in which they experienced severe sexual repression,[66] and they had less exposure to pornographic materials than other Americans.[67] Their heavy involvement in homosexual activities[68] leads one to believe that many of them are more interested in proving that they are "real men" to themselves than in "putting women in their place." This idea is further supported by Chappell and James's finding that the victim behavior reported as most likely to make rapists angry was not fighting back or threatening to involve the police, but instead was making negative references to the masculinity of the rapist.[69]

To recapitulate, high rape rates seem to be associated with high general criminality and a subculture of violence; urbanization and the variables associated with it in the United States including geographical mobility, impersonality, anonymity, and bystander apathy; a considerable degree of status differentiation so that there is an abundance of potential victims that are relatively low in status; and a complex of relatively severe personal problems in the rapist. Saying that rape is not commonly committed with the intent of sexual repression *per se* is not the same as saying that it could not possibly have the effect. The fear of rape is so widespread in America that it cannot help but add to the burden of sexual discrimination suffered by women in other contexts. The fact that so little was done about rape (except when committed by lower-class men against upper-class women) until the feminist movement awakened women to flex their political and ideological muscles is consistent with the interpretation that the criminal justice system was more concerned with "keeping women in their place" than with protecting their right to live undisturbed, law-abiding lives. American sexism is not a very good explanation for high rape rates. However, it is an excellent aid for understanding the inadequate response of the criminal justice system to rape complaints.

Femicide

It is not possible to use self-report victimization surveys to estimate homicide rates since the victims are unable to testify. This forces us to rely on police statistics, but that is much less of a disadvantage than it would be with other crimes because of the relatively high proportion of homicides that are reported to the police. Likewise, the comparatively high clearance rate for homicide (79 percent in 1976, as compared with 21 percent for all FBI Index crimes[70]) allows us to have more confidence in information about offender characteristics than would be true for any other American crime.

When Sutherland studied cases of femicide in the *New York Times* for 1930, 1935, and 1940, he found that 102 of 324 murders were committed by the victims' husbands, 37 by fathers and other close relatives, and 49 by lovers or suitors.[71] Wolfgang analyzed criminal homicide in Philadelphia's police files for the years 1948-1952, finding that women were more likely to be victims (24 percent) than offenders (18 percent) in homicide incidents. Black women constituted 69 percent of all female victims, and 85 percent of all female offenders. During the five-year period, only sixteen white women committed a murder. In terms of rates per 100,000 population, black women were ten times as likely as white women to be homicide victims and twenty-three times as likely to have committed homicide.[72]

Women were killed by men in 87 percent of the femicide cases. In only 6 percent of the cases were femicides judged by Wolfgang to have been victim precipitated, as compared with 31 percent of the murders of men. Four-fifths of the femicides occurred at home, as compared with less than half of the homicides involving male victims. More than two-thirds of the women killed at home were attacked either in the bedroom or the kitchen, and two of every five had been drinking before their death. Women who had consumed alcohol before being killed were proportionately more likely to suffer excessively violent deaths (severe beating, more than one act of violence involved, etc.) than men who similarly imbibed, perhaps because it lowered their inhibitions against "talking back" more than their (usually male) companions would tolerate. Almost none of the women were killed by strangers. Fifty-two percent were murdered by family members, 21 percent by lovers, and most of the rest by close friends or acquaintances. In contrast, only 16 percent of the men were killed by family members, but similar percentages were killed by acquaintances and by strangers, and 34 percent were murdered by close friends.[73]

In their survey of reported crimes in seventeen cities during 1967, the National Commission on the Causes and Prevention of Violence found that four of every five femicides were committed by men. A recalculation of data in several of the commission's tables indicates that between a third and a half of the female victims were murdered by their husbands. Men were about as likely to be murdered by their wives as women were by their husbands, but they were much more likely to be murdered by nonfamily members. Women comprised one-fifth of both the murderers and the victims, with black women being twice as likely as white women to be murder victims and five and a half times as likely to be murderers. These ratios do not take the relative number of blacks and whites at risk into account. If this were done, the racial differences would be even greater.[74]

Among black marital homicides, wives were more likely to be the aggressors than the victims. This relationship was reversed for whites, with white wives being three times as likely to be the victims of marital homicides as white husbands. Both husbands and wives who committed marital homicides used firearms more often than any other method. Wives were more likely to use sharp instruments and men were more likely to beat their wives to death with their fists. Poison was not used in any of the marital homicides. The majority of all femicides occurred in the home, as did about a third of the murders of men. This reflects not only the woman's ecological restriction to the home in many marriages, but also the larger proportion of women who are killed by family members. In marital homicides, wives were more likely to be killed in the bedroom or outside the house, while husbands were more likely to be killed in the kitchen or the living room. Victim precipitation was judged to have occurred in over a quarter of the murders of men, but less than a tenth of the murders of women. Victim precipitation was more common in marital murders than in any other kind. Women were more likely to be killed as a result of family quarrels, sexual motives, or jealousy, while men were more likely to be killed in self-defense, during a robbery, or in an altercation with the offender.[75]

These findings are completely consistent with the (less detailed) results of a study of female homicide victims in Philadelphia by Zahn,[76] and similar to sex ratios computed from the most recent edition of the *Uniform Crime Reports.* According to the FBI, 2,657 women were murdered in the United States during 1976, which was 24 percent of all reported homicides. Women made up only 19 percent of the murderers. Most homicide were intrasex, but femicides accounted for 58 percent of the cross-sex murders. Nine of every ten femicides were committed by men, as compared with the opposite situation in which only one in every five male homicide victims met his end at the hands of woman. Females were more heavily represented among homicide victims aged zero to nine than any other age group—44 percent. This was followed by age sixty-five and up (34 percent) and age ten to nineteen (29 percent). Between the ages of twenty and sixty-four, women consistently made up between one-quarter and one-fifth of the murder victims.[77]

We have already argued that rape is more common in the United States than elsewhere. Is the same thing true for femicide? America is an uncommonly violent society, but if we look only at the proportion of homicide victims that is female, American statistics are not unusually high. There are many nations that show homicide-sex ratios that are similar to those in the United States: for example, Finland from 1939 to 1944, Sweden from 1881 to 1900,[78] Poland before World War II,[79] Ceylon in 1946,[80] and Uganda in 1964.[81] Others show higher proportions of female homicide victims, such as Canada between 1961 and 1974,[82] the Nyoro and Soga tribes in Africa,[83] Germany from 1928 to 1930, England and Wales from 1885 to 1905,[84] and Baden-Württemberg in the German Federal Republic during 1970 and 1971.[85] Palmer found that females were underrepresented in homicide incidents in half of forty nonliterate societies selected from the Human Relations Area Files.[86] Unfortunately, he does not provide the details necessary to make a direct comparison with American homicide statistics.

There is nothing in these reports to suggest that women are proportionately more commonly the victims of homicide in the United States than in other countries. There is also considerable evidence that female victims are much more likely than male victims to be killed by social or sexual intimates, and family members in particular,[87] in other countries, just as they are in the United States. It is important to remember that although the proportion of female homicide victims is not unusually high in the United States, the general level of homicide is so high in this country that the risk factor is actually much higher for American women than for women in most other nations.[88]

Wife-Beating

Rape and homicide are acts of such a heinous nature that they are fairly well documented, which has eased our discussion of them in the preceding two sections. Wife-beating is not so easy to get at. It is not a legal category, so police statistics are of no help except where an investigator makes a special effort to sort through a mass of individual incident reports in order to identify those cases that fit whatever definition of wife-beating has been agreed upon for the study. The self-report victimization survey series sponsored by LEAA also does not include the necessary pieces of data to pinpoint wife-beating. As a result, the most comprehensive set of data on wife-beating is material on husband-wife aggravated assault in seventeen cities, collected in 1967 by the National Commission on the Causes and Prevention of Violence.

Marital homicides studied by the commission were equally distributed between the sexes, but aggravated assaults were overwhelmingly committed by husbands against their wives. This was the case in 68 percent of the marital assaults among blacks and 85 percent of white marital assaults. Husbands inflicted injuries on their wives with their hands in nearly half the cases, followed in frequency by blunt instruments, sharp instruments, and firearms. Because of their smaller size, lesser strength (on the average), and lack of training in self-defense, wives rarely used blunt instruments or their hands in assaulting their husbands. They preferred sharp instruments, followed by firearms. Nearly two-thirds of their assaults on their husbands occurred in the living room. Husbands also assaulted their wives in the living room more often than any other place, but they were much more likely than their wives to choose the bedroom or kitchen as the site of the assault.[89]

Researchers have used a wide variety of techniques to obtain data, including intensive studies of small samples of marital dyads, the examination of police incident reports, analyzing groups of cases from agency treatment files, and gathering data on families that are in the process of divorcing. Intensive studies of small samples of marital couples have been carried out by Gelles[90] and Adler.[91] Gelles conducted in-depth interviews with eighty couples, finding that slightly more than half had used physical force in disagreements, and a quarter did so with some degree of regularity. Those families experiencing higher stress and frustration levels, particularly those in which the husband has less education or occupational prestige than the wife, were the most likely sites of marital violence. The point is that family violence is structurally conditioned rather than random. Learning experiences such as exposure to family violence as a child also predispose family members to engage in marital violence.[92] Gelles found that wives were more likely to stay with their abusing husbands instead of seeking help if the violence was relatively infrequent or less severe, if they had a low level of educational and occupational resources, and if they had been beaten by their parents in their childhood.[93]

Adler studied fifty couples, of which at least one member of the marital dyad was a part-time graduate student. Although marital violence is generally associated with poverty,[94] this white, middle-class sample included a considerable amount of marital violence. Thirty-four percent of the husbands and 32 percent of the wives had used violence against their spouses during their marriage, including acts such as hitting, pushing, kicking, and punching. Although the incidence of violence was similar for husbands and wives, the definitions of the violence differed in six of sixteen cases of violence by wives; the husband defined it as ineffective, non-threatening, amusing, annoying. None of the wives who were assaulted defined the situation in this way.[95] One way to interpret these data is to say that violence had social control implications favoring husbands in 34 percent of the marriages and favoring wives in 20 percent of the marriages.

One reason why violence by husbands is more likely to be defined as threatening than violence by wives is that husbands are generally physically larger and stronger than wives. In Adler's sample, husbands were larger than wives in forty-eight of fifty cases. All but one of the husbands and two of the wives agreed that the husband was physically stronger than his mate. Except when dangerous weapons were used, which happened with only one of the wives in the study, the husbands had the capability of controlling their wives by force. As a test of the relationship between the use of violence and control of the marriage, Adler correlated the use of violence with degree of domination by first husbands and then wives. The use of violence by wives was essentially unrelated to the balance of power between husbands and wives (Yule's $Q = .09$), but the use of violence by husbands was strongly associated with their dominance over their wives (Yule's $Q = -.53$).[96] This is just the opposite of what Straus found in a study of parents of college students, which he seems to interpret as meaning that the husbands need to use their violence resources in order to assert themselves in marriages that are particularly threatening to them by virtue of their wives' high relative power in marital decisions.[97] At the moment, there is no evidence that would allow us to choose between these alternative interpretations.

Bard and Zacker did not deal with marital dominance in their study of 1,388 police reports handled by a special family-crisis unit. They found that assaults were only reported in 36 percent and substantiated in 29 percent of the incidents in which the police department was contacted. Alcohol was present in between one-third and one-half of the incidents, and police officers believed that it was only an important factor in one of every seven incidents. Alcohol use in the second party was associated with a decrease rather than an increase in the probability that the reporting party would be physically assaulted and thus become a victim in the legal sense of the term.[98]

Studies of cases from agency files have the disadvantage that only relatively extreme and unrepresentative forms of wife-beating are included. This is an important problem, but it is also important to study the more common use of lower levels of violence, threats of violence, and even implications of violence as social control devices in the family. In a study of a limited number of cases, Snell, Rosenwald, and Robey found that families in which wives were so severely beaten that they filed assault and battery complaints were characterized by passive, indecisive, sexually inadequate husbands and aggressive, masculine, frigid, masochistic wives. In these marriages, there was a frequent alternation of passive and aggressive roles between the spouses, with the husband becoming aggressive and abusive when drunk but being passive at other times.[99] This may be the pattern in a small number of cases, but it could hardly be true of wife-beating on a large scale. In addition, some of the terms used to describe the spouses are so value-laden that one is tempted to classify the study as ideology rather than the objective report of material obtained through the use of scientific procedures.

Gayford's study of 100 British battered wives seeking medical treatment shows greater care in separating fact from ideology. The women in his sample seem to have been unusual long before they became the victims of assaults by their husbands. Eighty-five of the women were legally married to the men they were living with, of whom only twenty-two had been engaged before marriage, and sixty were pregnant when the man either married them or moved in. Seventy-one had been to physicians, complaining of symptoms such as depression which led to their receiving prescriptions for tranquilizers, antidepressants, or both. A total of forty-two had attempted suicide.[100]

Nearly all of the women had fled from their homes, arriving at a shelter for battered women with their children and little more than the clothes they had on. More than a third of the women had previously fled from their homes on at least four occasions, and some had done so as often as ten to twenty times, returning because they had been located by their husbands, who either promised to reform or threatened additional violence if they did not return.[101] In nearly half the cases, the husbands regularly assaulted their wives when they were drunk.[102]

In the first of two studies of divorcing families, Levinger found that 37 percent of the wives alleged physical violence against them by their husbands. Wives with a lower-class background were approximately twice as likely to report physical abuse as wives from the middle class.[103] The second study covered those families in which one member applied for a divorce in a large urban, midwestern county during the first nine months of 1969. A sample of 150 families from this group was selected for detailed interviews, during which twenty-five spouses *spontaneously* mentioned suffering overt violence in their marriages. Twenty-one of the twenty-five assaulted respondents were women. Half of the incidents of violence were one-shot affairs, and the other half were part of a life-style that included the frequent use of violence. Violent behavior was most common in those families in which the husband was not performing the role of provider adequately and where the husband had lower educational achievement than the wife.[104] A study of parents of university students by Straus confirmed that the more dissatisfied a wife was with the family income the more she was likely to be beaten by her husband.[105]

Personality factors certainly are not irrelevant to the occurrence of marital violence, but the studies discussed above, plus a number of theoretical treatments of the subject, make clear that structural and cultural factors in American society strongly encourage wife-beating. Farrington emphasizes the simultaneous effect of high family stress and the proviolence norms in the subculture of violence on marital violence in the lower classes,[106] which is supported by the covariation between unemployment and reported cases of wife-beating during a six-month period in Birmingham, England. When unemployment rose sharply, wife-beating experienced an equally sharp rise, presumably because of the increased stress on families in which the breadwinner lost a job as well as a reaction by husbands to the loss of power within the family that accompanies the decline in occupational status.[107]

General values in American society also support marital violence. Straus has listed nine "specific ways in which the male-dominant structure of the society and of the family create and maintain a high level of marital violence."[108] These are: (1) the defense of male authority, (2) compulsive masculinity, (3) economic constraints and discrimination, (4) the burdens of child care, (5) the myth of the single-parent household, (6) the preeminence of the wife role for women, (7) negative self-images often held by women, (8) the conception of women as children, and (9) the male orientation of the criminal justice system.[109] These values and norms bind women into a position in which they are easily victimized at the same time that they encourage men to flex their muscles. Whitehurst combines structural and cultural elements in his suggestion that cultural elements favoring male dominance will persist in the face of an increase in structural factors favoring equality between the sexes, thereby causing an increase in the level of marital violence.[110]

How does the criminal justice system respond to wife-beating? LeGrand points out that many police departments follow a policy of no arrests in domestic-violence incidents, which has led to class-action suits against them in California and New York.[111] Prosecutors also screen out a disproportionate number of assault cases between married individuals. In a study of a run of assault cases in Washington, D.C., during 1967, Field and Field found that three-quarters of the nonmarital assaults resulted in a trial or a guilty plea, as compared with only one-sixth of all husband-wife-assault cases.[112] This difference is partially due to differential treatment of the cases by prosecutors, and also to the frequency with which wives drop the charges against their husbands. Only the provision of extensive support services that guarantee the safety of the victims of wife-beating and at the same time try to deal with the problems of the husband will allow more cases to be terminated positively.

This is, in turn, dependent on the public's coming to define wife-beating as a serious social problem. Historically, it was such an accepted practice that few thought of it as a social problem. In many countries, such as Scotland, Iran, and Italy, wife-beating was not made illegal until the 1970s. It was not outlawed in the United States until nearly the twentieth century, and there is still an ordinance on the books in one Pennsylvania town that forbids wife-beating on Sundays and after ten o'clock each evening.[113] These attitudes linger on, for even in Milwaukee, a city in which 1,294 cases of wife-beating were reported to the District Attorney's Office in a twelve-month period,[114] only two dozen people came to a public hearing on domestic violence that was conducted by the Special Committee on Domestic Violence of the Wisconsin Legislative Council.[115] The appearance of manuals for battered women[116] similar to those distributed a few years ago on rape suggests that a social movement focusing on wife-beating is beginning to take shape, and there is no reason to think that this movement will be any less successful than the antirape movement, which has already had a significant impact on the actions of criminal justice system personnel and the self-images of women.

Child Abuse

The thought of beating, starving, sexually molesting, or raping little girls is so upsetting to any normal human being that rational discussion of the subject is almost impossible. As with wife-beating, child-beating was not considered to be a problem until modern times. Children were not considered to have the right to grow up undamaged by their parents' disciplinary excesses. Even after minimum standards for child protection were established, the problem continued to be ignored. Few cases came to the attention of the authorities, so no reliable statistics on the problem were developed. During the last decade, national meetings such as the Symposium on Protecting the

Abused, the Neglected, and the Sexually Exploited Child that has been given annually for the past eight years by the American Humane Association and the National Conference on Child Abuse and Neglect that is sponsored by the Protective Services Resource Institute and the National Center on Child Abuse and Neglect have helped to focus the public's attention on child abuse. Standard data-reporting forms distributed and analyzed by the National Study on Child Neglect and Abuse Reporting of the American Humane Association's Children's Division have helped to simplify the data-gathering process. At the same time, this project has stimulated the states to upgrade their child-abuse reporting systems, most of which had begun to register cases between 1963 and 1966.[117]

As of early 1978, thirty-seven of the fifty states were currently sending full data to the AHA data center. Looking at some of the printout summaries for states in the Midwest, we see that male and female children are about equally likely to be victimized. At younger age levels, boys are more likely to be abused than girls. This turns around at the beginning of the teenage years, and girls make up an increasing portion of child-abuse victims as the age cohort rises from twelve to seventeen. As an example of the detail contained in the AHA files, abused girls in Ohio during 1976 were as likely as boys to suffer moderate (23 percent male, 24 percent female) or serious (6 percent female, 7 percent male) damage in a reported incident of child abuse, and they were equally likely to remain in their homes after the state had concluded its investigation (72 percent male, 70 percent female). As a group, girl victims of child abuse were more likely than boy victims to suffer subdural hemorrhage or hematomas, burns and scalds, rape, molestation, deviant acts, incest, and unspecified sexual abuse.[118]

The Department of Health and Social Services of the State of Wisconsin is exceptional in that it has produced comprehensive reports on child abuse in Wisconsin since the state legislature passed an amended child-abuse law in 1967. During the past decade, the number of reported cases of the abuse of female children in Wisconsin has risen from 118 to 1,078 per year. At the same time, the annual total of male child-abuse cases increased from 117 to 1,019. Sexual abuse, which is suffered mostly by girls rather than boys, has increased in both frequency and as a proportion of all child-abuse cases in every year since 1971.[119] The majority of abused youngsters were male at every age level up to seven to nine. In the ten to thirteen age cohort, females predominated in most years, and in the fourteen to seventeen age cohort, they completely dominated the statistics. In 1976, three-quarters of the abused teenagers were female, and that proportion has been steady since 1968.[120] Fathers or stepfathers committed 54 percent of all sexual-abuse incidents in 1975[121] and 55 percent in 1976.[122]

There have been a handful of attempts to estimate the national incidence of child abuse, but not one of these has been completely successful.

These include a survey of press clippings in 1965, a national sample interviewed in 1965 by the National Opinion Research Center, the 1967-1968 study of officially reported cases by Gil, and limited portions of the LEAA victimization surveys from the 1970s. Thirty-nine percent of the victims of child abuse reported in press clippings of 504 incidents were female,[123] but the selective factors in newspaper reporting are so great that this sample cannot be considered to be representative of the national distribution of child abuse in any way. The NORC study found that 58 percent of the Americans interviewed believed that "almost anybody could at some time injure a child in his care." Only one respondent in every 250 admitted personally abusing a child, and just one in every 34 reported personally knowing of a child-abuse incident in the previous year.[124] These figures do not permit us to make any accurate inferences about the national level of child abuse. The first rate is based on the self-admission of a serious crime, and as a result is almost certainly a gross understatement of the true rate. The second figure is essentially meaningless because there is no way to know what proportion of Americans who know of a child-abuse case overlap with others who know the same case. If, on the average, the ratio were four to one, then the national incidence in 1965 would have been between 600,000 and 1 million cases. This is so speculative that it cannot be considered to be more than a wild guess.

The study of officially reported cases in 1967 and 1968 by Gil is the most accurate information currently available for the nation as a whole. His cases, like all child-abuse cases, came to the attention of the authorities only after a long filtering process that removed the majority of the incidents from public view. Gil found that just over 50 percent of the abused children were boys in both 1967 and 1968. The age pattern in Gil's data is similar to more recent reports from individual states in that boys were more likely to be victimized up to age twelve, and just about half as likely as girls to be abused during their teenage years. Over half the youngsters suffered relatively minor injuries, and the classical "battered child" syndrome was infrequently identified.[125]

The LEAA victimization studies utilize a self-report technique that yields much more accurate estimates of citizen victimization than aggregations of police reports. The problem is that these surveys do not include interviews of individuals who are below age twelve. Actually, the self-report technology could never be extended too far down the age hierarchy because there are realistic limitations on the ability of children to respond to victimization questions and, in addition, there are ethical questions about the effects of victimization interviews on the mental health of youngsters. Another problem with the LEAA data is that not all violent crimes are child abuse. Fights between youngsters and many other kinds of incidents are far from the accepted meaning of the term child abuse. In 1973, young women between the ages of twelve and fifteen reported victimization rates of 1.3 per 1,000 for rape and 31.3 for assault. Rape increased to 2.7 in 1974 and then decreased to 1.6 in 1975, while assault decreased to 27.7 in 1974 and then rose to 34.1 in 1975. Young men suffered assault rates about 50 percent higher than young women, and essentially no rapes.[126]

The data examined so far in this section establish that girls are somewhat less likely to be beaten than boys, particularly at very young ages. It is also clear that girls and young women are much more likely to be sexually abused than their male counterparts, and that this abuse is more likely to come from fathers and stepfathers than from all other sources combined. The word for this type of sexual abuse is incest, which is an umbrella term that also includes sexual relations between nonmarital family members other than fathers and daughters.

DeFrancis examined official records of the sexual abuse of children in Brooklyn from mid-1962 to mid-1967. There were 5,567 documented cases, of which 68 percent were rapes, 17 percent were impairing-morals charges, 5 percent were carnal abuse, 5 percent were sodomy, and 3 percent were incest (there were a small number of cases that did not fit these five categories). Girls were about ten times as likely to be victimized as boys, and the sexual-abuse rate for Brooklyn was 149 per 100,000 children, or more than nine times the rape rate for the total population.[127] If these figures are representative of the entire nation, then the sexual abuse of children is a much greater problem than has been generally recognized. The true figure is probably much closer to Gagnon's top estimate of as many as 500,000 female children aged four to thirteen sexually abused per year[128] than Giaretto's estimate of 225,000 cases per year.[129] In an innovative strategy, Walters gave questionnaires to 412 college students, 21 percent of whom admitted receiving sexual approaches from adults prior to their own puberty. In four-fifths of these approaches, some type of physical sexual contact occurred. All the approaches to females were by adult males who were well known to them, mostly family members such as fathers and stepfathers.[130] Numerous other studies support the preponderance of girls and young women among victims of sexual abuse, as well as the heavy involvement of fathers and stepfathers in the sexual abuse of children.[131]

The great tragedy of these acts is not the physical damage, which actually occurs in only a small proportion of sex-abuse cases,[132] but rather the personality damage that often occurs. This emotional suffering has, in the past, often been due more to the way cases were handled than to the abusive incidents themselves. DeFrancis reports that 83 percent of the victims in his study suffered anxiety after the abuse, 58 percent felt lowered self-esteem and guilt, 28 percent felt completely rejected, and 55 percent became hostile and aggressive. Overall, two-thirds of the victims were judged to have been emotionally disturbed by the offense and its consequences.[133] Maisch found that incest increased the personality disturbances of just under a third of the girls he studied.[134] The tendency toward guilt and lowered self-esteem is heightened by the common stereotype that the victim (even a child) is at least partially responsible for the act.[135] Although most incidents of childhood sexual abuse probably have little long-term effect on personality development, there has been an increasing amount of evidence in recent years that adults sometimes suffer severe personality problems as a result of childhood experiences of sexual abuse.[136] Even Warren Farrell, who otherwise champions the positive effects of incest, admits that father-daughter incest is rarely welcomed by the daughter.[137]

Having broken one of the most strongly felt taboos in the history of human civilization, even though they were victims rather than offenders, are the child participants of incest more likely to break other important social norms in the future? Will their relations with men be severely damaged? The youngsters studied by DeFrancis showed increased tendencies toward delinquency and trouble in school after experiencing sexual abuse.[138] Studies by Foster[139] and Robey[140] suggest that fear of incest is a factor in the runaway behavior of some delinquent girls. It is traditional to ignore the persistent reports of prostitutes who claim they were sexually assaulted as children, but the continuing accumulation of evidence in support of the relationship between childhood sexual abuse and a later career in prostitution makes it imperative that the issue be taken seriously.[141] There is also some evidence that childhood sexual abuse is related to drug addiction[142] and rosaphrenia, which is the inability of a woman to accept her own sexuality regardless of how she practices sex.[143]

Conclusions

Women are heavily victimized by criminals in the United States. (It is little solace that men are even more heavily victimized.) They make up a higher proportion of the victims of property crime than violent crime. Variations in various victimization rates among cities are unexplainable at present, although they suggest the possible influence of cultural as well as structural factors. When victimization data from a large enough number of cities become available, it will be enlightening to use multiple-regression analysis to give us some hints about the causal sequences involved.

Americans have little empathy for the victims of personal crime. Most mass-media presentations concentrate on the mental processes and actions of offenders, not victims. We have sympathy, not empathy. We feel sorry from crime victims, but do not make much of an effort to understand their suffering. This seems to be the case for women even more than for men, and is most noticeable in rape cases.

Sexism in America may not be a major cause of rape; however, it is a major factor in the response of the criminal justice system to rape. Rape seems to be related to (1) high levels of crime in general and, in particular, a subculture of violence, (2) a group of variables that cluster around the process of urbanization in America, (3) a high degree of status differentiation, and (4) severe emotional problems in the rapist.

Very little is known about wife-beating, child abuse, and incest at this time. All three are much more common than has been supposed in the past, due to a combination of filtering factors that allowed few cases to come to the attention of the public. Females are heavily represented as victims in marital violence and incest, and appear in child-abuse statistics in approximately equal numbers with males. The place of wife-beating in the power conflict between marital partners has already been pointed out by several researchers. What is needed in the future is to continue to do research aimed at understanding the place of violence in marital conflicts. It is important to see wife-beating as a continuum involving most Americans in one way or another rather than as an extreme abnormality found only in a small number of poorly socialized individuals.

Because child abuse occurs so early in life, there needs to be a proportionately greater budgeting of research resources for ascertaining the problems caused by abusive incidents, including incest, than in conditions affecting adults. Incidence studies also need to be continued, inasmuch as the public will not admit that child abuse is a common problem unless the proof is obtained and presented with the backing of the scientific community. Of particular interest to the criminologist are the hints that child abuse and incest are causally related to a wide range of antisocial behavior. This has been tentatively studied by retrospective surveys of adults and adolescents. The most convincing evidence of this linkage cannot be obtained unless long-term cohort studies are funded that will enable researchers to follow child-abuse victims through a decade or more of later life, using a panel design to check on their progress from time to time. Such studies will also provide invaluable information about what interventive techniques have the most beneficial effects on child-abuse victims, both immediately and in the long run.

Notes

1. President's Commission on Law Enforcement and Administration of Justice, *Task Force Report: Crime and Its Impact—An Assessment* (Washington, D.C.: Government Printing Office, 1967), 17.
2. Ibid., 80.
3. Ibid., 82.

4. Donald J. Mulvihill, Melvin M. Tumin, and Lynn A. Curtis, *Crimes of Violence,* Volume XI (Washington, D.C.: National Commission on the Causes and Prevention of Violence, 1969), 207-215.

5. *Criminal Victimization in the United States, 1973* (Washington, D.C.: Government Printing Office, 1976), 80.

6. Ibid.

7. Ibid., 82-83.

8. Ibid., 114.

9. *Uniform Crime Reports* (Washington, D.C.: FBI, U.S. Dept. of Justice, 1976), 6, 16.

10. Mulvihill, 54.

11. *Criminal Victimization,* 69, 70, 73.

12. Ibid., 83.

13. Mulvihill, 217.

14. Menachan Amir, *Patterns in Forcible Rape* (Chicago: University of Chicago Press, 1971), 234.

15. Duncan Chappell, Gilbert Geis, Stephen Schafer, and Larry Siegel, "A Comparative Study of Forcible Rape Offenses Known to the Police in Boston and Los Angeles," in *Forcible Rape—The Crime, the Victim, and the Offender,* ed. by Duncan Chappell, Robley Geis, and Gilbert Geis (New York: Columbia University Press, 1977), 239.

16. *Criminal Victimization*, 82.

17. Amir, 62; Arthur F. Schiff, "A Statistical Evaluation of Rape," *Forensic Science* 2 (1973), 34-35; and Donald K. Nelson, Manuel Vega, and Ira J. Silverman, "A Study of Rape in a Southern City," paper presented at the annual meeting of the American Society of Criminology (Atlanta, 1977), 4.

18. Nelson, Table 3.

19. Michael W. Agopian, Duncan Chappell, and Gilbert Geis, "Black Offender and White Victim: A Study of Forcible Rape in Oakland, California," in *Forcible Rape—The Crime, the Victim, and the Offender,* 131.

20. Mulvihill, 212.

21. Charles Hayman, Charlene Lanza, Roberto Fuentes, and Kathe Algor, "Rape in the District of Columbia," paper presented at the annual meeting of the American Public Health Association, 1971, cited in Agopian, 131.

22. Amir, 44.

23. Ibid.

24. Agopian, 131.

25. Amir, 112; Nelson, 5.

26. Amir, 179; Nelson, 9; Schiff, 342-43; and Duncan Chappell and Susan Singer, "Rape in New York City: A Study of Material in the Police Files and Its Meaning," in *Forcible Rape—The Crime, the Victim, and the Offender,* 255-56.

27. Amir, 99; Nelson, 4.

28. G. Terence Wilson, "Alcohol and Human Sexual Behavior," *Behavior Research and Therapy* 15 (1977), 250.

29. Nelson, 6; Michael J. Hindelang and Bruce J. Davis, "Forcible Rape in the United States: A Statistical Profile," in *Forcible Rape—The Crime, the Victim, and the Offender*, 96. Amir reports that only 45 percent of the women physically resisted the attacker (p. 166). Hindelang and Davis are using self-report data from the 1971-72 and 1972 LEAA surveys of thirteen cities, while the other researchers present data only from cases reported to the police.

30. Amir, 148; Nelson, 5; Chappell and Singer, 261.

31. Hindelang and Davis report that more than half the victims were injured to the extent of requiring medical attention (p. 97); Schiff reports an injury rate of 39 percent (p. 344); and Chappell and Singer indicate that 15 to 20 percent of the victims required hospital treatment for injuries (p. 260).

32. Schiff, 344.

33. Amir, 152-55; Chappell and Singer, 260; Hindelang and Davis, 96.

34. Reported proportions of multiple offenders in rape incidents are Amir, 43 percent (p. 200); Nelson, 12 percent (p. 7); Schiff, 39 percent (p. 342); Chappell, Geis, Schaffer, and Siegel, 46 percent in Los Angeles and 28 percent in Boston (p. 239); and Chappell and Singer, 23 percent (p. 263).

35. Amir, 159; Nelson, 6.

36. *Criminal Victimization in the United States*, 1973, 114; Hindelang and Davis, 98.

37. Hindelang and Davis, 98.

38. Ann W. Burgess and Lynda L. Holmstrom, "Rape: The Victim and the Criminal Justice System," *In Victimology: A New Focus*, Volume III, ed. by Israel Drapkin and Emilio Viano (Lexington, Mass.: D.C. Heath, 1975), 22.

39. Kurt Weis and Sandra S. Borges, "Victimology and Rape: The Case of the Legitimate Victim," *Issues in Criminology* 8 (Fall 1973), 98-107.

40. Ann W. Burgess and Lynda L. Holmstrom, "Rape Trauma Syndrome," in *Forcible Rape—The Crime, the Victim, and the Offender*, 315-28.

41. Ibid., 319-25.

42. Weis, 103.

43. Pamela L. Wood, "The Victim in a Forcible Rape Case: A Feminist View," *American Criminal Law Review* 11 (1973), 348.

44. "Police Discretion and the Judgment that a Crime Has Been Committed—Rape in Philadelphia," *University of Pennsylvania Law Review* 117 (1968), 322-23.

45. Vicki M. Rose, "Rape as a Social Problem: A Byproduct of the Feminist Movement," *Social Problems* 24 (October 1977), 75-89.

46. Duncan Chappell, "Forcible Rape and the American System of Criminal Justice," in *Violence and Criminal Justice*, ed. by Duncan Chappell and John Monahan (Lexington, Mass.: D.C. Heath, 1975), 94.

47. Burgess and Holmstrom, "Rape: The Victim and the Criminal Justice System," 23.

48. Lisa Brokyaga, *et al., Rape and Its Victims: A Report for Citizens, Health Facilities, and Criminal Justice Agencies* (Washington, D.C.: Government Printing Office, 1975).

49. Cy Ulberg and Frank Albi, *Forcible Rape, A National Survey of the Response by Police* (Washington, D.C.: Government Printing Office, 1977), 28-35.

50. Ibid., 15-17, 27, 39.

51. Ibid., 20-24.

52. Larry David, Donna Schram, and Cy Ulberg, *Forcible Rape, A National Survey of the Response by Prosecutors* (Washington, D.C.: Government Printing Office, 1977), 11, 19, 24-25.

53. Ibid., 22, 26-32.

54. Burgess and Holmstrom, "Rape: The Victim and the Criminal Justice System," 28.

55. Carol Bohmer, "Judicial Attitudes toward Rape Victims," *Judicature* 57 (February 1974), 303-307.

56. Camille E. LeGrand, "Rape and Rape Laws: Sexism in Society and Law," *California Law Review* 61 (May 1973), 939.

57. Gerald D. Robin, "Forcible Rape, Institutionalized Sexism in the Criminal Justice System," *Crime and Delinquency* 23 (April 1977), 147-49.

58. Harry Kalven and Hans Zeisel, *The American Jury* (Boston: Little, Brown, 1966), 342, cited in Robin, 52.

59. See, for example: Diana E.H. Russell and Nicole Van de Ven, *Crimes Against Women: Proceedings of the International Tribunal* (Milbrae, Cal.: Les Femmes, 1976), 110-26; J.S. Brown, "A Comparative Study of Deviations from Sexual Mores," *American Sociological Review* 17 (1952), 135-36.

60. Arthur F. Schiff, "Rape in Other Countries," *Medicine, Science and the Law* 11 (1971), 139-43; and Arthur F. Schiff, "Rape in Foreign Countries," *Medical Trial Technique Quarterly* 20 (1973), 66-74. The best comparison would be with the *International Crime Statistics* (St. Cloud, France: Interpol, 1971-1972 and previous years), but the sex offense category in these reports is defined as rape plus trafficking in women plus other acts defined as sex crimes by the reporting countries. This means that "rape" rates given in the *International Crime Statistics* are exaggerations of the official rape rates, with the degree of exaggeration varying from country to country. In 1972, the official rape rate in the United States was 42 per 100,000 population, but the number of arrests for sex offenses other than

rape, prostitution, and commercialized vice was nearly three times the number of arrests for rape. This means that a rate calculated on the same basis as many other countries in the *International Crime Statistics* could possibly be as high as 115 or perhaps as low as 50 or 60. Data for 1972 in the *International Crime Statistics* show that most countries have sex offense rates below 25. Of the dozen highest countries, eight are small in size, ranging from less than 200,000 (Bahamas, British Solomons) to about 5 million (Tunisia). The four larger countries are West Germany, the Netherlands, Venezuela, and England (including Wales), which reported sex offense rates of 70, 60, 51, and 48, respectively. If the United States does not have the world's highest true rape rate, it must be very close to the top. More exact comparisons are not possible at this time.

61. Duncan Chappell, "Cross-Cultural Research on Forcible Rape," *International Journal of Criminology and Penology* 4 (1976), 295-304.

62. Marvin E. Wolfgang and Franco Ferracuti, *The Subculture of Violence* (London: Tavistock, 1967), 314-15.

63. K.K. Ray, "Feelings and Attitudes of Raped Women of Bangladesh towards Military Personnel of Pakistan," *Victimology: A New Focus*, Volume V, ed. by Israel Drapkin and Emilio Viano (Lexington, Mass.: D.C. Heath, 1975), 65-72.

64. See, for example, Benjamin Karpman, *The Sexual Offender and His Offenses* (New York: Julian Press, 1954); Paul H. Gebhard, John H. Gagnon, Wardell B. Pomeroy, and Cornelia V. Christenson, *Sex Offenders* (New York: Bantam Books, 1967); Duncan Chappell and Jennifer James, "Victim Selection from the Rapist's Perspective: A Preliminary Investigation," paper presented at the 2nd International Symposium on Victimology (Boston, 1976); and The Commission on Obscenity and Pornography, *Erotica and Antisocial Behavior*, Volume VII of the Technical Reports (Washington, D.C.: Government Printing Office, 1971).

65. Gebhard, 205.

66. Michael J. Goldstein *et al.*, "Exposure to Pornography and Sexual Behavior in Deviant and Normal Groups," in *Erotica and Antisocial Behavior*, 56.

67. Ibid.; C. Eugene Walker, "Erotic Stimuli and the Aggressive Sexual Offender," in *Erotica and Antisocial Behavior*, 130; and Robert F. Cook and Robert H. Fosen, "Pornography and the Sex Offender," in *Erotica and Antisocial Behavior*, 160.

68. Goldstein, 56; Gebhard, 191.

69. Chappell and James, Table 3.

70. *Uniform Crime Reports*, 1976, 160-61.

71. Edwin H. Sutherland, "The Sexual Psychopath Laws," *Journal of Criminal Law and Criminology* 40 (January-February 1950), 545-46.

72. Marvin E. Wolfgang, *Patterns in Criminal Homocide* (Philadelphia: University of Pennsylvania Press, 1958), 32-35, 56.

73. Ibid., 223-24, 256, 368-78.

74. Mulvihill, 210-22, 268-69, 293.

75. Ibid., 293-350.

76. Margaret A. Zahn, "The Female Homicide Victim," *Criminology* 13 (November 1975), 400-15.

77. *Uniform Crime Reports*, 1976, 9-11.

78. Veli Verkko, *Homicides and Suicides in Finland and Their Dependence on National Character* (Kobenhavn: G.E.C. Gads Forlag, 1951), 42-47.

79. Pawel Horoszawski, "Homicide of Passion and Its Motives," in *Victimology: A New Focus*, Volume IV, 7. The Polish data are only for a series of "homicides of passion."

80. Jacqueline Straus and Murray Straus, "Suicide, Homicide, and Social Structure in Ceylon," *American Journal of Sociology* 58 (March 1953), 461-69.

81. Ralph E.S. Tanner, *Homicide in Uganda, 1964* (Uppsala, Sweden: Scandinavian Institute of African Studies, 1970), 98.

82. Paul Reed, Teresa Bleszynski, and Robert Gaucher, *Homicide in Canada, A Statistical Synopsis* (Ottawa: Statistics Canada, 1976), 107.

83. Paul Bohannan, *African Homicide and Suicide* (New York: Atheneun, 1967), 240.

84. Wolfgang, 60.

85. Klaus Sessar, "The Familiar Character of Criminal Homicide," in *Victimology: A New Focus*, Volume IV, 35.

86. Stuart Palmer, "Characteristics of Homicide and Suicide Victims in Forty Non-Literate Societies," in *Victimology: A New Focus*, Volume IV, 45.

87. See, for example, Sessar, 36; Reed, 85; Tanner, 111-12.

88. William Goode, "Violence Among Intimates," in *Crimes of Violence*, Volume XIII, ed. by Donald J. Mulvihill, Melvin M. Tumin, and Lynn A. Curtis (Washington, D.C.: National Commission on the Causes and Prevention of Violence, 1969), 947.

89. Mulvihill, *Crimes of Violence*, Volume XI, 298-301, 319.

90. Richard Gelles, *The Violent Home: A Study of Physical Aggression Between Husbands and Wives* (Beverly Hills, Cal.: Sage, 1974).

91. Emily S. Adler, "Perceived Marital Power, Influence Techniques and Marital Violence," paper presented at the annual meeting of the American Sociological Association (Chicago, 1977).

92. Gelles, 188-89.

93. Richard J. Gelles, "Abused Wives: Why Do They Stay?" *Journal of Marriage and the Family* 38 (November 1976), 666-67.

94. Keith Farrington, "Toward a General Stress Theory of Intra-Family Violence," paper presented at the annual meeting of the National Council on Family Relations, 1975.

95. Adler, 18-20.

96. Ibid., 20-21.

97. Murray A. Straus, "Cultural and Social Organizational Influences on Violence Between Family Members," in *Configurations: Biological and Cultural Factors in Sexuality and Family Life*, ed. by Raymond Prince and Dorothy Barrier (Lexington, MA: D.C. Heath, 1974), 66-67.

98. Morton Bard and Joseph Zacker, "Assaultiveness and Alcohol Use in Family Disputes; Police Perceptions," *Criminology* 12 (November 1974), 281-92.

99. John Snell, Richard Rosenwald, and Ames Robey, "The Wifebeater's Wife," *Archives of General Psychiatry* 11 (August 1964), 107-12.

100. J.J. Gayford, "Battered Wives," *Medicine, Science and the Law* 15 (1975), 237-45.

101. Ibid., 243.

102. J.J. Gayford, "Wife Battering: A Preliminary Survey of 100 Cases," *British Medical Journal*, Number 5951 (1975), 194-97.

103. George Levinger, "Physical Abuse Among Applicants for Divorce," *American Journal of Orthopsychiatry* 36 (October 1966), 804-806.

104. John E. O'Brien, "Violence in Divorce-Prone Families," *Journal of Marriage and the Family* 33 (November 1971), 692-98.

105. Straus, 65.

106. Farrington, 39-45.

107. Suzanne Steinmetz and Murray Straus, "The Family as the Cradle of Violence," *Society* 10 (September-October 1973), 53.

108. Murray A. Straus, "Sexual Inequality, Cultural Norms, and Wife-Beating," *Victimology* 1 (Spring 1976), 62.

109. Ibid., 63-66.

110. Robert N. Whitehurst, "Violence in Husband-Wife Interaction," in *Violence in the Family*, ed. by Suzanne K. Steinmetz and Murray A. Straus (New York: Dodd, Mead, 1974), 75-82.

111. Camille LeGrand, "Rape and Other Crimes Against Women," in *Forgotten Victims: An Advocate's Anthology*, ed. by George Nicholson, Thomas W. Condit and Stuart Greenbaum (Sacramento: California District Attorneys Association, 1977), 162. See also Mary Van Stolk, "Beaten Women, Battered Children," *Children Today* 5 (May-June 1976), 8-12.

112. Martha H. Field and Henry F. Field, "Marital Violence and the Criminal Process: Neither Justice nor Peace," *Social Service Review* 47 (June 1973), 224-25.

113. Del Martin, *Battered Wives* (San Francisco: Glide, 1976), 31-33.

114. *Issues Relating to Domestic Violence* (Madison: Wisconsin Legislative Council, 1977), 4.

115. "Little Worry on Domestic Abuse Here," *The Milwaukee Journal* (December 3, 1977).

116. *Battered Women, Handbook for Survival* (Milwaukee, WI: Task Force on Battered Women, 1977).

117. Betty Simons and Elinor F. Downs, "Medical Reporting of Child Abuse, Patterns, Problems, and Accomplishments," *New York State Journal of Medicine* 68 (September 1, 1968), 234.

118. Unpublished data supplied by the National Study on Child Neglect and Abuse Reporting of the American Humane Association.

119. Karen Oghalai, "Ten Year Survey of Child Abuse Reporting in Wisconsin" (Madison: Wisconsin Department of Health and Social Services, 1977).

120. Ruth Robinson and Todd Kummer, "A Five Year Statistical Comparison of Child Abuse Reporting in Wisconsin" (Madison: Wisconsin Department of Health and Social Services, 1975); Karen Oghalai, Caryl Peterson, and Joyce Wills, *Child Abuse in Wisconsin, 1975* (Madison: Wisconsin Department of Health and Social Services, 1976); and Karen Oghalai, Caryl Peterson, and Joyce Wills, *Child Abuse in Wisconsin, 1976* (Madison: Wisconsin Department of Health and Social Services, 1977).

121. *Child Abuse in Wisconsin, 1975.*

122. *Child Abuse in Wisconsin, 1976.*

123. David G. Gil, "Incidence of Child Abuse and Demographic Characteristics of Persons Involved," in *The Battered Child*, ed. by Ray E. Helfer and C. Henry Kempe (Chicago: University of Chicago Press, 1968), 27-28.

124. Ibid., 58-60.

125. David G. Gil, *Violence Against Children: Physical Abuse in the United States* (Cambridge, MA: Harvard University Press, 1970), 104-105, 138.

126. *Criminal Victimization in the United States, A Comparison of 1973 and 1974 Findings*, 18; and *Criminal Victimization in the United States, A Comparison of 1974 and 1975 Findings*, 14-15.

127. Vincent DeFrancis, *Protecting the Child Victim of Sex Crimes Committed by Adults* (Denver: American Humane Association, 1969), 35-37, 217.

128. John H. Gagnon, "Female Child Victims of Sex Offenses," *Social Problems* 13 (1965), 176-92.

129. LeGrand, "Rape and Other Crimes . . . ," 162.

130. David R. Walters, *Physical and Sexual Abuse of Children, Causes and Treatment* (Bloomington: Indiana University Press, 1975), 116-17.

131. See, for example, Arthur C. Jaffee, Lucille Dynneson, and Robert ten Bensel, "Sexual Abuse of Children, An Epidemiologic Study," *American Journal of Diseases of Children* 129 (June 1975), 689-92;

J.E.H. Williams, "The Neglect of Incest: A Criminologists' View," in *Victimology: A New Focus*, Volume IV, 191-96; Carolyn Swift, "Sexual Victimization of Children: An Urban Mental Health Center Survey," *Victimology* 2 (Summer 1977), 322-27. For summaries of these and other studies of child abuse, see Emilio Viano, "The Battered Child: A Review of Studies and Research in the Area of Child Abuse," in *Victimology: A New Focus*, Volume IV, 145-64; and Marc F. Maden and David F. Wrench, "Significant Findings in Child Abuse Research," *Victimology* 2 (Summer 1977), 196-224.

132. LeRoy G. Schultz, "The Child as a Sex Victim: Socio-Legal Perspectives," in *Victimology: A New Focus*, Volume IV, 187.

133. DeFrancis, 159-69.

134. Herbert Maisch, *Incest* (New York: Stein and Day, 1972), 215-16.

135. Frederick H. Samuels, "Incest: Not a Private Matter," paper presented at the annual meeting of the American Sociological Association (Chicago, 1977).

136. See, for example, Joseph J. Peters, "The Philadelphia Rape Victim Study," in *Victimology: A New Focus*, Volume III, 181-99; and Barry Siegel, "Incest: A Family Sickness," *Milwaukee Journal* (August 28, 1977).

137. Philip Nobile, "Incest, the Last Taboo," *Penthouse* 9 (December 1977), 117-26, 157-58.

138. DeFrancis, 162-63.

139. R.M. Foster, "Intrapsychic and Environmental Factors in Running Away from Home," *American Journal of Orthopsychiatry* 32 (April 1962), 486-91.

140. Ames Robey, "The Runaway Girl," in *Family Dynamics and Female Sexual Delinquency*, ed. by Otto Pollak and Alfred S. Friedman (Palo Alto, CA: Science and Behavior Books, 1969), 127-37. See also Ames Robey, R.E. Rosenwald, J.E. Snell, and Rita E. Lee, "The Runaway Girl: A Reaction to Family Stress," *American Journal of Orthopsychiatry* 34 (July 1964), 762-67.

141. Henry Giaretto, "Humanistic Treatment of Father-Daughter Incest," in *Child Abuse and Neglect—The Family and the Community*, ed. by R.E. Helfer and C.H. Kemp (New York: Ballinger, 1976); T.C.N. Gibbens, "Juvenile Prostitution," *British Journal of Delinquency* 8 (July 1957), 3-12; and LeGrand, "Rape and Other Crimes . . . ," 161.

142. Jean Benward and Judianne Densen-Gerber, "Incest as a Causative Factor in Antisocial Behavior: An Exploratory Study," *Contemporary Drug Problems* 4 (Fall 1975), 323-40.

143. Major J. Baisden, *The World of Rosaphrenia: The Sexual Psychology of the Female* (Sacramento: Allied Research Society, 1971).

5 Gangs and Prostitutes: Two Case Studies of Female Crime

In this chapter, we leave the statistical study of female crime behind us to have an in-depth look at two categories of female criminal behavior. There are few studies of specific female crimes in the literature, and most of these are isolated from the mainstream of criminological thought.[1] We have chosen to look at gang girls at the delinquent level and prostitution at the adult level of female crime because these are two types of criminal involvement in which the illegal behavior *seems* to be less passive and more like the masculine crime model. For this reason the study of these topics may be particularly fruitful in terms of giving us some insights into female sex-role behavior as enacted in the underworld of criminal activity.

Young Women in Gangs

Almost everything that has ever been written on delinquent gangs has focused on male gangs. Many of the classic accounts in the field include just a few tantalizing tidbits on the participation of females in gang activities. For example, Thrasher devotes less than a page to the question of whether or not girls and young women form gangs. He found no more than half a dozen female gangs in the 1,313 groups he surveyed in Chicago. He believes that this is due to two factors: (1) young women are much more closely supervised than young men, and (2) the social traditions into which young women are socialized are inconsistent with gang behavior. Only two of Thrasher's female gangs were judged to be "true" gangs; he considered the others to be no more than social clubs. One of these gangs was formed around playing baseball and the other had stealing as its main activity.[2]

Females were occasionally admitted to male gangs. In young gangs, girls were tomboys who participated in gang activities on the same basis as the boys. As youngsters aged and overt sexual interests asserted themselves, sexual role differentiation occurred. Participation by young women was likely to be limited to sociosexual activity with gang members, with the females sometimes organized as auxiliaries rather than as full gang members. Thrasher mentions that young women are becoming a more important part of adult criminal gangs (remember that this was written in 1927), citing several famous female frontier outlaws and telling the story of Honey, one of his interviewees. Honey was the twenty-one-year-old "brains" of a male gang, which was officially led by Tom, who was husky and a good fighter. Honey started out in a more traditional role, sitting in the car while her boyfriend committed robberies. The fellow did so poorly that she took charge of the criminal operations, following which they recruited seven more members and formed the gang.[3]

There are occasional references to females in the voluminous writings of James F. Short and his associates on male gangs. In one article, Short and Cohen mention that female gangs are of both the sexual-activity and hoodlum types, neither of which has been studied by social scientists.[4] A small section in Short's introduction to a reader on gangs and delinquent subcultures discusses females. He cites some of the better-known female auxiliaries to male gangs, such as the Vice Queens (related to the Vice Kings), the Egyptian Cobrettes (related to the Egyptian Cobras), and the Lady Rocketeers (related to the Rocketeers), but presents no details about these groups.[5] There is a suggestion in an article by Short and Strodtbeck that young women are more likely to become gang girls if they are unattractive in physical appearance and inadequate in their social relations with peers.[6]

Short's research efforts centered in Chicago, continuing in the tradition begun by Thrasher. Three other publications from the early 1960s added comparative data from New York and Boston. Hanson wrote a documentary novel on an East Harlem group that she renamed the Dagger Debs. This was a tough, fighting female gang that could hold its own with male gangs in an open battle. At the same time, the gang was an auxiliary to the Daggers male gang. Hanson found the fourteen young women in the Dagger Debs to be poorly groomed and to exhibit physical movements that were typical of male rather than female sex-role behavior. The Dagger Debs had a measure of influence over their male companions in that they spread false rumors, goaded the boys by threatening their masculinity, and were seductive with rival gang members in order to provoke intergang warfare. Hanson notes that the Debs were becoming more aggressive and were beginning to take an active role in gang wars.[7]

Another New York female gang was the subject of a lengthy article by Rice in *The New Yorker*. This group was not violent, limiting its activities to what youth workers would call sexual delinquency. The author points out that females are doomed to lower status in the street-gang society, which is completely controlled by males and oriented toward male activities. There is nothing that a young woman can do to achieve power or prestige in the gang world. If they fight, the young men do not like them, and if they play a more feminine role, they are disregarded except for sexual purposes. Rice sees their structural position, which is oppressive, as causing them to have very low self-esteem. In his words " . . . because gang girls aren't boys, they are, in their own view, barely people, and this low self-esteem is naturally reflected in their personalities."[8] Perhaps some of the social dysfunctions, and, to the extent to which self-image is reflected in physical carriage and facial expression, even physical unattractiveness are effects of participation in the New York gang world rather than a cause of it.

Both the feminine and the masculine strategies were used by young women in two Boston gangs. The preadolescent girls behaved like tomboys, carrying knives and competing directly with the boys. The older gang was more loosely organized. The young women in this group played a more traditional feminine role, which included manipulating the young men into gang fights during which they carried weapons for them. They also encouraged their male companions to steal cars to take them for joy rides and to engage in other risky acts.[9]

Walter Miller has long been famous for his studies of lower-class delinquency. In several of his recent publications he has provided us with a considerable amount of information about the behavior of young women in gangs. The Molls, one female gang that he studied, used the pseudomasculine strategy to gain the approval of a male gang in the neighborhood, committing numerous minor crimes such as truancy, theft, and property damage. They only committed one physical assault in a thirty-month period, as compared with eighteen by another female gang in the same city. Their only status in the gang world came through their association with males, and, rather than resenting this condition, they seemed actively to seek and to glory in it. Miller found no evidence that these young women had been exposed to or influenced by the women's movement.[10]

A more recent research report by Miller indicates that this pattern is true for the six cities in the United States that have the worst problems with gangs. The total population of gang females in these cities was no more than a tenth of the number of gang males. Half of the male gangs in New York City had female auxiliaries. Of all the known gangs in the Bronx and Queens, only six were autonomous female gangs. There were some reports of increased violence by female gang members, but the overall distribution of female participation in gang activities did not differ from what existed in the past.[11] Adler draws the opposite conclusion, claiming that by the early 1970s "girls had become more highly integrated in male gang activity and were moving closer to parallel but independent, violence-oriented, exclusively female groups,"[12] and this is supported by data on female gang behavior in Prince George's County, Maryland. In Maryland, Thompson and Lozes found female gang members committing nonutilitarian thefts, malicious assaults, and sometimes using weapons. Female gang behavior in Maryland in the 1970s looked very much like male gang behavior from the 1950s.[13]

Maryland gangs were loosely organized into what Yablonsky called near-groups rather than tightly organized associations.[14] This was also true in Philadelphia, where gangs were more like cliques, with up to a few dozen young women hanging around together. These informal groups differed from male gangs in that they had no runners, warlords or any of the other rigid structural components often found in male delinquent organizations.[15]

The sources discussed thus far in this section offer either an in-depth literary treatment of female gang participation or a few isolated comments from larger social-science studies. Two additional bodies of information are available, the results of field research projects conducted in Los Angeles by Malcolm Klein in the mid-1960s and by John Quicker nearly a decade later. Much of this material was provided to the author by these investigators; it has not been published to date.

Klein's study was of black female delinquent gangs in a south central Los Angeles neighborhood. A number of gangs of young men existed in the area, supplemented by half a dozen sister gangs, with a total membership of perhaps 150 young women aged twelve to twenty-five. These gangs varied considerably in their structural characteristics, size, and degree of criminal involvement. They were less longlived than the gangs of young men, and all began with a relationship to a male gang. If the related male gang disbanded, the female gang generally disintegrated.[16] In one gang, 83 percent of the young women had been arrested, of which a third were in custody or on probation. Not all offenses by young women in the area were committed by gang members, but gang membership was associated with a higher probability of involvement in aggressive and violent behaviors.[17] Fourteen percent of 938 gang incidents reported to the police during a three-year period involved direct participation by a female.[18]

The methodology used in Klein's project involved interviews with male gang members to ascertain the effect of the presence of girls on the incidence of illegal acts, contact reports from Group Guidance workers, direct observations of gang meetings and activities, interviews with male and female gang leaders, and questionnaire and psychological test data from gang members, nongang delinquents, and nondelinquent controls.[19] Rather than being the instigators of gang violence, gang girls in this Los Angeles neighborhood seemed to inhibit the occurrence of violent acts.[20] They helped to plan only one aggressive incident out of each 50 reported and participated in just over one tenth of the actual incidents. Male gang members said that if young women happened onto the scene of an incident as it was in progress, they would be most unlikely to include them (5 percent). It was much more likely that the event would be called off or postponed (47 percent). The older the boys involved, the more likely they were to say that an incident would be terminated by the presence of young women.[21] This sounds as if females are a more powerful deterrent to crime than any other meaningful force in the immediate life-span of male gang members.

Quicker's study utilizes data gained from extensive, focused interviews with fifteen young women in Chicana gangs operating in East Los Angeles, plus less formal interviews with twenty-five other gang members, probation officers, sheriffs, gang workers, and teachers in the area. Chicana groups were semiautonomous, being more autonomous than mere auxiliaries but not fully independent of the male gangs to which they were related. Most of the male gangs had female members, and the trend seemed to be toward an increasing proportion of young women. In Chicana gangs, the young women made their own decisions on internal matters, usually via the democratic process. When they went along with their male affiliate gang to fight, they often fought against young women associated with the enemy gang or carried weapons for their fellows. Their dating activities were largely limited to the young men in their affiliate gang, unless they were peripheral members of the gang or the gang itself was weakly organized.[22]

Chicana gang members have a fierce loyalty to their gang. In fact, they refer to fellow members as "home-girls" and to male affiliates as "home-boys." Almost all the meaningful activities in their adolescent lives occur with gang members, including adaptive activities such as learning how to get along in the world, meeting prospective mates, and being psychosocially insulated from the harsh environment of the *barrio*. Why are the youngsters so devoted to their gangs? Quicker argues that there is not enough economic opportunity available in the *barrio* to meet the needs of the family unit. As a result, families are structurally disintegrating and, in addition, do not have the capability of providing access to culturally emphasized success goals for young people about to enter adulthood. The schools teach material that most Chicano youngsters consider to be irrelevant, and which also does not guarantee economic success if mastered. The Chicano gang fills this cultural power vacuum. It is a normal response to structural conditions in the *barrio* in that it is the most reasonable solution to the problems faced by the Chicanos.[23] Quicker sums it up nicely when he points out that gangs only thrive in areas where there are no other acceptable alternatives available to the young women, and that the only way to successfully do away with these "girl gangs" is to create viable alternatives for personal involvement and problem solving.[24]

We can summarize what appears to be true of female participation in gangs in the following propositions. First, female gang participation appears to be increasing in all its aspects—as independent gangs, as auxiliaries to male gangs, and as individual members in mixed-gender groups. Independent female gangs and mixed gender gangs seem to be increasing more rapidly than auxiliary groups. Second, female participation in gang violence seems to be up, although it is not clear to what extent this is an effect of the increase in female gang participation. Third, female gangs differ greatly, the primary differentiating factors being the age and ethnicity of the members, the socioeconomic and other characteristics of the neighborhood, and the availability and characteristics of the male gangs in the area. The fourth point is that female gang members have tried both traditionally masculine and traditionally feminine strategies to gain status in the gang world, with little success either way. There is some very tentative evidence that recent female gang behavior is more of an integration of the two than the swings between the two extremes that were true in the 1950s and 60s. The passive-aggressive "instigator" behavior of females attached to male gangs is most likely to be found where young women are not allowed to play a more meaningful role in gang activities. The fifth point is that the presence of females at the site of a potential criminal incident may actually inhibit rather than encourage criminal behavior. Finally, the changes noted above do not appear to be related to the women's liberation movement, which is largely a creature of the middle class. Most lower-class gang females have never been exposed to the doctrines or the leaders of the movement, and would probably consider them to be irrelevant if they came into contact with them.

Prostitution: New Wrinkles in the Oldest Women's Profession

In contrast to the very limited literature on female participation in delinquent gangs, there is an abundance of books and articles on the subject of prostitution. Most of these emphasize historical and psychoanalytic perspectives.[25] Our focus in this chapter will be upon the social roles played by prostitutes in contemporary American society. These are complicated by two interacting factors, the socioeconomic structure of the prostitution profession and the developmental stages through which people come to begin prostituting themselves and gradually redefine their role as they mature professionally in their occupational subculture. The basic socioeconomic structures common in prostitution are three in number—streetwalkers, house prostitutes, and call girls.[26] Streetwalkers are at the bottom of the status hierarchy, call girls are at the top, and house prostitutes fall in between. Working conditions improve, arrests decrease, and income increases as status increases. The madam represents a step out of the role of prostitute into the administration of the sexual service delivery system.

Houses of prostitution in the United States have been decreasing even more rapidly than farms. There is a considerable amount of historical material on brothels, but very little contemporary data. The only substantial body of recent scholarship on house prostitution is the series of articles and papers by Barbara Heyl.[27] She studied the operation of a brothel operating in "Prairie City," a middle-sized city in the rural Midwest. The brothel was a furnished apartment rather than a house, and was staffed by a madam and a group of young "turn-outs" who stayed an average of two or three months each. The "turn-outs" came to the house, or were sent by their pimps, to learn the skills of prostitution, of which the madam is a "famous" teacher. Most of the young prostitutes came via the pimp route, with three pimps in Prairie City and a like number in other communities supplying new converts to the trade on a regular basis.[28] The madam spent a considerable amount of time with the new employees, first while teaching them about the profession before they saw their first clients, then while they were with clients during the first several weeks, and intermittently for the rest of their stay in the house. There were three main content areas in the training sequence: physical skills and strategies, the verbal skills necessary for client management, and the teaching of "racket" values to help the neophyte fit into the world of prostitution. The physical skills and strategies included how to check the customer for venereal disease, how to satisfy him physically without allowing oneself to be bruised, and tactics for getting out of sex rapidly if the customer became abusive. The verbal skills were designed to hustle for the highest possible level of services and fees, being used as a form of sexual aggression to establish a certain degree of sexual dominance in the relationship. The values of the trade taught by the madam not only facilitated the development of a professional identity by the young prostitutes, but also minimized conflicts among the prostitutes and between them and their clients.[29]

Would houses like the one described by Heyl be any different if prostitution were legalized? Unlike most comparative questions of a "what if" nature, this one has an answer. Prostitution is legal in Nevada except for the two counties containing the largest cities and two others in the Reno-Lake Tahoe area. Thirty-three brothels were in operation in Nevada as of mid-1973. The largest town permitting brothels within its corporate boundaries was Elko, which had a 1970 census population of 7,621.[30] In 1969, Beth Duncombe, a student of the author, completed a study of prostitution in Elko, which was her home at the time.[31] Her father was a prominent Episcopal priest who had defended brothel prostitution in print, saying, "It may be a moral problem for those who patronize it, but it is no problem to the town as such,"[32] so she received uncommon cooperation from the madams and their employees.

From time to time, some people have tried to close the brothels in Elko, but never with any success. Duncombe interviewed a number of residents of the town, all of whom felt that legalized prostitution was better for Elko than having prostitutes be uncontrolled and underground. The prostitutes generally gave 60 percent of their earnings to the house, except for one establishment that was satisfied with a fifty-fifty split. An FBI agent who was interviewed indicated that pimps sent some of the women to Elko for training, much like those in the house described by Heyl, but the seven prostitutes who were interviewed denied any connection with pimps. These ladies registered with the police when they arrived in Elko, were required to have a cervix smear weekly and a monthly blood test for venereal disease, and agreed to go downtown only between noon and 6:00 P.M. and between 3:00 and 6:00 A.M., with no soliciting allowed at all. There was no crime associated with prostitution in Elko, and when an occasional customer became rowdy, the madam could call the police to come to take care of the matter without any problem.[33]

One of Duncombe's interviews was with a babysitter who took care of many of the prostitutes' children. These children ranged from age two to eleven and lived completely with the babysitter. Their mothers were only allowed to spend one afternoon a week with their children, generally taking them for walks. They frequently bought them presents, showed a strong interest in their progress in school, and wanted them to be brought up using traditional gender stereotypes. The children were told that their mothers' working hours as waitresses made it impossible for them to be together.[34]

In order to interview prostitutes in two of the brothels, Duncombe had to go to the back door, ring the buzzer, and be led to the prostitutes' individual rooms by the madam. This was because nonprostitute women are not allowed in Elko brothels. All of the prostitutes indicated that their parents were unaware of their occupation. One of the advantages of prostituting in Nevada may be that, since it is remote from major population centers, prostitutes can be fairly sure that word of their activities will not filter back home. Most of them saw their main function as social workers of a sort, indicating that they spent more time talking with customers than having sex with them. In a situation like Elko's, more of the money earned is directly available to the prostitution business because there are no payoffs to the police and government officials. Still, babysitting fees are a drain and the women indicated that they spent a large proportion of their money on clothing, hairstyling, and similar professionally related expenses.[35]

One of Duncombe's interviews was with a madam, a fifty-six-year-old white woman from New York who had been married five times. Her basic ideology was that good whores are made, not born, and it was her job to teach them the trade, including how to keep clean, to dress, to hustle, and what to do to please the customers in the back room. If any of her employees used drugs, they were fired. Nearly all of them had children when they arrived in Elko, many from broken marriages. For women in this situation, prostitution was the best way to support their children and themselves. The madam felt that one reason why they opted for prostitution instead of welfare was their high need to feel independent. She amplified the social-worker ideology of many of the prostitutes, saying that prostitution is the best way to keep unattractive adolescent males from becoming homosexuals because of their inability to secure dates and to avoid having marriages start out badly because of the sexual inexperience of the husband (no mention was made of the problems of unattractive adolescent females or sexually inexperienced brides). Her "girls" usually stayed only a short time, with a few staying for as long as two years. Several of them used their earnings to finance a college education and then "went square."[36]

Symanski's findings for Nevada as a whole indicate that the situation in Elko is not atypical. Prostitutes generally earn more in the less isolated areas where business is better, with earnings running to $350 a week after all house expenses are paid. Law-enforcement records for seventy-seven prostitutes revealed that more than a quarter of them worked ten days or less in one spot, and nearly 60 percent worked less than a month before moving on. The longest tenure known in one town was four years in a single house. There was a two-tiered circulation system, with prostitutes either rotating through the lower-class houses such as those at Mina, Eureka, and Battle Mountain, or the higher-class houses in towns like Winnemucca, Elko, and Wells. Upon entering one of these houses, a customer selects a prostitute from among those sitting in a parlor, at a bar, or in a more formal lineup, pays his fee before engaging in sexual activity, and is moved on out of the house as quickly as possible. The whole operation is low key in that advertisements are banned, the prostitutes' behavior outside the brothel is severely circumscribed by law and custom, and madams are careful to be good citizens by contributing freely to the charitable activities popular in town.[37] Some of the restrictions on the prostitutes are so severe that they are repressive, but everyone goes along with them in the interest of good public relations and high profits. The result is that legal prostitution is well established in Nevada and shows no evidence of being in danger of being outlawed in the future.

If house prostitutes are the middle class of the world of sex for sale, call girls are its upper crust. They earn so much money that they can afford to go to expensive psychotherapists, a luxury that house prostitutes and streetwalkers can rarely afford. This has led to a number of psychologically oriented studies, of which perhaps the most useful is Greenwald's *The Elegant Prostitute*. In his earlier work, he saw prostitution as the result of a highly self-destructive, irrational process. By 1970, he had revised his conception of the etiology of prostitution to include differential association, economic factors, and other environmental factors. He was not sure whether the severe personality problems he saw in his practice had encouraged the original choice of prostitution as a career or were instead a result of years in the profession.[38] He realized that prostitution was "not necessarily more degrading than working at a job one hated or being married to a man one found physically repulsive. . . ."[39]

He concludes that although prostitution has a complex etiology there is a simple prevention, for he has never known a call girl who had strong bonds of love and affection with her family.[40] Rosenblum takes an intermediate position on call girls, arguing that the etiology of their prostitution includes strong components of the need to be independent of men and to gain as much money as possible.[41]

A more fully sociological view of call girls is taken by Bryan, who studied how call girls learn their trade. In his sample of call girls, most of whom were pimpless "outlaw broads," one generally learned to be a call girl by serving as an apprentice to an established call girl, an arrangement that was broken off when the apprentice had developed a "book" of clients of her own or got into disagreements with her trainer, not terminated by the apprentice's mastery of the content of the training "curriculum." Bryan did not find much physical, sexual training to be occurring. Instead, the training consisted of two broad areas, verbal behavior and attitudes. The verbal behavior was difficult for many apprentices to master because it was more contrary to traditional sex roles than the overt sexual activity that was sold. Call girls had to learn to be verbally aggressive, to call men on the phone and to ask directly for dates.[42] The attitudinal component of the call-girl profession was enlarged upon in a later article by Bryan, in which he found that the women saw themselves as counselors, social workers, and sexual therapists whose services were sorely needed in American society. In a semantic differential test administered to twenty-eight active call girls, they rated themselves and their customers more positively than other men and women, with other call girls receiving much lower ratings. Of three dimensions tested—positive/negative evaluation, activity, and potency, the only one that was correlated with the amount of time spent in the trade was evaluation, and that was only correlated for men who were not customers. In contrast to what might be predicted based on the stereotype of the hard, cold, man-hating prostitute, these women became more positive toward men the longer they were in the profession. This low level of occupational socialization may be due to the fact that most call girls insulate themselves so well from moral condemnation that they have little need to justify their choice of profession through more than a rudimentary occupational ideology.[43]

The idea that prostitutes may not have as negative a self-image as might be expected is supported by an unpublished dissertation completed at the Ventura School for Girls in California, in which young prostitutes were found to have a better self-concept than nonpromiscuous delinquents and as positive a self-concept as "normal" females.[44] Streetwalkers are more likely to encounter moral condemnation than most other kinds of prostitutes. How do they deal with this? Jackman, O'Toole, and Geis report that they are socially and psychologically isolated even though they are physically integrated with "straights," and that those general social values that filter through to them are handled by a system of rationalizations in which values such as financial success and the unselfish support of relatives and friends are emphasized over those of conformity.[45]

Davis spent three months doing participant observation in another school for delinquent young women, which led to the formulation of a three-stage model of the development of a deviant identity. In the first stage, the young women drift from promiscuity to prostitution, experiencing motivations such as curiosity, desire to escape boredom and find new experience, and identification with hustler norms, which emphasize the desirability of high earnings. The second stage is transitional, during which the women vacillate back and forth between conventional and deviant behavior. The thing that keeps bringing them back to prostitution is their need for the kind of money that only prostitution can offer them. Professionalization occurs in the third stage, and with it the adoption of all the elements of the ideology of prostitution. This movement is encouraged by definitional situations such as being arrested, called a common prostitute, and imprisoned; being mistreated by one's pimp, who now feels that the woman is securely in his stable; and public exposure, with the attendant expressions of horror and rejection from one's relatives.[46]

Heyl's series of stages in becoming a house prostitute is similar, but leans more toward an occupational model. In her first stage, the woman is merely willing to suspend her traditional norms, values, and beliefs so she can flirt with the fast life. Stage two, the novice stage, includes increased deviant behavior. At this point, the prostitute has two sets of friends and acquaintances, one traditional and one in the racket. The third, or professional, stage completes the movement away from traditional society. All friends are now in the life or close to it, all the techniques of prostitutes are routine, and clients are processed with high frequency and efficiency. Heyl adds a fourth stage, the madam, which nicely rounds out the life of the prostitute. Like the elder statesperson on a college faculty, the madam broadens her social contacts out into the community and achieves a satisfactory level of respect both from her employees and from other community members. Sexual behavior is greatly decreased, and is replaced by business and management concerns.[47]

Three social scientists have conducted ethnographic studies of streetwalkers, one in the late 1950s and two in the early 1970s. The first study was a student project completed by Ross at Harvard in which he portrayed the life of the hustler in Chicago. Ross found that the hustler role could be played by either men or women. Its essence was a combination of prostitution, robbery, and extortion.[48] The teenagers in Seattle who were interviewed by Gray also combined robbery with prostitution, calling the technique "creeping" or "ripping-off." They had rather poor social relations with everyone in their lives—family, clients, pimps, and other streetwalkers. Their experiences with traditional occupations has been distressing and unrewarding. As a group, they were singularly uninterested in the possibility of living a traditional life in the future. Their past experiences with family, school, and jobs did not make traditional alternatives to streetwalking very attractive.[49]

These modest investigations serve as the prelude to an extensive set of publications on Seattle streetwalkers by James. She has completed several major studies and has been in continuous contact with the world of the streetwalker since 1969. Among her contributions to the understanding of streetwalking are: (1) an understanding of the varieties of streetwalker and pimp roles through linguistic analysis, (2) the first satisfactory explication of the pimp-prostitute relationship, (3) the part played by geographical mobility in the life of the streetwalker, and (4) analyses of the motivational patterns held by both prostitutes and customers. James identified thirteen argot roles played by prostitutes and ten played by pimps. Six of the thirteen argot prostitute roles were "true" prostitutes—"outlaw," "rip-off artist," "hype," "old-timer," "thoroughbred," and "lady." The others were part-timers, women "who had no style," or amateurs, all of which were subsumed under the term "ho." The "hype" is a prostitute who works to support her addiction to heroin or ritalin. A "lady" can be identified by her carriage, class, finesse, and professionalism. The "old-timer" is also a solid professional but lacks the class of the "lady." Prostitutes who are too young to be called "old-timers" are called "thoroughbreds" if they show the same professionalism. "Rip-off artists" are thieves who use prostitution as a come-on rather than as their major income producer. "Outlaws" refuse to work with pimps, and show considerable independence in their actions. These argot roles are not mutually exclusive, since they describe different dimensions of streetwalker behavior rather than complete behavioral sets, each containing elements from all relevant streetwalker behavioral dimensions.[50]

The pimp's argot roles are also multi-dimensional, revolving around elements of personal style, size of stable, and techniques used for keeping his "girls" in line. The most successful of the pimp roles analyzed by James are the "sugar pimp," who treats his women so well that he always has all the women he can handle; the "fast-steppin' pimp," who is a capable business manager, moving his women over a large circuit in the service of maximum profits; and the "boss pimp," who has as many as seven women in his stable. A "boss pimp" sends his women as far afield as Canada and the Bahamas, and employs less successful pimps, such as "half-steppers," to watch his business for him in faraway places.[51] The principle that geographic mobility is associated with social status in the world of the streetwalker applies to prostitutes as well as to pimps. Most of the streetwalkers studied by James moved a distance of at least 500 miles every three months, with moves of lesser distance interspersed in between. High geographic mobility is adventurous, minimizes the danger of arrests, increases income by putting the prostitutes in the right place at the right time to maximize the number of customers, decreases pressures from family and friends in their home towns, and gives prostitutes insurance against being attacked by customers they have recently robbed.[52]

James asked her sample of prostitutes what advantages and disadvantages there were in working for a pimp. The women named his taking care of business (25 percent), providing protection and generating respect for them from others (21 percent), and caring about them (8 percent) as advantages, and giving up one's earnings (20 percent), being beaten (15 percent), loss of individuality and independence (12 percent), lack of respect from them (11 percent), and the fact that pimps set work quotas for them (11 percent) as disadvantages. The similarity between these lists and parallel lists of the advantages and disadvantages of marriage is obvious. Amplifying this theme, James explodes a number of myths about the pimp-prostitute relationship. Based on her research, it is not true that pimps force women to work against their will, seduce young girls, turn women into drug addicts for the purpose of control, give no sexual satisfaction to their women, keep them from ever leaving their stable, and are never married to prostitutes who work for them.[53] Aside from the specific advantages and disadvantages of attaching oneself to a pimp, it appears that the severe social isolation that preprostitutes feel predisposes them to join up with someone who "plugs" them into the world, giving them a set of social relations, a place to call their own, and an ideology to make the world intelligible. There is something oppressive about pimping, but it is not so much the actions of the pimp himself (unless he is a "gorilla pimp" who subjects his prostitutes to severe violence) as it is the structure of the social environment from which these women come. It is the broader environment that closes off other occupational opportunities from them, makes prostitution a viable financial alternative, and conditions men to regard sex as something worthwhile even if impersonal and purchased, so that there are always many customers.

This leads to the question of motivation. James holds that "prostitution is more easily understood as an institutionalized occupational choice for women than a symptom of pathology."[54] Surveying the literature on the motivations of prostitutes, she identified three groups of motivations: conscious (economics, persuasive pimp, working conditions, and adventure), situational (early life experiences, parental abuse and/or neglect, and occupation), and psychoanalytic (general factors, latent homosexuality, oedipal fixation, and retardation).[55] In a studyof 131 prostitutes that she conducted herself, she found that the most commonly reported motivation for entering prostitution was to obtain money and material goods (56 percent), followed by the influence of a male friend (11 percent), to get money for drugs (9 percent), economic necessity at a basic level (8 percent), and curiosity (4 percent). Only 3 percent of the respondents said that their main motivation for entering prostitution was that they were attracted to the life-style. When asked for the main advantage of being a prostitute, 85 percent chose easy money and material goods, followed by the social life it affords (5 percent) and independence (4 percent).[56]

James also performed a literature search on the subject of customer motivations for visiting prostitutes, in which she was able to identify eleven separate motivational factors. These were: (1) while traveling away from normal sources of sexual contact, (2) to visit prostitutes in a group or gang in order to bring the group closer together, (3) customers too disabled to seek other sexual contacts, (4) the desire for highly deviant sexual acts not easily found among "straights," (5) impotency, (6) homosexuality, (7) therapy of an interpersonal nature, (8) to have many women with little effort, (9) to experience variety in sexual partners, (10) to avoid the interpersonal entanglements that commonly accompany sexual involvements, and (11) to combat loneliness.[57] Unfortunately, James has not yet published any empirical data on the subject, so this insightful list must remain untested for the moment.

Gender Differences in Prostitution: Implications for the Understanding of Sex Roles

Women are not the only prostitutes. Boys and young men also enter the trade in sizable numbers. Most of the larger works that have been written on male prostitution are of a journalistic or literary nature rather than the writing of a social scientist. For example there are Rechy's *City of Night*,[58] Lloyd's *For Money or Love: Boy Prostitution in America*,[59] Drew and Drake's *Boys for Sale*,[60] and Gerassi's *The Boys of Boise*.[61] The political analysis of factors in the Boise trials by Gerassi is particularly insightful. Raven's article in *Encounter* is also literary in style, though it is closer to some of the ethnographic accounts in the social-science literature. He identifies five types of male prostitutes operating in London around 1960: (1) young military men, often from the Queen's Household Troops, (2) young men who have traditionally effeminate jobs and prostitute themselves from time to time, (3) boys who are too poorly skilled to do more than drift from job to job, prostituting in between, (4) hustlers who make all their money in criminal activities, of which prostitution is one among many they engage in, and (5) the full-time male prostitute who, unlike all the others, works seriously and continuously at his trade, and derives all of his income from it.[62]

The publication of studies relevant to the sociology of male prostitution began in 1947 with Butts's article "Boy Prostitutes of Metropolis." In this article, he reported that few of the young men showed effeminate characteristics, most had other occupations, practicing prostitution as a sideline, and only four of them appeared to prefer homosexual over heterosexual behavior when they were not being paid for sex. More than three-quarters of the young men were under age twenty-one, and most of them came from incomplete homes. Butts comments that his subjects were a maladjusted, unhappy lot.[63]

Jersild also found that the male prostitutes in his sample of Danish cases were young. A third of them had entered the trade before age eighteen and more than three-quarters had begun before age twenty-one. Most came from inadequate or broken homes of low economic standing, and less than one in six had any salable occupational skills. Two percent were judged to be exclusively homosexual, 13 percent bisexual, and 85 percent heterosexual.[64] Jersild continued to accumulate cases after the publication of his book, which did not alter the pattern of variables discerned in his earlier work.[65]

A study of 103 male prostitutes in seven American cities by MacNamara found that the prostitutes were very young (the oldest was twenty-three), hostile to their parents, themselves, and society in general, with poor educational attainment, work history, and family background, and with a firsthand acquaintance with poverty. They did not, as a group, seem to be psychologically pathological, but rather had "found in prostitution a temporary and relatively satisfactory survival *modus vivendi*; a subcultural adjustment, perhaps, but neither as self-destructive as suicide, narcotics addiction or alcoholism nor as antisocial as an overtly criminal career."[66] In a British study, Craft concluded that boy prostitution was "an important but incidental feature of a general, social and personal maladjustment which by disposal to institutions is liable to increase any homosexual orientations."[67] Although these studies differ in their emphasis on psychological maladjustment, they agree that male prostitution is a way of coping with a crippling set of disadvantages that make competing in the legitimate world a losing battle.

This theme is further developed by Ginsburg, who argues that we should not assume that a homosexual prostitute is necessarily homosexual or that his primary motivation for engaging in it is anything other than economic. The young men interviewed by Ginsburg had been extensively rejected in their families of orientation, showed considerable disdain and antagonism toward the men they dealt with, and had an insatiable need for affection. Never having been wanted in their youth, they now want more than anything else to be desired, an object of worth in human relations. Bargaining for money is a facade, masking negotiations for the recognition of the prostitute's personal worth. If a very attractive, desirable person wants him, he will often go along for nothing since in this case his need for an affirmation of personal worth has already been met by the characteristics of the client. Ginsburg admits that although the initial motivation of the male prostitute may not be primarily economic or sexual, it is quite possible that one consequence of years of hustling may be the adoption of a permanent homosexual orientation.[68]

These young men sound very different from the delinquent prostitutes described by Reiss, who did not prostitute for a living but only to obtain spending money. They would permit an adult homosexual to perform fellatio on them for an appropriate fee, but would assault him if he tried to be affectionate with them or to coax them into playing a more active role in the sexual incident. In this setting, the prostitutes had no difficulty in maintaining their heterosexual identity, and really were not part of the sexual underworld. As they matured and became serious about a particular young woman, they stopped prostituting themselves and went on to a heterosexual life that seemed little affected by their experiences in prostitution.[69] It is possible that Reiss was misled by his informants. If he was not, then his findings are strong evidence that definitions of the situation are more important than overt sexual experience in the development of a stable pattern of sexual object choice.

The most recent study of male prostitution shows a remarkable similarity across time to earlier studies and cross-nationally with results obtained from England and Denmark. Deisher, Eisner, and Sulzbacher interviewed sixty-three male prostitutes in Seattle and San Francisco, paying each subject $5 for his time. The prostitutes had an average age of nineteen, were poorly educated, and had few job skills. Many of them came from broken families, and other families were probably destructive and disorganized even if formally intact. These young men exhibited a high degree of geographical mobility, much like the female prostitutes described by James.[70] When vocational counseling and job placement were offered to the young men, more than half accepted and were eventually placed in blue-collar jobs such as hospital attendant, waiter, and truck driver. The prostitutes who would not accept these services were either psychopathological or were so successful in their hustling careers that they would not consider a switch to a legitimate occupation.[71]

This completes our brief survey of the sociology of male prostitution. We are now in a position to say something about the similarities and differences between male and female prostitutes. The similarities are striking. Both male and female prostitutes generally come from the lower strata of society, have relatively poor relations with parents, began prostituting themselves in their teenage years, have performed poorly at school and failed to graduate, and possess few if any legitimate job skills. Were it not for their involvement in prostitution, they would be unlikely to be earning their present level of income. Male and female prostitutes both tend to travel an extensive circuit. For them, geographical mobility is not only profitable, it is a way of life. And why not float along, since the ties to friends and family are generally weak?

The process of drifting into prostitution seems similar for young men and women. The stages for males appear to be the same as the stages for females described by Heyl and James, although nobody has as yet undertaken to develop a sequential framework for analyzing the entrance into full-time male prostitution. The general pattern of hustler norms also seems to be similar for men and women. More important than any of these factors is the way in which the law of supply and demand determines success in prostitution. Youth sells better than experience; certain physical features are favored over others. The prostitute must go where the business is, and must provide the kinds of sexual services desired, or he/she will lose out in the competition. Finally, prostitutes of both sexes seem uncommonly in need of being physically desired by others as a crutch to a feeling of self-worth that is otherwise denied to them.

The differences between male and female prostitutes are fewer in number. First, male part-timers are less likely to go on to a fully developed career in the trade. At any given point in time, a larger proportion of the male prostitutes on the street are part-timers than their female coworkers. This may be partially due to the earlier age at which male prostitutes lose their ability to attract clients. It is more likely to be due to the greater availability of viable occupational opportunities to males than to females, and to the greater ease with which they can escape the stigma of having been a prostitute. Other contributing factors are that males seem to make less money in prostitution than females, and that their physical equipment is not as well adapted to servicing a high volume of clients in a short period of time.

A second male-female difference in prostitution is that social roles are elaborated to a much greater degree among women in the trade. There are more argot roles available for female prostitutes than males, which presumably accommodates a greater diversity of personality types. The role of the madam, though less common today than a few decades ago, gives women an opportunity to mature in the profession, to increase their profits, to survive the decline of youthful features, and to derive increased self-respect in the socially valued roles of teacher and administrator. Also related to role restriction among male prostitutes is the lack of any viable male prostitute defense organization analogous to COYOTE (Call Off Your Old Tired Ethics) for women. Just as gay-rights organizations have not rivaled women's-liberation organizations in any way, homosexual prostitution is organizationally inferior to heterosexual prostitution. There are not even a group of dedicated social scientists to champion the cause of homosexual prostitution in the scholarly community and the press. The day may come when the call-boy role is as well established (if not as popular) as the call-girl role, but it will not be soon.

The final difference (actually a group of related differences like the two previous points) is in the power positions of the two genders of prostitutes. There are no pimps to speak of in the world of homosexual prostitution. In entering into prostitution, a woman may escape boredom, poverty, and a sense of worthlessness. She is unlikely to escape domination by men. In a recent paper, Heyl detailed sexual stratification in the world of the female prostitute. These women are subject to the political power of male police officers, the physical and psychological power of their pimps (if they have any), and the economic/consumer power of businessmen and sexual clients. The combined power of men over prostitutes is greatest at the level of the streetwalker, declining up to the level of affluent call girl.[72] Even at that level, the prostitute is the servant of the male gender, and her continued success depends on her ability to please men in whatever ways they desire.

Sexual stratification in the larger society is at the very core of the etiology of prostitution. It is not the intent of the author to provide a comprehensive treatment of that subject. However, it is interesting that a number of the etiological factors that come up again and again in the literature (such as desire for economic self-sufficiency and social isolation) are related to the American system of sexual stratification. It is quite possible that differences between various types of female prostitutes are as great as differences between male and female prostitutes. If one were to do a study of differing motivational patterns among streetwalkers, house prostitutes, and call girls, it might be found that the higher the status of the prostitute, the higher the motivational component derived from the desire to escape the negative consequences of sexual stratification.

Gangs, Whores, and the Criminal Justice System

Girls and young women in delinquent gangs are processed by the criminal justice system just like other young female delinquents and criminals. This situation is fully discussed by Meda Chesney-Lind in chapter 6. Young women do not organize into political pressure groups to fight the system. Their age, inexperience, and lack of resources make it hard to organize a movement in their own interest. Equally important is the isolation of the gangs from each other, which is similar to the isolation of Native American tribal groups, and which dooms a broad-based cooperative movement arising from the grass-roots level.

Female prostitutes have been more successful in having their treatment by the criminal justice system publicized in the press and, more recently, in organizing themselves for political action. There are many reasons for this difference other than those noted above, not the least of which is that many upper-class prostitutes have friends (clients) in high places. Another point is that prostitution is a victimless crime, while gang activities are generally thought of as involving crimes of violence. This distinction is misleading because some prostitutes conspire to commit violence against clients and many young women do nothing violent in their gang activities, but this refinement has not become part of the general understanding of the difference between gangs and prostitution. As perpetrators of victimless crimes, prostitutes have benefited from the campaign to legalize all victimless crimes, which has been led by scholars such as Skolnick,[73] Schur,[74] Duster,[75] Lindesmith,[76] and Ploscoe,[77] and from the organizational activities of groups like the American Civil Liberties Union, the National Council on Crime and Delinquency, and some units of the American Bar Association. The basic stance of this social movement is that crimes without victims do no necessary harm to their participants, and are therefore a matter of private consenting behavior between adults that is of no interest to the state.

Prostitution in the United States expanded greatly in connection with the massive migration of Europeans into eastern cities in the late nineteenth century. Many of the immigrants were men who were either unmarried or who had left their wives at home. They needed sexual contacts and also a little feminine sympathy, both of which were well supplied by a growing cadre of prostitutes. These same conditions obtained in the frontier regions of the western states, with the same results. The only women in many mining towns were prostitutes, a number of whom have been immortalized in American folklore because of their outstanding contributions to their communities, which included great generosity in charitable affairs and willingness to expose themselves to fatal diseases in order to nurse the sick during epidemics.

The movement to curtail prostitution in the eastern states was not unrelated to the rise of nativism and a high degree of prejudice and discrimination directed toward recent migrants from the countries of Mediterranean Europe. As the sex ratio became less unbalanced in the West, the antiprostitution forces gained strength there too. The *Readers Guide to Periodical Literature* lists 341 articles on prostitution from the years 1890-1968, 157 of which were published between 1909 and 1914, the peak of public agitation about prostitution. Similarly, the *International Index* lists 322 prostitution articles from the years 1908-1968, with a peak of fifty-six articles in 1915-1920. The *Journal of Social Hygiene* published nearly half of these articles until it ceased publication in 1954. When the American Vigilance Association and the American Federation for Sex Hygiene merged into the American Hygiene Association in 1913, the movement to abolish prostitution took on new vigor.[78] The evils of sin were united in the public mind with the ravages of venereal disease. Around this time prostitution began to go underground, thus increasing the difficulty in monitoring the quantity and quality of services delivered. "Red light" districts in the major American cities were closed down between 1912 and 1917.[79] The pressure on prostitutes continued through the two world wars, with increasing sentiment in favor of liberalizing laws and enforcement policies in the 1950s, leading to a national debate in the 1960s that continues today.

Roby, who had detailed the history of prostitution laws in New York State in her doctoral dissertation,[80] analyzed the recent legal debate over prostitution in that state in an article in *Social Problems.* After extensive study and politicking, a new prostitution law was passed in 1965. This law reduced the penalty for prostitution from three years (a crime) to fifteen days (a violation), included patrons as violators, allowed either males or females to be prosecuted for prostitution, and limited the basis for arrests of prostitutes to observing a couple while the prostitute accepted payment from the customer for the promised sexual act. This was surprisingly close to legalizing prostitution, perhaps more than would be so if prostitution were to be decriminalized. It may be that this attracted an increased number of prostitutes to New York City. The police seemed to think so, although there was no objective evidence available. In any case, the prostitutes who were there became bolder, which gave the appearance of increased numbers, and businessmen complained that streetwalkers were hurting business.[81] In late summer 1967, the police responded to these complaints by picking up the prostitutes *en masse* under the state's disorderly conduct and loitering statutes. The women would be held overnight and then be released the next day for lack of evidence, only to run the danger of being rearrested the following evening.[82] This harassment was as costly as it was unpleasant for the prostitutes. Patrons and prostitutes who kept off the streets were not harassed. An amendment increasing the penalty for prostitution and also making soliciting a crime was passed in 1969, which reestablished the status quo.[83] The most recent development in the New York prostitution circus is a ruling by Judge Taylor that portions of the state's prostitution laws are unconstitutional because they deprive unmarried adults of their constitutional right to privacy in the pursuit of pleasure. In her ruling, she noted that only sixty-two of 3,219 individuals arrested in prostitution cases between January and June 1977 were patrons. All the rest were prostitutes.[84]

In recent years, there have been a number of articles in which the legal underpinnings of prostitution laws have been undermined.[85] More important for our purposes are studies that reveal how prostitutes are treated by criminal justice system personnel. For example, La Fave reports that suspected prostitutes were the largest category of offenders arrested for purposes other than prosecution in Detroit in the early 1960s. Women walking in areas known to be frequented by prostitutes were subject to arrest under the disorderly persons investigation law if they were accompanied by men who were not their relatives, if they had no evidence of regular employment, and especially if they were racially different from the men.[86] This shows how policemen can mistreat law-abiding women in their zeal to harass prostitutes, a serious occurrence in a democracy, in addition to the mistreatment of the prostitutes themselves. A participant observation-interview study in a southern town by Atkinson and Boles documents how the need that vice officers have for information about criminal activities leads them to engage in quasi-ethical and even illegal activities.[87] It is a sad commentary on the law that many of the most humanistic actions of vice officers in their official capacity are on the dark side of the letter of the law.

To summarize the argument, the attempt to enforce laws against prostitution leads police officers to unconstitutionally harass prostitutes, unconstitutionally harass nonprostitutes who happen to be in the wrong place with the wrong people at the wrong time, and engage in illegal behavior with some prostitutes in order to get information that will be used to prosecute other prostitutes, drug dealers, and so forth. Considering these points, and also the high incidence of unsolved crimes of violence, it is hard to see why city police departments continue to spend sizable amounts of money on prostitution. In San Francisco, where there were 12,511 robberies and 69,700 burglaries (counting only official reports) in 1971, the police spent $375,000 to arrest and transport prostitutes to jail. Bryant states that ". . . the continued enforcement of anti-prostitution laws is not justified in terms of its overall effect on crime and that while prostitution may be considered an act of deviant behavior, the present criminal sanctions should be removed. . . ."[88]

Scholars and "straight" activists are not the only groups that are interested in the issue of decriminalizing prostitution. The National Organization for Women (NOW) approved a resolution on prostitution in 1973 which supported the decriminalization of prostitution and recognized that it grows out of a socioeconomic structure that keeps women in a lower-status caste in which they have attenuated opportunities to develop themselves as productive human beings. An action group that focuses directly on the legal problems of prostitutes is COYOTE, which grew out of WHO (Whores, Housewives and Others) in 1973. In addition to lobbying for the decriminalization of prostitution, COYOTE puts on an annual hookers' convention and the famous Hookers' Ball. By handing out a "Trick of the Year Award" and a giant keyhole to the "Vice Cop of the Year," COYOTE showed a healthy sense of humor that is unfortunately lacking in action programs peopled by "true believers."[89] The organization also publishes an intermittent newspaper with the unlikely name of *Coyote Howls,* which had a circulation of 8,000 in late 1977. The achievements of COYOTE to date have been more local than national and more publicized than they deserve on the basis of their impact on society. Still, it has been much more successful than most other organizations of "unrepentant deviants," and it can look forward to increased impact in the future. Because of the broad support of the decriminalization of prostitution from many power groups, it is not improbable that some states will carry this through in the coming decade, in which case the coyote will have eaten the bear.

Notes

1. See, for example, William J. Deadman, "Infanticide," *Canadian Medical Association Journal* 91 (September 5, 1964), 558-60; Harvey Greenberg, "Pyromania in a Woman," *Psychoanalytic Quarterly* 35 (1966), 256-62; Werner Tuteur and Jacob Glotzer, "Murdering Mothers," *American Journal of Psychiatry* 116 (1959), 447-52; Eddyth P. Spears, Manuel Vega, and Ira J. Silverman, "The Female Robber," paper presented at the annual meeting of the American Society of Criminology, Atlanta, 1977; P.T. d'Orban, "Baby Stealing," *British Medical Journal* 2 (1972), 635-39; P.T. d'Orban, "Child Stealing: A Typology of Female Offenders," *British Journal of Criminology* 16 (July 1976), 275-81; Rudi G. Denys, "Lady Paperhangers," *Canadian Journal of Corrections* 11 (1969), 165-92; and Ellen Rosenblatt and Cyril Greenland, "Female Crimes of Violence," *Canadian Journal of Criminology and Corrections* 16 (1974), 173-80.

2. Frederic M. Thrasher, *The Gang* (Chicago: University of Chicago Press, 1963), 161.

3. Ibid., 155-70.

4. Albert K. Cohen and James F. Short, Jr., "Research in Delinquent Subcultures," *Journal of Social Issues* 14 (Summer 1958), 35.

5. James F. Short, Jr., *Gang Delinquency and Delinquent Subcultures* (New York: Harper and Row, 1968), 4.

6. James F. Short, Jr., and Fred L. Strodtbeck, *Group Process and Gang Delinquency* (Chicago: University of Chicago Press, 1965), 242.

7. K. Hanson, *Rebels in the Streets: The Story of New York's Girl Gangs* (New York: Prentice-Hall, 1964), 6-14.

8. Robert Rice, "A Reporter at Large: The Persian Queens," *New Yorker* 39 (October 19, 1963), 153.

9. Ethel Ackley and Beverly R. Fliegel, "A Social Work Approach to Street-Corner Girls," *Social Work* 5 (1960), 29-31.

10. Walter B. Miller, "Race, Sex and Gangs," *Society* 11 (Nov.-Dec. 1973), 32-35.

11. Walter B. Miller, *Violence by Youth Gangs and Youth Groups as a Crime Problem in Major American Cities* (Washington, D.C.: U.S. Government Printing Office, 1975), 23-27. Richard Deming, *Women, The New Criminals* (New York: Thomas Nelson, 1977), 108-109, gives a slightly different set of figures for New York City. According to him, the New York City police know of 278 male youth gangs, 23 of which have female aux-

iliaries, and 13 gangs composed exclusively of females. He states that the female gangs engage in basically the same kinds of activities as the male groups.

12. Freda Adler, *Sisters in Crime* (New York: McGraw-Hill, 1975), 99.

13. Robert J. Thompson and Jewel Lozes, "Female Gang Delinquency," *Corrective and Social Psychiatry and Journal of Behavior Technology Methods and Therapy* 22, 3 (1976), 1-5.

14. Ibid., 1. For more information on Yablonsky's theory of gang structure, see Lewis Yablonsky, *The Violent Gang* (New York: Macmillan, 1962).

15. Adler, 99.

16. Malcolm W. Klein, Helen E. Shimota, and Gay Luce, "Delinquent Girl Gangs," in Julius Segal (ed.), *The Mental Health of the Child* (Washington, D.C.: U.S. Government Printing Office, 1971), 395-97.

17. Malcolm W. Klein and Barbara G. Myerhoff, "The Nature and Roles of Female Delinquent Gangs," a proposal submitted to the National Institutes of Health, 1963.

18. Joseph Donato, "A Study of Girl Involvement in Juvenile Gang Incidents," Los Angeles County Probation Department, Division of Research, 1963 (Mimeo.). Cited in Klein and Myerhoff, 2, 19.

19. Malcolm W. Klein and Helen E. Shimota, "The Nature and Roles of Female Delinquent Gangs: Summary of Second Year's Progress," interim grant report from the Youth Studies Center of the University of Southern California 1965, 1-2; and Helen E. Shimota, "Delinquent Acts as Perceived by Gang and Non-Gang Negro Adolescents," paper presented at the annual meeting of the California State Psychological Association (Los Angeles, 1964), 2-3.

20. Malcolm W. Klein, *Street Gangs and Street Workers* (Englewood Cliffs, N.J.: Prentice-Hall, 1971), 77.

21. Shimota, 6-7, reported in Klein, 1971, 77-79.

22. John C. Quicker, "The Chicana Gang: A Preliminary Description," paper presented at the annual meeting of the Pacific Sociological Association, San Jose, 1974, 1-4, 8.

23. John C. Quicker, "Home-girls and Home-boys: A Theory of Female Gang Membership," which is a revision of "Chicana Gang Membership as a Function of Institutional Failure," paper presented at the annual meeting of the Pacific Sociological Association (Victoria, 1975), 11-18.

24. Ibid., 18-19.

25. See, for example, Fernando Henriques, *Prostitution and Society* (New York: Grove Press, 1962); Maryse Choisy, *Psychoanalysis of the Prostitute* (New York: Philosophical Library, 1961); Harold Greenwald, *The Elegant Prostitute* (New York: Ballantine Books, 1970); and William W.

Sanger, *The History of Prostitution* (New York: Eugenics Publishing Co., 1937). Bridges from historical and psychoanalytic perspectives to sociological perspectives are provided by two comprehensive volumes, Charles Winick and Paul M. Kinsie, *The Lively Commerce: Prostitution in the United States* (Chicago: Quadrangle Books, 1971); and Harvey Benjamin and R.E.L. Masters, *Prostitution and Morality* (New York: The Julian Press, 1964), and a pioneering article by Kinsley Davis, "The Sociology of Prostitution," *American Sociological Review* 2 (1937), 744-55.

26. Jennifer James has correctly pointed out that the varieties of prostitutes are almost endless, including bar girls, masseuses, studio models and escorts, stag party workers, hotel girls, convention prostitutes, illegal house and apartment prostitutes, and circuit travelers, in addition to the three basic types. See: Jennifer James, "Prostitutes and Prostitution," in Edward Sagarin and Fred Montanino (eds.), *Deviants: Voluntary Actors in a Hostile World* (Morrison, N.J.: General Learning Press, 1977), 383-87.

27. Two journal articles and three papers by Barbara Sherman Heyl are at hand, and a book summarizing and enlarging upon these writings is in press as of this writing. The articles are "The Madam as Entrepreneur," *Sociological Symposium* (Spring 1974), 61-83; and "The Madam as Teacher: The Training of House Prostitutes," *Social Problems* 24 (June 1977), 545-55. The papers are "Becoming and Being a Prostitute: A Sequential Model of Identity Transformation," presented at the annual meeting of the Midwest Sociological Society (Chicago, 1975); "The Training of House Prostitutes," presented at the annual meeting of the American Sociological Association (San Francisco, 1975); and "Prostitution: An Extreme Case of Sex Stratification," presented at the annual meeting of the Southwestern Sociological Association (Dallas, 1976).

28. "The Madam as Entrepreneur," 61-69.

29. "The Madam as Teacher . . . ," 546-53.

30. Richard Symanski, "Prostitution in Nevada," *Annals of the Association of American Geographers* 64 (September 1974), 361-65.

31. Beth Duncombe, "A Descriptive Study of Seven Prostitutes in Elko, Nevada," unpublished paper (Whitman College, 1969).

32. "Pastor—A Crusade Against Shady Ladies," *San Francisco Chronicle,* November 8, 1964. This article described an attack on brothels by one outspoken minister and then added two more moderate opinions by members of the clergy, one of whom was Rev. David Duncombe.

33. Duncombe, 2-4.

34. Ibid., 6-7.

35. Ibid., 8, 10-12.

36. Ibid., 19-22.

37. Symanski, 368-75.

38. Harold Greenwald, *The Elegant Prostitute: A Social and Psychoanalytic Study* (New York: Walker, 1970), xiii-xviii.

39. Ibid., xx.

40. Ibid., 242.

41. Karen E. Rosenblum, "Female Deviance and the Female Sex Role: A Preliminary Investigation," *British Journal of Sociology* 26 (1975), 173-78.

42. James H. Bryan, "Apprenticeships in Prostitution, *Social Problems* 12 (Winter 1965), 287-97.

43. James H. Bryan, "Occupational Ideologies and Individual Attitudes of Call Girls," *Social Problems* 13 (Spring 1966), 441-50.

44. H. Kagan, *Prostitution and Sexual Promiscuity among Adolescent Female Offenders,* unpublished doctoral dissertation, University of Arizona, 1969. Abstract available from the reference service of the Law Enforcement Assistance Administration.

45. Norman R. Jackson, Richard O'Toole, and Gilbert Geis, "The Self-image of the Prostitute," *Sociological Inquiry* 4 (1963), 150-61.

46. Nanette J. Davis, "The Prostitute: Developing a Deviant Identity," in James M. Henslin (ed.), *Studies in the Sociology of Sex* (New York: Appleton-Century-Crofts, 1971), 297-322.

47. "Becoming and Being a Prostitute," Table A.

48. H. Lawrence Ross, "The 'Hustler' in Chicago," *Journal of Student Research* 1 (1959), 13-19.

49. Diana Gray, "Turning-Out: A Study of Teenage Prostitution," *Urban Life and Culture* 1 (January 1973), 401-405.

50. Jennifer James, "Two Domains of Streetwalker Argot," *Anthropological Linguistics* 14 (1972), 174-75.

51. Ibid., 178-79.

52. Jennifer James, "Mobility as an Adaptive Strategy," *Urban Anthropology* 4 (1975), 349-64.

53. Jennifer James, "Prostitute-Pimp Relationships," *Medical Aspects of Human Sexuality* 7 (November 1973), 147-63.

54. Jennifer James, "Motivations for Entrance into Prostitution," in Laura Crites (ed.), *The Female Offender* (Lexington, MA: D.C. Heath, 1976), 177.

55. "Prostitutes and Prostitution," 390-91.

56. "Motivations for Entrance into Prostitution," 200-202.

57. "Prostitutes and Prostitution," 402-409.

58. John Rechy, *City of Night* (New York: Grove Press, 1963).

59. Robin Lloyd, *For Money or Love: Boy Prostitution in America* (New York: Vanguard Press, 1976).

60. Dennis Drew and Jonathan Drake, *Boys for Sale* (Farmingdale, N.Y.: Brown Book Co., 1969).

61. John Gerassi, *The Boys of Boise* (New York: Macmillan, 1968).

62. Simon Raven, "Boys Will Be Boys, The Male Prostitute in London," *Encounter* 15 (November 1960), 19-24.

63. W.N. Butts, "Boy Prostitutes of the Metropolis," *Journal of Clinical Psychopathology* 8 (1947), 673-81.

64. Jens Jersild, *Boy Prostitution* (Copenhagen: G.E.C. Gad, 1956), 53-59.

65. Harry Benjamin and R.E.L. Masters, *Prostitution and Morality* (New York: Julian Press, 1964), 299-302.

66. Donal E.J. MacNamara, "Male Prostitution in American Cities: A Socioeconomic or Pathological Phenomenon?" *American Journal of Orthopsychiatry* 35 (1965), 204.

67. Michael Croft, "Boy Prostitutes and Their Fate," *British Journal of Psychiatry* 112 (1966), 1114.

68. Kenneth N. Ginsburg, "The 'Meat Rack': A Study of the Male Homosexual Prostitute," *American Journal of Psychotherapy* 21 (1967), 179-83.

69. A.J. Reiss, "The Social Integration of Queers and Peers," *Social Problems* 9 (1961), 102-20.

70. Robert W. Deisher, Victor Eisner, and Stephen I. Sulzbacher, "The Young Male Prostitute," *Pediatrics* 43 (1969), 936-41.

71. Patrick Gandy and Robert Deisher, "Young Male Prostitutes—The Physician's Role in Social Rehabilitation," *Journal of the American Medical Association* 212 (June 8, 1970), 1661-66.

72. "Prostitution: An Extreme Case of Sex Stratification," 7-21.

73. Jerome H. Skolnick, *Coercion to Virtue: A Sociological Discussion of the Enforcement of Morals* (Washington, D.C.: President's Commission on Law Enforcement and Administration of Justice, 1967).

74. Edwin M. Schur, *Crimes Without Victims: Deviant Behavior and Public Policy* (Englewood Cliffs, N.J.: Prentice-Hall, 1965).

75. Troy Duster, *The Legislation of Morality: Law, Drugs, and Moral Judgment* (New York: Free Press, 1970).

76. Alfred A. Lindesmith, *The Addict and the Law* (Bloomington: Indiana University Press, 1965).

77. Morris Ploscowe, *Sex and the Law* (New York: Ace Books, 1962).

78. Charles E. Reasons, "A Developmental Model for the Analysis of Social Problems: Prostitution and Moral Reform in Twentieth Century America," unpublished manuscript (Washington State University, 1971), 3-6.

79. Kay A. Holmes, "Reflection by Gaslight: Prostitution in Another Age," *Issues in Criminology* 7 (Winter 1972), 96.

80. Pamela A. Roby, *Politics and Prostitution: A Case Study of the Formulation, Enforcement and Judicial Administration of the New York State Penal Laws on Prostitution, 1870-1970,* unpublished doctoral dissertation, New York University. 1971

81. Pamela A. Roby, "Politics and Criminal Law: Revision of the New

York State Penal Law on Prostitution,'' *Social Problems* 17 (Summer 1969), 90-93.

82. Sidney E. Zion, "Prostitution: The Midtown Roundup," *New York Times* (October 1, 1967).

83. Jennifer James, "The History of Prostitution Laws," in Jennifer James, Jean Withers, Marilyn Haft, Sara Theiss, and Mary Owen, *The Politics of Prostitution* (Seattle: Social Research Associates, 1975), 16.

84. "N.Y. Prostitution Ruling Stirs Fuss," *Milwaukee Journal* (January 27, 1978).

85. See for example: Marilyn G. Haft, "Hustling For Rights," *Civil Liberties Review* 1 (Winter-Spring 1974), 8-25; Marilyn G. Haft, "Legal Arguments: Prostitution Laws and the Constitution," pp. 20-36 in *The Politics of Prostitution*; Women Endorsing Decriminalization, "Prostitution: A Non-Victim Crime?" *Issues in Criminology* 8 (Fall 1973), 137-62; and Madeline S. Caughey, "Criminal Law—The Principle of Harm and Its Application of Laws Criminalizing Prostitution," *Denver Law Journal* 51 (1974), 235-62.

86. Wayne R. La Fave, *Arrest: The Decision to Take a Suspect into Custody* (Boston: Little, Brown and Co., 1965), 451-56.

87. Maxine Atkinson and Jacqueline Boles, "Prostitution as an Ecology of Confidence Games: The Scripted Behavior of Prostitutes and Vice Officers," in Clifton Bryant (ed.), *Sexual Deviancy in a Social Context* (New York: Franklin Watts, 1977), 219-31.

88. Marshall A. Bryant, "Prostitution and the Criminal Justice System," *Journal of Police Science and Administration* 5 (December 1977), 388.

89. Jean Withers and Jennifer James, "Three Organizations Working to Change Prostitution Laws: N.O.W., A.C.L.U., and C.O.Y.O.T.E.," in *Politics of Prostitution,* 68-74.

Young Women in the Arms of the Law

Meda Chesney-Lind

Juvenile Courts and Female Delinquency

The problem of juvenile delinquency has always claimed a large share of the public's attention, but historically this concern has been limited to discussions of the male delinquent and his behavior. Reports of startling changes in the female crime picture, however, have generated substantial interest in the female delinquent, and this interest is not misplaced. While overall female arrests are increasing more rapidly than male arrests, this increase has been especially marked for juvenile women. Between 1960 and 1975, arrests of adult women were up 60.2 percent; during this same period, arrests of women under the age of eighteen were up 253.9 percent.[1]

These dramatic increases were immediately defined by some as indicative of a "rising female crime rate" caused by the women's liberation movement.[2] While this explanation seems plausible, it is clearly premature. The interpretation of official rates of deviant or criminal behavior requires an understanding of two sociologically distinct processes: "the social conduct which produces a unit of behavior (the behavior producing processes)" and "the organizational activity which produces a unit in the rate of deviant behavior (the rate producing processes)."[3]

Unquestionably, challenges to traditional female roles have affected the juvenile female crime rate. To attribute the increasing arrest rate of juvenile women solely to "the steady erosion of the social and psychological differences between men and women" as does Freda Alder is, however, clearly unsatisfactory.

Given the complicated nature of official record-keeping and the sensitivity of this process to changes within law-enforcement agencies, the behavior and attitudes of those within these systems must also be scrutinized when changes in rates of arrest are noticed.[4] Advocates of this approach, John Kitsuse and Aaron Cicourel, have explained the importance of this consideration by observing that rates of deviant behavior are produced by actions taken by personnel within agencies who are empowered to define, classify, and record certain behaviors as deviant or criminal. If these individuals choose to ignore a particular behavior it will not appear as a unit in the set of rates the sociologist attempts to explain.[5] Likewise, these individuals could choose to label as deviant or criminal a behavior which had previously been ignored. This perspective argues that changes in the volume and character of female arrests should not be assumed, automatically, to mirror changes in adolescent behavior. An equal amount of attention should be focused on those who possess the authority to label particular behaviors as strange, deviant, or "delinquent."

This chapter will review available research on this often-neglected side of the interaction which produces female delinquency. Studies on the attitudes and behavior of those who label young men and women as delinquent will be examined so as to develop both a coherent picture of this important activity and to determine if any part of the rising adolescent female crime rate could be attributed to changes in the behavior of those who produce rates of female delinquency.

Shifting attention from the young woman labeled as delinquent to those within the juvenile system who define behavior as delinquent necessitates an understanding of the unique history of this organization. Established in the late 1800s, the juvenile or family court has become a judicial body with broad powers over not only the criminal youth but all adolescents.[6] Assuming the natural dependence of youth, the court's founders created a unique system charged not only with judging the guilt or innocence of those accused of criminal behavior but also with acting for or in place of the defendant's parents (*parens patriae*).

The actual intent of the founders' paternalism went far beyond a concern for removing the adolescent criminal from the horrors of the adult criminal justice system, as Anthony Platt notes:

> Many of the child savers' reforms were aimed at imposing sanctions on conduct unbecoming youth and disqualifying youth from the benefit of adult privileges. The childsavers were more concerned with restriction than liberation, with the protection of youth from moral weaknesses as well as from physical dangers. The austerity of the criminal law and criminal institutions were not the major target of their concern, nor were they especially interested in problems relating to "classical" crimes against person and property. Their central interest was in the normative behavior of youth—their recreation, leisure, education, outlook on life, attitudes to authority, family relationships, and personal morality.[7]

The importance of the court's concern for the morality of youth and its commitment to parental authority is not simply of historical interest. Many of the values which gave rise to family courts across the nation in the late 1900s still permeate the structure of modern courts and the day-to-day activities of persons in the juvenile justice system.

For example, juveniles in America can be taken into custody for a wide range of behaviors which are not crimes but rather violations of parental authority. Often called "status" or "uniquely juvenile offenses," these include: "running away from home," "ungovernability," "incorrigibility," being a "truant," in danger of becoming "morally depraved," or a "person (child, minor) in need of supervision." Obviously these offense categories invite substantial amounts of both parental and official discretion, and they have been extensively criticized for this reason.[8] But more to the point, the uncritical acceptance of familial authority represented by these offense categories is particularly ominous for young women.

Families have always had very different expectations and made different demands of their male and female children. From their sons, parents expect achievement, aggressiveness, and independence, but from their daughters obedience, passivity, and, implicitly, chastity.[9] It is this pattern of differential expectations which produces most of the observable variation in male and female behavior. But more to the point, the female sex role is clearly more restrictive than its male counterpart. While a substantial amount of adventurous behavior and defiance of authority is expected of young men ("boys will be boys," "sowing wild oats"), the family has always tried to control these impulses in their daughters so as to protect their "reputations."

Thus, the family has always possessed a double standard for evaluating the significance of male and female misbehavior. From sons, defiance of authority is almost normative whereas from daughters it may be seen as an extremely serious offense. And because so much of the adolescent female sex role evolved to control female sexual experimentation so as to guarantee virginity upon marriage,[10] such defiance is virtually always cast in sexual terms. terms.

Within this perspective, it becomes significant that young women have always been more likely than their male counterparts to be referred to the juvenile court for offenses which represent violations of parental authority (often called "status offenses") rather than for violations of the law. One recent national study, for example, found that 75 percent of the females in the juvenile institutions were referred for noncriminal, status offenses.[11] In fact, it may be that young women, who are only about a quarter of the juvenile court populations across the country, constitute a clear majority of those charged with these offenses.[12] Young men, on the other hand, are more likely to find their way into the juvenile justice system for criminal offenses such as burglary, larceny, and car theft.[13]

Criminologists who studied the female offender long believed that those young women referred to courts were representative of female delinquents in the larger community and generated theories of female delinquency based on the characteristics of these young women. Consequently, a substantial body of literature has accumulated on female delinquency which emphasizes the fact that young women are more likely to violate their sex roles and act out sexually while males are likely to violate the law. As Albert Cohen, a recognized expert on deliquency, put it, "The delinquent is the rogue male."[14]

A sampling of comments from authoritative and widely cited studies on the subject of female delinquency indicates the widespread nature of the assumption that young women violate their sex role rather than the law:

As compared with male delinquency (stealing, assault, robbery) female delinquency is largely sexual delinquency and running away. The juvenile male delinquent tends to hurt others, while the female delinquent tends to hurt herself.[15]

The problems of adjustment of men and women, of boys and girls, arise out of quite different circumstances and press for quite different solutions. It is time now to consider some of the differences between male and female roles which make the delinquent subculture which we have described peculiarly appropriate to problems of the male child . . . boys collect stamps, girls collect boys.[16]

The women are themselves on the whole a sorry lot. The major problem in the delinquency and criminality of our girls is their lack of control of their sexual impulses.[17]

The predominant expression of delinquency among girls in our society is promiscuous sexual behavior. The sexual behavior of young girls is of great concern to their parents, and the current status of standards and practices of premarital sexual behavior is an issue of great concern for society in general.[18]

The consistent focus on sexuality found in these characteristics of female delinquency is understandable. Students of the court recognized that while most young women in the court were charged with status offenses, these were simply buffer charges to mask a concern for sexual behavior. In an important article on the meaning of these labels, Albert Reiss commented:

The categories of "ungovernability," "loitering," "immoral or indecent conduct," "runaway," and similar designations are frequently the preferred charges, particularly if the court has a policy to avoid stigmatizing an individual with a sex offense.[19]

Reiss also observed that this pattern weighed far more heavily on young women than young men. Examining 1,500 cases of alleged sexual misbehavior heard by a metropolitan juvenile court judge, he noted that this judge

refused to treat any form of sexual behavior on the part of boys, even the most bizarre forms, as warranting more than probationary status. The judge, however, regarded girls as the "cause" of sexual deviation in boys in all cases of coition involving an adolescent couple and refused to hear the complaints of the girl and her family; the girl was regarded as a prostitute.[20]

Reiss's relatively critical perspective on the manner by which most young women found their way into the juvenile justice system is not typical of those academics who studied female delinquency. Virtually all of his counterparts accepted the courts' population as representative and condoned the judicial intervention as benign and necessary:

> While studying delinquent girls, we should keep this in mind; when you train a man you train one individual; when you train a woman, you train a family.[21]

> The literature on the subject of delinquency in girls is not more than a small fraction of that relating to crime and delinquency in the male. This is so for many reasons. In the first place, the delinquent girl is much less frequent than her male counterpart, and in the second place she is criminologically much less interesting. Her offenses take predominantly the form of sexual misbehavior; a kind to call for her care and protection rather than her punishment.[22]

> On first examination it would appear from these data that the court discriminates heavily against the female sex offender, even though the offense that brings her to the court is seldom, if ever, bizarre sex behavior characteristic of the male offender. Such an interpretation is, in our opinion, totally at variance with the facts. Training schools are more frequently needed for the promiscuous female for her own protection.[23]

> [The] sexually delinquent girl violates the caring and protective attributes of her maternal role in a way which will harm her and her offspring for the remainder of her life.[24]

Gradually the theory that female delinquency was typically a violation of parental authority and sexual norms rather than the law began to be challenged by those who were studying the extent of unreported delinquency. Utilizing questionnaires which asked school children to report on the types of frequency of delinquent activities, researchers encountered a puzzling pattern. While it was clear that males were reporting more delinquent acts than females it was also clear that young women appeared to be more delinquent in self-report samples than official statistics would indicate.[25] Another consistent and surprising finding of these studies was the type of delinquent activity that both males and females reported. In brief, girls consistently reported far more delinquent acts of a criminal nature than the researchers expected. As Martin Gold, author of one of the most complete of these studies, summarized his findings:

> Discussions of girls' delinquency have emphasized the preponderance of running away, incorrigibility, and fornication among their offenses. For this reason, these offenses have come to be regarded as "girls' offenses" and their nature has provided the foundation for thinking about the causes for girls' delinquency. However, in the

present data, running away, incorrigibility . . . and fornication account for only eight percent of girls delinquent acts, and not much less of boys, six percent.[26]

More recent research[27] has confirmed these findings and also indicated that, contrary to Alder's contention, there has been little change in the types and volume of male and female delinquency since these surveys began: "A comparison of self-report studies of delinquent behavior conducted around 1960 . . . 1964 . . . 1968 . . . and 1971, shows that the mean sex ratios across all delinquent acts and for theft and aggression items have not changed in the direction predicted by the "liberation" theories for this time period."[28]

In essence, these studies indicate that if the agents of the juvenile justice system were randomly sampling male and female delinquent activity, there would be more males than females in court populations but they would be referred for roughly the same kinds of offenses. In view of these data, it is all the more important that the bureaucratic or "rate producing" processes which result in the labeling of certain young women as delinquent be examined.

An appropriate starting point in the analysis of the official responses to male and female delinquency, and one that will begin to explain the unusual character of the courts' female population, would be to review the way in which many young women find their way into the court system: they are placed in or "referred to" the court by their own parents.

Parents and Daughters in Conflict

Exemplary of the pervasive effect of the philosophy *parens patriae* on the day-to-day operation of the modern juvenile court is the phenomenon of parental referral. In this court system, unlike its adult counterpart, there are two distinct mechanisms of entry; the first and most widely understood is apprehension and arrest by the police. A lesser-known, but in the case of female delinquency, highly significant form of entry is one wherein the parent initiates a complaint against his or her own child.

Since young women are more likely than young men to be referred to the court for status offenses such as "running away" or being "incorrigible," it would follow that they would also be more likely to be referred to the court by parents and nonlegal sources (such as school and welfare officials). Parents obviously play major rather than peripheral roles in defining a particular series of acts as constituting ungovernable or incorrigible behavior, and the structure of the juvenile court system allows parents to approach either the police or a court officer with these concerns. A parental complaint is often all that is necessary to initiate police court activity.

While national data on this are unavailable, a study of the family court system in Delaware revealed that nearly one-fourth of the girls (23 percent) were referred to that court by their parents, compared to less than one-twentieth of the young men (3.5 percent).[29] Another study of ungovernability referrals in New York State revealed that the majority of those charged with this offense were female (62 percent) and that parents brought four times as many of these complaints as did the police (59 percent compared to 16 percent).[30]

The importance of the parental role in the initiation of noncriminal complaints is significant. Because parents possess different standards of obedience for their male and female children and because there are few legal guidelines as to what constitutes a reasonable parental request, parents are able to refer young people to court for a wide variety of activities. The New York study revealed, for example, that parents would come to intake interviews angry and armed with a long list of offenses which ranged from relatively serious offenses such as running away from home and truancy to such things as "refusing to bathe regularly, having an abortion against parental wishes, sleeping all day, refusing to do household chores, being selfish and self-centered, banging a door in reaction to a parental command, wanting to get married, attempting suicide, and being an 'invertebrate' (sic) liar."[31]

It is clear, then, that the court's structure allows for considerable parental discretion in the definition of delinquent behavior. Consequently, offense categories which appear neutral on their face may, in practice, be discriminatory because parents have different standards of obedience for their male and female children. Parents, however, may not be the only ones who participate in differential evaluation of male and female misbehavior. Kratcoski's study of an urban midwestern court revealed that 24 percent of the young women but only 9 percent of the young men in the court's population had been referred for truancy. He concluded by commenting that a double standard appeared to be operating with "truancy on the part of boys perhaps being overlooked or handled through informal means by school officials while such offenses are dealt with strictly when committed by girls."[32]

At this point, it might be appropriate to suggest that the phenomenon of parental referral could account for a portion of the rise in the number of female arrests. In a world where norms which restrict female sexuality are criticized daily, young women might be increasingly likely to challenge arbitrary demands which reflect traditional values and morality.

The comments of one runaway seem indicative of what might be a growing strain between modern young women and parents who require them to conform to a restrictive sex role:

You have to learn how to lie . . . you have to be a goody goody when they want you to be good and cry when they want you to cry. When I go home, I cry a little but I am still a little defiant. I act sorry I left and they're satisfied. You learn how to be yourself but make it fakey enough so it'll pass. Because if your parents knew what you were really like, they'd lock you up. I mean, I'm really crazy.[33]

Another irony in the juvenile court's legal commitment to the enforcement of parental authority and traditional adolescent sex roles is that it may actually be fueling the dramatic rise in adolescent criminal conduct. The existence of laws which insist on the dependence of young women may actually be one cause of increases in female property and drug offenses. Young women "on the run" from homes characterized by sexual abuse and parental neglect are forced, by the very statutes designed to protect them, into the life of an escaped convict.[34] Unable to enroll in school or take a "straight" job to support themselves because they fear detection, young female runaways are forced into the streets. Here they engage in panhandling, petty theft, and occasional prostitution in order to survive.[35] Young women in conflict with their parents may actually be forced by present laws which implicitly support a restrictive female sex role into petty criminal activity.

Young Women and the Police

Most young women and virtually all young men who enter the juvenile justice system are referred to the court by the police after arrest. While many might assume that, in comparison to parental referrals, less discretion characterizes police interactions with juvenile women, this is actually an oversimplification of routine police work. Many, if not most, police arrests of juveniles are made in response to complaints filed with them rather than by apprehension at the scene of a crime,[36] and of police interactions with juveniles in the street, many do not result in arrest. One study in Philadelphia, for example, revealed that between 60 to 70 percent of the police contacts with juveniles on the street were handled informally by the officer.[37] Consequently, it is important to examine carefully police responses to female misbehavior.

Those criminologists who have considered police-female interactions always assumed that police tended to act "chivalrously" when dealing with female suspects, and that they were less likely to define situations they encountered on the streets as crimes if they involved females. Pollak, author of one of the few works on the subject of female criminality, stated the position quite clearly:

Men hate to accuse women and thus indirectly to send them to their punishment, police officers dislike to arrest them, district attorneys to prosecute them, judges and juries to find them guilty and so.[38]

Pollak's formulation has been widely accepted, as these statements from other criminologists indicate:

> Female offenders have a much better chance than male offenders of not being reported, of not being arrested and of dropping out of the judicial process, that is of remaining uncommitted.[39]

> Finally, in crime a certain degree of chivalry prevails. Some people dislike to report a woman criminal to the police and the police are more likely to release women or turn a young woman over to her parents or release to a social agency than would be true for boys or men.[40]

Few of these authors examined actual records of police-juvenile interactions to test the chivalry hypothesis. A look at empirical research in this area, however, provides a different and more complicated picture.

Police officers make independent decisions about the disposition of juvenile suspects at two separate points: (1) the decision to make an arrest and (2) the decision to refer an arrested juvenile to family court.

Studies of police behavior in the field are quite rare and many of these did not examine the effect of the sex of the suspect on the decision to make an arrest. One exception to this generalization is Monahan's study of police dispositions of juvenile offenders in Philadelphia. His work revealed that police were more likely to release a young woman than a young man they suspected of a crime, equally likely to apprehend male and females they suspected of running away, and more likely to arrest girls they suspected of sex offenses.[41] Another important dimension of police discretion was discovered by DeFleur in her study of the informal disposition of males and females suspected of drug offenses. She observed that there was a tendency to avoid arresting females as often as males if they behaved in "stereotypic ways." If female suspects cried during drug raids, claimed to have been led astray by men, or expressed concern for their children this appeared to have a direct influence on the officers' decision to not arrest the suspect. If, however, the female suspect was aggressive or hostile, DeFleur observed that they were more likely to be arrested and processed.[42]

While DeFleur was discussing both juvenile and adult arrests, her point is especially significant for juvenile women. One of the areas where female arrest rates have climbed most steeply in the last few years is in the area of drug offenses, and female juvenile arrests for these offenses climbed 5,378 percent between the years of 1960 and 1975.[43]

Clearly, at the level of the decision to arrest, studies of police behavior do not support the contention that officers ignore all female delinquent acts. Rather, they may be selectively arresting those young women who are acting out sexually or those who are behaving in nontraditional ways while ignoring those they suspect of criminal misconduct.

Police decisions after arrest also reflect a curious pattern which in some ways continues the distortion of female delinquency referrals. Several studies indicate that police tend to refer young women charged with violations of parental authority to the court and release those charged with crimes. In 1965, young women charged with status offenses were approximately one-third of those arrested but they were about 50 percent of those who were referred to juvenile courts. Only about 20 percent of the young men were referred to court for these offenses. Males were more likely to find their way to court for criminal offenses: burglary, larceny, and car theft.[44]

More recent statistics from Honolulu, Hawaii, indicate that the situation has not changed. During 1972, young women charged with noncriminal offenses were almost three times as likely as young women charged with crimes to be referred to juvenile court. Only 6.1 percent of the females arrested for the most serious adult offenses and 12.7 percent of the females arrested for less serious adult offenses were referred to court, compared to 33.7 percent of those arrested for juvenile or status offenses. The police were also a good deal more likely to refer a female than a male arrested for a juvenile offense to court (33.6 percent compared to 22.7 percent).

Less specific was Goldman's study of police dispositions of male and female delinquency arrests. Without identifying offense, he noted that males were generally less likely to be referred to court than females (35.1 percent compared to 54.2 percent). While the number of women in his study was small, Goldman concluded that his data "suggested that girls brought to the attention of the police are more liable to court referral than boys."[45]

Finally, Terry, in his study of police dispositions of male and female arrests in a large midwestern community juvenile court, noted that proportionally fewer females than males were released (84.9 percent compared to 89.7 percent), and that nearly twice as many young women than young men were referred either to a social agency or the family court.[46]

The relatively harsh police response to the predominantly noncriminal activity of young women that these studies reflect is, in some respects, the result of parental attitudes. Young men and women who are brought to the attention of the police for criminal offenses have natural advocates in their parents; but youths charged with "running away from home" or being "incorrigible" are frequently brought to the attention of the police by their parents.

Much of the police response to female delinquents, then, is a result of  police paternalism; police, like other officers of the juvenile court, tend to overlook female misbehavior of a criminal sort but are concerned, or are encouraged by a young woman's parents to be concerned, about situations which appear to endanger a young woman's "reputation."

Focusing on the breadth of police discretion—both at the level of the decision to arrest and at the disposition of arrest—suggests some fertile areas of inquiry regarding the rising female arrest rate. Self-report data consistently indicate that previous arrest and court statistics both underestimated the volume of female delinquency and overestimated its sexual character. These data, coupled with evidence that police routinely released women suspected of crimes, especially those who behaved in traditional ways, suggest one possible reason for the increasing number of young women arrested for crimes. Police could simpy be reacting to changes in the demeanor of female suspects rather than to substantive changes in their behavior. Comments of law-enforcement officers to the press certainly give evidence of a new approach to the female suspect. Saying that the criminal justice system was becoming "less tolerant" of women, one officer told a *New York Times* reporter: "They are being apprehended more frequently and not as sheltered as in the past, when we tended to overlook women."[47]

Whether or not the demeanor of women is affecting the increased arrests of women, it is clear that increasing numbers of young women are entering the juvenile justice system. Once in this system, as this chapter will show, they will be exposed to a paternalistic style of justice that characterizes not only police behavior but every step in the judicial process of the juvenile justice system.

Detention: Protection or Punishment

While it would appear logical that those charged with the most serious offenses should be more likely to be held in secure detention or jail until their hearing, this is not the case in the juvenile system. Instead, the paternalism which resulted in a higher rate of court referral for women charged with violations of parental authority and sexual morality also results in an overrepresentation of these women among those held in juvenile detention facilities and jails.

Young women were only 21.2 percent of all juvenile arrests in 1974, but they constituted 30.1 percent of those held in juvenile detention centers during the year.[48] Detailed analysis of those held in these facilities during the year of 1971 revealed that 75 percent of the young women held in detention, but only between 20 and 30 percent of the young men, were charged with noncriminal offenses.[49] Other research on the decision to detain in Denver and Memphis family courts revealed that females charged with property and violent offenses faced a substantially lower than average risk of being detained compared to males, but females referred to the court for status or "decorum" offenses (alcohol, drug, or loitering) were more likely than males to be detained.[50]

Further, once in detention, young women appear to be held longer than young men. Velimesis's study of juvenile detention in Philadelphia revealed that status offenders, especially females, were detained longer than males charged with crimes.[51] This finding was confirmed by Lerman's study of detention in New York; he found that adolescents charged with juvenile offenses were twice as likely as youth charged with crimes to be detained for more than thirty days.[52] Since young women are the majority of those charged with these offenses, it seems likely that they remain longer in detention than do their male counterparts.

This pattern, while initially puzzling, is again explained by the paternalistic ideology of the juvenile justice system. Court officers, like good parents, feel the need to "protect" their "daughters"—usually from sexual experimentation. Indeed this rationale is found even in academic papers which report the phenomenon:

> Girls picked up as runaways are held if the parents cannot be reached immediately, and if the girl is fleeing from a punishing or a sexually aggressive parent, she may need the protection the detention center offers. When it seems imperative not to return a girl to her home and a temporary foster home is not readily available the detention center is utilized because alternative facilities do not exist. The court personnel and police said some girls found the detention center environment more comfortable and less threatening than that of their own homes. Therefore, what may appear to be differential treatment of female offenders may in fact be the juvenile court's response to girls' special needs and its utilization of the limited alternatives available.[53]

This protective rationale might seem plausible until additional data are considered. First, despite the fact that young women generally pose no threat to community well-being, they are comparatively underrepresented in nonincarceratory shelters and farms. Thus, while they are about a third of those held in detention, they are only 6.8 percent of those sent to ranches, camps, and farms, 22.8 percent of those placed in half-way houses, and 28.6 percent of those in group homes.[54]

Second, the conditions in the nation's detention facilities are by no means characterized by the protective atmosphere described by proponents of the practice of detaining young women. One recent review of conditions in these facilities conducted by the American Bar Association concluded:

> We found conditions for young women equally unsuitable: the facilities had cells with only a bed and blanket and no toilet; limited or no opportunities for recreation; few changes to be in the company of other inmates; and long periods of time behind locked doors. The impressions of one detained girl describe the problem more vividly: "I thought I was going crazy for a while just being locked up all the time. . . . I was up on the upper floor because the boys were down below. And I was just locked in day and night. An the only time I saw anybody was when they brought my food up to me.[55]

In addition to the jaillike atmosphere that confronts all young people held in detention facilities across the country, young women experience an extra and significant violation of their civil rights: pelvic examinations. Elizabeth Gold reported that all young women brought before the family court in New York were given vaginal smears, even young women brought before the court for nonsexual offenses.[56] Similarly, in Philadelphia, each young woman who enters the Youth Study Center, regardless of age, must submit to an internal examination. Given the problem of venereal disease among teenagers this procedure might seem reasonable. However, it must be remembered that these examinations take place in an institutional setting and in concert with other entry rituals and, thus, are both degrading and depersonalizing.

One detention center surveyed by the National Council of Jewish Women, for example, required all young women to undergo a pelvic exam "to determine if they are pregnant" and at the same time required the children to go through a Cuprex Delouse test, "where a yellow burning substance [is] sprayed on bodies. This is done in a group."[57] The director of the Philadelphia Youth Study Center was a little more specific about the administration of the pelvic exam required of all women who entered his institution: "We do put a girl on the table in the stirrups and we do have a smear. . . . We do have a swab. You go in and get a smear." When he was questioned about whether young women refused to submit to this pelvic examination would be placed in solitary confinement ("medical lock-up"), he responded, "Yes, we may have to."[58]

At least three separate lawsuits have been filed on behalf of teenage women who did not wish to submit to these internal examinations. Their cases are illuminating. In one, a young woman was examined internally while she was in a detention center for four days awaiting trial. Said her attorney, "The doctor had reported that she was not a virgin and that she was promiscuous. She did not have venereal disease. This report was sent to (the young woman's) parochial school."[59] This same attorney reported on another thirteen-year-old youngster who had been arrested and detained after throwing a snowball at a neighbor. She refused, at intake, to submit to an internal examination and continued to resist this until, after two weeks in solitary confinement, "the matrons held her legs and the doctor made the examination."[60]

Finally, Kenneth Wooden, in his nationwide review of juvenile justice systems, commented:

> Examinations for venereal disease are carried out with outrageous frequency. Young ladies in custody have been known to undergo as many as three and four pelvic exams for the disease. At some facilities, ten- and eleven-year olds are forced to submit to "vaginals" each time they are transferred to a new facility, even though they have not been released between placement. In one town in Louisiana two detectives complained to me about the county coroner, who forcefully examined all runaways: "You know when he is working because you can hear the young girls screaming at the other end of the hall."[61]

These incidents clearly suggest that the administration of pelvic examinations, in the context of entry into detention, is, at best, of questionable medical value. But aside from being a degrading experience for the young women, and probably a violation of her right of privacy, the routine administration of pelvic exams indicates that court personnel tend to equate female delinquency with sexuality. It is their assumption that young women who come to the attention of official agencies are quite probably engaging in "promiscuous" sexual activity. Like their adult counterparts, young women are frequently labeled as "carriers" of venereal disease and at fault if they are pregnant and unwed.

Detaining young women charged as "runaways" or "persons in need of supervision" is logical because these legal categories cover the court's real interest in the young women's obedience to sexual norms and parental authority. This same concern explains why court personnel see no problem with lengthy incarceration of young women who have not been charged with crimes. While they frequently assert that the young women "have no place to go," it is actually the case that the officials demand that the young women choose between some form of court-arranged and court-approved living situation or continued incarceration. They, like a young woman's parents, feel that she must be controlled and "protected" from the temptations of the street. Only rarely does the court manifest the same concern for the protection of young men in its jurisdiction, and in any case empirical accounts of conditions in juvenile detention facilities do not suggest that they afford protection for troubled young women.

Judicial Paternalism

Criminologists consistly suggested that the juvenile court, as well as the other elements of the juvenile justice system, treated young women chivalrously, ignoring all but the most serious female misbehavior. Again, a careful review of research on the official response to young men and women referred to court reveals a more complex pattern.

By the time young women appear in court, those charged with status offenses constitute anywhere from half to three-quarters of those in the juvenile justice system[62] despite the fact that young women arrested for these offenses were, in 1975, only about a quarter of all female arrests.[63] These young women have been "referred" to juvenile court, which means that they must meet with a probation officer who will determine whether they will be "counseled and released," placed on informal supervision, or officially adjudicated in a court hearing. Obviously, these are responses of increasing severity, and one would assume that those juveniles charged with noncriminal offenses would be the most likely to have their cases handled informally.

Studies of the responses of probation officers to males and females referred to them, however, do not confirm this expectation. Yona Cohn's study of probation officers' recommendations to the judge at the Bronx Family Court, conducted in the early 1950s, revealed that while young women constituted only a sixth of the court's population, they were nearly half of those recommended for institutionalization. Put another way, she found that three times as many young women as young men were recommended for institutions.[64]

Conducted at about the same time, Robert Terry's study of a midwestern court's probation department revealed that while young men were slightly more likely than women to be referred to court (25.3 percent compared to 32.9 percent) young women were less likely than young men to be released and substantially more likely to be placed on informal supervision (42.6 percent compared to 28.6 percent).[65] Similar findings were reported by Cohen in a more recent study of the Denver County Family Court; he reported that females were less likely than males to be released by probation officers (40 percent compared to 50 percent), more likely than males to be placed on informal supervision (30 percent compared to 15 percent), and equally likely to be formally adjudicated.[66] Finally, data collected in Honolulu by the author revealed that, during 1972, young women were six times more likely than young men to appear before a juvenile-court judge on an initial referral.

While most of the these studies failed to control either on the type of offense or on the number of previous referrals, it is clear that the court officers were responding at least as severely to females, most of whom have been referred for noncriminal or status offenses, as they were to the males who were, for the most part, referred for criminal misconduct. In attempting to explain this puzzling pattern, Yona Cohn explained:

> Girls who appeared before the court usually had committed delinquent acts against their parents or against sexual taboos—acts which the probation officer generally considered products of social background and personality make-up beyond the range of effective probation treatment. Indeed, sexual delinquents were *never* recommended to probation.[67]

These studies clearly refute the notion that juvenile courts are reluctant to adjudicate females. If anything, probation officers are responding as harshly to the noncriminal conduct of females as to the criminal conduct of males. This impression is confirmed by a detailed review of the disposition of cases involving status offenders, the majority of whom (62 percent) were female, in selected New York family courts. Researchers involved in the study noted that, in general, court officials appeared to have a difficult time resisting parental demands that the court intervene in family disputes and punish their child.

Despite the fact that many of these parents appeared to be troubled individuals themselves, and their children could have been easily labeled as neglected rather than delinquent, the researchers noted that court officials were encouraged by parental rage and the existence of vague offense categories such as "incorrigible" or "person in need of supervision" to label the child as offender rather than victim. Consequently, youths charged with noncriminal offenses were, in the New York study, more likely to be referred to court than their counterparts charged with criminal misconduct:

> None of the cases alleging shoplifting, possession of a dangerous weapon, or burglary were referred to court. The charge of having a boyfriend objectionable to parents (64 percent referred to court) is treated more seriously than the charge of larceny (57 percent referred to court). Verbal abuse (100 percent referred to court) is treated more seriously than assault (73 percent referred to court). Refusal to obey (62 percent referred to court) and coming home late (59 percent referred to court) are treated more seriously than arson and illegal entry (50 percent referred to court).[68]

This pattern of severe response to the relatively minor offenses is surprising but not illogical. Children charged with crimes have natural allies in their parents at every step in the judicial process. Parents of young people charged with status offenses are, themselves, the complainants and they not only impune the moral character of their children but frequently refuse to take them home in an attempt to force the court official to retain jurisdiction. Since the determination of good moral character is pivotal in the determination of guilt or innocence in the juvenile justice system,[69] this parental orientation is significant.

While it is clear that parents play a major role in the dynamic which retains young women in the juvenile justice system, probation officers and judges are by no means reluctant partners in this process. They too participate in a differential standard of evaluating male and female misbehavior. Like good parents, they view female "acting out" as more significant than its male equivalent and as requiring more drastic intervention.

Juvenile court judges, for example, seem to participate enthusiastically, though perhaps unconsciously, in the judicial enforcement of the female role. Part of their behavior, while discriminatory, is understandable. Their legal background provides them with clear guidelines when confronting youths charged with crimes. Standards of evidence are clear, elements of the crime are laid down by statute, and the youth's civil rights are, at least to some extent, protected by law.

But in the case of a young woman or man charged with incorrigibility or ungovernability, the court is without legal guidelines. Many of these judges find themselves in a legal never-never land and, in this void, fall back on the role of benevolent but harsh parent, which is built into the juvenile justice system.

Andrews and Cohn's review of the handling of cases of ungovernability in New York concluded with the comment that judges were acting "upon personal feelings and predilections in making decisions," and gave as evidence for this claim several courtroom lectures they recorded during the course of their study:

> She thinks she's a pretty hot number; I'd be worried about leaving my kid with her in a room alone. She needs to get her mind off boys.[70]

Similar attitudes expressing concern about premature female sexuality and the proper parental response are evident throughout the comments. One judge remarked that at age fourteen some women "get some crazy ideas. They want to fool around with *men,* and that's sure as hell trouble." Another judge admonished a young woman:

> I want you to promise me to obey your mother, to have perfect school attendance and not to miss a day of school, to give up these people who are trying to lead you to do wrong, not to hang out in candy stores or tobacco shops or street corners where these people are, and to be in when your mother says. . . . I don't want to see you on the streets of this city except with your parents or with your clergyman or to get a doctor. Do you understand?[71]

As more young women enter the juvenile justice system, this unapologetic judicial paternalism is of growing significance. It may be that this judicial overreach is one reason why many young women "on the run" so assiduously avoid the court. Experiences with those agencies specifically empowered to protect them may teach young women not to turn to the police or courts for help:

> Last year Mia, a 17 year old girl who lived with her boyfriend with parental consent, was kidnapped and raped by another man. When she reported it to the police, they arrested her as a runaway and shipped her off to juvenile hall instead of going after the rapist. Wilma had a similar experience on the East Coast, when she went back for a visit. Raped and dumped by a man who gave her a ride, she made her way to the nearest police station, where she was promptly arrested. The judge seeing her past record, said he would sentence her to a state reformatory until she was 21—unless the social worker put her on a plane to California within 24 hours.[72]

Judicial paternalism also explains why juvenile women, unlike their adult counterparts, are frequently sentenced to adolescent prisons or "training schools." In 1974, young women accounted for over 20 percent of those held in training schools with nearly 6,000 young women incarcerated at any time.[73] Looking at these data differently, while young women comprise only about 40 percent of all arrests of women, they constitute about 60 percent of all women in prison.[74]

That court judges appear as likely to sentence young women as young men who come before them to training school was first documented by Robert Terry, who, in examining court dispositions, noted that 76.7 percent of the females who appeared before the judge but only 59.7 percent of the males were institutionalized, even though females tended to have less extensive prior records of delinquent behavior.[75]

This harsh pattern of judicial response is even more puzzling when it is remembered that the majority of women who appear before juvenile court judges have not been charged with crimes but rather status offenses. But, in fact, it is precisely because these young women have been charged with these offenses that they are sentenced to institutions. They have been imprisoned, according to court officials, "for their own protection," which translates into "protection" from the "temptation" of their own sexuality. The comments of a judge in sentencing a young woman to a training school in New Jersey illustrate this quite clearly: "The Court does not want to put you in another situation where you might get pregnant or where you would fail. It is my feeling that you might be better at Long Lane."[76] Another judge added that because most of the women he committed were status offenders, he kept them the maximum term. As he saw it, "I figure if a girl is about to get pregnant we'll keep her until she's sixteen,"[77] after which time he felt that welfare would pick up the case.

As a consequence of this judicial paternalism, those "convicted" of status offenses constitute roughly half of those young women doing time in the nation's training schools, compared to less than one-quarter of the men.[78] Further, women appear to be overrepresented in these closed, correctional institutions compared to less incarceratory options. The National Assessment of Juvenile Corrections Project found a significantly lower percentage of young women in day-care programs than young men—8 percent compared to 16 percent—and few women in group homes in the community.[79]

Taken together, these data on the characteristics of young women in the nation's juvenile prison population provide impressive evidence that the court routinely imprisons young women who have not committed criminal offenses and who pose no threat to community well-being. Despite this, juvenile justice officials appear reluctant to change their orientation toward juvenile female offenders. Comments made by Hunter Hurst, Director of the Juveniel Justice Division of the National Council of Juvenile Court Judges in June of 1975, are very revealing in this regard. He says that the reason society reacts so strongly against female status offenses is that these offenses offend our values, particularly where sexual behavior is involved. It is his feeling that the courts protect the rights of the young women more than any other social agency would, so they are, in a sense, making the best of a bad situation.[80] Mr. Hurst's enthusiasm about the quality of the court's commitment to the rights of women should be tempered by the legal controversy presently surrounding the issue of the rights of minors charged with juvenile status offenses. He should also be somewhat troubled by an argument that lumps the juvenile justice system with vigilante groups in the enforcement of community prejudices against women. The fact that these sexist community norms exist is no justification for involving agencies of the law in their enforcement, any more than community prejudices would justify judicial racism.

Conclusions

This chapter has reviewed research on the treatment of young women by agents of the juvenile justice system. It has been suggested that this review is useful in two distinct ways. First, it supplies information about a critical and neglected area in criminological research—the treatment of women having long been ignored by most criminologists. Second, it provides a vital perspective on the dramatic increase in the number of juvenile females arrested in recent years.

With regard to the rising female crime rate, this chapter has reviewed evidence which suggests that police until recently ignored much of the criminal misconduct of young women, particularly if the young women behaved in a traditionally female manner at the point of apprehension. Consquently, changes in this routine police behavior, perhaps triggered by changes in the demeanor on the part of female suspects, may be artificially inflating the number of arrests of juvenile women without a comparable shift in behavior on the part of young women.

This chapter has also suggested, though with less empirical support, that the rising number of female arrests could be fueled, in part, by archaic laws which insist on juvenile dependence and prohibit young people from living away from their parents. The existence of the juvenile court may itself be forcing young women into petty criminal activity so as to avoid the detection which would inevitably accompany attempts to live a normal teenage life.

Perhaps more importantly, this chapter has reviewed the judicial responses to female misbehavior. While police may be arresting more young women for criminal conduct, these women tend not to remain in the system unless this misbehavior is defined either by parents or court officials as part of a larger pattern of defiance to parental authority. Women who violate an adolescent sex role which requires obedience to this authority are seen by court officials as more serious offenders than their counterparts who have committed crimes. Consequently, while some young women are accorded chivalrous treatment within the juvenile justice system, every piece of evidence seems to indicate that it is those young women charged with crimes who are the beneficiaries of this, the positive side of paternalism. Routine police and court procedures seem to select out young women whose offenses threaten parental authority and young men whose offenses cannot be explained away as "boys will be boys." The court does this because both its history and its structure encourage extralegal paternalism rather than law enforcement.

The evidence is clear that young women who present the possibility of becoming sexual delinquents receive harsher treatment than their sisters suspected of crimes at the level of referral to court, pretrial detention, and incarceration. It is also apparent that those females brought before the court for violation of parental authority and sexual norms are more harshly censured than the few males who have been charged with these offenses.

This confusing pattern acquires meaning only when placed within the context of the court's role in the enforcement of parental authority and adolescent morality. If the court is committed to traditional sex roles which require that adolescent females be protected from sexual experimentation, then it has little choice but to view female "delinquency" as indicative of greater moral lassitude, and in need of more drastic treatment, than male delinquency.

This process of differential perception constitutes sexual discrimination in two separate ways. First, the court is clearly applying the law in an unequal manner. But more importantly the court is punishing the noncriminal behavior of females as harshly as the criminal behavior of males. Incarceration, glamorized with such phrases as "for her own protection," is incarceration nonetheless. Most of the women doing time in American training schools have not violated any major law or committed any crime. They are there because they cannot live with their parents and the court will not allow them to be free.

But the question then arises: "If the court does not retain jurisdiction over status offenders, who will help these children?" The assumption behind this question is that the court acts only because other agencies are willing to intervene. This reasoning, according to Judge David Bazelon of the U.S. District Court of Appeals, is incorrect. Bazelon suggests that precisely because the court retains jurisdiction it is unlikely that others will become involved, noting that schools and public agencies refer their problem cases to the juvenile court because the court has jurisdiction, because the court exercises its jurisdiction, and because the court holds out promises that it can provide solutions.[81]

Judge Bazelon's formulation seems persuasive. There is a pressing need for runaway shelters, halfway houses, and other community resources to deal with problems in a nonjudicial context. Parents and children who are in conflict with each other, or children who are in conflict with society during adolescence, should have resources available to them for their *voluntary* use. Shelters of this sort are already in existence in many parts of the country. Their success points to nonjudicial alternatives to a community problem, as well as a way to curb certain forms of adolescent female criminality which are more likely products of street living than women's liberation.

In conclusion, this review of the treatment of women who come into the juvenile justice system clearly indicates that a retention of the status quo is not desirable. At all levels in this system, officials seem unable to restrain themselves from becoming involved in family matters and because of this often find themselves enforcing a double standard of justice. Routine procedures in the juvenile justice system encourage the evaluation of male and female misbehavior in different ways, and as a consequence they are systematically violative of the civil rights of women.

Notes

1. Federal Bureau of Investigation, *Uniform Crime Reports* (Washington, D.C.: U.S. Department of Justice, 1976), 183.

2. A number of recent articles and books have appeared in response to the dramatic increases in female arrests rates. Some of these have quite clearly linked this increase to the Women's Liberation Movement. The most notable proponent of this position is Freda Adler in her book, *Sisters in Crime: The Rise of the New Female Criminal* (New York: McGraw Hill, 1975). Others have made similar observations, however, including P.K. Wilson, "Is Crime a Man's World?" *Journal of Criminal Justice* 3 (1975), 131-39, and George Noblit and Janie Burcart, "Women and Crime: 1960-1970," *Social Science Quarterly* 56 (1976), 650-57.

3. John Kitsuse and Aaron Cicourel, "A Note on the Use of Official Statistics," *Social Problems* 11 (1963), 131-39.

4. Interest in the role of labeling institutions in the production of rates of deviant behavior was spurred by a number of influential books and articles on this process. Among the most widely cited is Howard Becker's *The Outsiders* (New York: Free Press, 1962), and Donald S. Black, "Production of Crime Rates," *American Sociological Review* (1970) 733-47. Articles and books with focus on the importance of these processes in the production of rates of juvenile delinquency include Aaron Cicourel, *The Social Organization of Juvenile Justice* (New York: John Wiley, 1968), and Robert M. Emerson, *Judging Delinquents* (Chicago: Aldine Press, 1969).

5. Kitsuse and Cicourel, 135.

6. A number of insightful critiques of the structure of the juvenile justice system are available; three excellent reviews of the major issues can be found in Nicholas Kittrie, *The Right to Be Different* (Baltimore: John

Hopkins Press, 1971); Orman Ketcham, "The Unfulfilled Promise of the American Juvenile Court," *Justice for the Child*, ed. Margaret Rosenheim (New York: The Free Press, 1962), and F.A. Allen, *The Borderland of Criminal Justice* (Chicago: The University of Chicago Press, 1964).

7. Anthony Platt, *The Child Savers: The Invention of Delinquency* (Chicago: University of Chicago Press, 1969), 199.

8. See Nora Klapmuts, "Children's Rights: The Legal Rights of Minors in Conflict with Law or Social Custom," *Crime and Delinquency Literature* 9 (1972), 449-476; Kathryn W. Burkhart, *The Child and the Law: Helping the Status Offender* (New York: Public Affairs Pamphlet, 1975); Milton G. Rector, "Jurisdiction over Status Offenses Should be Removed from the Juvenile Court" (Hackensack, New Jersey: National Council on Crime and Delinquency, 1974); "The Dilemma of the 'Uniquely Juvenile Offender,' " *William and Mary Law Review* 14:2 (1972), 386-408.

9. See Eleanor Maccoby, ed., *The Development of Sex Differences* (Stanford: Stanford University Press, 1966), and Lenore J. Wietzman, "Sex Role Socialization," *Women: A Feminist Perspective* (Palo Alto: Mayfield, 1975).

10. The existence of the sexual double standard in patriarchial societies meant that while men were permitted and encouraged to experiment sexually prior to marriage, they demanded that their wives be virgins. Parents, in response to this reality, sought to guarantee the marriageability of their daughters by developing elaborate mechanisms of control over their behavior. This, it was hoped, would preserve if not their virginity then at least their virginal reputation. A daughter who could not be married off was of no value whatsoever in these societies.

11. Rosemary Sarri and Robert Vinter, "Juvenile Justice and Injustice," *Resolution* 1 (1975), 47.

12. Recent statistics cited by R.H. Andrews and A.H. Cohn, "Ungovernability: The Unjustifiable Jurisdiction," *Yale Law Journal* 83 (1974), 1383-1409, for the New York area indicate that young women are 62 percent of those charged with status or ungovernable offenses. In Hawaii, during 1976, young women were 55 percent of those charged with status offenses.

13. The most recent national data on this are provided in Children's Bureau, Department of Health, Education and Welfare, *Statistics on Public Institutions for Delinquent Children, 1965,* (Washington, D.C.: U.S. Government Printing Office, 1967). However, recent offense data from various jurisdictions indicate that the pattern persists.

14. Albert K. Cohen, *Delinquent Boys* (New York: The Free Press, 1955), 140.

15. Clyde B. Vedder and Dora B. Somerville, *The Delinquent Girl* (Springfield, Illinois: Charles B. Thomas, 1970), 89.

16. Cohen, 139-42.

17. Sheldon Glueck and Eleanor Glueck, *Five Hundred Delinquent Women* (New York: Knopf, 1934).

18. Herbert H. Herskowitz, "A Psychodynamic View of Sexual Promiscuity," *Family Dynamics and Female Sexual Delinquency,* eds. Otto Pollak and Alfred S. Friedman (Palo Alto: Science and Behavior Books, 1969), 89.

19. Albert J. Reiss, "Sex Offenses: The Marginal Status of the Adolescent," *Law and Contemporary Problems* 25 (1960), 309.

20. Ibid., p. 316.

21. Vedder and Somerville, viii.

22. John Cowie, Valarie Cowie and Eliot Slater, *Delinquency in Girls* (Chicago: Aldine Press, 1968), 1.

23. J.D. Acheson and D.C. Williams, "A Study of Juvenile Sex Offenders," *American Journal of Psychiatry* 3 (1954), 370. Copyright 1954, the American Psychiatric Association. Reprinted by permission.

24. P. Bloss, *On Adolescence: A Psycho-Analytic Interpretation* (New York: The Free Press, 1962).

25. Among the most significant of these self-report studies were the following: J. Short and I. Nye, "Extent of Unrecorded Juvenile Delinquency," *Journal of Criminal Law, Criminology and Police Science* 49 (1958), 296-302: John P. Clark and Edward Haurek, "Age and Sex Roles of Adolescents and their Involvements in Misconduct: A Reappraisal," *Sociology and Social Research* 50 (1966), 496-508: Nancy Wise, "Juvenile Delinquency Among Middle-Class Girls," *Middle-Class Juvenile Delinquency,* ed. Edmund Vaz (New York: Harper and Row, 1967).

26. Martin Gold, *Delinquent Behavior in an American City* (Belmont, California: Wadsworth, 1970).

27. Michael J. Hindelang, "Age and Sex and the Versatility of Delinquent Involvements," *Social Problems* 18 (1971), 522-35; Martin Gold and David J. Reimer, "Changing Patterns of Delinquent Behavior Among Americans 13 through 16 Years Old: 1967-1972," *Crime and Delinquency Literature* 7 (December 1975), 483-517.

28. Joseph G. Weis, "Liberation and Crime: The Invention of the New Female Criminal," *Crime and Social Justice* 6 (Fall-Winter 1976), 24.

29. Susan K. Datesman and Frank R. Scarpetti, "Female Delinquency and Broken Homes: A Re-Assessment," *Criminology* 13 (1975), 40.

30. Andrews and Cohn, 1385.

31. Ibid., 1383.

32. P.C. Kratcoski, "Differential Treatment of Boys and Girls by the Juvenile Justice System," *Child Welfare* 53 (1974), 19.

33. David Riley, "Runaways: And Then There Were Thousands," *Delinquency Prevention Report* (Washington, D.C.: U.S. Department of Health, Education and Welfare, 1972), 3.

34. Celest MacLeod, "Street Girls of the 70s," *The Nation* (April 20, 1974), 486.

35. Ibid., 487.

36. Robert M. Terry, "Discrimination in the Handling of Juvenile Offenders by Social Control Agencies," *Becoming Delinquent,* eds. Peter G. Garabedian and Donald C. Gibbons (Chicago: Aldine, 1970), 84.

37. Thomas P. Monahan, "Police Dispositions of Juvenile Offenders," *Phylon* 31 (1970), 134.

38. Otto Pollak, *The Criminality of Women* (Philadelphia: University of Pennsylvania Press, 1950), 151.

39. Walter C. Reckless, *The Crime Problem* (New York: Appleton-Century-Crofts, 1961).

40. Ruth S. Cavan, *Criminology* (New York: Crowell, 1962). The development and significance of the "chivalry proposition" is well documented in Etta A. Anderson, "The Chivalrous Treatment of the Female Offender in the Arms of the Criminal Justice System: A Review of the Literature," *Social Problems* 23 (1976), 349-57.

41. Monahan, 139.

42. Lois B. DeFleur, "Biasing Influences on Drug Arrest Records: Implications for Deviance Research," *American Sociological Review* 40 (February 1975), 101.

43. Federal Bureau of Investigation, 183.

44. U.S. Department of Health, Education and Welfare, *Delinquency Prevention Report.*

45. Nathan Goldman, "The Differential Selection of Juvenile Offenders for Court Appearances," *Crimes and the Legal Process*, ed. William J. Chambliss (New York: McGraw Hill, 1969), 285.

46. Terry, 85.

47. Steven Roberts, "Crime Rate of Women Up Sharply Over Men's," *New York Times,* June 13, 1971, 72.

48. Law Enforcement Assistance Administration, U.S. Department of Justice, *Children in Custody: Advance Report on the Juvenile Detention and Correctional Facility Census of 1974* (Washington, D.C., Government Printing Office, 1977), 34.

49. Law Enforcement Assistance Administration, U.S. Department of Justice, *Children in Custody: A Report on Juvenile Detention Facility Census, 1971* (Washington, D.C.: Government Printing Office, 1973), 9.

50. Lawrence E. Cohen and James E. Kluegal, "The Detention Decision: A Study of the Impact of Social Characteristics and Legal Factors in Two Juvenile Courts," paper presented at the 1977 Meetings of the American Sociological Association.

51. Margery Velimesis, *Report on Survey of 41 Pennsylvania County Courts and Correctional Services for Women and Girl Offenders* (Philadelphia: Pennsylvania Division of the AAUW, 1969).

52. Paul Lerman, "Child Convicts," *Transaction* 8 (July 1971), 35-44.

53. Kratcoski, 20.

54. Rosemary Sarri, "Juvenile Law: How It Penalizes Females," in *The Female Offender,* ed. Laura Crites (Lexington, Mass.: Lexington Books, D.C. Heath, 1966), 67-87.

55. Female Offender Resource Center, *Little Sisters and the Law* (Washington, D.C.: American Bar Association, 1977), 11.

56. Sarah Gold, "Equal Protection for Juvenile Girls in Need of Supervision in New York State," *New York Law Forum,* 17 (1971), 593.

57. Edward Wakin, *Children without Justice: A Report by the National Council of Jewish Women* (New York: National Council of Jewish Women, 1975), 45.

58. Loretta Schwartz, "The Kids Nobody Wants," paper distributed by the Philadelphia Program for Women and Girl Offenders.

59. Lois G. Forer, *No One Will Listen* (New York: John Day Co., 1970), 125.

60. Ibid., 126.

61. Kenneth Wooden, *Weeping in the Playtime of Others* (New York: McGraw Hill, 1976), 121.

62. Recent statistics reported by Kratcoski (p. 18) in his study of a midwestern juvenile court indicated that 52 percent of the females in his sample but only 28 percent of the males were referred to court for "status" offense. In Honolulu, during 1976, 56 percent of the females were referred to court for status offenses.

63. Federal Bureau of Investigation, 183.

64. Yona Cohn, "Criteria for the Probation Officer's Recommendation to the Juvenile Court," in *Becoming Delinquent,* 193.

65. Terry, 85.

66. Lawrence E. Cohen, "Juvenile Dispositions: Social and Legal Factors Related to the Processing of Denver Delinquency Cases" (Washington, D.C.: U.S. Department of Justice, 1975), 21.

67. Cohn, 199.

68. Andrews and Cohn, 1397.

69. Robert Emerson noted that, in juvenile court proceedings, the determination of moral character is pivotal to the disposition of cases since a young person who is "fully discredited" is far more easily committed to a training school.

70. Andrews and Cohn, 1404.

71. Ibid.

72. MacLeod, 487.

73. Law Enforcement Assistance Administration, 1977, 36.

74. These figures were compiled by comparing statistics on juvenile and adult female offenders contained in the U.S. Department of Justice, *Sourcebook on Criminal Justice Statistics, 1973* (Washington, D.C.: U.S. Government Printing Office, 1973).

75. Terry, 85.

76. Kristine Rogers, "For her own protection . . . ": Conditions of Incarceration for Female Juvenile Offenders in the State of Connecticut," *Law and Society Review* (Winter 1972), 229.

77. Ibid., 227.

78. Sarri, 1976, 11.

79. Female Offender Resource Center, 33.

80. Hunter Hurst, "Juvenile Status Offenders," a speech given to the New Mexico Council on Crime and Delinquency, June 20, 1975.

81. David Bazelon, "Beyond Control of the Juvenile Court," *Juvenile Court Journal* 21 (1970), 44.

7 Chivalry Reexamined: Women and the Criminal Justice System

Meda Chesney-Lind

There has been great interest in the rise of the new female criminal. Most of the discussion of this phenomenon, appropriately or not, has focused on the dramatic increases in the number of adult women arrested for criminal misconduct.[1] Comparatively less interest is expressed by the public at large over the manner in which adult women come to the attention of the agents of law enforcement and what happens to them once they enter the criminal justice system.

The question of the treatment of adult women who are arrested, tried, and sentenced has been ignored primarily because of the small number of women involved in these processes. Whether or not this was ever a valid reason for neglecting this aspect of the official response to criminality, it becomes increasingly less convincing as larger numbers of women are swept into the criminal justice system.

Those few who did speculate on the treatment of women suggested, often with little support, that adult women were treated "chivalrously" by agents of the criminal justice system. This hypothesis was perhaps best articulated by Otto Pollak:

> Men hate to accuse women and thus, indirectly, to send them to their punishment, police officers dislike to arrest them, district attorneys to prosecute them, judges and juries to find them guilty and so on.[2]

Pollak's formulation, as the chapter on the treatment of juvenile women demonstrated, is still widely accepted.[3] While it certainly does not describe the criminal justice system's response to young women, a quick glance at the statistics on adult women at each state in the criminal justice system appears to support the chivalry interpretation.

Adult women comprised about 14.9 percent of those arrested in 1975.[4] During roughly the same period, however, they were only 5.9 percent of those held in the nation's jails,[5] 11 percent of those convicted,[6] and only 3.4 percent of those incarcerated in state and federal prisons.[7]

There are problems with this analysis, however, as this chapter will show. The most obvious shortcoming is that women tend to be arrested for different, and less violent, sorts of offenses than males.[8] Recently, however, female arrest statistics seem to indicate some movement away from this pattern. First, in sheer numbers, more women are being arrested, and the rate of increase for female arrests far outstrips the male figure. Between 1960 and 1975, for example, male arrests were up 22.8 percent but female arrests were up 101.7 percent. Secondly, these same FBI statistics appear to report startling increases in nontraditional female misbehavior. For example, between 1960 and 1975, the number of women arrested for murder was up 105.7 percent, forcible rape up 633.3 percent, and robbery up 380.5 percent.[9]

The media has made much of these changes, but more careful analysis reveals that they are not all that startling. Rita Simon, for example, has calculated that the percent of females arrested for violent crime as a percentage of all female arrests has remained virtually unchanged for the past twenty years.[10]

How are Simon's findings possible? The answer is that most of the dramatic percentage increases in female misbehavior, and particularly those in nontraditional areas, were based on extremely small base numbers. The number of women arrested for robbery, for example, went up from 1,439 in 1960 to 6,915 in 1975, but these 7,000 women constitute less than 1 percent of the total number of women arrested during that year.[11] Percentage increases of this sort, then, present a rather incomplete picture of the meaning of changes in female arrest patterns.

Another approach might be to look at increases in particular offense categories as a percentage of the total increase in the number of female arrests. Looking at the figures this way, it can be seen that virtually all of the increase in females arrested for serious crime has been the product of a dramatic increase in the number of women arrested for larceny theft. This one offense category accounts for fully 40 percent of the increase in female arrests. Arrests for drug offenses accounted for another 10 percent, and fraud, 6.5 percent. By contrast, robbery arrests (which increased by nearly 400 percent) accounted for only 1.4 percent of the increase in the total number of female arrests.

Finally, changes in arrest rates must be scrutinized for evidence that a change might be occurring in either victim or police behavior. Essentially, official arrest rates are products of an interaction first between the victim (if any) and the offender, and second between an officer of the law and the suspect.[12] As the product of these interactions, rates are colored by many factors, including victim and police attitudes, and, as this chapter will show, minor changes in either victim or police practices could result in dramatic changes in official rates of female criminality.

This chapter will examine studies which focus on the unofficial and official reactions to the female labeled as criminal. The extent to which changes in the number of women arrested might be explained by shifts in victim and police behavior will be explored. But more importantly, the chapter will review the facts on the treatment of women who enter the criminal justice system to determine whether, throughout this process, they are the beneficiaries of chivalry.

Women and Their Victims

An extremely important factor to consider in the discussion of male and female entry into the criminal justice system is the possible bias introduced at the level of victim. Are victims less likely to report offenders to the police if they are female? This thought seems to be supported by at least one laboratory study which could be seen as replicating a criminal encounter.[13] It is unclear, however, whether these findings could be extended to an authentic crime situation. Unfortunately, though the effects of ethnicity on the victim's decision to refer his or her complaint to the police have been examined, no such study has been conducted on the effect of sex of this decision.[14]

There have, however, been several studies of the decision-making behavior of corporate victims and/or their private security forces. These indicate not only that a substantial amount of prearrest screening takes place, but also that this behavior could have a substantial impact on the numbers of males and females formally placed under arrest for particular offenses.

First, it is clear the official statistics substantially underestimate the volume of larcenous behavior. Mary Cameron in her early study of shoplifting in Chicago found, for example, that only one department store in her study arrested fully half as many women per year as were officially charged with all types of larceny in the entire city of Chicago.[15] This pattern was explained by the fact that department stores generally wished to prosecute "as few arrested persons as possible."[16] As a consequence, store officials referred only about 12 percent of those they arrested for shoplifing to the police for prosecution. Similar figures on the reluctance of corporate victims to refer offenders to the police are reported in other studies of shoplifting.[17]

In the determination of which offenders to refer to the police, Cameron found that informal practices tended to favor women suspected of shoplifting over their male counterparts. Store detectives, for example, referred only 10 percent of the women they apprehended but 35 percent of the males to the police for prosecution.

Cameron also found that the bias of store detectives favored white over nonwhite women. Black women comprised 4.4 percent of all women arrested in the store, but 17.8 percent of all women officially charged. Stating these percentages differently, only 8.8 percent of the white women apprehended for shoplifting, but 42 percent of the black women, were officially charged with shoplifting. Further, this pattern was not the product of difference in the value of items stolen or prior criminal record of the offender.[18]

Variations were found, however, in the magnitude and style of male and female shoplifting which could, in turn, have had a significant effect on the number of women caught for the offense and also on the store official's response to that behavior. Women, Cameron observed, tended to steal more items than men, to steal items from several stores, but to steal items of lesser value.

Store detectives explained this pattern by saying that people tended to "steal the same way they buy."[19] Men came to the store with one thing in mind. They would see it, take it, and leave the store. Women, on the other hand, would shop around. Since the chance of being arrested obviously increases with each item stolen, Cameron felt that store figures might actually have underestimated the number of male shoplifters.

Though women stole more items, the median value of adult male theft was significantly higher than that of the females ($23.36 compared to $16.40).[20] This, coupled with the fact that more males than females were defined by store detectives as "commercial shoplifters" (people who stole merchandise for possible resale), seemed to Cameron to affect the decision to prosecute these particular shoplifters.

The importance of these two variables has been established by later studies of shoplifting. These clearly indicate that stores tend to select out those shoplifters who steal larger amounts and those whom store detectives suspect were stealing items for resale. Robin's study of shoplifting in Philadelphia, for example, revealed that the stores in his study prosecuted only about 30 percent of those who stole items worth less than $30 but nearly 75 percent of those who stole items worth more than that amount.[21]

Cameron's study of shoplifting was one of the first to examine the discretion in the victim's response to criminal activity. Additionally, she was one of the first to explore official responses to females suspected of criminal misconduct (her research indicated that fully 80 percent of the women, and 40 percent of the men arrested for petty larceny, were shoplifters).[22]

Hindelang's more recent study of files in the data bank of a private security corporation adds another dimension to Cameron's findings. Analyzing data from the years 1963, 1965, and 1968, Hindelang was able to chart trends in corporate response to male and female shoplifting. He found that in 1963, even after controlling for the effect of value of the theft on the referral decision, women enjoyed a significant advantage compared to men; only 28 percent of the women accused of "large thefts" were referred to police compared to 44 percent of the males.[23] By 1968, however, the effect of sex on the decision-making had disappeared and the referral decision was clearly related to the value of the object stolen, what was stolen, and the method of theft.[24]

Another recent study, conducted in California, confirmed Hindelang's findings. Cohen and Stark found that male shoplifters were slightly more likely to be referred to the police (67 percent compared to 52 percent), but this was explained by the fact that males tended to be unemployed and were more likely to steal expensive goods.[25]

Additional evidence of diminishing effect of sex on the victim's decision to report deviance is found in Steffensmeier and Terry's study of public reactions to shoplifters. Basically, the researchers discovered that while the dress of the offender (hippie versus straight) had an effect on the willingness of observers to report incidents of shoplifting, sex had no such impact. Customers in their study were equally willing to report male and female shoplifters.[26]

It is clear that these studies do not necessarily contradict Cameron's findings. What they do suggest are possible shifts in both female behavior and the official response to female misbehavior. Particularly significant is the fact that, in Hindelang's study, five years erased a differential not necessarily in female behavior but in the official response to that behavior.

Closely related to shoplifting and of equal interest to the study of informal reactions to male and female criminality is Gerald Robin's work on employee theft.[27] Depending upon the status of the employee, Robin found that the type of theft would vary; lower-status employees would steal merchandise or small amounts of money whereas executives would embezzle funds. He also discovered that despite the fact that virtually all employees engaging in these sorts of activities confessed once apprehended, only 17 percent of these violators were referred to the police for prosecution.

While Robin noted wide variation among companies with reference to the willingness to involve the police in their affairs, he did not discover any pattern of "chivalry" toward female employees. Women were 18 percent of those apprehended by the businesses and 17 percent of those prosecuted. However, while in general the size of the theft increased the likelihood of prosecution for males, this was not so for females. Women who stole more than $100 were less likely than males who committed the same offense to be prosecuted (47 percent compared to 60 percent).[28] In essence, this could be seen as the product of another pattern that Robin located. He discovered that the amount of theft increased with the social position of the employee. Thus, what could be happening is that high-status female thieves were enjoying some benefits of chivalry while their lower-status counterparts were being censured as harshly as male thieves.

In all, these studies indicate that victims exercise a significant amount of discretion in the decision to refer offenders to the police. This discretion results in large numbers of both males and females who may be guilty of property offenses being diverted from the criminal justice system. Further, these studies indicate that in the past women may have enjoyed some extra benefits in this filtering process. However, recent research on the subject of shoplifting, in particular, seems to indicate that this pattern is being eroded. If this is the case, the large increase in the number of women arrested for larceny could be explained at least partially as a product of an erosion of chivalry rather than as a dramatic upswing in female criminality. If this pattern is extended to other areas of criminal misconduct as well, the possibility exists that while female criminal behavior may have changed very little as a result of the women's movement, the response of the victim or, as the next section will discuss, the response of the police officer, might well have been affected.

Women and the Police

Studies of police behavior in arrest situations have most often focused on issues of brutality[29] or discretion in the decision to take a suspect into custody.[30] Unfortunately, nearly all neglect to mention the effect of the suspected offender's sex on this crucial interaction. There is, however, some evidence that police officers' "discretionary enforcement," employed in an attempt to meet the public's demand for law and order with limited enforcement resources, could substantially affect the number of women arrested for criminal misconduct.

Studies of discretionary enforcement reveal, for example, that officers in the field routinely ignore or release without arrest large numbers of individuals suspected of "minor" or victimless crimes.[31] It is also clear, however, that many of these offenses are also those for which large numbers of women are arrested (for example, shoplifting, drunkenness, prostitution, and drug use). Clearly, an examination of the effect of the sex of the suspect on the officer's decision to make arrests for these types of offenses is important.

Leaving aside, for the moment, the substantial body of literature on the complex issue of prostitution, studies of police enforcement of drug laws provide the most interesting perspectives on the effect of sex on the arrest decision. Recently arrests of women for this offense have been climbing rapidly. In 1960, for example, drug offenses accounted for less than 1 percent of all female arrests. By 1975, women arrested for drug offenses accounted for 5.9 percent of all arrests—an increase of over 1,000 percent.[32]

Fortunately, two excellent studies, one on self-reported drug use[33] and another on bias in police drug records,[34] allow an examination of how factors other than the commission of an illegal act might result in an underestimation of female criminality. They also indicate that minor changes in police practice might result in large increases in the number of women arrested for drug violations.

Johnson and his associates combined questionnaire data on the extent of marijuana usage with arrest statistics in three metropolitan areas to estimate arrest probabilities. They discovered that differences in male and female drug use were exaggerated by official statistics and concluded this pattern was explained almost entirely by the fact that males are far more likely than females to be arrested.[35]

Their data on the circumstances of arrest suggest that males tended to use marijuana in settings that made them more vulnerable to arrest. Since men were using marijuana "on the streets," they were more likely than women to be arrested by general patrolmen, more often arrested in vehicles, and more often arrested alone.[36]

Women were more likely to be arrested as a result of raids on private residences. Since use of marijuana in private locations is, generally speaking, less visible than public use or transport, and since police raids into private domiciles are more strictly regulated by statute, fewer women are arrested. In essence, the restrictions on female mobility, as well as social norms which encourage women to rely on men to procure marijuana for them,[37] cushion women from arrest.

Another source of bias in police decisions to arrest drug offenders, and one which may also affect the number of women arrested, was discovered by Lois DeFleur. In her study of police drug enforcement in Chicago, DeFleur noted the clear affect of political pressure on the dramatic increase in the numbers of white youths arrested for possession of marijuana. But more to the point, DeFleur's research revealed that police were also sensitive to the arrestees' demeanor during the raid. When suspects were uncooperative, she noted that "the police were almost certain to be harsh in their written reports and to press all possible charges against the participant."[38]

This last point was especially important in the case of female suspects. She noted that there was a tendency not to arrest females as often as males if they behaved in expected, stereotypic ways. Women who "cried, claimed to have been led astray by men or expressed concern about the fate of their children" were often released, whereas young women who were "aggressive and hostile" were arrested and processed.[39] DeFleur also noted that, according to the police, young women were increasingly likely to behave in nonstereotypic ways. Clearly, this might go a long way toward explaining the dramatic increases in the number of women arrested for drug offenses.

Both of these studies indicate that minor changes in female mobility or demeanor (rather than drug use *per se*) could result in dramatic increases in the number of women arrested for drug offenses. But, perhaps more importantly, this research indicates that the police might be involved in punishing women who violate their sex-role expectations rather than those who violate the law. In essence, women who conform to the female role which requires them to eschew responsibility and plead incompetence escape punishment despite their criminal behavior. These women, it appears, are the beneficiaries of chivalry. Women who refuse to play this role, on the other hand, are arrested.

The police role in the enforcement of female sex-role expectations is, however, not limited to the drug raid. Indeed, it is perhaps clearest when viewing police interaction with women they define as prostitutes. Much of their behavior in this area is startling and significant. In general, an overview of police interactions with women reveals that, contrary to the chivalry hyothesis, police officers routinely violate the civil rights of women they suspect of prostitution. As this section will show, harassment is a highly significant reminder to women that paternalism accrues only to women who conform to a sex role which requires their obedience to men, their passivity, and their acceptance of their status as the sexual property of only one man. Should they step outside of this boundary, as have women who attempt to survive economically by selling their sexual favors,[40] chivalry is replaced by harsh exploitation and harassment.

Attempts to discourage the practice of prostitution through the use of criminal law are as timeless as the activity itself. Clearly, though, agents of law enforcement have not elected to arrest both parties engaged in the activity. Indeed, whenever jurisdictions have attempted to arrest patrons public outcry has been sufficient to stop the practice.[41] So, despite the fact that every year over 100,000 women are arrested for prostitution (either explicitly or implicitly), the comparable male figure is only one-tenth this amount.[42] Yet, if Kinsey's data are correct, 70 percent of all men have been to a prostitute at least once.[43]

The law, then, punishes only the women engaged in prostitution; this legal hypocrisy is possible because women who engage in the activity have so little power. The situation is made all the more disturbing by the fact that legal proscriptions against prostitution have had no appreciable effect in discouraging the activity. Kinsey, again, estimated the volume of prostitution in America to be 1,659,000 contacts per year per million population.[44] Katchadourian and Lunde noted that this meant that in an average American community of 500,000 there would be 16,000 acts of prostitution per week.[45]

Given these data on the volume of prostitution in America it becomes clear that police cannot hope to effectively enforce laws against the practice. Police forces, as a consequence of their assignment to enforce an essentially unenforceable law, have devised certain modes of relating to women they define as prostitutes. These routine procedures are designed to control the practice or to render it slightly less publicly visible; and they are extremely relevant to any discussion of police interactions with women in the streets.

Because prostitution is a victimless or consensual crime, for example, there is no victim to seek police assistance. This means that the enforcement of laws against prostitution requires that police must often pose as customers in order to make an arrest. Decoys, undercover, or plainclothes police officers accounted for over half of the prostitution arrests in jurisdictions studied by Winick and Kinsie[46] in their classic work on prostitution. But clearly this method of law enforcement is troublesome and controversial. Police must avoid identifying themselves while attempting to enter into an agreement with a prostitute to purchase sexual favors.

In order to avoid charges of "entrapment," courts frequently require that police engaged in this sort of law enforcement prove that the prostitute was the initiator in the interaction, that the specific nature of the immoral act was suggested, and that a specific price was agreed upon.[47] Prostitutes often complain that police misrepresent the interaction which led to their arrest while police, on the other hand, become frustrated at the sophisticated language employed by prostitutes so as to avoid apprehension.[48] It is clear that conflicting testimony will be the norm in prostitution trials, and rumors of police "framing" women so as to obtain a necessary number of arrests do nothing to dissipate the concerns that arise about such arrests.[49]

But, because of the difficulty in making prostitution arrests, police generally fall back on harassment of women suspected of prostitution so as to keep the activity less visible and under control. Wayne LaFave's research on police behavior in Detroit, for example, revealed that while police rarely made arrests for prostitution *per se*, they did arrest large numbers of "suspected prostitutes." In fact, LaFave observed that suspected prostitutes were "the largest category of offenders arrested for purposes other than prosecution."[50]

LaFave observed that "whore squads" in Detroit arrested every night forty to fifty women "believed to be prostitutes" and booked these women on "Disorderly Persons Investigation." This category was always used in this precinct for prostitutes who were not going to be prosecuted. LaFave noted that women arrested in this manner were not searched at the time of booking but were instead "immediately placed in a large detention area reserved for women prisoners. When the number of women apprehended had reached ten, then the patrol wagon returned to the police station where the women were searched and fingerprinted."[51]

The morning after arrest, LaFave observed that a nurse would appear at the women's detention quarters and administer a pelvic examination to all female prisoners. While awaiting the results of the examination, police would interrogate the women and then return them to the streets. As to the significance of this practice, LaFave noted that these "DPI" arrests constituted "nearly half" of the total precinct arrests. In one six-month period, LaFave noted that the precinct reported 2,942 "DPI" arrests but made only 53 arrests for either prostitution or soliciting.[52]

Aside from the volume of female arrests, LaFave also found that the methods employed by the police in making such street sweeps were somewhat unconventional. In interviews with the officers, he discovered that police did not limit themselves to arresting women seen soliciting men for purposes of prostitution. All that was necessary was that a woman be "found in an area in which prostitution is practiced" or that the woman be "known" as a prostitute. Sometimes women so identified were arrested while eating in restaurants.

Occasionally, police would suspect and arrest women, even if their occupations were unknown, solely because they were "found late at night" in areas with a high incidence of prostitution. LaFave noted that *any* woman walking slowly down the street, standing on a corner, or standing in a doorway might be arrested by police regardless of her previous record. Additionally, a woman in the company of a man of a different race was, according to the officers interviewed, risking almost certain arrest, particularly if the woman was black:

> If a Negro woman is found in the company of a white man, she is usually confronted by the police and taken to the station unless it is clear that the association is legitimate.[53]

LaFave's article on police discretion reveals a startling pattern of racism and sexism in routine police encounters with women. Undoubtedly, practices such as this in jurisdictions across the United States explain why Winick and Kinsie found that blacks were grossly overrepresented in prostitution arrests. They noted that while blacks accounted for about 11 percent of the population, they constituted 53 percent of all urban arrests for prostitution. They further noted that in Los Angeles, 33 percent of the women arrested for prostitution were black while blacks accounted for only 9 percent of the population.[54]

Other studies confirm these findings about the harassment arrests and routine examinations for venereal disease. Additionally, recent revelations concerning police corruption, most notably in New York, add two important points to the pattern revealed by LaFave's research.

The Knapp Commission found that plainclothes police officers in New York had "informal arrest quotas," which meant that any officers on prostitution details had to produce a stipulated number of arrests a night and would, as a consequence, arrest "obvious" prostitutes without obtaining sufficient legal evidence.[55] The commissioners also reported that police, on occasion, took payment from brothels in exchange for warnings of impending raids and took money from prostitutes they had apprehended in exchange for not arresting them.[56]

Other studies of prostitution have established that police extortion of higher-class prostitutes and exploitation and harassment of "streetwalkers" is a common pattern.[57] The routine enforcement of prostitution laws, then, tends to victimize the least-skilled and lowest-paid of the prostitute community—the streetwalker—while ignoring the prostitute who works out of a brothel or as a "call girl." Women in these latter categories tend to be far less vulnerable to arrest and of higher social class background than their sisters who walk the streets.[58]

Embedded in the routine police practices for "dealing" with prostitution, as well as police responses to women who are apprehended for nonsexual crimes, is an important theme. Police appear to be willing to overlook the trivial criminal offenses of women who are able to establish themselves as conforming to one or more of the attributes of traditional femininity. If, however, the nature of the woman's offense (as in the case of prostitution) or the woman's demeanor (in criminal offenses) suggests that she does not conform to her role as obedient and subservient woman, she stands a greater chance of being arrested.

Police, then, harass women who violate the norms which require them to remain sexually monogamous and indoors at night. As LaFave's research has shown, women who got out alone at night, like blacks found in the "wrong" part of town, are subject to arrest and detention with little or no regard for their civil rights. Likewise, women apprehended for criminal offenses are not released if they refuse to play the traditional female role. In this fashion, police are not so much responding chivalrously to women as they are patrolling the boundaries of the female sex role.

Women in Jail

Surprisingly little is known about the women who are awaiting trial or serving time in the nation's jails. It is clear, however, that women are proportionately underrepresented in jail populations: women comprised about 6 percent of those held in the nation's jails during 1972, but during that same year they constituted about 12.8 percent of the arrests.[59] These figures seem to support the suggestion that women receive "chivalrous" treatment at this point in the judicial process. A more systematic analysis of the data is, however, essential before such a conclusion is drawn. First, the reasons for incarceration in jail must be reviewed, as must the conditions of male and female jails. Finally, a detailed comparison of the pre- and posttrial judicial decision-making processes (some of which involve incarceration in jail) in both male and female cases must be undertaken.

This section will briefly analyze the reasons for the incarceration of women in jails and the conditions of those jails and jail quarters where women are held (leaving the detailed discussion of court decision-making for the next section).

A review of the available data on the reasons for incarceration provides little support for the notion that courts are responding chivalrously or less harshly to women. Nearly half of all the males incarcerated in the nation's jails were confined for offenses which the Law Enforcement Assistance Administration classifies as "major crimes of violence" (23.9 percent) or "major property offenses" (20.6 percent). Less than one-fourth of the incarcerated women were confined for either of these offense categories (22.9 percent). The remaining three-fourths of women in the nation's jails were charged with minor crimes such as petty larceny, drug offenses, and "other" offenses.[60] So while males are jailed or waiting trial for offenses which are serious, this is clearly not the case for women, the vast majority of whom have been jailed for nonviolent and relatively less serious property and deportment offenses.

This pattern of jailing women for trivial offenses is confirmed by the few studies that have been done on the subject. During 1964, for example, 72 percent of the white and 49 percent of the black women sentenced to jail in Chicago were incarcerated for offenses against "public order" (which for the most part were immorality, drunk and disorderly charges, and drug offenses).[61] An earlier study of a Minnesota workhouse showed that drunkenness was the chief offense for which commitment was made, followed by a variety of sex offenses including "common prostitution, lewd and indecent conduct, or false hotel registration (used when evidence for prostitution was less than complete). This study also revealed that minority women were tremendously overrepresented, constituting approximately half of those imprisoned in a city that was more than 96 percent white.[62]

National data on the characteristics of incarcerated women are unfortunately unavailable. A 1972 study conducted by the Women's Prison Association, for example, found that most institutions do not keep socioeconomic information on women in prison.[63] Preliminary data are, however, available from a twelve-state study conducted by Ruth Glick which revealed that "most incarcerated women are poor, uneducated, unskilled, minority group members who have dependents."[64] A slightly earlier review of the few studies available on incarcerated women, conducted by Margery Velimesis, concluded that "most studies find that poor self image, parental neglect, disrupted family and a background of poverty are typical of incarcerated females."[65]

The conditions in women's jails certainly do little to ameliorate these problems and may actually exacerbate them. Because of the small numbers of incarcerated women, states are often forced either to transport women long distances to the nearest female facility or to place them in special segregated sections of male facilities. The latter option, employed most often in the case of women sentenced to jail, has a wide variety of negative consequences. A study of women's jails conducted by the Pennsylvania Program on Women and Girl Offenders revealed, for example, that "very often women are not provided with exercise yards, day rooms or religious services because women were an afterthought in the construction of a jail that was built primarily to hold men."[66] The study went on to note that this often meant that women's cells were the most isolated and least maintained in the facility. Also, in many jails women were forced to eat in their cells while men were able to go to a dining hall, and were often idle 75 to 100 percent of their time in jail.

This pattern was found in Gates's survey of the women's section of the county jail in Riverside, California. She noted that as many as twelve women were held in cells measuring ten by six feet.[67] In this jail there was no exercise area for women, so they were, as a consequence, confined to their cells most of the day. Also, while judges in California could sentence minor male offenders to the country road camp, this option was not available to women. Similarly male inmates were able to become trustees and work at the county hospital or do maintenance work at the courthouse. These men also earned a small wage for their work. None of these options was available to women inmates.[68]

Similar problems were also reported by Linda Singer in her study of women's jail conditions. She found different visiting hours for men and women and also noted that, while roughly two-thirds of jailed women have children, many jails either prohibit visits by children entirely or force mothers to see children through glass.[69] The study also noted that in some states where the number of women convicted of felonies is small, these women may be sentenced to local jails for terms exceeding one year. Consequently, they are mixed with pretrial detainees and first offenders—a situation rarely found in male prisons.[70]

Also, women in rural jurisdictions may have little or no privacy from male staff when a separate section for women does not exist in the jail. The consequences of this kind of situation were graphically illustrated by the case of Joann Little, who was accused of murdering her jailer in North Carolina. The plight of women forced to serve time in local jails staffed only by male guards must be carefully monitored to avoid the sexual exploitation of female inmates.

Because jails fear the mixing of male and female inmates, women rarely enjoy the same vocational opportunities or recreational opportunities as male inmates. Sometimes enforced segregation in small rural jails can even result in solitary confinement for women.

These practices have been the object of legal challenges that they deny incarcerated women with equal protection. In one successful case in San Francisco (*Dawson* v. *Carberry*), female jail inmates sued in federal court to gain participation in a work-furlough program. Jail officials argued, predictably, that they lacked the resources to create such a program for women and that their small numbers made special arrangements unfeasible. The judge, however, rejected this argument. Saying that exclusion from the program was "almost blatantly unconstitutional," he gave the officials three months to create the program for women.[71]

Perhaps the most startling and graphic revelations about the conditions of women's jails came from publicity surrounding the Women's House of Detention in New York. Sparked by accounts of terrible jail conditions made by young civil rights workers who spent several days in the jail, the controversy was further fueled by a bizarre request from a convicted prostitute that she be allowed to serve up to five years in a women's prison rather than serving six months in the House of Detention.[72]

Accounts of the conditions in this one women's jail were collected by Sara Harris. She described conditions of degrading entry conditions, filth, overcrowding, unhealthy and poorly prepared food, and poor medical conditions. These charges eventually sparked a New York grand jury investigation into the facility and ultimately led to its closure a few years later.

Perhaps the most startling thing to the women who entered the jail was the practice of routine vaginal examinations for venereal disease. This experience was graphically described by Andrea Dworkin, then an eighteen-year-old civil rights worker:

> In the examination room they took our temperature rectally, asked us whether we were virgins and told us to sit down and wait. . . . I was taken into the [examining] room first. The examining doctor was sitting down and the other doctor was standing there. I was made to get on the examining table and spread my legs. While he began exerting pressure on my stomach and my breast, I told him he was hurting me. . . . But he continued to exert the pressure. The examination consisted of his inserting his hand in both the rectum and vagina. He used a rubber glove. Then the use of forceps was brutally applied to the vagina.[73]

Such coercive examinations are apparently common,[74] and cannot be justified by the institution's concerns for the health of jailed women. For example, other sorts of medical care in the same jail were woefully inadequate.[75] Other jails are apparently no better. Male institutions, because of their size, are more likely than female institutions to have complete hospital and dental facilities,[76] or a doctor on duty. Jailed pregnant women are frequently denied important medical care and those who desire abortions are sometimes prevented from obtaining them.[77]

Overall, the women in America's jails (over a third of whom are pretrial detainees)[78] are confined in deplorable and harsh conditions despite the fact that most are incarcerated for minor offenses. Clearly most of these women should qualify for in-community programs rather than incarceration. Yet studies of these programs suggest that they function as supplements rather than alternatives to confinement for both men and women.[79]

In general, the failure of women to be sentenced to jail appears to be less a product of chivalry than the combined product of the trivial offenses committed by women and the harsh conditions found in women's jails. Indeed, from one perspective, that which compares the types of offenses for which men and women are incarcerated, women appear to be more harshly censured than men. Nearly three-quarters of the women in jail, but only about one-half of the men, are incarcerated for trivial offenses. A complete investigation of the relative harshness of the treatment accorded male and females, however, necessitates an examination of the entire range of judicial responses to male and female criminality.

Women and the Courts

Much of the research which suggested that women were treated chivalrously by agents of the criminal justice system focused on what appeared to be clear evidence of judicial reluctance to sentence women harshly. Criminology texts and the like routinely state that women are less likely to be held in custody at the pretrial stage, less likely to be convicted if tried, and, if convicted, more likely than men to avoid imprisonment.[80]

There are several ways to evaluate the adequacy of this chivalry argument. First, one could catalogue numerous examples of legislation governing the sentencing of men and women for the same offenses. Quite frequently, these allow for greater use of the indeterminant sentence in handling female offenders, and occasionally they specifically prescribe more severe sentences for women. In Maine, for example, as late as 1972, the sentence for intoxication for men was two years while for women it was three years.[81] Iowa statutes permit women to be confined for five years for a misdemeanor whereas men can only be imprisoned for a maximum of one year.[82] Nor are these examples extreme; Clements, in his review of this type of legislation, observed that fourteen states had or have sentencing statutes applicable to women calling for indeterminant sentences, usually resulting in more severe sentences for women than men found guilty of the same offense.

Such legislation was bound to be challenged as unconstitutional; and examination of one of these cases demonstrates both the importance of such challenges and the difficulty in establishing the constitutional case. In 1966, Jane Daniel was convicted of simple robbery in Pennsylvania, an offense which carried a maximum ten-year sentence. The judge initially sentenced her to serve a one- to four-year term in the county prison but then, a month later, brought her back to court and vacated the original sentence. He resentenced her to serve a maximum of ten years with no minimum term specified at the state's prison for women. This was the result of the state's Muncy Act, which required that women receive the maximum legal penalty if convicted of a crime punishable by more than three years and that the sentence be served in a state penitentiary.[83] This action was appealed, and eventually the Pennsylvania Supreme Court determined that

> while legislative classification on the basis of sex alone did not violate the equal protection clause, it [the court] could find no reasonable justification for a statute which imposed longer sentences on women than on men convicted of the same crime.[84]

Unfortunately, this finding is by no means typical of court responses to such sentencing statutes. Clements, for example, in his review of this and other such challenges, concluded that equal protection challenges to unequal sentencing statutes have "generally failed,"[85] and Carolyn Temin in another study of these cases went further, saying, "The history of the fight against sex-based discrimination in criminal sentencing statutes presents a strong example of the absolute necessity for the equal rights amendment."[86] Indeed, even the ultimate resolution of the *Daniels* case proves this to be true; the Pennsylvania legislature responded to the court's decision by enacting a new law that provided for another type of indeterminant sentence for women.[87]

While these pieces of legislation seem almost unbelievable, they have been largely ignored by criminologists, perhaps because so few adult women entered the criminal justice system. This situation, however, no longer obtains and the potential for abuse that it represents in many ways just being realized. These statutes are based on a protectionist logic reminiscent of the juvenile court's approach to women. Because of their special nature, these statutes argue, women should be protected, not punished. Curiously, however, this protection often seems to involve greater use of the indeterminant sentence and even, in some cases, lengthier incarceration. Certainly the existence of these statutes indicates that the legal chivalry could result in harsher, not less severe, punishment of females labeled as criminal.

But it is not sufficient to review legislation governing the sentencing of women. The actual effect of these statutes on the decision-making of the courts must also be examined. Unfortunately, while there have been a great many studies of the effect of both legal and extralegal variables on court sentencing, few of these studies seriously considered sex with the same weight as racial or ethnic background. Recently, however, research on this important area has begun.

Typical of the studies which establish sex as an important factor in sentencing is the Texas study. Investigators accumulated data on 1,720 felony cases (ninety-eight of which involved female defendants) from twenty-seven courts during the 1960s and determined that women receive much better treatment than men, with "a substantially higher percentage of women receiving suspended sentences." Judges, the researchers continued, showed "something of a chivalrous attitude toward women," and as a consequence a substantial higher percentage of women offenders receive sentences that do not involve incarceration.[88] The authors in this study, however, failed to control for either the type of felony charged or for the prior record of the defendants.

This, according to Edward Green, who conducted a study of sentencing patterns in Philadelphia, is a serious flaw. Green, in his research, controlled these variables and discovered that "a comparison of the two sexes in cases with no prior convictions of a felony with the grade of offense controlled yield results affirming the equality of the sexes before the criminal law."[89] Green discovered, for example, virtually identical percentages of penitentiary sentences for men and women once he controlled for the effects of these two variables.

Unfortunately, most sentencing studies do not employ the controls recommended by Green. Rita Simon's chapter on the sentencing of women in her book on women and crime, for example, simply analyzed conviction rates drawn from federal and state court records. These do provide a few interesting facts. Between 1967 and 1971, conviction rates of women in the federal system went up dramatically (62.4 percent, compared to only 20.3 percent for male convictions). In California during roughly the same period the pattern was more mixed, with convictions of women for violent offenses up 29 percent but a decline of 13 percent in the convictions of women for property offenses.[90] The meaning of these trends is, however, somewhat obscure since there was no way to control for the effect of the defendant's prior records on the conviction decisions. Similarly, there was no way to determine the relative harshness of the sentence imposed as a result of the conviction.

The most widely cited investigation of the effect of sex on judicial behavior, and one which has supplied support for the chivalry hypothesis, is Nagel and Weitzman's analysis of national data collected to analyze procedures for providing attorneys to indigent defendants.[91] Nagel and Weitzman examined the experience of criminal defendants charged with either grand larceny or felonious assault and concluded that the courts were treating women "paternalistically" rather than punitively. Fewer women when compared to men were sentenced to jail, more women than men were held less than two months before trial, and more received suspended sentences or probation. They also noted, however, that substantially more of the women charged with assault than those charged with larceny were jailed after trial (89 percent compared to 53 percent), and, more importantly, they noted that these women were significantly less likely to receive a jury trial.[92]

Their interpretation was that women were in general being treated "paternalistically" by the court. This was especially true of women who committed traditionally female crimes. Their research, however, was not able to control on a number of important variables known to affect judicial outcome (prior record and criminal status). Despite this, the amount of support for the paternalistic hypothesis, even in their data, seemed weak. For example, out of sixteen possible court actions only seven confirmed the paternalistic hypothesis, and at several points, the court response seemed harsher toward women. This is certainly a more complex pattern than sheer paternalism or judicial chivalry.

This complexity was confirmed by another study conducted by Rottman and Simon which examined, in part, women and men accused of theft and deceptive practice in a single court. These data did not confirm Nagel and Weitzman's findings with reference to women avoiding jail, nor was there any significant difference in the percentage of males and females obtaining a jury trial. Rottman and Simon conclude that the proportion of men and women in the pretrial release categories are examined, no "evidence of the paternalistic treatment is evident. If anything, some support is found for the view that judges treated women defendants more harshly."[93]

Significantly, once certain sorts of control (on offense and prior record) are introduced, as Green suggested, many of the apparent benefits which many suggested accrue to women as a product of chivalry appear, upon closer examination, to be the court's recognition of less serious prior records and more trivial current charges.

Perhaps one of the strongest indications of this came from a study of judicial processing of felony offenders in twelve counties in California.[94] In an impressive monograph on the activities of two types of courts during 1969 and 1971 in both rural and urban counties, Pope developed a mechanism for controlling for the effects of original charge, criminal status, and prior record. The ability to control for the effects of these variables across a wide variety of current offenses makes this study very significant.

The impact of controlling for the effects of these three factors in the analysis of court activity is clear; the influence of sex on sentencing was significantly reduced. So, for example, unstandardized data on rural lower-court activity indicated that 45 percent of the males and only 38 percent of the females were sentenced to jail. However, when this was corrected to control for the effects of prior record and offense type, the figures changed to 45 percent of the males sentenced to jail and 41 percent of the females. Similar though less dramatic charges also occurred in the lower courts in urban areas.[95]

When the same standardization was applied to the upper or superior courts, the changes were even more dramatic. Prison sentences, the most frequently cited figures when the chivalry hypothesis is discussed, are a case in point. In rural superior courts, for example, the unstandardized figures indicated that 19 percent of the males were sentenced to prison compared to only 8 percent of the women. But when these data were standardized by prior record, the figures became 18 percent of the males and 17 percent of the females sentenced to prison. Similar changes were produced in the data on superior-court decision-making in urban settings. As Pope summarized his results, "Apparently, the discrepancy between male and female prison dispositions observed in the unstandardized bivariate table was largely accounted for by prior record, since the percentage of each sex receiving a prison commitment is about equal when prior record is introduced as a test factor."[96]

Pope's research concluded that women were likely to fare slightly better than men in lower courts (especially in the urban courts), but were treated equally in superior courts. Similar conclusions were reported by Green, who noted that among those convicted of misdemeanors women faired "slightly though not significantly better than men," with only 5.3 percent of the women misdemeanants, but 7 percent of the males, sentenced to jail. Also, a larger percentage of females (78.9 percent) received nonprison sentences, compared to 69.7 percent of the males.[97]

More sophisticated studies of the influence of sex on court response indicate the complexity of this issue and emphasize the importance of careful analysis. Bernstein and her associates have been pioneers in this rigorous approach. In their first study on charge reduction (plea bargaining)[98] in a typical court in New York between 1974-1975, they focused on individuals charged with larceny, burglary, assault, and robbery. Among defendants whose cases were disposed upon the first hearing, sex had no effect once researchers had controlled for the effects of fourteen variables known to be related to judicial decision-making (such as the defendant's attributes, offense type, criminal status, and prior imprisonment record).

When the researchers examined the severity of the most serious charge for which the defendant was convicted (controlling for the severity of the most serious of the original charges), it was found that women were being convicted of more serious charges. The researchers concluded that since the offenses being examined were, for the most part, non-feminine offenses, women were being, in effect, more harshly punished. Drawing on court observations, the authors noted that when women "are prosecuted for the kinds of serious non-female typed offenses here examined, they may be more severely responded to because they are violating expectations for approximate sex-role behavior as well as appropriate law abiding behavior."[99]

In another more recent piece of research on a wider range of offenses, Bernstein, Cardacia, and Ross examined the role that sex played in court decision-making. Again, the researchers controlled for the effects of a wide variety of independent variables on this official response. With respect to the harshness of the sentence, they concluded that while the decision was determined similarly for both sexes, females appeared to enjoy an advantage over men. Males were 12 percent more likely than females to receive a harsh sentence.[100] In general, they felt this supported the paternalistic hypothesis.

Apparent support for the paternalistic hypothesis was also found when considering whether the defendant ever spent time in prison. They found that males were more likely than females to be imprisoned. But in this instance, the researchers found considerable differences in the manner in which the court responded to males and females.

First, they determined that while the severity of the offense was strongly related to the likelihood of a male spending time imprisoned, this variable had no significant effect for females. In essence, they found that women charged with felonies were neither more nor less likely to be imprisoned than those charged with misdemeanors. Indeed, a whole range of variables that have traditionally affected this decision for males (seriousness of offense, possession of a weapon, prior convictions, etc.), had no significant effect on the severity of sentence for women. Instead, marital status, a variable not significant among male defendants, had a strong effect on a woman's likelihood of being imprisoned.

Another significant variable in examining the likelihood that a woman would spend time in prison was the type of offense. Bernstein and her associates determined that there was a "strong adverse effect" for females charged with personal crimes (as compared to those charged with property offenses) with respect to imprisonment. They concluded that there exists a strong possibility that among women defendants a kind of sex discrimination exists, so that those women engaging in personal crimes are being punished more harshly than their counterparts who commit property offenses because the former represent a violation of their sex role as well as the law. She also noted that this finding is quite different from the way in which courts normally treat disadvantaged persons. Typically, personal offenses in powerless communities tend to evoke less severe condemnation while property offenses are considered more serious.[101] For women, just the reverse appears to be the case.

Bernstein's research provides the most thorough examination of the effect of sex on sentencing both in view of the breadth of offenses (twelve) that they considered and the rigor of the control over the effects of other variables known to affect sentencing. Their findings are therefore enlightening. Some caution, however, with reference to their findings which support the paternalistic hypothesis seems in order. First, they did not include prostitution or other public-order offenses among the twelve crimes they investigated. Given the evidence that many women but few men are routinely arrested for these trivial offenses, this oversight seems significant. If, as some studies of female jails indicate, a significant portion of the women in these facilities are either explicitly or implicitly held for prostitution, the failure to include this offense in the study compromises the findings.

What seems to be emerging from all of these studies is that far from treating women chivalrously the courts have been engaging in a more complex response to female criminality. It would appear that some women, particularly those who engage in traditionally female offenses, may enjoy some benefits before the court, particularly if they can establish themselves as "women" by fulfilling other traditional roles.

For women who are arrested for nontraditional female offenses, the court's reponse is less chivalrous. What appears to be happening is that the courts are indeed engaging not so much in chivalry as in the judicial enforcement of female sex-role expectations. Like their counterparts in the juvenile court, judicial bodies seem willing to overlook female criminality as long as the behavior is not totally inconsistent with female sex-role expectations. When the woman commits "male" crimes, however, the advantage of being female deteriorates rapidly, and, in some cases, the courts may be responding more harshly to female than to male behavior.

Conclusions

At the beginning of this chapter, statistics on the processing of women through the criminal justice system were cited. These appeared to give strong support to the contention that adult women, unlike their adolescent counterparts, were the recipients of chivalrous treatment in the official response to their criminal misconduct. This chapter has examined the evidence for this contention at four stages in the criminal justice decision-making process (prearrest, arrest, jail, and court sentencing).

What has been revealed by reviewing the admittedly uneven research about the official response to female misbehavior has been intriguing. First, at the level of the victim's response, it appears that until recently some women may have enjoyed some benefits as a result of their sex, particularly white and upper-status women, but much of this was a product of the type of criminal misbehavior in which these women engaged.

The research which focused on shoplifting, for example, revealed that women tended to steal more items than men and to steal items of less value. Once the value of the items was controlled for, much of the apparent advantage enjoyed by women evaporated. The other significant element in these studies was that even minor change in store or company policies regarding the prosecution of female offenders could result in a dramatic increase in the number of women arrested. Indeed, if women did enjoy any advantage in the response to their misbehavior, it is possible that the women's movement may have shattered this—resulting in a dramatic increase in the number of women prosecuted for shoplifting.

At the level of police behavior, the few studies which exist indicate that police tend to fall into patterns of enforcing female sex-role expectations rather than the law. Clear evidence has been presented to show that police certainly respond in anything but a chivalrous attitude toward women they label as prostitutes. Routine violation of the civil rights of these women appears to be the norm, and, if LaFave's data are correct, a staggering number of "arrests" (which may not even be recorded) of these women occur every week. Efforts to arrest the patrons of prostitutes have never seriously been attempted, producing a totally hypocritical and costly legal game in which outcast women are the victims.

Other women suspected of criminal misconduct, particularly if they possess proper feminine deportment in the arrest situation, may enjoy some benefits. Again, however, if women act like adults and refuse to conform to the female sex-role expectations (powerlessness, dependency, weakness) they are responded to harshly.

The conditions in women's jails provide another repudiation or at least correction of the chivalry hypothesis. Judges may be reluctant to imprison women in jails precisely because this is a far harsher sentence than its male equivalent. Because of their small numbers, women in jail do not possess the same opportunities as men for recreation, visitation, and prerelease furloughs. Because they cannot mingle with the men, they often spend virtually all of their sentence in their cells. Added to this is the fact that three-quarters of these women in jail are held for minor offenses, compared to only about half of the males. This does not give strong support to the chivalry hypothesis.

Finally, when women come before the bar of justice, the court again appears to be less lenient than early studies seem to indicate. Much of the empirical support for the chivalry hypothesis was, in actuality, the product of the fact that women have less serious offenses. When the effects of these variables are controlled, the advantage enjoyed by women is either significantly reduced or completely eliminated.

But, perhaps most significantly, there appears to be discrimination against some women defendants and favoritism toward others. Bernstein's research demonstrates that the type of offense (rather than its severity) seems to be a major factor in the court's response to female defendants. If the activity is unfeminine (for example, violent) the court seems likely to respond harshly. This seems particularly to be the case if the woman cannot provide other evidence of her conformity to the standards of womanhood (for example, marriage). Clearly what is being examined is the degree to which the defendant can prove conformity to a role which requires her to be nonviolent and subservient toward men. When this is not possible, she is punished harshly.

This chapter must be seen as a tentative first step in the examination of official responses to the woman labeled as criminal. Much more research will be necessary before firm conclusions can be drawn. It appears, however, that facile comments about women defendants' benefiting from male tolerance are incorrect. Indeed, there is much compelling evidence in the opposite direction. Again, what may be happening is judicial enforcement of sex-role expectations as well as, and sometimes in place of, the law, with court personnel's overlooking female criminal misconduct of the woman who conforms to female sex-role expectations, but responding harshly to women who deviate from sexual and behavioral components of the female sex role. That these clear patterns, particularly in the case of prostitution, have so long been ignored is itself evidence that chivalry never accrued to all women, but only to "good" women. That the formulation was so widely accepted as indicative of the need for more systematic and objective research in this important area.

Notes

1. A number of recent books have appeared in a response to the dramatic increases in female arrest rates. The most notable of these include Freda Adler, *Sisters in Crime: The Rise of the New Female Criminal* (New York: McGraw Hill, 1975); Rita James Simon, *Women and Crime* (Lexington, Mass.: Lexington Books, 1975); and Richard Deming, *Women: The New Criminals* (Nashville: T. Nelson, 1977).

2. Otto Pollak, *The Criminality of Women* (Philadelphia: University of Pennsylvania Press, 1950), 151.

3. See for example comments made in Walter C. Reckless, *The Crime Problem* (New York: Appleton-Century Crofts, 1961) or Ruth S. Cavan, *Criminology* (New York: Crowell, 1962). The widespread acceptance of the chivalry hypothesis is well documented in Etta A. Anderson, "The Chivalrous Treatment of the Female Offender in the Arms of the Criminal Justice System: A Review of the Literature," *Social Problems* 23 (1976), 349-57.

4. Federal Bureau of Investigation, *Uniform Crime Reports* (Washington, D.C.: U.S. Department of Justice, 1976), 183.

5. U.S. Department of Justice, *Sourcebook of Criminal Justice Statistics* (Albany, New York: Criminal Justice Research Center, 1977), 633.

6. Female Offender Resource Center, American Bar Association, *Female Offenders: Problems and Programs* (Washington, D.C.: American Bar Association, 1976), 1.

7. U.S. Department of Justice, 686.

8. Dale Hoffman-Bustamante, "The Nature of Female Criminality," *Issues in Criminology* 8 (1973), 117-36 and Dorie Klein and June Kress, "Any Woman's Blues: A Critical Overview of Women, Crime and Criminal Justice System," *Crime and Social Justice* 5 (1976), 34-49.

9. Federal Bureau of Investigation, 183.

10. Simon, 37.

11. Federal Bureau of Investigation, 183.

12. John Kitsuse and Aaron Cicourel, "A Note on the Use of Official Statistics," *Social Problems* 11 (1963), 131-39.

13. A.H. Buss, "Physical Aggression in Relation to Different Frustrations," *Journal of Abnormal and Social Psychology* 67 (1963), 1.7.

14. Michael J. Hindelang, "Race and Involvement in Crimes," *American Sociological Review* 43 (1978), 93-109.

15. Mary B. Cameron, *Department Store Shoplifting,* unpublished Doctoral Dissertation (Indiana University, 1953), 126.

16. Cameron, 16.

17. Referral rates to police for prosecution for shoplifting rarely exceed 30 percent of those apprehended. For example, Gerald Robin in "Patterns of Department Store Shoplifting," *Crime and Delinquency* 9 (1963), 163-72, reported a referral rate of 14 percent; Lawrence E. Cohen and Rodney Stark in "Discriminatory Labelling and the Five Finger Discount, *Journal of Research in Crime and Delinquency* 11 (1974), 25-39, reported 46 percent referred to the police, and Michael J. Hindelang, "Decisions of Shoplifting Victims," *Social Problems* 21 (1974), 580-93, reported a referral rate of 26 percent.

18. Cameron, 159.

19. Ibid., 75.

20. Ibid., 62.

21. Robin, 169.

22. Cameron, 163.

23. Hindelang, 588.

24. Ibid., 591.

25. Cohen and Stark, 35.

26. Darrell J. Steffensmeier and Robert M. Terry, "Deviance and Respectability: An Observational Study of Reactions to Shoplifting," *Social Forces* 51 (1973), 417-26.

27. Gerald D. Robin, *Employees as Offenders: A Sociological Analysis of Occupational Crime,* unpublished Doctoral Dissertation (University of Pennsylvania, 1965).

28. Ibid., 171.

29. The classic study on police brutality is Albert J. Reiss, "Police Brutality: Answers to Key Questions," *Trans-action* 5 (1968), 10-19. See also U.S. Commission on Law Enforcement and Administration of Justice, *Task Force: Police* (1967), 178-89.

30. Studies of police discretion are generally descriptive. Two of the most complete are James Q. Wilson, "Police Discretion," in Leon Radzinowicz and Marvin Wolfgang, *The Criminal in the Arms of the Law* (New York: Basic Books, 1971), 253-68; and Wayne LaFave, "Arrest: The Decision to Take a Suspect into Custody," in Lawrence M. Friedman and Steward Macaulay, *Law and the Behavioral Sciences* (Indianapolis: Bobbs-Merrill and Co., 1969), 97-116.

31. LaFave, 102-106.

32. Federal Bureau of Investigation, 183.

33. Weldon T. Johnson, Robert E. Petersen, and L. Edward Wells,

"Arrest Probabilities for Marijuana Users as Indicators of Selective Law Enforcement," *American Journal of Sociology* 83 (1977), 681-99.

34. Lois B. DeFleur, "Biasing Influences on Drug Arrest Records: Implications for Deviance Research," *American Sociological Review* 40 (1975), 88-103.

35. Johnson *et al.,* 691.

36. Ibid., 693.

37. Lee H. Bowker, *Drug Use at a Small Liberal Arts College* (Palo Alto, California: R and E Research Associates, 1976).

38. DeFleur, 101.

39. Ibid.

40. Charles Winick and Paul M. Kinsie, in *The Lively Commerce: Prostitution in the United States* (New York: Signet, 1972), 14, estimate that the average prostitute makes approximately $9,300 annually. This compares favorably to the $4,000 to $6,000 that women in other traditionally female occupations earn.

41. Pamely Roby and Virginia Kerr, "The Politics of Prostitution," *The Nation* (April 10, 1972), 463-66.

42. Federal Bureau of Investigation, 183.

43. A.C. Kinsey, W.B. Pomeroy, and C.E. Martin, *Sexual Behavior in the Human Male* (Philadelphia: W.B. Saunders and Co., 1948), 391-92.

44. Ibid., 391.

45. Herant A. Katchadourian and Donald T. Lunde, *Fundamentals of Human Sexuality* (New York: Holt, Rinehart and Winston, 1975), 521.

46. Winick and Kinsie, 190.

47. LaFave, 114.

48. Harry Benjamin and R.E.L. Masters, *Prostitution and Morality* (New York: Julian Press, 1964).

49. Commission to Investigate Allegations of Police Corruption and the City's Anti-Corruption Procedures, *Commission Report (Knapp Commission Report on Police Corruption)* (New York: George Braziller, 1972), 28.

50. LaFave, 110.

51. Ibid.

52. LaFave, 111.

53. Ibid., 113.

54. Winick and Kinsie, 191.

55. Knapp Commission, 122.

56. Ibid., 117-20.

57. Benjamin and Masters, 387-99, and Marilyn Haft, "Hustling for Rights," *American Civil Liberties Review* 1 (1974), 8-26.

58. Gail Sheehy, "The Economics of Prostitution: Who Profits? Who Pays?" in Erich Goode and Richard R. Troiden, *Sexual Deviance and Sexual Deviants* (New York: Wm. Morrow and Co., 1974), 110-23.

59. U.S. Department of Justice, 641; and Federal Bureau of Investigation *Uniform Crime Reports* (Washington, D.C., 1973), 124.

60. U.S. Department of Justice, 641.

61. Charles O'Reilly, Frank Cizon, John Flanagan, and Steven Pflanczer, "Sentenced Women in a County Jail," *American Journal of Correction* 30 (1968), 23-25.

62. Barbara Knudson, *Career Patterns of Female Misdemeanant Offenders,* unpublished Doctoral Dissertation (University of Minnesota, 1968).

63. National Prisoner Statistics, *Prisoners in State and Federal Institutions for Adult Felons* (Washington, D.C.: U.S. Government Printing Office, 1972), Bulletin No. 47.

64. Quoted in Female Offender Resource Center, 9.

65. Margery L. Velimesis, "The Female Offender," *Crime and Delinquency Literature* (March 1975).

66. Margery L. Velimesis, "Women in County Jails and Prisons," quoted in *Women Behind Bars* (Washington, D.C.: Resources for Community Change, 1975), 75.

67. Dorothy Gates, *Theft and the Status of Women,* unpublished Doctoral Dissertation (University of Hawaii, 1976).

68. Ibid., 100.

69. Linda Singer, "Women and the Correctional Process," *American Criminal Law Review* 11 (1973), 300.

70. "The Sexual Segregation of American Prisons," *Yale Law Journal* 82 (1973), 1229-73.

71. *Dawson v. Carberry,* No. C-71-1916 (N.D. Cal., filed September 1971).

72. Sara Harris, *Hellhole* (New York: Tower, 1967), 8-9.

73. Ibid., 14.

74. LaFave; Margery Velemesis, "Criminal Justice for the Female Offender," *Journal of the American Association of University Women* (October 1969), 15.

75. Harris, 41-75.

76. *Yale Law Journal,* 1234.

77. Female Offender Resource Center, 15; Singer, 302.

78. U.S. Department of Justice, 633.

79. Gene Kassebaum, "Sex Status and Community Based Correctional Supervision," paper presented at the American Sociological Association Meetings (September 1977).

80. Examples of these statements were included in the chapter on the treatment of juvenile women. See also note 3, chapter 6.

81. Mark Clements, "Sex and Sentencing," *Southwestern Law Journal* 26 (1972), 897.

82. Carolyn Temin, "Discriminatory Sentencing of Women Offenders," *American Criminal Law Review* 11 (1973), 361.

83. The major components of the Muncy Act are found in Temin, 360-61.

84. 430 Pa. at 649, 243, A2d. at 403.

85. Clements, 898.

86. Temin, 357.

87. Ibid., 367-69.

88. George W. Baab and William Furgeson, "Texas Sentencing Practices: A Statistical Study," *Texas Law Review* 45 (1967), 496.

89. Edward Green, *Judicial Attitudes in Sentencing* (London: Macmillan, 1961), 53.

90. Simon, 54-56.

91. Stuart Nagel and Lenore Weitzman, "Women as Litigants," *Hastings Law Review* 23 (1971), 171-81.

92. Ibid., 174.

93. D.B. Rottman and R.J. Simon, "Women in the Courts," *Chitty's Law Journal* 23 (1975), 52.

94. Carl E. Pope, *Sentencing of California Felony Offenders* (Washington, D.C.: Criminal Justice Research Center, 1975).

95. Ibid., 18.

96. Ibid., 21.

97. Green, 53.

98. Ilene Bernstein, Edward Kick, Jan T. Leong, and Barbara Schulz, "Charge Reduction: An Intermediary State in the Process of Labelling Criminal Defendants," *Social Forces* 56 (1977), 362-84.

99. Ibid., 379.

100. Ilene Nagel Bernstein, John Cardascia, and Catherine Rose, "Institutional Sexism: The Case in Criminal Court," paper presented to the American Sociological Association Meetings (September 1977), 14.

101. LaFave, for example, noted that many of the minor offenses overlooked by police involved assaults in low-income communities. Studies of societal reactions to homicide also confirm this pattern. See Harold Garfinkle, "Research Notes on Inter- and Intra-racial Homicides," *Social Forces* 27 (1949), 369.

8 Females in Corrections

There has never been a time when women were more than a small proportion of the total population of state and federal prisoners in the United States. Information on male and female prisoners from 1950 to 1975 is summarized in table 8-1. In 1950, females comprised 3.5 percent of all adult prisoners; in 1960, 3.7 percent; in 1971, 3.2 percent; and in 1975, 3.6 percent. If anything characterizes this trend, it is consistency, not a great rise in the proportion of female prisoners. In the years from 1960 to 1975, the number of incarcerated women formed a shallow, U-shaped curve, declining from 7,700 in 1960 to 6,269 in 1972, and then rising to 8,850 in 1975. This could not have strained the capacities of any correctional facilities, except perhaps in 1975. During most of the years between 1960 and 1975, the average women's prison operated at well under its rated capacity.

Table 8-1 also shows that changes in female incarceration rates parallel changes in male incarceration rates. Both increased slowly up through about 1960, then decreased slightly until 1973, when they began a rise of increasing steepness which has continued up through the present. In the twenty-five-year period, the number of women incarcerated in state and federal institutions increased 52.4 percent and the number of men increased 45.9 percent. In absolute terms, this meant a rise of 73,585 male prisoners but only 3,042 female prisoners.

As punishments became more severe, the percentage of females among those being punished decreased. The proportion of females in state and federal prisons is just under 4 percent. The only more severe punishment than long imprisonment in the United States is execution. Between 1930 and 1973, 3,827 men were executed, as compared with only thirty-two women (0.8 percent).[1] On the other side of long-term imprisonment, one finds short sentences served in local jails. In 1970, 5.7 percent of the 153,063 adults incarcerated in American jails were women,[2] which was about the same proportion as was found in a 1972 survey.[3]

Juvenile punishments are thought to be still less severe, though in practice they may turn out to be worse than jail terms. At mid-century, there were 14,098 girls and 42,566 boys in American correctional facilities (24.9 percent female). By 1960, these figures had risen to 16,751 girls and 70,951 boys (19.1 percent female).[4] In 1971, the first expanded census of correc-

An earlier version of this chapter appeared in the *International Journal of Women's Studies* 1 (6), Nov.-Dec. 1978, under the title "Women and Girls Behind Bars: Theory and Practice."

Table 8-1
Prisoners in U.S. Federal and State Facilities, 1950-1975

	Prisoner Counts		*Annual Percentage Change*		
Year	*Male*	*Female*	*Interval*	*Male*	*Female*
1975	233,900	8,850	1974-75	+10.8	+19.8
1974	211,077	7,389	1973-74	+6.8	+9.6
1973	197,527	6,684	1972-73	+4.1	+6.6
1972	189,823	6,269	1971-72	−1.0	−0.9
1971	191,732	6,329	1965-71	−1.1	−3.3
1965	203,327	7,568	1960-65	−0.2	−0.3
1960	205,253	7,700	1955-60	+3.0	+1.6
1955	178,655	7,125	1950-55	+2.3	+4.5
1950	160,315	5,808			

Source: *Prisoners in State and Federal Institutions* (Washington, D.C.: U.S. Department of Justice, Law Enforcement Assistance Administration, 1976-1977); *National Prisoner Statistics* (Washington, D.C.: U.S. Department of Justice, Bureau of Prisons, 1969).

tional facilities was conducted under the auspices of the Law Enforcement Assistance Administration. It included detention centers and shelters as well as the traditional correctional facilities portrayed in earlier surveys conducted by the Department of Health, Education and Welfare. At this time, 41,781 boys and 12,948 girls were in custody (23.7 percent female). By 1973, the numbers had decreased to 10,637 girls and 35,057 boys (23.3 percent female), and in 1974, to 34,783 boys and 10,139 girls (22.6 percent female).[5] As juvenile decarceration progressed during the last decade, the decrease in institutionalized young women has almost exactly matched the decrease in institutionalized young men.

The parallels between males and females in adult and juvenile incarceration statistics suggest that the force of correctional policy developments affects males and females in the same way. Although there are many differences between the sexes at the point of the commission of the crime, by the time they have gone through the multiple processing procedures of the criminal justice system, these have been ironed out to a considerable extent. Apparently the basic decisions about how many offenders will go to prison and how soon they will be released are made for offenders in general rather than for male and female offenders separately. Otherwise, the changes in the levels of incarceration for males and females would probably not follow each other quite so closely. There has been practically no relationship between trends in incarceration and trends in crime in recent years (see Chapter 1).

Female Correctional Institutions and Their Programs

Local jails are the least tolerable of the three levels of institutions for females. State and federal facilities are generally better, and youth programs, although they vary from place to place, are the best of all. At least half of the incarcerated women on a given day are in local jails,[6] yet almost nothing is known about the conditions and programs current in those facilities.

Of the miscellaneous publications on women in county jails, the most vaulable are those by Hendrix, O'Reilly, Velimesis, and the Commission on Correctional Facilities and Services of the American Bar Association.[7] Hendrix surveyed women in the New York City Correctional Institution for Women in 1972, finding that 9 percent were white, 77 percent had neither a GED nor a high-school diploma, 74 percent were unmarried, and 67 percent had children. Twenty-two percent of the women were accused or convicted of crimes against persons, and 62 percent of the detainees and 80 percent of the sentenced women were recidivists.[8] In a national questionnaire sample which unfortunately had a low response rate, Hendrix found that 42 percent of the incarcerated women were white, 46 percent had less than tenth-grade educations, and 67 percent had children.[9]

In a similar study in the Cook County Jail in Illinois, about a quarter of the women were married and two-thirds were black. Racial differences were acute. Half the blacks and three-quarters of the whites were incarcerated for public order crimes. Fifty-nine percent of the whites and 85 percent of the blacks were recidivists. An amazing 29 percent of the blacks had been in jail fourteen or more times, yet none of them had ever been imprisoned for a felony. In comparison, 25 percent of the whites had served previous felony sentences.[10]

Although the best study on women in local jails is not generally available, it has been summarized in a number of periodicals and reports.[11] In the mid-1960s, Margery Velimesis surveyed forty-one county court and correctional services in Pennsylvania. The sample was composed of 2,407 of 6,226 women and girls who entered the court and correctional process in 1965 and 1966. Out of the 2,407 females, 1,100 were detained, 626 received a sentence to a county jail, and 40 were sent to the state institution at Muncy. Only females detained in a county jail were counted in this sample. Young women who were processed by the juvenile courts were studied in a separate sample.[12]

The most common offense was disorderly conduct, with 387 cases, followed by prostitution (214), larceny (104), shoplifting (81), drunk and disorderly (79), burglary (79), worthless checks (58), and assault and battery (57). Crimes against persons constituted only 9.3 percent of all offenses, of which two-thirds were misdemeanors. Bonds were set for 615 offenders, the most common amount being between $1,000 and $1,500. Average sentences ranged from seventeen days for summary offenses to fifty-two days for misdemeanors and 109 days for felonies. Females rarely served the full length of their sentences, and the longer the sentence, the smaller the proportion served. Fifty-nine percent of the misdemeanants and 68 percent of the felons were released before they had served three-fifths of their sentences.[13]

Few of the women were able to pay bail, so many were needlessly forced away from their families. About 80 percent had children, though some of these youngsters were no longer living with them. In many jails, women were not allowed to visit with any of their own children who were under age sixteen. Most of the women were unemployed at the time of their arrest, and those who did work were commonly employed as domestics or waitresses. Blacks were overrepresented, but were a majority only in urban jails. Matrons were poorly trained, and did little other than enforce punitive rules and act as gateways to special services such as those provided by physicians. Very few locational programs were available, so that the women were idle most of the time. Recreation and other services were poor or completely lacking, and there were not more than one or two institutions in which medical services were adequate. Women who attempted suicide were punished rather than helped.[14]

State and federal prisons for women have been studied more extensively than local jails, but only in recent years. Except for a few articles in the *American Journal of Correction,*[15] very little was published on the subject between Lekkerkerker's 1931 book, *Reformatories for Women in the United States,*[16] and 1973. At that time, Chandler's *Women in Prison*[17] appeared, along with a *Yale Law Journal* survey of prisons for women.[18] This was followed in 1976 by the *National Study of Women's Correctional Programs* by Glick and Neto.[19] Chandler sent questionnaires to all thirty-four American prisons for women, receiving answers from thirty of them. The questionnaire and tables summarizing the responses are included in an appendix to her book. At the time of the survey (probably 1972), only Georgia, Kentucky, Missouri, South Carolina, Tennessee, and Texas had more women incarcerated than the rated capacities of their women's institutions. Some states were as low as 36 percent of their rated institutional capacity. Although a few of the institutions were surrounded by fences, none had walls similar to those in fortress-type men's prisons. Some institutions had liberal rules for visits by family and friends, but others allowed as few as two visits a month. There were many institutions in which a high-school degree was not required for matrons and a college degree was not required for administrators. Very few institutions had full-time physicians on their staffs and only five employed psychiatrists full time or shared them with nearby men's facilities.[20]

Five of the state women's prisons had no organized recreation at all, and some of the others that had programs did not have a staff person assigned to them. Most of the institutions had academic education programs available through the high-school level and vocational training in traditional women's jobs such as laundry, secretarial work, hotel baking and cleaning, sewing, domestic service, and nurses' aides. The women were permitted to receive money from friends and relatives, and were paid for their labor in most states. Wages were generally between 50 cents and a dollar a day, with some institutions paying nothing or as little as 10 cents a day and others paying as much as $2.40 per day. Release money ranged from bus fare in South Carolina to $100 in Colorado, Minnesota, and Iowa.[21]

In the other 1973 study, Arditi and Goldberg surveyed fifteen females and forty-seven male prisons in the United States. They found a number of differences due to the primary factors of stereotyping and scale. The small number of female prisoners as compared with males leads to differences in remoteness, heterogeneity, and institutional services. Some states have so few incarcerated female offenders that they house them in adjacent jurisdictions. Even in the larger states, there are not enough women offenders to permit classifying them into different institutions by custody grading the way it is done with men. It is difficult for states to provide adequate religious, medical, and other specialized institutional services to small groups of female prisoners. Female stereotying in corrections has both good and bad results. The physical environment in women's prisons is generally less oppressive than in institutions for men, and there is more of an emphasis on rehabilitation, but there are fewer recreational facilities, and the educational and vocational programs prepare women to support themselves after release even less than programs in men's institutions. An advantage of sexual stereotyping and smaller scale is that staff-inmate ratios are more favorable in women's prisons than in men's institutions.[22]

Glick and Neto studied sixteen state prisons, forty-six county jails, and thirty-six community-based programs located in fourteen states in their *National Study of Women's Correctional Programs.* The populations of the institutions studies ranged from sixteen to 979 offenders, in almost all cases less than the rated institutional capacity. Prisons generally provided single cells for female inmates, but jails did not. Physical facilities varied directly with richness of programs. In the fourteen major state women's prisons, only three had a stable administration for twenty-four months ending in March 1976. No wonder that program continuity was difficult to maintain in the other eleven facilities.[23] In general, Glick and Neto report the same things that were discovered earlier by Chandler and by Arditi and Goldberg. They differ from those authors in that they have provided more detail on women's prisons than has ever before been available to readers. Their survey revealed that 79 percent of the institutions commonly dispensed pain medication and 58 percent distributed tranquilizers and other psychotropic drugs to their prisoners, which enabled them to venture the interpretation that ". . . tranquilizers and mood elevators are widely used in some institutions as a means to facilitate control of large inmate populations."[24]

Half of the female prisoners in the institutions surveyed were black, two-thirds were under age thirty, and 20 percent were currently married. Six out of every ten had been married once or more in the past, of which only one was living with her husband at the time of arrest. Some would say that this shows that married women are more law-abiding than single women, but class biases and the probability that marriage serves as a shield against arrest make it dangerous to hold to such a simple conclusion. Seventy-three percent of the women had children, but only 56 percent still had them at home with them at the time of the arrest. Sixty percent had not been employed during the two months prior to their incarceration, and over half had been on welfare during their adult lives.[25]

We do not have the kinds of data about programs in institutions for delinquent girls that are now available for women's prisons. However, there are indications that the two situations are similar in many ways. The same effects of smaller scale and ideological biases about proper female role behavior that are found in adult prisons are also present in juvenile institutions. In 1976, the Female Offender Resource Center completed their "Survey of Educational and Vocational Programs in State Juvenile Correctional Institutions," in which they analyzed twenty-two female, thirty male, and fifty-five coeducational institutions. At that time, nearly half of the young women in state training schools were status offenders, as compared with less than one-fifth of the young men, yet males served shorter sentences on the average.[26]

The male institutions offered a larger variety of vocational training programs than the female institutions. The programs most commonly offered in male institutions were auto shop, welding, and small engine repair. In female institutions, they were cosmetology, business education, nurses' aide instruction and food services. If the young women were allowed to work at a job while incarcerated, they were more likely to be unpaid than young men, and if paid, it was almost always at a lower rate. Academic education was generally of poorer quality in female institutions than male institutions, as were other specialized institutional services such as those in the areas of counseling, religion, and medicine.[27]

The other national study of juvenile corrections is an assessment of forty-two juvenile correctional programs by the National Assessment of Juvenile Corrections staff, led by Robert Vinter and Rosemary Sarri, at the

University of Michigan. A breakdown of program components by sex is not included in *Time Out, A National Study of Juvenile Correctional Programs,* but the characteristics of the juveniles in their sample are often presented separately for males and females. They found the same difference in the proportion of incarcerated young men and women that was obtained by the ABA's Female Offender Resource Center, and added the fact that only 8 percent of the young women in the sample were in day treatment programs (a community alternative to incarceration) as compared with 16 percent of the young men.[28]

Adolescent males and females in the sample were about equally likely to report skipping school, drinking alcohol, and smoking marijuana or hashish at least three times. Males were more than twice as likely as females to report recurrent incidents of breaking and entering or robbing someone. The one category in which young women predominated was recurrent running away from home. Fifty-six percent of the young women and 28 percent of the young men reported running away from home at least three times. The males had been arrested more often than the females (8.7 to 4.6 times per person), and were also higher on times placed in detention (4.6 to 3.8), jail (3.2 to 2.0), appearances in court (5.6 to 4.7), and previous institutionalizations (1.6 to 1.3).[29] In the conclusion to the report, Vinter writes that "we can think of no straight-forward and adequate explanation for why girls who have not committed offenses against others and who do not threaten community safety should be incarcerated to such an extent."[30]

Case Examples of Individual States

South Carolina. The number of women admitted to the South Carolina Department of Corrections rose from 107 in fiscal year 1973 to 145 in 1974, 181 in 1975, 282 in 1976, and 346 in 1977. Paralleling this growth in the number of admissions, the number of female prisoners rose from 150 in 1973 to 341 in mid-1977. Because the number of male prisoners also rose steeply, the percentage of females in South Carolina prisons held steady at about 4.5 percent during this period. At the beginning of 1973, all female prisoners were housed at the Harbison Correctional Institution for Women, which had a design capacity of 110. When this was replaced in November 1973 with the Women's Correctional Center, converted from a former junior college in the area, the capacity temporarily decreased to ninety-six, and then was increased to 168 at the beginning of 1976. At no time during this period did the average daily population ever dip down to the design capacity. In June 1977, the population at the Women's Correctional Center was operating at slightly more than twice the design capacity. Sixty percent of the incarcerated women were nonwhite, 10 percent were youthful offenders, and 48 percent were serving sentences of more than ten years. The most common offense was homicide, at 27 percent in 1977, followed by larceny (13 percent), robbery (12 percent), forgery/counterfeiting (10 percent), and dangerous drugs (8 percent).[31]

When Baunach and Murton visited the Women's Correctional Center in 1973, they found that the ladies were earning between $2 and $21 a month by making their own prison uniforms, plus those for male prisoners in other institutions. Training programs included child care, furniture refinishing, cooking, sewing, money management, hygiene, and makeup application. They also recorded several complaints about inadequate medical services.[32]

Texas. In Texas, there are two women's prisons. One, which is located near Huntsville, is called the Goree Facility. It has 5 dormitories, 132 individual cells, 208 double cells, 34 isolation cells, and 34 quarantine cells. The capacity is rated at 709.[33] A survey of all incarcerated female offenders in September 1974 revealed that 58 percent were black and 11 percent were Mexican-American. Approximately 39 percent were married, including common-law marriages, and 69 percent had children. Only 15 percent had completed high school or passed the GED examination, and 55 percent had IQs of under 100. Murder was the most common offense (20 percent), followed by drug offenses (just under 20 percent), robbery (15 percent), larceny (12 percent), burglary (10 percent), and forgery (9 percent). Nearly half the sentences were one to five years, and most of the rest were six to ten years. Slightly under 42 percent of the women were recidivists, with approximately four in every ten of them having previously served time in the Texas Department of Corrections.[34]

In 1960, there were 340 females in the Texas Department of Corrections. This rose to 423 in 1962, slowly decreased to 370 in 1966, and then rose to 637 in 1974, at which time females constituted 3.7 percent of all incarcerated offenders.[35] By December 1976 this had risen to 823, which was 4.0 percent of all prisoners. At this time, the most common offense was drugs (23 percent), followed by robbery (17 percent), homicide (16 percent), and larceny (15 percent). Sentences received by women in 1976 were shorter than in 1974, as might be expected from the rise of the less serious crimes and the relative decline of offenses against persons.[36]

A 1974 summary of the services available at Goree is uninspiring. The basic correctional services are all mentioned, but there is no reference to serious vocational training programs. The emphasis is on "female skills" such as needlecraft, knitting and quilting, and an academic education through the Windham School District.[37] Chandler lists cosmetology, floristry, horticulture, nurses' aide, licensed vocational nurse, domestic service, sewing, laundry, and hotel baking and cleaning as available to females in the Texas Department of Corrections.[38]

Minnesota. Minnesota judges do not send a great many people to prison, either male or female. At the time of the Glick-Neto survey, there were only thirty-nine women in the Minnesota Correctional Institution for Women, which is located at Shakopee, half an hour's drive from Minneapolis. This is an unusual institution, in that it has more staff than prisoners, the average time served is only ten months, and the annual cost per prisoner is $20,281. In comparison, the inmate/staff ratio at Goree is 6.6 to 1, the average time served is sixteen months, and the annual cost per prisoner is $1,675. A minimum-security facility built in 1923, the Minnesota Correctional Institution for Women has nine double rooms, forty-two single rooms, and seven isolation cells.[39]

The number of admissions to MCIW rose from twenty-seven in 1971 to forty-nine in 1972, and then held steady through 1975. During this period, the proportion of offenses against persons were also steady, averaging 21 percent of all admissions, nearly half of which were homicides. Twenty-seven percent had been convicted more than once, and 24 percent had been imprisoned on a previous conviction. Nearly one-third of the women had previously been full-time psychiatric or drug-dependency patients, and almost half of them were judged to be chemically dependent upon admission. Only 55 percent did not have a high-school diploma or its equivalent. Vocational programs at MCIW decreased between 1971 and 1975, being replaced by treatment programs of one sort or another. Two-thirds of the women were mothers, and almost all of their children were removed from the nuclear family upon their incarceration. An innovation in programming was that children were permitted to visit their mothers often, and to stay overnight with them at the institution on weekends.[40]

Iowa. In 1960, the Women's Reformatory at Rockwell City held sixty-seven prisoners, which rose to a peak of eighty-five in 1963, declined to fifty-seven in 1969, rose to seventy-three in 1971, and then dipped below seventy until 1976. In fiscal year 1976, the Women's Reformatory admitted seventy-two prisoners, released sixty-three, had an average population of sixty-nine, and a one-day population on June 30, 1976, of seventy-eight.[41] Since 1960, more women have been admitted with sentences in excess of ten years, though in the last decade the actual amount of time served has been declining and more women have been released on parole. Other population trends include an increasing proportion of black admittees, more women in the twenty to twenty-nine age bracket, and more women who are single. Less than 15 percent of the women paroled from the institution since World War I have been returned to the institution, with women serving longer sentences being much more likely to recidivate than those serving shorter sentences.[42]

The Iowa Women's Reformatory looked like a relatively benign institution in 1973. There were no bars on the windows, no guns, no fences, no cells, and no uniforms on staff or prisoners. Pay for work in the kitchen, laundry, drapery factory, garden, and powerhouse, as well as general maintenance, ranged from 30 cents to $1.40 a day. The general quality of the facility was high, though prisoners complained that there was not enough to do and that it was not always possible to earn enough money to buy the necessary clothing and other personal items.[43] By 1976, the institution had moved to give the prisoners more to do by opening up a shirt factory in the chapel and greatly expanding the offerings of the education department. At this time, the inmate/staff ratio was 1.8 to 1 and the annual cost per prisoner was $9,954.[44]

Washington, D.C. Female crime in Washington, D.C., has decreased in recent years, and just over a quarter of these offenses have been FBI index (serious) crimes in each year since 1971. Despite this, female admissions to the D.C. Department of Corrections rose 86 percent between 1973 and 1976. The evidence suggests that the increased number of incarcerations is almost entirely due to changes in judicial and/or prosecutorial policy in the sentencing of females. At the same time, the sentencing of more minor offenders to incarceration has resulted in a lowering of the average maximum sentence. The increase of 101 incarcerated Washington, D.C., women between 1975 and 1976 added $1,469,200 to the budget, a high price for a change in criminal justice system policy.[45]

Most female prisoners in Washington, D.C., are housed in the Women's Detention Center, though the new D.C. Detention Facility has two units for females and can take up to 160 women at maximum capacity.[46] The average population in the Women's Detention Center was ninety-nine in the last quarter of 1975, and 167 one year later.[47] Since the capacity of this facility is rated at sixty-six, this means that it was operating at 253 percent of capacity, a horrible imposition for women living there.

In *Woman Offender,* the staff of CONtact present a detailed summary of the programs available at the Women's Detention Center. These include community activities, social services, education, religious services, medical services, vocational training, and a series of postrelease program units. The community activities consist of programs like work release and special-purpose furloughs. High-school courses and a program leading to the GED test are available, and prisoners can take college courses by mail. There is a full-time psychologist and nurse. A physician drops in three times a week. Vocational training programs prepare the women for jobs as secretaries, factory workers, and cooks. Programming is more difficult at the Women's Detention Center than at state women's prisons because the population includes women being booked and processed, as well as those awaiting trial. State prisons generally hold only sentenced felons.[48]

Florida. Except for a slight dip in 1972, the female prisoner count in the Florida Department of Offender Rehabilitation rose steadily from 306 in 1967 to 712 in 1976, at which time 6 percent of all admissions to Florida correctional institutions were women.[49] In the decade before 1967, the female population had fluctuated only slightly, varying between 286 in 1964 and 331 in 1959.[50] Less than 9 percent of the 712 incarcerated women in 1976 had previously been committed to the department, as compared with nearly a quarter of the 16,097 incarcerated men. Approximately half of both the men and women were judged to have problems with alcohol and/or other drug use.[51]

The Florida Correctional Institution at Lowell (near Ocala) has a capacity of 842, which has now been reached. At the time of the Glick-Neto survey, the inmate/staff ratio was 2.76 to 1 and the annual cost per prisoner was $5,720. Most of the women were housed in dormitories rather than single or double cells.[52] At the end of 1975, 62 percent of the population was black, 70 percent had received sentences of less than five years, and 82 percent had no prior felony commitments. The most common offense was murder/manslaughter (29 percent), followed by narcotics (23 percent) and forgery (12 percent). Nearly half of the women had a problem with heavy alcohol and/or narcotics use, and an equal percentage had confirmed physical or mental disability.[53] Programs provided at the Florida Correctional Institution included an honor unit for selected residents, work and study release, four career laboratories, and a drug-treatment program.[54]

Pennsylvania. Pennsylvania is unusual in that it has collected correctional information on both the state and the local levels. The number of women in county and city facilities decreased from 293 in 1960 to 157 in 1970, and then rose unevenly to 198 in 1975.[55] In the state's Bureau of Correction, there were 267 females in 1960, which declined to 105 in 1971 and then rose steadily to 220 in 1975, at which time females made up 3.2 percent of all prisoners. The most common offense among those committed in 1975 was narcotics (16 percent), followed by criminal homicide (13 percent) and prison escapes (13 percent). Sentences of less than five years were received by 44 percent of the women. The average time actually served was 11.6 months.[56]

The Pennsylvania institution for women is at Muncy. Chandler reports that women at Muncy are trained in nursing, sewing, laundry work, typing, shorthand, and keypunching. Academic education programs are provided through high school.[57] In 1971, Kitsi Burkhart quoted the matron in charge of the punishment unit at Muncy as saying that the girls in her unit were never allowed outdoors, except to sweep the walks in the summer. She said, "They have kitchen work to do here . . . cleaning, trays to wash and silver to wash, linens to distribute . . . *the same as in your own house practically.*"[58]

The Federal Prison System

Until 1927, female federal offenders were housed in state institutions. At that time, the Federal Reformatory for Women at Alderson, West Virginia, opened with a capacity of 500 prisoners. By September 30, 1976, 1,448 women were incarcerated in the Federal Prison System, an increase of approximately 3 percent a year over the last decade. The two major racial/ethnic groups represented in the system in 1976 were blacks (54 percent) and whites (34 percent). More than half of the women had a history of problem drug use, most of whom had been involved with narcotics. A self-report survey of these women revealed that 73 percent had dependent children, about two-thirds of whom were living with them prior to their current arrest; nearly a third were on welfare at the time of arrest, three-quarters claimed to have a GED or high-school diploma, and 22 percent had experienced some type of vocational training while incarcerated. The majority of the women had earned less than $5,000 in the year prior to their arrest. The most common offense committed was the violation of drug laws (27 percent), robbery (9 percent), and embezzlement/fraud (3 percent).[59] These crimes are not representative of all American female arrests, since the federal government handles only a restricted range of offenses.

With a current design capacity of 660, Alderson could never hold all these women, so additional facilities have been built or reassigned in Texas, Kentucky, and California. In 1976, there were 537 women in Alderson, 203 at Forth Worth, 339 at Lexington, 101 at Pleasanton, 164 at Terminal Island, and 7 in three Metropolitan Correctional Centers. Terminal Island was the only one of these facilities that was beyond capacity. All of the institutions except Alderson are cocorrectional, which means that they house men and women in different parts of the same institution, not that they live together. Dining, study, and work, plus some program activities are organized so that men and women can interact in supervised settings. Cocorrections has a major impact on the women in the Federal Prison System, with nearly two-thirds of them serving their time in cocorrectional institutions. Unfortunately, since only 4.3 percent of all federal prisoners are women, there is no parallel opportunity available to the male prisoners in the system.[60]

Alderson is a maximum-security facility consisting of cottages and small dormitories. It is without the towered walls that characterize maximum-security prisons for men. Fort Worth contains medium- and minimum-security prisoners whose records show no violence, who are unlikely to escape, and who desire to participate heavily in institutional programs. Terminal Island is in between Alderson and Forth Worth in its security classification, Lexington has programs for drug abusers, alcoholics, and other special types of prisoners, and Pleasanton specializes in young offenders who require only a minimum-security facility. These institutions are organized using the unit management approach, in which groups of fifty to 250 prisoners are housed together, with a multi-disciplinary staff team permanently assigned to the unit. By having staff specialize in the problems of a relatively small group of prisoners, a greater degree of individualization of treatment can be achieved.[61]

Women in the Federal Prison System are exposed to a wider range of services than their sisters in most of the state institutions. Fifty-six percent are involved in academic education programs, 49 percent in occupational education, 26 percent in industries, and a handful in work and study release. Many women participate in more than one counseling program, so that the enrollment figure for fiscal year 1976 was 13 percent higher than the total female population. While women are much less likely than men to receive adequate correctional services in state facilities, they participate almost twice as heavily as men in programs in the Federal Prison System. Federal prison industries employ 302 female prisoners, 111 in automatic data processing (keypunching, keytaping, and clerical data-control clerk work) at four institutions, 107 in the garment factory at Alderson, 48 in electronics assembly at Lexington, 6 in metal work at Terminal Island, and 10 in graphics at Fort Worth. These programs are less traditionally oriented than most of the vocational programs offered to incarcerated women. Another unusual program is Artists-In-Residency, partially funded by a grant from the National Endowment for the Arts, which placed a professional artist in Alderson (in addition to a number of male institutions) in fiscal year 1977.[62]

This account of women in the Federal Prison System suggests that women are much better off there than in state or local facilities. The information presented was derived from an official publication, which means that negative commentary was omitted. There is no reason to doubt any of the statistics or program descriptions, but it may be that the picture thus constructed is incomplete. Is it more difficult for women to deal with an impersonal national system in which they have no contact at all with higher level administrators than with a single small state facility? The Gulaglike characteristics of a national system such as this one could permit a variety of administrative abuses. A rather important consideration is the crucial variable of sentence length. The average sentence length for women in the Federal Prison System increased from fifteen months in 1967 to forty-two months in 1976.[63] Because of differences in the crimes committed by women sentenced to state prisons and the Federal Prison System, a direct comparison of sentence length cannot be made with the information at hand. It would be wise to reserve final judgment on what appears to be an advanced penal system for women until more reports are published by external observers who do not have a stake in preserving the status quo in the Federal Prison System.

Sociological Approaches to the Study of Female Correctional Institutions

Sociology has been the major academic discipline to study incarcerated women and girls, though not all sociological studies have been performed by sociologists or published in the standard sociological journals. The first important study of this kind is "A Perversion Not Commonly Noted" by Otis, published in 1913. Otis was amazed to find that in a reform school there were regular courting patterns in which black and white girls dated just as if they were boys and girls.[64] Ford found that there was a considerable amount of nonphysical coercion used to convince new prisoners to become the homosexual partners of more experienced women in an Ohio institution. Some of these relationships never became overt, the participants gaining considerable pleasure from the exchange of love notes. More interesting than this was the way in which the women formed pseudofamilies of role relationships, complete with brothers, sisters, fathers, mothers, aunts, uncles, and grandparents.[65] Selling showed that few of the young women who participated in the dating system, known as the "honies," or in pseudofamilies were interested in engaging in overt sexual behavior. Those who played a masculine role in one relationship did not necessarily continue to play masculine roles in succeeding relationships.[66]

Among the best of the remaining early studies of female prisoner subcultures are those by Kosofsky and Ellis, Halleck and Hersko, and Taylor. Kosofsky and Ellis examined 100 "script" notes written between young women in a New Jersey state institution, finding that romanticism was far more important to them than overt lesbianism. The "studs" and "frails" discussed many incidents relating to the pseudofamilies at the institution, but few items from their family relations in the outside world.[67] At the Wisconsin School for Girls, Halleck and Hersko found that the majority of the prisoners participated in homosexual relationships, most of which did not actually involve overt sexual behavior. This "girl stuff," as it was called, was defined by the young women as including such things as kissing, hand-holding, and imaginary sexual involvement.[68] Even in New Zealand, Taylor found the same kinds of social structures. Young women at the Arohata Borstal Institute distinguished between "darl" relationships, which were moderate friendships, and "special darls," in which intensely emotional relationships developed.[69]

Of the four major published works on female prisoner subcultures, two were written by Rose Giallambardo. Her first book, *Society of Women: A Study of a Women's Prison,* is about social relations at the Federal Reformatory for Women in Alderson, West Virginia. She presents convincing evidence that much of what is found in female prisoner subcultures is derived from sex-role stereotypes imported into the prison from American society. She believes that the subculture in men's prisons is designed to combat the detrimental effects of the pains of imprisonment, while the subculture in women's prisons is more oriented toward establishing a substitute social world in which the women can play roles that are relevant to their social lives outside the institution. At Alderson, mutual aid was the norm for friends or lovers, but was rarely extended to cover relations with women outside of the pseudofamily system.[70]

In her second book, Giallombardo replicated her original study, this time in three institutions for female juvenile delinquents. She found additional evidence in these facilities for her position that female inmate social organization mirrors sex roles in the outside world. The pseudofamily system was called the "racket" in one institution, the "sillies" in the second, and the "chick business" in the third, but the kinship networks in the three institutions were quite similar.[71] There is a certain confusion in Giallombardo's work between pseudofamilies and homosexual behavior, and there is not enough openness to alternative hypotheses. These weaknesses notwithstanding, Giallombardo's work is preeminent in the field of female correctional studies.

Ward and Kassebaum completed their study of the California Institute for Women at Frontera in the mid-1960s, about the same time as Giallombardo's first book. Their results are very different from hers. They did not find any pseudofamilies, but there was quite a bit of overt homosexuality and many fights. The sociosexual roles at Frontera included the "butch," "femme," "jail house turn-out," and "true homosexual." There was a strict line of differentiation between the "butches" and the "femmes," with the former expected to be strong, controlled, and independent and the latter to be as weak, passive, and emotional as possible. The relationships were not very long in duration, often ending in violent fights. Ward and Kassebaum hypothesize that psychological and social benefits are what make homosexuality attractive as a way of life for female prisoners, much more so than the deprivation of heterosexual outlets.[72]

The great contribution made by Heffeman in her study of prisoners at the District of Columbia Women's Reformatory at Occoquan is that there were three major subcultural systems there rather than a single unitary prisoner subculture. These were the "square," the "cool," and the "life." Like "square Johns" in men's prisons, the members of the "square" subsystem accepted the basic norms, values, and beliefs of the straight society on the streets. Women in the "cool" subsystem were professional criminals who tried to make as few waves as possible while doing "easy time" until they could return to their criminal pursuits. In the "life" subsystem, habitual criminals who had been in and out of prison for most of their lives participated in a rich subculture that amounted to colonizing the institution. At Occoquan there were pseudofamilies, but overt lesbianism was ridiculed among the prisoners. The homosexual alliances that formed were more economic and social than sexual.[73]

Aside from a number of recent journal articles,[74] the only other major sources of information on subcultures in women's prisons are doctoral dissertations and masters' theses. A few of these are summarized in journal articles,[75] and one has been reprinted by R & E Research Associates,[76] but the others are not available in either public or university libraries.[77] Other difficult-to-obtain sources of information include papers given at professional meetings[78] and papers informally printed by research centers.[79] Since the primary purpose of this chapter is not to survey the history of female prisoner studies, only a few of the most significant publications will be discussed here.

Dorothy Coutts applied Sykes's theory of the pains of imprisonment[80] to the prisoner social system at the Oakalla Prison Farm in British Columbia. This was a strange population to study, for 59 percent of the women were narcotics addicts and 33 percent were excessive alcohol users, no prisoners were detained for more than two years, and most were released within six months. Despite the short sentences, about a quarter of the women entered into overt lesbian relationships in which there was little role differentiation into passive and active types. Nonsexual argot roles were so informal that some were not even given names. The only stable nonsexual roles were ones commonly found in male prisons or in the addict subculture. There were few violent incidents at Oakalla, and when they did occur the women tended to see them as indicative of mental illness rather than as a legitimate part of the prisoner subculture.[81] In general, the women at Oakalla suffered lower levels of deprivation than the men described by Sykes in *The Society of Captives.*

In one of the two California institutions for female juvenile delinquents, Rochelle administered questionnaires to 268 inmates. There were six cottages, and the proportion of young women participating in pseudofamily relationships varied from 81 percent in the lowest cottage to 96 percent in the highest. An inmate would be a "husband" in one relationship and a "honie" in another at the same time, which made it hard for Rochelle to produce a sociometric chart of the relationships in the cottages. Half of the young women taking a masculine name took a feminine name in another relationship in which they were engaged at the same time. Despite this confusion, young women taking masculine names were more likely to be high status than those taking feminine names. Inmates who participated heavily in the pseudofamilies, called the "chick-business," were also more likely to be high status. The only three prisoner code items to achieve a high degree of consensus were (1) never "fink" regardless of provocation, (2) try to keep others from "messing-up," and (3) if you engage in "chick-business" relationships, appear to take them seriously.[82]

In her study at a discipline-oriented institution for female juvenile delinquents in New England, Carter found young women making trouble just to pass time and carving crude but permanent tattoos on their bodies. Blacks were high status, played pseudomasculine roles, and largely ran the institution. Approximately 70 percent of the young women played "butch" and "femme" courting roles, but few went as far as overt lesbianism. Though Carter did not find the same degree of role confusion that Rochelle did, she noted that inmates changed from "butches" to "femmes" from time to time. Few lovers lived in the same cottage, so they sent a constant stream of love notes back and forth. There were overlapping micro and macro kin family systems in existence at the same time. In these kin networks, one role that was conspicuously absent was the role of "son." The courting relationships varied in their degree of generality, some being limited only to the cottage and others being just physical "fooling around" without a serious emotional commitment.[83] When Carter revisited the institution three years later, a more treatment-oriented program and shorter sentences had been instituted, and the prisoner subculture described above had almost completely vanished.[84] This is a strong piece of evidence in favor of the proposition that the inmate subculture really is subject to administrative controls.

At the State Industrial Farm for Women at Goochland, Virginia, Simmons found that the inmate leaders were more likely than nonleaders to be black, recidivists, from urban areas, and not currently married. They were also more likely to display high levels of interaction with other prisoners, and to play "stud" roles in homosexual diads. There were no pseudofamilies at Goochland, which may be related to the high incidence of inmate violence there. Simmons believes that many of the fights were caused by staff moves to break up known homosexual couples by forcing one member of each couple to relocate to a different part of the institution. When this was accomplished, one of the old partners would take a new lover, temporarily creating a lovers' triangle that often led to a fight. Simmons also found that the longer a woman was in prison, and the larger her number of previous commitments, the more likely she was to engage in overt lesbianism.[85]

The most recent unpublished doctoral dissertation is Propper's study of four female and three coeducational institutions for juvenile delinquents. Propper was unable to find structural factors to account for the differences between institutions in the level of overt homosexuality, which ranged between 6 and 2.9 percent of the institutional populations. This may be due to the fact that since all of the institutions were relatively treatment-oriented, the range of institutional structural characteristics was not great. By far the best predictor of participation in overt homosexuality during the current term of incarceration was previous homosexual behavior. There was relatively little overlap between pseudofamily membership and overt lesbianism. The only pseudofamily role-players who were likely to be involved in overt homosexuality were husband-wife diad members. Mother-daughter role players were much less likely to participate in overt sex than would be expected by chance.[86]

Looking at all these studies, it is amazing how the pseudofamily pattern has grown up in diverse types of institutions and populations around the country. The pattern described in 1913 by Otis is not much different from the one detailed in many studies conducted in the 1970s. There are evidently a few institutions where there are no pseudofamilies, but these are only a small number among hundreds. Since there is no way that the same pattern could be found in a small institution for young first timers on the East Coast and a large women's prison on the West Coast by cross-fertilization, it must be that structural similarities in the conditions of incarceration plus similarities in sex roles and the personalities that develop to be consistent with sex-role stereotypes combine in the institution to produce the same symbolic kinship structures over and over. This is strong evidence in favor of the enviromentalist position on the determinants of human behavior.

Other Approaches to the Study of Female Correctional Institutions

Not all studies of women in corrections take the sociological approach. Some take a psychological stance, and others are social-work or therapy oriented. There has been an increasing number of contributions to the literature using a biological model in recent years.

Psychological Studies. Psychological studies conducted in women's institutions focus on topics such as self-concepts,[87] general personality,[88] and sociopathy.[89] In addition, most of the studies comparing male and female offenders are psychological in nature. Perhaps the most valuable of the pure psychological studies is Earnest's unpublished dissertation, based on a 1964 survey of the female prisoners at the Wisconsin Home for women, Taycheedah. These women were mature criminals. Their average age was thirty, and only two of 105 in the sample did not have a previous felony conviction. Earnest found that offense characteristics were less important in determining criminal self-concept than the opinions of significant others. Thirty-seven percent of the women identified significant others who thought of them as criminals. Only 15 percent of the women with a noncriminal self-conception at entry developed a criminal self-conception during the *present* prison term, which translated into just a 66 percent rise in the proportion of criminal self-concepts (65 to 71 percent) in the total population. Unfortunately, it was not possible to estimate the contribution of previous incarcerations to the development of criminal self-concepts among these women.[90]

A study that would more properly be labeled social psychological than psychological is Toch's *Men in Crisis,* in which he found that women were more likely than men to injure themselves because of psychological problems encountered in prison. The women who were the most likely to injure themselves were young, of Latin extraction, and with a history of drug abuse. Approximately four of every five women who experienced psychological breakdowns reported that these events were accompanied by a substantial and explosive release of pent-up emotions. As compared with male self-injuries, the women were more likely to experience crises in the areas of coping, self-linking, and self-release, and to reinjure themselves at a later date.[91]

Most of Toch's data concern male prisoners, but the female data set is analyzed separately in a chapter by Fox, in which he reports that women in crisis situations were more concerned about support from significant others than were men. Perhaps inspired by the work of Giallombardo, he believes that the inability to play accustomed meaningful social roles in prison is more of a problem for women than the physical pains of imprisonment. When role participation and interpersonal security and responsiveness are restricted, imprisoned women are forced to regress to a more immature level of behavior, which in some cases is self-destructive.[92]

Comparative Studies. Since so many levels of discretion exist between criminal behavior and incarceration, imprisoned criminals can in no way be considered representative of criminals in general. What happens when groups of male and female prisoners are compared is that these biasing factors become hopelessly confused. There is no way that such studies can shed light on sexual differentiation among criminals on the streets, though they can say something about the differential effects of imprisonment on specific groups of men and women, and that can have value for correctional policymakers. Examining these studies, we learn that institutionalized male delinquents are not more poorly socialized than female delinquents nor do they use more neutralization techniques.[93] As compared with male prisoners, female prisoners in Ohio were more antilaw and slightly more moralistic and powerless.[94] In Michigan, male and female prisoner value systems resembled each other more than they did the value systems of control groups of street people. In addition, the female prisoners were judged to have a more "masculine" value system than the street female control group.[95]

Finding few gender differences among institutionalized delinquents, Clark concluded that by the time the youngsters were processed to the ultimate point of incarceration, the filtering process left largely hard-core and high-risk delinquents regardless of sex.[96] In another study, a similarly high proportion of incarcerated men and women felt that their sentences were too harsh, were dissatisfied with their lawyers, and believed that the poor could not get fair trials in America.[97] Though some studies show significant male-female prisoner differences,[98] the best summary statement on contemporary prisoner sexual differentiation is Wilson's conclusion that "when men and women do time in a similar environment, the differences in their styles of doing time are not great." Differences in criminal roles and offense types are associated with greater variability in prison behavior than male-female differences.[99]

Therapeutic Approaches. There have been a number of reports published of therapeutic techniques used specifically with female prisoners. Some of these are general,[100] but most deal with a specific technique, such as drug therapy,[101] moral education,[102] self-management,[103] group psychotherapy,[104] social work,[105] dance therapy,[106] or specialized programs for drug addicts.[107] These articles tend to be descriptions of programs that are specific to a particular facility, without general theoretical relevance. An outstanding exception to this is the moral development program implemented at the Niantic State Farm for Women in Connecticut. In this program, the researchers managed to get administrators, line staff, and prisoners to agree to a program in which the prisoners would have a considerable degree of control over disciplinary actions and living conditions in their own cottage. Decisions were made by majority vote in community meetings. Scharf *et al.* found that this type of self-government resulted in increased social role-taking and moral development by the women. The first group studied showed an improvement of approximately one-third of a stage on Kohlberg's six-stage scale of moral maturity. In an eight-month follow-up study, only 15 percent of the program graduates had recidivated, and all of them had been reinstitutionalized for parole violations rather than new offenses.[108]

Biological Approaches. The biological theories of female criminality put forth by Lombroso have already been discussed in chapter 2. Other early studies are discussed by Pollak, who cites diverse empirical studies linking female criminal behavior to menstruation.[109] Due to methodological inadequacies, these cannot be considered to be more than suggestive of the relationship between the female biological cycle and criminal behavior.[110] The recent literature on the influence of menstruation on crime includes two summary articles[111] and half a dozen field research reports.

Several of these reports have been authorized by Katharina Dalton. In a study of 386 newly convicted prisoners, she found that 49 percent of their crimes were committed during the premenstruum period or during menstruation. By chance, only 29 percent of the crimes would have been committed during these eight days in the normal twenty-eight-day cycle. All types of crimes were overrepresented during the premenstruum and menstruation, with theft being the most overrepresented of all. Within the institution, citations for bad behavior were also higher than expected during this period, and the overrepresentation was greater for women who had more than one citation than for those who had only a single "tag."[112] The same pattern was found by Dalton in a study of the misbehavior of schoolgirls as recorded by school authorities.[113]

Ellis and Austin also found that female prisoner aggressive behavior (both verbal and physical) was concentrated around the time of menstruation. The rate of aggressive behavior was above average during the four days of premenstruum, the day of menstruation, and the day after. There was an uneven period with generally below-average levels of aggression between menstruation and ovulation, and then a considerable dip in aggression between ovulation and the premenstruum. The authors were not able to link this to sexual frustration or irritability, but they did find an association with the experience of nonspecific body pain or discomfort.[114]

In two alternative approaches to the study of the relationship between biological factors and crime, Climent *et al.* found a high incidence of medical disorders among female prisoners[115] and Cavior *et al.* found relationships between the physical attractiveness of female delinquents and a number of measures of institutional performance.[116] At the Massachusetts Correctional Institution in Framingham, 42 percent of the women had major infectious diseases, 22 percent had ear trouble, 39 percent had headaches, 76 percent had head injuries, and so on. In this population, offender violence was related to neurological disorders and other medical disorders in the family, in addition to a number of nonmedical variables.[117]

Cavior *et al.* had front-facial pictures of seventy-five delinquent girls rated by a panel of ten white males (the same sex and race as the majority of the correctional workers at the Kennedy Youth Center, where the young women were housed). They found that high physical attractiveness was associated with early paroles and expirations, but the differences were not large enough to be statistically significant. Physical attractiveness was significantly related to both escorted and unescorted town trips for whites, but not for blacks. It was also related to two kinds of negative behavior reports—high-stigma aggressive and high-stigma nonagressive actions.[118]

In evaluating these studies, it is important to remember that they are exploratory and fragmentary, not definitive. They establish that the menstrual cycle is associated with crime in some women, but they also suggest that it is inconsequential for others. There is no way that studies with limited populations of incarcerated women can be generalized to all female criminals or to women as a whole. There is also the distinction between biological variables and the socially created arbitrary categories of criminal offenses. Any biopsychological predisposition to engage in antisocial behavior has to go through an internal interpretive process within the offender as well as by observers of the act and officials of the criminal justice system to whose attention the case is brought. Because of these multiple interpretive processes, biological factors can only interact with social variables to produce what is defined as a criminal act. They cannot do so in any direct fashion.

This is true for biological studies other than those of menstruation. For example, in Cavior *et al.*'s study of physical attractiveness, the female delinquents had to be judged to be more or less attractive. There was no possible way to measure directly and uninterpretively the variable because beauty is still in the eye of the beholder, even in science. The kinds of distortions that arise from this are exemplified by the fact that race was correlated with the judges' ratings of the young women's physical attractiveness. Blacks received a mean rating of 3.35 and whites received 4.04 on a scale of 1 to 7, with 1 being least and 7 most attractive.[119] With a set of judges that was all black instead of all white, the rating might have been different, and that would have changed the results of the study.

Probation, Parole, and Community Corrections

It is generally agreed that few delinquent girls and young women require institutionalization. Community corrections programs are a preferable alternative for most of them. Upshur indicates that these programs should include family counseling, vocational and educational programs, sex and woman's role education, and coeducational activities.[120] Comparatively little is known about the effectiveness of community programs that act as substitutes for incarceration, but there have been a number of studies of young women who have been released to parole by the California Youth Authority in 1961 and 1962, finding that the released young women had worse backgrounds than the young men, presumably because of greater selection in the criminal justice process. The young women were more likely to be from broken homes and from homes rated as undesirable for their return. They were also more likely to show serious emotional disturbances, to have been members of more than one household, to have disliked school intensely, and to have committed truancy persistently. Probation violation was less related to actual behavior for young women than for men, which is another way of saying that the authorities used more discretion in their cases and used it to violate them excessively rather than to keep them out of institutions. Very few of the females committed serious antisocial acts while on parole.[121] A later California study found that female delinquents with the highest chance of recidivating were younger, had more delinquencies in their records, and were more likely to have cooffenders in the commitment offense.[122]

In the most comprehensive of the remaining studies of recidivism among female juvenile delinquents, Sepsi studied the experiences of 210

Ohio juveniles for twelve months after their release from the Scioto Village institution. His sample was selected so that half the young women were recidivists. Only eleven of the 104 variables studied showed a significant difference between the successful and unsuccessful parolees. The most meaningful of these were previous commitment to a training school or mental hospital, previous sentence of probation, poor education, and young age at first court appearance and commitment.[123]

Parole recidivism studies have been more extensively done for adult women than for adolescents. The most broadly based of these studies are the summary reports for all U.S. state institutions published in the *Uniform Parole Reports Newsletter.* A one-year followup of 1972 male and female parolees showed that 79 percent of the men and 81 percent of the women were still continued on parole. By offense, the most successful parolees were those convicted of willful homicide (91 percent female, 90 percent male) and negligent manslaughter (91 percent female, 89 percent male), and the least successful were those convicted of forgery, fraud, or larceny by check (76 percent female, 71 percent male), and unarmed robbery (69 percent female, 79 percent male). In a three-year followup of 1969 parolees, 66 percent of the women and 63 percent of the men had successfully avoided getting into trouble. Interestingly, the homicide and manslaughter success rates were about the same after three years as after one for women, but approximately 10 percent lower for men. Excluding those offenses for which there were less than fifty cases, the least successful women were those who had been convicted of narcotics (52 percent still on parole after three years), burglary (59 percent), and forgery, fraud, or larceny by check (61 percent).[124] For both men and women, parole success declined as the number of prior prison sentences increased.[125] Prior drug use reduced the three-year success rate from 78 to 45 percent for women and from 65 to 50 percent for men. Neither gender showed much difference associated with prior alcohol abuse.[126]

Why do women fail on parole? Christine Rasche developed a multiple-factor theory which linked recidivism to the number and immediacy of the problems suffered by the releasees, the nature of these problems, and the availability of resources with which to deal with the problems.[127] In an Ohio sample, Robison concluded that the best predictor of success on parole was interpersonal competence—faring well in interpersonal relationships and increasing one's ability to relate to people.[128] Other factors that have been found to be associated with parole failure include sociopathy, drug dependence, homosexuality,[129] younger age, white ethnicity, low education, longer commitments,[130] and perceived social isolation.[131]

It is difficult to find much literature on females in community corrections. The general textbooks on the subject largely ignore women's problems and programs.[132] The best information available at this time has been collected under the sponsorship of the American Bar Association and the Law Enforcement Assistance Administration. In one ABA publication, Hudes and Monkman point to educational and vocational training as one of the most effective ways of getting women out of the criminal justice system forever by releasing them from economic dependency. These training programs are much more easily provided in the community than in isolated insituations housing only a small number of offenders. Hudes and Monkman also demonstrate that the costs of such programs can be significantly less than their benefits.[133] Another ABA pamphlet briefly describes female community-based programs such as the Bay Area Quest Program, the Hopper Home of the Women's Prison Association, and Sojourn, Inc.[34]

Thirty-six community corrections programs were included in the LEAA survey conducted by Glick and Neto. They found that these fell into six categories—halfway houses, work-release/prerelease centers, academic prerelease centers, therapeutic communities for drug abusers, mixed-modality drug programs, and programs for alcoholics. Though still control oriented, these programs differed from correctional institutions in that the racial distribution of the staff was close to that of the prisoners, ex-offenders were more likely to be employed as staff members, family and community resources were more likely to be involved, and these substantially replaced inhouse resources in many programs. Cost per year per offender was as low as $2,500 and as high as $14,350, the variation being partly determined by whether or not the program used in-house services, which naturally cost much more than making use of already-existing community services. Of the thirteen halfway houses in the sample, five used reality therapy, two practiced transactional analysis, one used gestalt therapy, two practiced a combination of gestalt and transactional analysis, and the rest implemented a combination of reality therapy and transactional analysis.[135] These programs are but a drop in the bucket compared with the need for community corrections facilities designed to serve females in unisex or coeducational programs.

Conclusions

In this chapter, we have seen that women and girls fare poorly in American corrections, whether behind the walls or in the community. Adolescents receive better correctional services than adults, but this is counteracted by the fact that many incarcerated youngsters are not guilty of any real crime at all, only status offenses such as being incorrigible or a runaway. The small number of scientific studies of females in corrections up until the mid-1960s gave way to a respectable level of scholarly output in the 1970s. If all the unpublished and obscure dissertations are included, there is now in existence a more-than-adequate literature on female prisoner subcultures. In contrast, there is little information available on institutional programs for females and almost no serious consideration of correctional policy development for women and girls. To fill in areas about which little is known at present, future research in female corrections should give particular attention to (1) racial differences among incarcerated females, (2) the problems that incarceration creates for children of female offenders, (3) drug and alcohol problems and programs, (4) extending the concept of conjugal visits to include husbands visiting incarcerated wives, (5) training and educational programs, (6) the effect of pseudofamily participation on the subsequent community adjustment (including recidivism) of released offenders, and (7) sex-linked differences in offender needs.

There is no need at this time for further studies of lesbianism in institutions for women and girls. Though it may be true that pseudosex roles are more important in institutions for females than in institutions for males, it is unlikely that the same could be said for overt homosexuality. In view of that fact, a continued emphasis on lesbianism would have to be considered as another case of the oversexualization of female behavior. At a time when so many of the traditional myths about women have been exposed by representatives of the women's movement and undermined by social-science research, it is inexcusable to continue to oversexualize the behavior of female prisoners.

Notes

1. *National Prisoners Statistics Bulletin—Capital Punishment 1973* (Washington, D.C.: Government Printing Office, 1975), 16, 17, 22.

2. *National Jail Census—1970* (Washington, D.C.: Government Printing Office, 1971), 10.

3. *Survey of Inmates of Local Jails, 1972, Advance Report* (Washington, D.C.: Law Enforcement Assistance Administration, 1974), 1.

4. *America's Children and Youth in Institutions*, 1950-1960-1964 (Washington, D.C.: Government Printing Office, 1965), 36.

5. *Children in Custody, Advance Report on the Juvenile Detention and Correctional Facility Census of 1974* (Washington, D.C.: Government Printing Office, 1977), 24.

6. Linda R. Singer, "Women and the Correctional Process," *American Criminal Law Review* 11 (1973), 300.

7. Other publications are literary treatments, such as Lillian Rubin, "The Racist Liberals—An Episode in a County Jail," *Transaction* 5 (September 1968), 39-44, or unpublished items like Marvin E. Ketterling, *Rehabilitation of Women in the Milwaukee County Jail: An Exploratory*

Study, unpublished doctoral dissertation (Colorado State College, 1964) and B. Knudson, *Career Patterns of Female Misdemeanant Offenders*, unpublished doctoral dissertation (University of Minnesota, 1968). Additional material on women in jails is contained in Ruth M. Glick and Virginia V. Neto, *National Study of Women's Correctional Programs* (Sacramento, Cal.: California Youth Authority, 1976), which is discussed later in this chapter, along with other studies of state and federal women's prisons.

8. Omar Hendrix, *A Study in Neglect: A Report on Woman Prisoners* (New York: The Women's Prison Association, 1972), 11-18

9. Ibid., 38.

10. Charles O'Reilly, Frank Cizon, John Flanagan, and Steven Pflanczer, "Sentenced Women in a County Jail," *American Journal of Correction* 30 (March-April 1968), 23-25.

11. See, for example, *Women in Detention and Statewide Jail Standards* (Washington, D.C.: Commission on Correctional Facilities and Services of the American Bar Association, 1974) and two articles by Margery L. Velimesis, "Criminal Justice for the Female Offender," *Journal of the American Association of University Women* (October 1969), 13-16, and "The Female Offender," *Crime and Delinquency Literature* 7 (1975), 94-112.

12. Margery L. Velimesis, *Report on the Survey of 41 Pennsylvania County Court and Correctional Services for Women and Girl Offenders, January 1, 1965-December 31, 1966* (Philadelphia: Pennsylvania Program for Women and Girls Offenders, 1969), 2-3.

13. Ibid., 12-13, 60, 65, 71.

14. *Women in Detention and Statewide Jail Standards*, 16-19.

15. A typical article in this journal is Isabel H. Gauper, "Missouri State Penitentiary for Women," *American Journal of Correction* 24 (November-December 1962), 26-30. A more recent article in this journal is Joann B. Morton, "Women Offenders: Fiction and Facts," 38 (July-August and November-December 1976), 32-34, 36-37.

16. Eugenia Lekkerkerker, *Reformatories for Women in the United States* (Groningen, The Hague: J.B. Wolter, 1931).

17. Edna W. Chandler, *Women in Prison* (Indianapolis, Indiana: Bobbs-Merrill, 1973).

18. "The Sexual Segregation of American Prisons," *Yale Law Journal* 82 (1973), 1229-73.

19. Ruth M. Glick and Virginia V. Neto, *National Study . . . .*

20. Chandler, 103-21.

21. Ibid., 122-41.

22. "The Sexual Segregation of American Prisons," 1229-43. Though originally published anonymously, the authors later summarized it in R.R. Arditi and F. Goldberg, "Sexual Segregation of American Prisons," *Mental Health Digest* 5 (September 1973), 18-26.

23. Glick, xii-xvii.

24. Ibid., 68-69.

25. Ibid., xvii-xx. For more information on the families of female prisoners, see Serapio R. Zalba, *Women Prisoners and Their Families* (Los Angeles: Delmar Pub. Co., 1964); and Carol Gibbs, "The Effect of the Imprisonment of Women upon Their Children," *British Journal of Criminology* 11 (1971), 113-30. Additional information on this topic is available in Elmer H. Johnson, "Childbirth to Women under Sentence: Characteristics and Outcome," Center for the Study of Crime, Delinquency and Corrections, Southern Illinois University, 1969.

26. *Little Sisters and the Law* (Washington, D.C.: Female Offender Resource Center, American Bar Association, 1977), 15-16.

27. Ibid., 16-18.

28. Robert D. Vinter, *Time Out, A National Study of Juvenile Correctional Programs* (Ann Arbor, Michigan: National Assessment of Juvenile Corrections, University of Michigan, 1976), 23-24.

29. Ibid., 41-45.

30. Ibid., 201.

31. "Summary of Statistical Data on the SCDC Female Inmate Population" (Columbia, S.C.: South Carolina Department of Corrections, 1977).

32. Phyllis Jo Baunach and Thomas O. Murton, "Women in Prison: An Awakening Minority, *Crime and Corrections* 1 (Fall 1973), 5.

33. Glick, 341.

34. "Profile of the Female Offender" (Huntsville, TX: Texas Department of Corrections, 1974), 4-26.

35. Ibid., 3.

36. "1976 Annual Statistical Report" (Huntsville, TX: Texas Department of Corrections, 1977), 49-55, 79-85.

37. "Profile of the Female Offender," 32-34.

38. Chandler, 130-31.

39. Glick, 333, 341.

40. "Women Offenders at Minnesota Correctional Institution for Women, 1976" (St. Paul, MN: Minnesota Department of Corrections, 1976).

41. "Annual Report" (Des Moines, Iowa: Iowa Department of Social Services, 1967-1976).

42. Laurel Rans, "Implications of Findings and Recent Trends—Iowa Historical Population Profile" (Des Moines, Iowa: Entropy Limited, 1975).

43. Baunach, 6-7.

44. "Annual Report, 1976," 20-21.

45. Michael A. Hagstad, "Women in the Criminal Justice Process in the District of Columbia: A Preliminary Analysis of Some Recent Trends" (Washington, D.C.: D.C. Department of Corrections, 1977).

46. "Annual Report, 1975-1976" (Washington, D.C.: District of Columbia Department of Corrections, 1977), 4, 35.

47. Michael A. Hagstad and Sandra P. Hall, "Population Report" (Washington, D.C.: District of Columbia Department of Corrections, 1977), 3.

48. CONtact staff, *Woman Offender* (Lincoln, Nebraska, CONtact Publications, 1976), 53-57.

49. "Annual Report, 1975-1976" (Tallahassee, Florida: Florida Department of Offender Rehabilitation, 1977), 53-56.

50. "Eighth Biennial Report" (Tallahassee, Florida: Florida Division of Corrections, 1972), 80.

51. "Annual Report, 1975-1976," 59-75.

52. Glick, 324.

53. "Statistical Report, Demographic Data Series, Florida Correctional Institution—Women, Population as of 12/31/75" (Tallahassee, Florida: Department of Offender Rehabilitation, 1976).

54. "Annual Report, 1975-1976," 24.

55. "Prisoners in Pennsylvania County Prisons and Jails" (Harrisburg, Pa.: Bureau of Criminal Justice Statistics, Pennsylvania Department of Justice, 1973-1975).

56. "Populations in the Bureau of Correction" (Harrisburg, Pa.: Bureau of Criminal Justice Statistics, Pennsylvania Department of Justice, 1974-1975).

57. Chandler, 126-31.

58. Kitsi Burkhart, "Women in Prison," *Ramparts Magazine* 9 (June 1971), 25.

59. Euphesenia Foster, *Female Offenders in the Federal Prison System* (Washington, D.C.: Federal Bureau of Prisons, 1977), 5-9, 28.

60. Ibid., 9, 19-20.

61. Ibid., 10-14, 18.

62. Ibid., 22-25.

63. Ibid., 6.

64. Margaret Otis, "A Perversion Not Commonly Noted," *Journal of Abnormal Psychology* 8 (1913), 113-16. For a more detailed discussion of sociological studies of female prisoner subcultures see Dee C. Thomas-Bowker and Lee H. Bowker, "Subcultures in Women's Prisons," in Lee H. Bowker, *Prisoner Subcultures* (Lexington, Mass.: Lexington Books, D.C. Heath, 1977), 77-92. A lengthy bibliography of studies on the subject is contained in Lee H. Bowker, *A Bibliographical Guide to Prisons and Prisoners* (Palo Alto, Cal.: R & E Research Associates, 1978).

65. Charles A. Ford, "Homosexual Practices of Institutionalized Females," *Journal of Abnormal and Social Psychology* 23 (1929), 442-48.

66. Lowell S. Selling, "The Pseudo-Family," *American Journal of Sociology* 37 (1931), 247-53.

67. Sidney Kosofsky and Albert Ellis, "Illegal Communication Among Institutionalized Female Delinquents," *Journal of Social Psychiatry* 48 (1958), 155-60.

68. Seymour Halleck and Marvin Hersko, "Homosexual Behavior in a Correctional Institution for Adolescent Girls," *American Journal of Orthopsychiatry* 32 (1962), 911-17.

69. A.J.W. Taylor, "The Significance of 'Darls' or 'Special Relationships' for Borstal Girls," *British Journal of Criminology* 5 (1965), 406-18.

70. Rose Giallombardo, *Society of Women: A Study of a Women's Prison* (New York: John Wiley and Sons, 1966), 14-17, 102-104, 125-27 and 148-51.

71. Rose Giallombardo, *The Social World of Imprisoned Girls* (New York: John Wiley and Sons, 1974).

72. David Ward and Gene G. Kassebaum, *Women's Prison: Sex and Social Structure* (Chicago: Aldine, 1965), 141-201.

73. Esther Heffernan, *Making It in Prison, The Square, The Cool and The Life* (New York: John Wiley and Sons, 1972), 41-43, 87-104.

74. Among the best of these are Thomas W. Foster, "Make-Believe Families: A Response of Women and Girls to the Deprivations of Imprisonment," *International Journal of Criminology and Penology* 3 (1975), 71-78; and Linda Norris, "Comparison of Two Groups in a Southern State Women's Prison: Homosexual Behavior Versus Non-Homosexual Behavior," *Psychological Reports* 34 (1974), 75-78.

75. See, for example, Barbara Carter's "Race, Sex and Gangs, Reform School Families," *Society* 11 (Nov.-Dec. 1973), 38-43, based on her brilliant dissertation, *On The Grounds: Informal Culture in a Girl's Reform School* (Brandeis University, 1972).

76. Arlene E. Mitchell, *Informal Inmate Social Structure in Prisons for Women: A Comparative Study* (Palo Alto, Cal.: R & E Research Associates, 1975).

77. See, for example, L.L. LeShanna, *Family Participation: Functional Response of Incarcerated Females*, unpublished M.A. thesis (Bowling Green State University, 1969); D.J. Wentz, *The Role of Incarcerated Female Juvenile Delinquents' Self-Acceptance and Their Participation in the Sillies and the Make-Believe Family*, unpublished M.A. thesis (Bowling Green State University, 1965); Sara W. McDonnell, *The Female Prisoners at Tipton and the Inmate Code*, unpublished M.A. thesis (Central Missouri State College, 1971); Imogene Simmons, *Interaction and Leadership Among Female Prisoners*, unpublished doctoral dissertation (University of Missouri-Columbia, 1975); Dorothy Mae Coutts, *An Examination of the Social Structure of the Women's Unit, Oakalla Prison Farm*, unpublished M.A. thesis (University of British Columbia, 1961); Phyllis A. Rochelle, *A Study of the Social System of an Institution for Adolescent Delinquent Girls*, unpublished D.S.W. dissertation (University of California, Berkeley,

1965); Linda Almy *et al.*, *A Study of a Coeducational Correctional Facility*, unpublished M.S. thesis (Boston University, 1975); Nancy Brandon *et al.*, *A Study in a Coeducational Correctional Facility: Differential Effects of Psychotherapy and Other Programs*, unpublished M.S. thesis (Boston University, 1977); and Alice Propper, *Importation and Deprivation Perspectives on Homosexuality in Correctional Institutions: An Empirical Test of Their Relative Efficacy*, unpublished doctoral dissertation (University of Michigan, 1976).

78. Among the best of these are Gary F. Jensen, "Perspectives on Inmate Culture: A Study of Women in Prison," paper presented at the annual meeting of the Society for the Study of Social Problems (Montreal, 1974); J. Robert Lilly and Richard A. Ball, "Norm Neutralization, Anomia and Self-Concept Among Institutionalized Female Delinquents," paper presented at the annual meeting of the American Society of Criminology (Tucson, 1972); and Alice Propper, "Importation vs. Deprivation: A Test of Perspectives of Causes of Institutional Lesbianism," paper presented at the annual meeting of the American Sociological Association (Chicago, 1977).

79. See, for example, two papers by Nanci K. Wilson published at the Center for the Study of Crime, Delinquency, and Corrections, University of Southern Illinois at Carbondale, "Styles of Doing Time in a Co-Ed Prison: Masculine and Feminine Alternatives" and "Unanswered Questions About Differences in Male/Female Inmate Cultures," both published in 1975; and Sally Davis, "Girls in Detention: A Sociological Study of a Juvenile Hall" (Berkeley, Cal.: Center for the Study of Law and Society, University of California, 1963).

80. Gresham M. Sykes, *The Society of Captives* (New York: Atheneum, 1966), 63-83.

81. Coutts, 47, 197, 231-45.

82. Rochelle, 43-58, 97, 102.

83. Carter, *On The Grounds*, 78, 87, 118-64.

84. Ibid., 199-204.

85. Simmons, 125-27, 153-55, 165, 190-93.

86. Propper, *Importation and Deprivation Perspectives*, 107, 137-38, 153-54, 200-201.

87. See, for example, John R. Snortum, Thomas E. Hannum, and David H. Mills, "The Relationship of Self-Concept and Parent Image to Rule Violations in a Women's Prison," *Journal of Clinical Psychology* 26 (1970), 284-87; R.N. Cassell and Julia Clayton, "A Preliminary Analysis of Certain Self-Concepts of Women in a Correctional Institution," *Sociology and Social Research* 45 (1961), 316-19; and Marion R. Earnest, *Criminal Self-Conceptions in the Penal Community of Female Offenders: An Empirical Study*, unpublished doctoral dissertation (University of Iowa, 1971).

88. Sybil B.G. Eysenck and Hans J. Eysenck, "The Personality of Female Prisoners," *British Journal of Psychiatry* 122 (1973), 693-98; Thomas E. Hannum and Roy E. Warman, "The MMPI Characteristics of Incarcerated Females," *Journal of Research in Crime and Delinquency* 1 (1964), 119-26; and W. Cecil Johnson, "Descriptive Study of 100 Convicted Female Narcotic Residents," *Corrective Psychiatry and Journal of Social Therapy* 14 (1968), 230-36.

89. Thomas C. Sannito and Thomas E. Hannum, "Relationship between the WAIS and Indices of Sociopathy in an Incarcerated Female Population," *Journal of Research in Crime and Delinquency* 3 (1966), 63-70; John P. Stefanowicz and Thomas E. Hannum, "Ethical Risk-Taking and Sociopathy in Incarcerated Females," *Correctional Psychologist* 4 (1971), 138-52; and Christine Schultz, *Sociopathic and Non-Sociopathic Female Offenders,* unpublished doctoral dissertation (Ohio State University, 1973).

90. Earnest, 50-55, 71, 79-80.

91. Hans Toch, *Men in Crisis* (Chicago: Aldine, 1975), 128-41.

92. James G. Fox, "Women in Crisis," in Toch, *Men in Crisis,* 193-203.

93. Shirley A. Merritt, *Systematic Comparison of Female and Male Delinquency by Selected Components*, unpublished doctoral dissertation (Ohio State University, 1971); and Henry W. Mannle, *An Empirical Exploration and Interpretation of Neutralization Theory Predicated upon Sexual Differences in the Socialization Process*, unpublished doctoral dissertation (Florida State University, 1972).

94. Barbara A. Kay, "Can You Change This Image? A Report of Male-Female Differences in Attitude toward the Police and Legal Institutions," *Police* 10 (Nov.-Dec. 1965), 30-32; Barbara A. Kay, "Female Prisoners: Their Concepts of Self," *Police* 7 (Nov.-Dec. 1962), 39-41, 70; Barbara A. Kay, "Value Orientations as Reflected in Expressed Attitudes Are Associated with Ascribed Social Sex Roles," *Canadian Journal of Criminology and Corrections* 11 (July 1969), 193-97; Barbara A. Kay, *Differential Self-Perceptions of Female Offenders*, unpublished doctoral dissertation (Ohio State University, 1961); and Barbara A. Kay and Christine G. Schultz, "Divergence of Attitudes toward Constituted Authorities between Male and Female Felony Inmates," in Walter C. Reckless and Charles L. Newman, *Interdisciplinary Problems in Criminology: Papers of the American Society of Criminology* (Columbus, Ohio: Ohio State University Press, 1965), 209-15.

95. Raymond Cochrane, "The Structure of Value Systems in Male and Female Prisoners," *British Journal of Criminology* 11 (1971), 73-79.

96. Shirley M. Clark, "Similarities in Components of Female and Male Delinquency: Implications for Sex-Role Theory," in Reckless and Neuman,

217-27. See also Anthony Catalino, "Boys and Girls in a Coeducational Training School Are Different—Aren't They?" *Canadian Journal of Corrections* 14 (1972), 120-31; and Gordon H. Barker and William T. Adams, "Comparison of the Delinquencies of Boys and Girls," *Journal of Criminal Law, Criminology and Police Science* 53 (1962), 470-75.

97. P.C. Kratcoski and K. Scheuerman, "Incarcerated Male and Female Offenders' Perceptions of Their Experiences in the Criminal Justice System," *Journal of Criminal Justice* 2 (1974), 73-78.

98. See, for example, D.W. McKerracher, D.R.K. Street, and L.J. Segal, "A Comparison of the Behavior Problems Presented by Male and Female Subnormal Offenders," *British Journal of Psychiatry* 112 (1966), 891-97; D. Offer and R.C. Marohn, "Violence among Hospitalized Delinquents," *Archives of General Psyhiatry* 32 (1975), 1180-86; Harjit S. Sandhr and Lewis H. Irving, "Female Offenders and Marital Disorganization: An Aggressive and Retreatist Reaction," *International Journal of Criminology and Penology* 2 (1974), 35-42; Morris Weitman, "Extent of Criminal Activity, Sex, and Varieties of Authoritarianism," *Psychological Reports* 13 (1963), 217-18; Patricia B. Sutker and Charles E. Moan, "A Psychosocial Description of Penitentiary Inmates," *Archives of General Psychiatry* 29 (1973), 663-67; and James H. Panton, "Personality Differences between Male and Female Prison Inmates Measured by the MMPI," *Criminal Justice and Behavior* 1 (1974), 332-39.

99. Wilson, "Styles of Doing Time," 21-22.

100. Camilla M. Anderson, "The Female Criminal Offender," *American Journal of Correction* 29 (Nov.-Dec. 1967), 7-9; and Marvin E. Ketterline, "Rehabilitating Women in Jail," *Journal of Rehabilitation* 36 (1970), 36-38, 56.

101. Constantine Iliopoulos and Robert L. Gatski, "Fluphenazine Treatment of Behavioral Disorders," *Comprehensive Psychiatry* 2 (1961), 364-67; and H. Brick, W.H. Doub. Jr., and W.C. Perdue, "A Comparison of the Effects of Amitriplyline and Protriplyline on Anxiety and Depressive States in Female Prisoners," *International Journal of Neuropsychiatry* 1 (1965), 325-36.

102. Peter Scharf, Joseph E. Hickey, and Thomas Moriarity, "Moral Conflict and Change in Correctional Settings," *Personnel and Guidance Journal* 51 (1973), 660-63; and Lawrence Kohlberg, Peter Scharf, and Joseph Hickey, "The Justice Structure of the Prison—A Theory and an Intervention," *Prison Journal* 51 (1971), 3-14.

103. Sarah R. Carpenter,"An Experiment in Successful Living," *Youth Authority Quarterly* 19 (1966), 9-14; and Sheryl Moinat and John R. Snortum, "Self-Management of Personal Habits by Female Drug Addicts: A Feasibility Study, *Criminal Justice and Behavior* 3 (1976), 29-40.

104. Roger Dennett and Janet S. York, "Group Therapy in One

Women's Correctional Institution,'' *American Journal of Correction* 28 (1966), 21-25; and Kent G. Bailey, ''Audiotape Self-Confrontation in Group Psychotherapy,'' *Psychological Reports* 27 (1970), 439-44.

105. F.J. Peirce, ''Social Group Work in a Women's Prison,'' *Federal Probation* 27 (1963), 37-43; and Allan P. Webb and Patrick V. Riley, ''Effectiveness of Casework with Young Female Probationers,'' *Social Casework* 51 (1970), 566-72.

106. Mary E. Montague, ''Women Prisoners Respond to Contemporary Dance,'' *Journal of Health, Physical Education and Recreation* 34 (1963), 25-26, 71.

107. Harold W. Demone, ''Experiments in Referral to Alcoholism Clinics,'' *Quarterly Journal of Studies on Alcohol* 24 (1963), 495-502; Ben I. Coleman, ''Helping Women Addicts in New York City,'' *International Journal of Offender Therapy and Comparative Criminology* 18 (1974), 82-85; and Houston Brummit, ''Observations on Drug Addicts in a House of Detention for Women,'' *Corrective Psychiatry and Journal of Social Therapy* 9 (1963), 62-70.

108. Scharf, 662-63.

109. Otto Pollak, *The Criminality of Women* (Philadelphia: University of Pennsylvania Press, 1950), 129.

110. Ibid., 135.

111. Jocelynne A. Scutt, ''A Factor in Female Crime,'' *Criminologist* 9 (Nov. 1974), 56-71; and Aleta Wallach and Larry Rubin, ''The Premenstrual Syndrome and Criminal Responsibility,'' *UCLA Law Review* 19 (1971), 209-312.

112. Katharina Dalton, ''Menstruation and Crime,'' *British Medical Journal* 2 (1961), 1752-53.

113. Katharina Dalton, ''Schoolgirls' Misbehavior and Menstruation,'' *British Medical Journal* 2 (1960), 1647.

114. Desmond P. Ellis and Penelope Austin, ''Menstruation and Aggressive Behavior in a Correctional Center for Women,'' *Journal of Criminal Law, Criminology and Police Science* 62 (1971), 388-95.

115. Carlos E. Climent, Ann Rollins, Frank R. Ervin, and Robert Plutchik, ''Epidemiological Studies of Women Prisoners, I: Medical and Psychiatric Variables Related to Violent Behavior,'' *American Journal of Psychiatry* 130 (1973), 985-90.

116. Helene E. Cavior, Steven C. Hayes, and Norman Cavior, ''Physical Attractiveness of Female Offenders, Effects on Institutional Performance,'' *Criminal Justice and Behavior* 1 (1974), 321-31.

117. Climent, 987.

118. Cavior, 326-28.

119. Ibid., 324, 326.

120. Carole Upshur, ''Delinquency in Girls: Implications for Service

Delivery," in Yitzhak Bakal, *Closing Correctional Institutions* (Lexington, MA: D.C. Heath, 1973), 26-28.

121. Evelyn S. Guttman, "A Comparison of Youth Authority Boys and Girls: Characteristics and Their Relationship to Parole Violation" (Sacramento: California Youth Authority, 1965), 1-2.

122. Martin J. Molof, "Statistical Prediction of Recidivism among Female Parolees in the California Youth Authority" (Sacramento: California Youth Authority, 1970).

123. Victor J. Sepsi, Jr., *Archical Factors for Predicting Recidivism of Female Juvenile Delinquents,* unpublished doctoral dissertation, Kent State University, 1971; and Victor J. Sepsi, Jr., "Girl Recidivists," *Journal of Research in Crime and Delinquency* 1 (1974), 70-79.

124. *Uniform Parole Reports Newsletter,* National Council on Crime and Delinquency Research Center, March 1975, Table I for Males and Females. For a comparison of 1970 parolees by sex, see William H. Moseley and Margaret H. Gerould, "Sex and Parole: A Comparison of Male and Female Parolees," *Journal of Criminal Justice* 3 (1975), 47-58.

125. Ibid., Table III for Males and Females.

126. Ibid., Tables V and VI for Males and Females.

127.Christine Rasche, *Problems, Expectations, and the Post-Release Adjustment of the Female Felon,* unpublished doctoral dissertation (Washington University, 1972).

128. Elizabeth B. Robison, *Women on Parole: Reintegration of the Female Offender,* unpublished doctoral dissertation (Ohio State University, 1971), 170.

129. C. Robert Cloninger and Samuel B. Guze, "Psychiatric Disorders and Criminal Recidivism," *Archives of General Psychiatry* 29 (1973), 267.

130. Imogene L. Simmons and Joseph W. Rogers, "The Relationship between Type of Offense and Successful Postinstitutional Adjustment of Female Offenders," *Criminology, An Interdisciplinary Journal* 7 (1970), 70-71.

131. Betty H. Metz, "Alienation among Female Probationers," *Journal of the California Probation, Parole and Correction Association* 4 (1967), 37-45. For other studies of parole recidivism, see the literature summary for Margery L. Velimesis, "The Female Offender," *Crime and Delinquency Literature* 7 (1975), 99-102.

132. See, for example, Hassim M. Solomon, *Community Corrections* (Boston: Holbrock Press, 1976); Louis P. Carney, *Corrections and the Community* (Englewood Cliffs, N.J.: Prentice-Hall, 1977); and Vernon Fox, *Community-Based Corrections* (Englewood Cliffs, N.J.: Prentice-Hall, 1977).

133. Karen Hudes and Gail S. Monkman, *Community Programs for Women Offenders: Cost and Economic Considerations* (Washington,

D.C.: Correctional Economics Center, American Bar Association, 1975).

134. *Female Offenders: Problems and Programs* (Washington, D.C.: Female Offender Resource Center, American Bar Association, 1976), 20-25.

135. Glick, 181-89.

9 International Perspectives on Female Crime and Its Correction

We have seen in chapter 1 that Adler's theory of the new female criminal receives only limited support from official crime data derived from the *Uniform Crime Reports.* In this chapter, we will see how it fares in the explanation of international female crime trends. The chapter concludes with a section on correction treatment for women in Canada, India, Denmark, Australia, and New Zealand.

Female Crime around the World

Interpol has been publishing reports on world crime since 1950. Participation is naturally voluntary, so the list of reporting nations is incomplete, and in addition varies from year to year according to administrative and political factors in the reporting countries. As an example of this, the United States sent summary statistics to Interpol for a number of years but no longer participates. The *International Crime Statistics*[1] are issued by Interpol every two years. Two tables summarize the annual crime statistics for each nation. These tables include data for only a limited list of crimes. Interpol has standardized crime categories as much as possible, considering the wide differences in the definitions of criminal acts from one nation to another. Despite this effort, definitional differences in crime among nations make cross-national comparisons tenuous at best. There are also international differences in enforcement policies, and in the criminal justice process, not the least of which is the proportion of the incidents reported to the police. These differences among nations are complicated by further changes in these factors over time within individual nations.

Our interest is in the second of the two tables, which breaks down offender statistics by age and sex of offender. These data were abstracted from the *International Crime Statistics* for the years 1950, 1955, 1960, 1965, and 1972. Nations were included in the analysis if they reported sex-specific crime rates for at least two years that were a minimum of a decade apart. Because so many countries either did not make a report to Interpol in some years or made reports that did not include breakdowns by sex of offender, only thirty nations met the criteria for inclusion in the sample. Three crime categories were selected for analysis—murder (which excludes manslaughter and abortion, but includes infanticide and attempted murder), major larceny (robbery, burglary, etc.), and total criminal offenses. Each of these data sets was transformed from crude female crime statistics to ratios of female crime over total crime in order to control for the general level of national criminal behavior at each measurement point. Murder was chosen because it is the most violent of violent crimes. However, many murders are passion crimes by law-abiding citizens and have no implication for the involvement of the offender in a life-style of antisocial behavior. For this reason, major larceny was added as the second data set. Major larceny is a good index of "professional" commitment to a criminal career, and includes offenses in which the use of violence is instrumental (in traditional sex-role stereotypic terms, masculine) rather than expressive, or passionate (in traditional sex-role stereotypic terms, feminine). Total crime was added as the third crime category for analysis as the best available measure of general female criminal behavior and, at the same time, a rough index of female property crime. The usefulness of total crime as an index of property crime is not greatly affected by the violent crime rate, since violent crime is but a small proportion of total female crime. What does impact this relationship is the extent to which public-order crimes are part of the total crime rate, and this is not clear from the data contained in the *International Crime Reports.*

Table 9-1 shows murders committed by females as a proportion of all murders in the thirty nations that met the criteria for inclusion in the sample. The proportions of murders committed by women are well below .50, except for Luxembourg in 1950, and that is an effect of the small number of murders committed in this tiny nation. Smaller nations tend to show a greater degree of variability in their murder rates than larger nations, especially if they have a high transient population such as one sees in population tourist centers. On the other end of the scale, Guyana, Ireland, Sweden, Hong Kong, Israel, Malaysia, and Norway have all reported years in which none of the murders were known to have been committed by women. Six of the thirty nations showed an increase of at least .03 in the proportion of murders committed by females over a period of a decade or more, and ten showed a decrease of the same magnitude. Nearly all the decreases are in European countries that reported unusually high proportions of female murders in the years after World War II and have returned to more "normal" levels since then. Changes in the sex and age distribution of the population, as well as other social effects of World War II, are probably largely responsible for this pattern. Taken as a whole, table 9-1 suggests that the female proportion of murderous acts is declining rather than increasing worldwide. It could be that this would not be true if all nations were included in the analysis. At the moment, the available statistics do not permit us to undertake the analysis of a more extensive sample of nations.

Females commit a much smaller proportion of major larcenies than murders. The range of proportions in table 9-2 is from .25 (Luxembourg) to .00 (Pakistan, Netherlands Antilles, Malaysia, Hong Kong, and Israel).

Table 9-1
Murders Committed by Females as a Proportion of All Murders

	Year				
Nation[a]	*1950*	*1955*	*1960*	*1965*	*1972*
West Germany	.27	.31	.21	.18	.12
Denmark	.12	.27[b]	–	.31[b]	.05
Egypt	–	.02	.02	.02	.02
Finland	–	.19	.24	.25	–
France	–	.11	.08	.15	.12
Ireland	.33[b]	.33[b]	.25[b]	.00	–
Israel	–	.10	.09	.07	.00
Japan	–	.15	.14	.17	.19
Luxembourg	.67[b]	.00	.18	.09	.20
Netherlands	–	.16	.13	.09	.04
England/Wales	.39	.34	.18	.17	.17
Scotland	.10	.33[b]	.04	.15	.13
Sweden	.23[b]	.27[b]	–	.00	.06[c]
Morocco	–	.24[b]	–	.07	.20
Philippines	.03	–	.01	.02	.02[c]
Netherlands Antilles	–	.10	.11	.07	.13
Austria	–	.32	.29	.23	.16
Australia	–	.18	–	.18	.11[c]
Hong Kong	–	–	.00	.00	.02
Indonesia	–	.06	.08	.05	.09
Kenya	–	–	.08	–	.10
Pakistan	–	.01	–	.01	–
Libya	–	.14	.11	.18	.17
Guyana	–	–	.00	.20	.11
Madagascar	–	–	.25	.22[b]	.11
Malaysia	–	–	.29	.02	.00
Nigeria	–	–	.03	.04	.09
Tunisia	–	–	.19	.22	.11
Burma	–	–	.01	.01	.01
Norway	–	–	.18	.40[b]	.00[c]

Source: Interpol, *International Crime Statistics* (St. Cloud, France: Interpol General Secretariat, 1950-1952, 1955-1956, 1959-1960, 1965-1966, and 1971-1972).

[a]Only nations listed at least twice with a minimum span of ten years were included. Monaco was excluded because of its small size and high transient population.

[b]These relatively high proportions are based on less than twenty-five female offenses.

[c]1971 statistics were substituted where 1972 statistics were not available.

Five nations showed rises of .03 or more in the proportion of major larceny committed by females over a period of at least ten years, and four showed declines. In 1972, the average nation experienced a female contribution to

Table 9-2
Major Larcenies Committed by Females as a Proportion of All Major Larcenies

	Year				
Nation[a]	*1950*	*1955*	*1960*	*1965*	*1972*
West Germany	.07	.06	.04	.04	.04
Denmark	.04	.01	–	.11	.07
Finland	–	.05	.05	.03	–
France	–	.10	.09	.09	.09
Ireland	.02	.05	.02	.03	–
Israel	–	.10	.09	.07	.00
Japan	–	.01	.01	.01	.08
Luxembourg	.06	.25	.07	.16	.05
Netherlands	–	.04	.04	.04	.04
England/Wales	.03	.03	.03	.02	.03
Scotland	.02	.02	.03	.04	.05
Sweden	.03	–	–	.02	.03[b]
Morocco	–	.09	–	.01	.03
Philippines	.02	–	.03	.02	.02[b]
Netherlands Antilles	–	.03	.00	.02	.02
Austria	–	.01	.12	.09	.09
Australia	–	.02	–	.03	.03[b]
Hong Kong	–	–	.01	.00	.01
Indonesia	–	.05	.06	.05	.03
Kenya	–	–	.01	–	.03
Pakistan	–	.00	–	.01	–
Libya	–	.02	.03	.02	.20
Madagascar	–	–	.16	.08	.13
Malaysia	–	–	.00	–	.00
Nigeria	–	–	.02	.02	.02
Tunisia	–	–	.06	.06	.14
Burma	–	–	.01	.01	.05
Norway	–	–	.04	.04	.04

Source: Interpol, *International Crime Statistics* (St. Cloud, France: Interpol General Secretariat, 1950-1952, 1955-1956, 1959-1960, 1965-1966, and 1971-1972).

[a]Only nations listed at least twice with a minimum span of ten years were included. Monaco was excluded because of its small size and high transient population.

[b]1971 statistics were substituted where 1972 statistics were not available.

the major larceny rate of approximately .05. In contrast, the lowest female proportion of total crime in table 9-3 is .04 (the Philippines and Kenya), and most of the proportions are above .10. Six nations experienced proportionate rises in female crime of .03 or greater over a ten-year period, and

Table 9-3
Crimes Committed by Females as a Proportion of All Crimes

	Year				
Nation[a]	*1950*	*1955*	*1960*	*1965*	*1972*
West Germany	.18	.10	.13	.15	.18
Denmark	.10	.10	–	.08	–
Egypt	–	.03	.03	.03	–
Finland	–	.05	.05	.05	–
France	–	.13	.10	.12	.16
Ireland	.11	.11	.10	.10	–
Israel	–	.11	.11	.12	.11
Japan	–	.14	.03	.10	.14
Luxembourg	.17	.20	.12	.14	.15
Netherlands	–	.13	.12	.10	.10
England/Wales	.13	.13	.12	.14	.14
Scotland	.10	.09	.10	.01	.14
Sweden	.04	–	–	.12	–
Morocco	–	.06	–	.19	.27
Philippines	.21	–	.06	.07	.04[b]
Netherlands Antilles	–	.10	–	.07	.06
Austria	–	.10	.14	.14	.13
Australia	–	.10	–	.10	–
Indonesia	–	.08	.09	–	.05
Kenya	–	–	.04	–	.04
Pakistan	–	.03	–	.02	–
Libya	–	.08	.06	.10	.09
Guyana	–	–	.09	.08	.10
Tunisia	–	–	.12	.13	.14
Burma	–	–	.11	.12	.13
Norway	–	–	.08	.08	.10

Source: Interpol, *International Crime Statistics* (St. Cloud, France: Interpol General Secretariat, 1950-1952, 1955-1956, 1959-1960, 1965-1966, and 1971-1972).

[a]Only nations listed at least twice with a minimum span of ten years were included. Monaco was excluded because of its small size and high transient population.

[b]1971 statistics were substituted where 1972 statistics were not available.

four experienced declines. The consistency in proportionate female crime over the years is much more significant than the changes that are found.

There are few apparent patterns in tables 9-1, 9-2, and 9-3. As a result, it was decided to cross-tabulate proportionate female crime with a series of three independent variables in order to understand better the structure of causal forces at work. The independent variables were degree of male-female social/educational equality, degree of male-female economic equality, and state of national socioeconomic development. The state of a nation's socioeconomic development was based on a combination of three variables: urbanization, industrialization, and number of annual kilowatt hours consumed per capita.[2] In the process of analysis, socioeconomic develoment was dichotomized into "more developed" and "less developed." The two indexes of male-female equality were developed by Stewart and Winter in their pioneering study, "The Nature and Causes of Female Suppression."[3] Stewart and Winter combined years women have had full suffrage, whether or not an alien bride acquires nationality, the female/male illiteracy rate, and the percentage of females in educational institutions at the primary, secondary, and college levels (all derived from United Nations data) into their social/educational equality scale. The economic equality scale was also a composite index, subsuming the percent of males/females who were economically active, percent of married women who were economically active, degree of sexual differentiation in industry, and extent of occupational sexual differentiation.

The female proportion of murders was related to all three of the independent variables. It was inversely related to socioeconomic development (gamma = —.65), directly related to the economic equality index (gamma = .52), and inversely related to the social/educational equality index (gamma = –.68). An increase in the female contribution to murder statistics was associated with low social/educational equality between the sexes, high male-female economic equality, and low socioeconomic development. The two inverse relationships are consistent, indicating that modernized societies, which typically have a high degree of social and educational equality between the sexes, tend to experience decreased proportionate female contributions to the murder rate. On the face of it, one might expect the economic equality index to be related to female proportionate murders in the same fashion instead of in the opposite (direct instead of inverse) direction. One reason why this is not so is that not all modernized societies receive high marks on economic equality between the sexes. For example, Denmark, Ireland, the Netherlands, Norway, Sweden, and Australia all have above-average ratings on social/educational equality and *below*-average ratings on economic equality between the sexes. Conversely, Nigeria, Malaysia, and Indonesia have below-average ratings on social/educational equality and *above*-average ratings on cross-sex economic equality.[4] It appears that although modernization is strongly associated with a narrowing of the social and educational gaps between the sexes it is no guarantee of a high level of economic equality. Modernization benefits both women and men in the economic sphere, but because it benefits men more than women, the differential between the sexes may increase rather than decrease.

The strong relationships between proportionate female murder and the three independent variables were not repeated for proportionate female major larceny. These relationships were all zero or close to zero. However, comparatively few nations were included in this analysis because of missing data, so these results must be viewed with even more skepticism than the other correlations reported in this chapter. Only one of the three variables had a strong association with total proportionate female crime, and that was the state of socioeconomic development (gamma = .88). Modernized nations tended to have an increasing female contribution to the total crime rate.

Aside from the impact of these variables on female criminal behavior, there is the issue of the effect that an increase in female criminality may have on female victimization. Do men respond to movement toward sexual equality in crime by victimizing women more heavily, partly because they have become more worthwhile targets for victimization and partly as a social control to "keep them in their place"? Unfortunately, the *International Crime Reports* do not include crime data by sex of victim, except that their sex-offense category is essentially limited to male victimizations of females. Sex offenses, as defined in the *International Crime Reports,* are mostly rapes, with the addition of trafficking in women, and perhaps some other crimes of a similar nature.

Forty-six nations with sex-offense data contributed the necessary murder statistics to Interpol for 1972, forty-four reported major larceny data, and thirty-two reported statistics on total crime. The correlations between the sex-offense rate and the proportion of female contributions to both the major larceny and total crime rates were near zero. The relationship between the proportionate female murder rate and the sex-offense rate was somewhat stronger (gamma = .33), indicating a weak tendency for the proportionate female murder rate and the sex-offense rate to covary. Thirty percent of the nations with high (.11 and up) proportionate female murder rates had high (more than 50 per 100,000) sex-offense rates, as compared with 15 percent of the nations that reported low or moderate proportionate female murder rates. It appears that there is no general tendency for men to increase their rate of the sexual victimization of women as a response to rising rates of proportionate female criminality.

There are a number of methodological problems with the analysis presented in this chapter other than those associated with comparability over time or between nations. These include: (1) inability to exclude alternative interpretations, (2) the ecological fallacy, and (3) skewed distributions. When analyzing official records *ex post facto,* one operates by fitting a theory to the data rather than by creating an experimental design to test a theory by collecting data on behavior in the future as it occurs. When collecting data on ongoing behavior, it is possible systematically to exclude extraneous variables from the analysis by using methodological structuring devices such as classical control-group experimental design. If properly designed, these experiments greatly reduce the possibility that alternative theoretical explanations will be confused with the theory being tested. Historical research simply does not permit this degree of methodological precision. As a result, alternative theories may well explain the patterns observed in the data. As an example of this, Wolfgang and Ferracuti's theory of the subculture of violence[5] could explain away any association between a rise in proportionate female crime and female victimization, the argument being that both rise as females are admitted into the social system in subcultures of violence, or as those subcultures expand and become more influential in a given society. It is not that one causes the other, but rather that both are caused by a third variable—in this case, variations in the composition and extent of subcultures of violence. The increased victimization of women in this case would not be repressive. It could be seen instead as a sign of the progressive acceptance of women into the subculture of violence which is the dominant culture in many areas.

The ecological fallacy occurs when people generalize relationships that obtain between large ecological units to smaller units of analysis, such as individual actors or subgroups within populations. Processes occurring within subgroups are often very different from those that are apparent if correlations are calculated between nations taken as a whole. Most modern nations are complex political and social entities, with many subgroups within them. These subgroups vary in their characteristics, and also in the relationships between characteristics. In the United States, for example, the relationship between sex of victim and sex of offender is not the same for black marital assaults and homicides as it is for whites. Nations are not the best units to choose for analysis. Culturally and regionally homogeneous units within nations would be better. Nations are used in macro-level analyses on the international level for the simple reason that no data on more homogeneous units of analysis are available.

The final problem is that women commit only a small proportion of most crimes. This skewed distribution can lead to misleading results when correlations are calculated. Very small differences in female crime rates and ratios can produce ordinal-level correlations and trends that are substantively accurate. This is further complicated by the fact that most of the nations at the extremes of proportionate female crime distributions are small and many of them have high transient populations which undermine the meaning of criminal statistics. A similar false impression is given by figures on the rise of female crime that are based on low initial female crime statistics. This issue was discussed in chapter 1 with respect to American crime statistics. It is equally applicable to international data. Table 9-4 shows how this can happen, using statistics on female murder, major larceny, and total crime from all the nations that submitted sex-specific

Table 9-4
Crimes Committed by Females in 1960 and 1972

	Murder			Major Larceny			Total Crime		
Nation[a]	*1960*	*1972*	*% Change*	*1960*	*1972*	*% Change*	*1960*	*1972*	*% Change*
West Germany	238	337	+42	2,422	5,970	+146	158,757	170,022	+7
Austria	54	29	–46	1,903	1,810	–5	29,423	25,590	–13
Burma	214	208	–3	429	2,964	+590	26,010	32,781	+26
France	132	154	+17	1,043	3,248	+211	45,782	116,799	+155
Guyana	0	17	–	182[b]	169[b]	–8	3,369	3,827	+14
Indonesia	128	88	–31	3,440	975	–72	13,575	3,473	–74
Israel	5	0	–	148	187	+26	5,141	4,749	–8
Japan	400	425	+6	67	63	–6	98,648	71,373	–28
Kenya	15	63	+320	29	142	+390	987	878	–11
Libya	24	8	–67	4	225	+5,525	1,560	657	–42
Luxembourg	12	11	–8	19	45	+137	439	976	+122
Madagascar	87	30	–66	75	58	–23	442	935	+112
Malaysia	51	0	–	0	0	–	239	115	–52
Morocco	27	58	+115	74	138	+86	4,048	15,682	+287
Nigeria	18	377	+2,094	44	60	+36	513[c]	2,348[c]	+358
Norway	2	0	–	61	173	+184	738	1,403	+90
Netherlands	41	30	–27	514	1,311	+155	10,406	12,059	+16
Philippines[d]	102	109	+7	146	56	–62	5,585	1,585	–72
England/Wales	24	32	+33	829	1,895	+129	19,617	46,621	+138
Scotland	2	16	+800	236	416	+76	2,772	4,634	+67
Tunisia	27	8	–70	74	97	+31	4,048	5,158	+27

Source: Interpol, *International Crime Statistics* (St. Cloud, France: Interpol Secretariat, 1959-1960 and 1971-1972).

[a]Monaco was excluded from the list because of its small size and high transient population.

[b]Includes major and minor larcenies.

[c]This is a summary of categories A through F in the *International Crime Statistics.* Only the category sum was available for 1972, so it was also used in 1960 for the sake of comparability. The true rate in 1960 was eight times the sum of categories A through F. If that ratio held true for 1972, the number of female crimes in that year would be over 18,000.

[d]Since 1972 data were not available, 1971 data were substituted.

crime reports to Interpol for 1960 and 1972. Total female crime increased in thirteen and decreased in eight of these countries during the twelve-year period. Major larcenies committed by women increased in fourteen nations, decreased in six, and held even at zero in Malaysia. Murder decreased in most of the nations (twelve of twenty-one). These trends do not correlate strongly with whether a nation is African, Asian, or European, or economically developing or highly modernized.

In those nations in which female crime registered large percentage increases between 1960 and 1972, the original base figures are quite low. As with American crime statistics, the seeming steepness of the rise is an artifact of the small baseline figure, and the absolute increase in female criminals is really quite small. Female crime seems to be increasing much more quickly than male crime, and this is true in proportionate terms. However, the absolute rise in female crime is actually much smaller than the absolute rise in male crime. The gender difference in the absolute number of crimes committed is increasing at the same time that it is decreasing in terms or percentage changes in crime rates. For example, total female crime in France rose 155 percent between 1960 and 1972, a rise of 71,017 crimes applied to a base of 45,782 crimes. During this same period, total French male crime rose only 51 percent, from 404,432 to 610,355 crimes. The rise in male crime is 205,923 cases, as compared with a rise in female crime of only 71,017 cases. In Madagascar, a Third-World country, total female crime rose from 442 to 935 between 1960 and 1972, an increase of 112 percent. Male crime increased 28 percent, but this represents an increase of 701 crimes, quite a bit more than the 493 crime rise for females. It would be dangerous for criminal justice planners to assume that what might be likened to a rapid start-up rate would be continued into the infinite future, and that female crime rates would therefore quickly overtake male crime rates. The fact that the absolute sex difference in criminal behavior seems to be increasing almost everywhere may prove to be a more important prediction of the future than percentage rate changes.

In a recent article, Freda Adler amplified her theory of the new female criminal and explicitly applied it to the international scene. She stated that "data from other nations concur with the American experience that as the social and economic disparity between the sexes decreases, there is a correlative increase in female criminality."[6] Furthermore, "developing countries are not immune to the phenomenon of rising female crime."[7] The analysis of the proportionate female crime statistics provides only limited confirmation for her theory. The crude female crime rates are somewhat more supportive of the image of the new female criminal, but that support is not terribly convincing. The two strongest supportive elements in this picture are: (1) female major larcenies, a sure sign of entrance into "masculine" professional crime, are up more than the other crime measures, and (2) the rises in national levels of female crime are much larger than the declines.

Women in Prisons Outside America

In this section, we will present material on the incarceration of women in Canada, India, Denmark, Australia, and New Zealand in order to demonstrate the extent to which our comments on the imprisonment of women in America in chapter 6 can be taken as generally applicable to the entire world. Biles states that Australian prisons rarely include more than 2 percent females.[8] In July 1977 there were 235 females incarcerated out of 8,858 prisoners, a rate of 2.6 percent.[9] This is partially due to the smaller number of crimes committed by women, along with two additional factors. Women in Australia are less likely than men to receive prison sentences, and if they are sent to prison, they serve terms that are considerably shorter. In Queensland from 1972 to 1973, one female appeared in the lower courts for each 7.36 males. The ratio of offenders sentenced to imprisonment was much more favorable to the women, 1 to 13.80, and the ratio of offenders committed to higher courts was even more so, 1 to 22.58. Women served "life" sentences and indeterminate detention periods (following a verdict of not guilty on the grounds of insanity) that were approximately half the length of male sentences in New South Wales and Victoria, Australia.[10]

Female prisoners in New Zealand increased from 121 in 1970 to 154 in 1976. Since the increase in the number of male prisoners was much sharper, the female proportion of prisoners declined from 5.1 to 4.1 percent during this period.[11] A detailed census of all prisoners was carried out in 1972 by the New Zealand Department of Justice, which showed that most incarcerated females were adolescents in borstals rather than women in prison. The number of females on probation and parole was almost ten times the number in institutions, as compared with two and a half times as many males in community supervision as in institutions. Only sixteen of the 108 incarcerated females had been found guilty of crimes against persons. Sixty-five of them were Maoris. Three-quarters of all the women in prison had sentences of two years or less.[12]

A detailed analysis of data from the Magistrates' Courts in 1964 shows that convicted females are much less likely to be sent to prison than convicted males. Eight percent of all convictions were of females, as compared with 3 percent of all prisoners. Nearly one in every three male cases dealt with by means other than a fine in 1964 resulted in a sentence of imprisonment, as compared with less than one in every six female cases. Of 143 females imprisoned in 1964, twenty-eight had been convicted of theft, forty-three of vagrancy, and no more than seven of any other specific offense.

Many of the vagrancy cases were of "ship girls" found in or around ships in dock, and are analogous to prostitution offenses. Most of these women were housed together at Dunedin, which meant that they were generally too far removed from their homes to receive regular visitors. Because of the small number of female prisoners, New Zealand was unable to provide the same quality of services to them that they did to male prisoners.[13]

In India, women made up 3.0 percent of the convicted prisoners in 1961 and 4.3 percent in 1965.[14] Detailed statistics for one Indian state, Rajasthan, show that women there varied only from 1.4 to 1.9 percent of the convict populations between 1958 and 1966. The length of female prison sentences was quite short, with more than three-quarters of the women serving less than a year. In 1965-1966, the most common crimes for which women in Rajasthan were imprisoned were theft (20 percent of all incarcerations), vagrancy (18 percent), and murder (6 percent). All other crimes were infrequently found.[15] In Maharashtra, nearly 2,500 women were admitted to prisons and jails during 1968. About half of them had been convicted of violations of the Railway Act, the Bombay Police Act, or the Prohibition Act. Nine percent had been convicted of housebreaking or theft, and not more than one percent had been convicted of any other crime.[16]

Sohoni reports that most correctional facilities in India house women and men, with provisions made to keep the sexes separate from each other. Women and girls, the mentally ill and "normal" female prisoners are all mixed together. Child-care services for children of convicts are rare. Vocational training is limited to traditional female skills such as weaving, tailoring, laundry, and embroidery—skills of only limited value on the labor market.[17] The Female Reformatory in Rajasthan is probably typical. There, female convicts in the mid-1960s learned such skills as sewing and button-stitching, earning money only if they worked overtime, and then averaging only two or three rupees a month. The educational program there, greatly needed, had been discontinued at the time of Ahuja's study.[18]

Women made up 2.2 percent of the people admitted to the Danish penal system in 1972. Of the total of sixty-four women, thirty-eight were convicted of forgery, larceny, or embezzlement. The most interesting thing about Denmark's imprisoned women is not their small number, but rather the advanced-treatment philosophy under which they live. All female prisoners are kept in a section of the State Prison at Horserod, which also houses men. A fence separates the sexes, and living quarters are not mixed. However, edcuation, work, and recreation are coeducational, and both male and female corectional officers are assigned to each unit. In addition to the usual liberal Danish prison policies, women are allowed to keep their infants with them at Horserod.[19]

When Johnson visited Horserod in 1972, there were forty women incarcerated there, along with 213 men, most of whom were serving short sentences for drunken driving. The women ranged from thirty to fifty years of age, and included a few drug addicts, mentally ill individuals, and pretrial detainees who were sent to Horserod because of inadequate conditions in some of the Danish local jails. The diversity within the female prisoner population caused difficulties for staff members, and doubtless for the prisoners too. Some of the women operated the institution's cooking facilities and did sewing work of a simple nature, being paid a modest wage according to how much work they did. Three women represented the female population on the inmate council, which met bimonthly to discuss issues of mutual concern with the administrators of the institution.[20]

Canada had only 131 women incarcerated in its penitentiary system at the end of 1974, plus an additional 376 in adult provincial institutions. Those women were 1.5 and 4.6 percent of all incarcerated individuals, respectively. Thirty-eight of the 81 women admitted to Canadian penitentiaries in 1974 were convicted of narcotic control act violations, with no other crime category producing more than seven female admissions.[21] These low figures misrepresent the total number of women imprisoned during the year, which is as much as eighteen times the year-end population count.[22] The most significant characteristics of incarcerated Canadian women is the high proportion of Indian and Metis offenders—a quarter of all female prisoners in one study[23] and from forty-six to 100 percent in a sample of six selected prisons in 1965-1966.[24]

Canada is a nation of enormous size and relatively low population density, which exacerbates the problem of servicing its female prisoners. Except for drug abusers in the western provinces, all women receiving sentences of two years or more are incarcerated at the Prison for Women in Kingston, Ontario. The Canadian Committee on Corrections has drawn attention to a number of problems associated with this system, including (1) unreasonable separation from families and friends, (2) difficulties in serving French-speaking women, and (3) lack of an internal segregation method for classifying offenders by age, criminal sophistication and emotional stability.[25] A more positive case is the Vanier Centre for Women, a provincial institution in Ontario. This institution was developed around the model of the therapeutic community. A number of problem-solving problems are provided for the women at Vanier, and a recent follow-up study indicates that participation in the program is associated with increased community adjustment after release.[26]

The information that has been presented here is admittedly sketchy. However, there is enough detail to assure us that prison systems in countries located on four continents incarcerate roughly the same proportion of females. It is safe to assume that women are universally incarcerated at rates well below their crime rates, which are in turn well below the crime rates exhibited by men. In all these nations and others for which criminal justice system information is available, it appears that women are subjected to a number of filtering processes as they move through the criminal justice system, each filter reducing the size of the offender cohort proportionately more than it does the parallel male offender cohort. The very small number of women in prison systems around the world suggests that problems of limited programs and facilities described for the United States in chapter 6 may be taken as representative of the situation of imprisoned women worldwide.

Notes

1. *International Crime Statistics* (St. Cloud, France: International Criminal Police Organization, 1950-52, 1953-54, 1955-56, and so forth. The most recent issue covers the years 1971-72).

2. For an earlier use of kilowatt hours in a similar setting, see Cathy S. Widom and Abigail J. Stewart, "Female Criminality and the Changing Status of Women," paper presented at the annual meeting of the American Society of Criminology (Atlanta, November 1977).

3. Abigail J. Stewart and David G. Winter, "The Nature and Causes of Female Suppression," *Signs: Journal of Women in Culture and Society* 2 (Spring 1977), 531-53.

4. The Philippines differ from this pattern in that they are a less-developed nation, have approximately an average amount of cross-sex economic equality, and have an above-average level of sexual equality in the social/educational sphere.

5. Marvin E. Wolfgang and Franco Ferracuti, *The Subculture of Violence* (London: Tavistock, 1967).

6. Freda Adler, "The Interaction between Women's Emancipation and Female Criminality: A Cross-Culture Perspective," *International Journal of Criminology and Penology* 5 (1977), 103.

7. Ibid., 106.

8. David Biles, "Women Offenders," paper presented to a seminar on Women as Participants in the Criminal Justice System, Academy of Science (Canberra, Australia, 1975), 3.

9. David Biles, "Australian Prison Trends—No. 14" (Phillip, Australia: Australian Institute of Criminology, 1977).

10. Biles, 1975, 4-6.

11. New Zealand, *Justice Statistics 1970* (Wellington: Dept. of Statistics, 1972), 67; and Dept. of Statistics Information Sevice Leaflet No. 77/206 (Wellington, 1977).

12. New Zealand, *Justice Department, Penal Census,* 1972 (Wellington: Research Section, Dept. of Justice, 1975), 1, 7, 13, 39.

13. New Zealand, Dept. of Justice, *Crime in New Zealand* (Wellington: R.E. Owen, 1968), 235-64.

14. N.K. Sohoni, "Women Prisoners," *Indian Journal of Social Work* 35 (July 1974), 139-40.

15. Ram Ahuja, *Female Offenders in India* (Meerut, India: Meenakshi Prakashan, 1969), 9-11.

16. Sohoni, 143.

17. Ibid., 145.

18. Ahuja, 115-17.

19. Arne Lonberg, *The Penal System of Denmark* (Copenhagen: Dept. of Prison and Probation, Ministry of Justice, 1975), 54, 60, 63, 105.

20. Elmer H. Johnson, *Community-Based Corrections in Western Europe* (Carbondale: Center for the Study of Crime, Delinquency, and Corrections, Southern Illinois University, 1973), 60-62.

21. Canada, Judicial Division, *Correctional Institution Statistics, 1974* (Ottawa: Statistics Canada, 1976), 14-15, 24.

22. Canadian Committee on Corrections, *Toward Unity: Criminal Justice and Corrections* (Ottawa: Queen's Printer, 1969), 46.

23. Canadian Corrections Association, "Brief on the Women Offender," *Canadian Journal of Corrections* 11 (1969), 46.

24. Canadian Committee, 46.

25. Ibid., 400.

26. L.R. Lambert and P.G. Madden, "The Adult Female Offender: The Road from Institution to Community Life," *Canadian Journal of Criminology and Corrections* 18 (1976), 319-31.

10 A Concluding Note

Anyone attempting to deal with sexual differentiation in criminal behavior has to consider two analytically distinct problems. First, there are the quantitative differences between men and women on the various legal categories of crime. The second problem is of lesser interest to criminal justice professionals but of greater interest to sex-role theorists. It is how to explain the sexual differences in role performance within crime categories. Conflict theory, opportunity theory, and a number of macrosociological theoretical systems have been shown to be useful in understanding quantitative differences in rates.[1] These theories are specific to crime and deviance rather than general theories of human behavior. In contrast, the explanation of gender differences is likely to come from general theories of sex-role performance that have nothing to do with criminal behavior.

Not many women commit robbery and burglary. In 1966, official statistics indicated that only 5 percent of the arrests for robbery and 4 percent of the arrests for burglary were made of women. By 1976, these statistics had risen only to 7 percent for robbery and 5 percent for burglary.[2] When women do commit these crimes, do they play the same criminal roles that are played by male robbers and burglars? Ward, Jackson, and Ward found that the criminal roles played by female robbers and burglars were more consistent with general female sex-role behavior than with the behavior of male robbers and burglars. In the majority of the cases, the women were partners rather than the sole perpetrators of the acts, and there were also a number of cases in which they were only accessories (who played secondary roles) or conspirators (who did not participate at all in the criminal acts). In only one case out of every seven did a woman carry out a robbery or burglary on her own.[3] These results were largely replicated in a recent study of robbers in the Florida Correctional Institution at Lowell by Spears, Vega, and Silverman.[4]

Ward, Jackson, and Ward found that about three-quarters of the assaults and homicides were carried out by unaccompanied women. The deviation from the male criminal model occurs when one looks at the characteristics of the victims and finds that nine out of every ten victims were known to the female offender before the crime, more than half of them were close intimates, and more than a third were husbands or lovers. Most of these crimes took place at home rather than in a public place, only about a quarter were premeditated, and although the victims were commonly adult males, they were often incapacitated by being drunk, ill, asleep, or otherwise off-guard.[5]

The ratio of property to violent crimes is higher among women than among men. The most recent FBI data indicate that women account for 37 percent of fraud, 31 percent of embezzlement and larceny-theft, and 30 percent of forgery and counterfeiting arrests.[6] Little is known about the sociology of these crimes as committed by men, and even less when they are committed by women. In fact, the only area of property crime by women that has received more than a passing glance is shoplifting. Most studies indicate that adult shoplifting is a predominantly female crime.[7] There is some evidence that female shoplifters apprehended by store detectives are less likely than male shoplifters to be turned over to the police,[8] but this may be due to the tendency of women to steal items of lesser value.[9] Women who shoplift are less likely than male shoplifters to have previous convictions,[10] and, if arrested and convicted, are less likely to recidivate.[11] It appears that women who shoplift are rarely career criminals, commonly take items of little value, and only contribute heavily to shoplifting statistics because they comprise most shoppers.[12]

Women are rarely found among members of organized crime syndicates, a situation in which discrimination presumably plays more than a minor role. It may be that women were more prominent in organized crime in the early 1900s than more recently.[13] An example mentioned by Plate suggests that women may have to form their own organizations in order to break into organized crime in significant numbers. He describes a smuggling ring delivering cocaine from Latin America to Miami and New York in which all the members were women, including stewardesses, high-school teachers, nurses, and actresses.[14]

Public order crimes are well-represented in the distribution of crimes committed by women. One of these crimes, prostitution is dominated by women. Although upward mobility to the level of the madam allows a small number of women to become criminal administrators[15] and others to maintain themselves as independent businesswomen,[16] a significant number of prostitutes continue to engage in relationships with pimps, all of whom take their money and some of whom assault them if they do not turn their quota of tricks in an evening. COYOTE notwithstanding, the impression one gets from reading the literature on prostitution is that most prostitutes have not entirely overcome their psychosocial dependence on men.

Hoffman-Bustamente's conclusions on women in crime still stand as the best summary of the fragmentary empirical data available at this time. These are: (1) women are greatly underrepresented among arrestees for crimes that require stereotyped male behavior; (2) on the occasions when they are arrested for their crimes, they are likely to have played secondary, supportive roles; and (3) women are less underrepresented or even overrepresented among arrestees for crimes that are consistent with stereotyped female behavior.[17] If we accept these conclusions as reasonable ones, then we are driven to the position that any adequate theoretical understanding of female criminal behavior must take general theories of sex-role differentiation into account. This book has concentrated on developing an understanding of structural and psychosocial aspects of the three-way relationship among women, crime, and the criminal justice system. The task of fully integrating female criminal behavior with general theories of sex-role differentiation must be left to a future investigation. When this occurs, one of the more interesting aspects of the project will most certainly be an examination of the roots of sexual oppression in childhood socialization experiences and how this relates to gender differences in criminal role performance.

Showing the way in which sexual oppression begins in childhood does not explain how it is determined in women's adult lives. Following this logic, adult female criminality cannot be satisfactorily explained by reference only to microsociological variables drawn from childhood socialization experiences. Etiological factors in the criminality of women could be discussed in terms of the great schools of criminological thought, such as differential opportunity theory, anomie theory, containment theory, and so forth. One could then reason that since women and men differ on many of these factors (differences on degree rather than kind), they differ in their levels of criminality. Aldridge summarizes these differences under the headings of "differential socialization, differential social control, and differential access or opportunities for committing offenses,"[18] and Cavanagh demonstrates the similarities in the castelike status of present-day women and blacks before the Civil Rights Movement.[19] The point is that the dependency effect created in females by childhood socialization experiences is prolonged throughout their lives by structural conditions and psychosocial processes existing in their adult lives. In this respect, we would be wise to heed Heidensohn's comment on the wisdom of taking "female deviance as an aspect of the female sex role and its relationship with social structure, rather than trying to make it conform to patterns apparently observed in the male role and its particular articulation with social structure."[20]

It is important to avoid taking an unrealistically deterministic position on this issue, given the current limitations on knowledge in the field. Harris and Hill argue correctly that female access to illegitimate opportunity structures has been even more limited than their access to legitimate opportunity structures, which is one reason why gender differences in white-collar crimes are much smaller than gender differences in street crimes. Yet they go on to say that there is no reason why females could not innovate highly criminal activities, overcoming structural blockages and, if necessary, even forming segregated enclaves of criminals.[21] In a study of British criminal statistics, Chiplin found a remarkable similarity in the legal and illegal distribution of female economic activities, and concluded that women self-select themselves into certain types of illegal behavior even when structural barriers to a wide variety of criminal activities are easily overcome.[22] To the extent that this is true, we may attribute it to the effects of childhood socialization into dependency plus the effects of a series of informal psychosocial pressures applied to women in their adult lives.

In this book we have explored alternative explanations of female crime and delinquency, we have presented statistics about illegal female behavior in the United States and elsewhere, and we have analyzed the criminal victimization of women. We have also examined topics that are bounded by the interaction among women, crime, and the criminal justice system. We gave considerable attention to the treatment of women in the criminal justice system—by the police, in the courts, and in prison. This included their interactions with representatives of criminal justice agencies as the victims of crime (rape, wife-beating, etc.) as well as the offenders (prostitution, shoplifting, etc.). Our general position is that developmental, situational, and macrostructural variables are all operative in the etiology of female illegal behavior and in female role occupancy within criminal behavior systems. By and large, these variables operate in ways that can arguably be referred to as oppressive. This tradition of female oppression is continued and amplified by the way in which women are processed in the criminal justice system.

Notes

1. Cathy S. Widom and Abigail J. Stewart, "Female Criminality and the Changing Status of Women," paper presented at the annual meeting of the American Society of Criminology (Atlanta, 1977).

2. Federal Bureau of Investigation, *Uniform Crime Reports* (Washington, D.C.: Government Printing Office, 1966, 1976).

3. David A. Ward, Maurice Jackson, and Renee E. Ward, "Crimes of Violence by Women," in Donald J. Mulvihill and Melvin M. Tumin (eds.), *Crimes of Violence* 13 (Washington, D.C.: Government Printing Office, 1969), 867, 906.

4. Eddyth P. Spears, Manuel Vega, and Ira J. Silvermann, "The Female Robber," paper presented at the annual meeting of the American Society of Criminology (Atlanta, 1977).

5. Ward, 868-71.

6. Federal Bureau of Invetigation, 1976, 211.

7. See, for example, Mary O. Cameron, *The Booster and the Snitch* (New York: Free Press, 1964); T.C.N. Gibbens, Clare Palmer, and Joyce Prince, "Mental Health Aspects of Shoplifting," *British Medical Journal* 3

(September 11, 1971), 612-15; Pat Mayhew, "Crime in a Man's World," *New Society* 41 (June 16, 1977), 160; C.N. Peijster, "Theft in Department Stores," in *Fourth International Criminological Congress: Preparatory Papers* (The Hague: International Society for Criminology, 1960), 1-16; and Gerald D. Robin, "Pattern of Department Store Shoplifting," *Crime and Delinquency* 9 (April 1963), 163-72.

8. Lawrence E. Cohen and Rodney Stark, "Discriminatory Labeling and the Five-Finger Discount," *Journal of Research in Crime and Delinquency* 11 (January 1974), 25-39; and Peijster, 9.

9. Cohen, 25; and Cameron, 84. This conclusion is supported by a study which is the exception to the rule in shoplifting investigations. Michael Hindelang ("Decisions of Shoplifting Victims to Invoke the Criminal Justice Process," *Social Problems* 21 [April 1974], 580-93) studied random samples of shoplifting cases drawn from the 1963, 1965, and 1968 files of Commercial Service Systems. The cases analyzed were from grocery and drug stores in Southern California. Females committed only 47 percent of the crimes recorded, were much more likely than males to steal items of large ($1.90 or more) value, and were almost as likely to be referred to the police for prosecution. This study suggests that differential referrals to the police are more due to the value of the stolen items than to the sex of the offender.

10. Cameron, 106; and T.C.N. Gibbens and Joyce Prince, *Shoplifting* (London: Institute for the Study and Treatment of Delinquency, 1962), 25.

11. Gibbens, Palmer, and Prince, 612, 614.

12. Mayhew, 160.

13. Alan Block, "Aw! Your Mother's in the Mafia: Women Criminals in Progressive New York," *Contemporary Crises* 1 (January 1977), 5-22.

14. Thomas Plate, *Crime Pays!* (New York: Ballantine, 1975), 180.

15. Barbara S. Heyl, "The Madam as Entrepreneur," *Sociological Symposium* 11 (Spring 1974), 61-82; "The Madam as Teacher: The Training of House Prostitutes," *Social Problems* 24 (June 1977): 545-55; and *The Madame as Entrepreneur: Political Economy of a House of Prostitution* (Chicago: Aldine, 1977).

16. James H. Bryan, "Apprenticeships in Prostitution," *Social Problems* 12 (Winter 1965), 287-97; James H. Bryan, "Occupational Ideologies and Individual Attitudes of Call Girls," *Social Problems* 13 (Spring 1966): 441-50; Harold Greenwald, *The Elegant Prostitute: A Social and Psychoanalytic Study* (New York: Walker and Co., 1970); and Karen E. Rosenblum, "Female Deviance and the Female Sex Role: A Preliminary Investigation," *British Journal of Sociology* 26 (June 1975), 169-85.

17. Dale Hoffman-Bustamente, "The Nature of Female Criminality," *Issues in Criminology* 8 (Fall 1973), 131.

18. Delores P. Aldridge, "Trends in Deviant Behavior among Women," paper presented at the annual meeting of the American Sociological Association (Chicago, 1977), 12.

19. Barbara K. Cavanagh, " 'A Little Dearer than His Horse': Legal Stereotypes and the Feminine Personality," *Harvard Civil Rights-Civil Liberties Law Review* 6 (1971), 274-75.

20. Frances Heidensohn, "The Deviance of Women: A Critique and an Enquiry," *British Journal of Sociology* 19 (1968), 170.

21. Anthony R. Harris and Gary D. Hill, "Women and Deviance: Empirical Trends and Paradigm Poverty," paper delivered at the annual meeting of the American Sociological Association (Chicago, 1977), 18-19.

22. Brian Chiplin, "Sexual Discrimination: Are There any Lessons from Criminal Behavior?" *Applied Economics* 8 (1976), 132.

Index

About the Contributors

Meda Chesney-Lind teaches sociology at Honolulu Community College. Her original research on the treatment of female juvenile delinquents in the criminal justice system has made her a leader in the field. Among her recent publications are articles in *Psychology Today* and *Crime and Delinquency.*

Joy Pollock is a Lehman Fellow at S.U.N.Y., Albany, in criminal justice. She was the senior author's research assistant at Whitman College in the months when this book was taking shape. She previously coauthored a chapter in *A Guide to the Social Science Literature on Prisons and Prisoners,* which was published by R & E Research Associates in 1978.

About the Author

Lee H. Bowker is the Coordinator of the Criminal Justice Program at the University of Wisconsin-Milwaukee. He is the author of *Prisoner Subcultures, Drug Use at a Small Liberal Arts College,* and several other monographs, as well as articles in journals such as the *International Journal of the Addictions,* The United Nations *Bulletin on Narcotics,* the *International Journal of Women's Studies, Addictive Behaviors,* and *the Journal of College Student Personnel.*

About the Author